T3-BHM-208

PENGUIN BOOKS

THE WORLD OF THE SHINING PRINCE

The world of Genji was the Japanese Heian period (fl. c. A.D. 950–1050), when the rest of the world, except China, lay in cultural darkness. Using *The Tale of Genji* as a frame of reference, Dr Ivan Morris outlines the political and social life, the religion and superstitions of the period, the everyday life of the court, its cult of beauty and the relations between men and women in Heian (Kyoto). His detailed study miraculously unfolds for us one of the most unusual and engaging patterns in the whole kaleidoscope of history.

'The people of the Heian period in Japan . . . evolved a civilization – at least the tiny percentage of the privileged – which was almost unbelievably aesthetic, and was pervaded by a sense of the transitoriness of things, combined with an awareness of beauty so sharp that it was poignant. . . . Ivan Morris's book is a very complete study of this period. It is as elegant as its theme. He manages to make this strange world thinkable: he even manages to make its people sympathetic' – Guy Wint in the *Observer*.

Ivan Morris wrote widely on modern and ancient Japan, where he lived for four years, and translated numerous works from both classical and contemporary literature. He was born in London in 1925 and began the study of Japanese language and culture at Harvard University. Having received his B.A. degree, he returned to England and received his doctorate from the School of Oriental and African Studies and afterwards worked in the BBC and the Foreign Office. Dr Morris lived in New York City for many years, where he was a member of the faculty of Columbia University from 1960 to 1973 and chairman of its Department of East Asian Languages and Cultures from 1966 to 1969. In 1966 he was elected a Fellow of St Antony's College, Oxford, and in 1968 the University of London awarded him a D.Litt. *The World of the Shining Prince* won the Duff Cooper Award. Ivan Morris died in 1976.

IVAN MORRIS

THE WORLD OF
THE SHINING PRINCE

Court Life in Ancient Japan

PENGUIN BOOKS

Penguin Books Ltd, Harmondsworth,
Middlesex, England
Penguin Books, 40 West 23rd Street,
New York, New York 10010, U.S.A.
Penguin Books Australia Ltd, Ringwood,
Victoria, Australia
Penguin Books Canada Limited, 2801 John Street,
Markham, Ontario, Canada L3R 1B4
Penguin Books (N.Z.) Ltd, 182–190 Wairau Road,
Auckland 10, New Zealand

First published in Great Britain by Oxford University Press 1964
First published in the United States of America by Alfred A. Knopf, Inc., 1964
Published in Peregrine Books 1969
Published in Penguin Books 1979
Reprinted 1983

Printed in the United States of America by
Offset Paperback Mfrs., Inc., Dallas, Pennsylvania
Set in Monotype Plantin

To Arthur Waley

Preface

THIS book is intended mainly for the general reader. Detailed factual information has therefore been consigned to the notes, which can be read *pari passu* with the text, or later – or indeed can be omitted entirely by the reader who is interested in having an overall impression of the world of the shining prince rather than in knowing about the details of the annual ceremonies, for instance, or the intricacies of directional taboos. My complete translation of Sei Shōnagon's *Pillow Book* will contain considerably more factual material about the period.

I should like to express my thanks to Professor Hans Bielenstein, Mr John Black, Dr R. H. van Gulik, Professor Yoshito Hakeda, Professor Donald Keene, and Professor Burton Watson for reading certain chapters of this book and for giving their valuable suggestions. I am also grateful to the Editor of *History Today* for permission to include three passages which were first printed in that periodical.

Contents

PREFACE   7

INTRODUCTION   11

I   THE HEIAN PERIOD   17

II   THE SETTING   31

III   POLITICS AND SOCIETY   56

    A. The Emperors   56
    B. The Fujiwaras   62
    C. Society   78
    D. Administration   84
    E. Economy   87
    F. Provincials and the Lesser Breeds   93

IV   RELIGIONS   103

V   SUPERSTITIONS   136

VI   THE 'GOOD PEOPLE' AND THEIR LIVES   153

VII   THE CULT OF BEAUTY   183

VIII   THE WOMEN OF HEIAN
       AND THEIR RELATIONS WITH MEN   211

IX   MURASAKI SHIKIBU   262

X   ASPECTS OF 'THE TALE OF GENJI'   275

    APPENDIXES

      1. Periods of Far Eastern History, and Rulers
        in Japan during the Heian Period   299

Contents

2. A Note on the Tenth Century   301

3. Is 'The Tale of Genji' Complete?   306

4. Genealogical Tables   309

5. Murasaki on the Art of Fiction   315

6. Glossary   318

BIBLIOGRAPHY   327

INDEX   333

Introduction

WHEN the first Westerners set foot in Japan in the sixteenth century, they found a country in many ways as strange and unpredictable as the moon, yet which at the same time had certain remarkably familiar features. They saw a land divided into great feudal baronies, a land dominated by military men who for over a century had kept the islands in a state of almost perpetual warfare. War indeed was the main fact of life, and with it came all the horrors and misery that Europe too had known for so long. The visitors from the West recognized much else that was familiar: a well-established Church, for example, contending with the secular authorities for riches and power; an ignorant peasantry producing nearly all the country's wealth but for the most part leading a squalid and precarious existence; burgeoning urban centres in which a growing merchant class was beginning to assert itself. And whenever they entered a large Japanese town one of the first sights to greet them would be the shambles of the execution grounds, strewn with the gory remains of some criminal, which no doubt served to reassure them, like Candide and his companions, that at least in one respect this was a civilized country.[1]

No such comforting tokens would have welcomed the visitor from the courts of King Harold or of the Emperors Otto who had been wafted to

1. The German physician, Engelbert Kaempfer, describes his arrival in the suburbs of Edo in 1691:
  'Just before we came to *Sinagawa*, the place of publick executions offer'd to our view a very shocking and unpleasing sight, human heads and bodies, some tending to putrefaction, some half devour'd, lying among other dead carcasses, with multitudes of dogs, ravens, crows, and other ravenous beasts and birds, waiting to satisfy their devouring appetites upon these miserable remains.' *The History of Japan . . . , ii.* 519.
In the Heian period executions were extremely rare, and the approaches to the capital were never disfigured by sights like these.

the other end of the planet and deposited in the city of Heian, the capital of Japan in Murasaki's time. He would have been confronted with a world totally different from anything he knew, a world which culturally was many centuries in advance of his own and which in customs, beliefs, and social organization was more alien than anything that Gulliver discovered on his travels. For Japan one thousand years ago had developed in a pattern that was almost totally unrelated to the experience of the West.

For us who inhabit a planet which, at least so far as communications are concerned, has become a single unit it requires a real effort of the imagination to picture a state of affairs in which men in most parts of the world linger in a state of cultural obscurity, absorbed almost entirely in the brute struggle for survival and power, while here and there, often on widely separated points of the globe, civilizations shine or flicker like ships' lights on a dark ocean. Yet so it has been during a great part of human history. So it was one thousand years ago.

If we exclude China and Japan, a bird's-eye view of the world in the tenth century would not lead us to regard the cultural situation with any great enthusiasm.[2] Much of western Europe is in a precarious state, while in many of the stronger, more stable societies the peak has been followed by a period of aridity or decadence. Here and there we find scattered lights of culture; elsewhere some of the famous works of world literature are first being committed to writing; and the culture of Islam is still vigorous. Yet on the whole the tenth century would appear to be one of the bleaker periods in cultural history.

The picture changes entirely when we include the Far East in our purview. In China, as well as in Korea, the tenth century was a period of political transition. Though it is associated with few outstanding works of literature, and is admittedly one of the less exciting centuries during the immensely productive era that spanned the dynasties of T'ang and Sung,[3] it is far from being a time of cultural stagnation or decline. Above all it contains the seeds of the great flowering that is to reach its climax later in the Sung period.

Some three hundred miles across the sea from Korea, in another of the peripheral areas of East Asian civilization, the Heian period is reach-

2. See Appendix 2.
3. See Appendix 1 for a chart of dynasties and periods.

ing its half-way mark. While China and Korea are undergoing dynastic changes, the kingdom of Japan is enjoying one of its great periods of political stability and has developed a remarkably advanced culture. One might expect that after several centuries of contact the prestige and power of China would have exerted so overwhelming an influence on the little islands to the east that this culture could be no more than a pale copy, or at the best a variant, of the T'ang model. If that were so, a study of the world of the shining prince would have little interest for anyone except the specialist. What makes this such a fascinating period is that, despite all the cultural riches from China, Heian Japan is in many ways original and even unique. The popular cliché about the Japanese being no more than skilful imitators is particularly misleading when applied to the time of Murasaki Shikibu. It is true that many of the outer forms – the layout of the capital city, for example, and cere-monial observances at the imperial court – had been taken over whole-sale from T'ang China. Yet the aspects that make the tenth and eleventh centuries in Japan so memorable are on the whole indigenous.

Murasaki's period has reminded some observers of the great cultural flowering in the century of Louis XIV. The comparison is dubious from almost every point of view. Fujiwara no Michinaga, the most powerful ruler of his time in Japan, was no *roi soleil* (much as he would have relished the image), and in comparison with Versailles the imperial court of Heian was simple to the point of austerity. Above all, the values that dominated the people in Murasaki's circle and those of the aristo-cracy in seventeenth-century France were in most respects as different as any two sets of standards could be in highly cultivated societies like these.

Far more valid parallels have been suggested by Sir George Sansom. He compares Heian with Islamic life in Persia, but considers that the closest resemblance is to be found in the court of Akbar, the sixteenth-century Mogul emperor.[4] It is an intriguing comparison; and certainly the same type of aesthetic values would seem to have prevailed in the two courts, widely separated though they were in time and space. Yet on the whole a study of Heian civilization does not impel us to look for

4. G. B. Sansom, *A History of Japan*, i, 196. *Akbar Nameh* (*The Book of Akbar*), written by the vizier Abulfazl, gives a detailed description of the great Mogul's court.

parallels; rather it leads to the conclusion that this was one of the most unusual and engaging patterns that the kaleidoscope of history has produced. If any society in the world can be described as unique, it was that of Heian Kyō in the time of Murasaki Shikibu.

*

It is not often that a culturally rich and diversified period lends itself to representation by a single work of literature or art. Murasaki's novel, however, apart from being the greatest literary product of its time, gives us so real a picture of what it was like to be a member of aristocratic Japanese society in the tenth and eleventh centuries that we may be justified in referring to this society as the world of *The Tale of Genji* or (to use the evocative name that was given to the novel's hero, Prince Genji) as the 'world of the shining prince'. In reconstructing a period or a society it would of course be dangerous to rely on any single book, let alone on a work of fiction in which idealization and a strongly personal viewpoint have played their part. I have leant heavily on Murasaki's novel in my effort to understand certain aspects of Heian society, and it has provided a good part of my references and quotations. But the material in this book is drawn from many other sources as well. These include works of fiction, diaries by court ladies of the time, and most important of all, Sei Shōnagon's *Pillow Book*, which, apart from being a minor literary masterpiece, is our main factual document about daily life in the capital. I have also used the more solemn types of writing in which Murasaki's male contemporaries specialized, notably chronicles and journals in Sino-Japanese, the respectable literary language for men of the time.

The Tale of Genji was written in the early decades of the eleventh century, but the society it describes belongs on the whole to the tenth. To what specific years, then, does the 'world of the shining prince' correspond? While there is no clear-cut line of demarcation at either end, my book deals with the period from the middle of the tenth century to the middle of the eleventh. Much that belonged to this world had, of course, developed well before the year 950, and much continued until the end of the twelfth century or even later. This is particularly true of religious beliefs and attitudes, which belong to the general Japanese tradition rather than to any particular era. Here and in most other ways these hundred years or so blend indistinguishably into the surrounding decades and centuries. Yet politically the period is marked by the acme of power of one great family, the family that produced both Murasaki herself and the Empress whom she served; and culturally it represents the flowering of Heian civilization, an unusual and significant chapter in the history of world culture.

I

The Heian Period

IN 784 the emperor gave orders that his capital should be moved from the temple city of Heijō (Nara), where it had been during most of the century, to Nagaoka, some thirty miles to the north. Like Heijō the new centre was to be modelled on the Chinese capital of Ch'ang-an; but, in accordance with the increased wealth of the island kingdom, it was to be on a far larger and grander scale than any previous town in Japan. Elaborate and expensive plans were drawn up for the construction of the new buildings, and these were carried out under the supervision of Tanetsugu, a member of the growing Fujiwara family.

The court and the government offices were duly moved to Nagaoka. Tanetsugu appears to have been a vigorous and efficient organizer, but he had acquired many enemies. Among these was the emperor's brother, Crown Prince Sawara, and members of certain rival families which resented the rise of the Fujiwaras. The taint of scandal soon attached itself to Tanetsugu: it was rumoured (perhaps quite correctly) that a certain rich family of Chinese descent had offered him the land on which the new capital was built in return for future favours that he might procure for them at court. These rumours were fanned by his enemies and only one year after the move to the new city Tanetsugu was attacked by a group of bravos and murdered. The real culprits were believed to be members of rival families, instigated by Prince Sawara. With typical acumen the Fujiwaras turned the murder to their advantage by removing these families from the scene. There were several arrests. Some of the suspects were executed, but most were sent into exile, which under the kindly influence of Buddhism had become the more normal form of punishment. Among them was Prince Sawara, who, after being imprisoned for some time in a Buddhist temple, was sent under escort to the island of Awaji on the Inland Sea. He never reached his destination. It appears that in the course of his journey he was put to death on official instructions. Shortly afterwards illness and other misfortunes started to plague the imperial family and the Fujiwaras. The primitive medical knowledge of the time, combined perhaps with a guilty conscience, led the government to attribute all this to Sawara's vengeful spirit. Efforts were made to placate the dead prince, and in the year 800 the government went to the extent of appointing him head of state with the title of Emperor Sudō, thus giving him the distinction of being the only man to become emperor after five years in the grave.

Prince Sawara's death had already helped to produce another, and far more significant, effect. Hardly a decade after the capital had been moved to Nagaoka, with all the work and expense this entailed, the emperor ordered that it be moved once again, this time to a little village some ten miles to the north. The site had been discovered in much the same way as Versailles – in the course of a hunting expedition. It seemed to fulfil the 'wind and water' topographical requirements better than the existing city; also its situation was more strategic and allowed for greater expansion. The main reason for the move, however, was superstition. The princely ghost, and also Tanetsugu's, still seemed to hover over Nagaoka; and no doubt the emperor and his advisers felt that their baleful influence might prevent the capital from developing into the splendid political and cultural centre they envisaged.

In 794, the year of the second move, an imperial edict announced that the new capital would be called Heian Kyō, the City of Peace and Tranquillity. Apart from having an auspicious ring (the latter part of the eighth century had witnessed a great deal of political strife and bloodshed), the name combined the first and last syllables of *Hei*jō, Japan's earliest real city, and Ch'ang-*an*, the great T'ang metropolis on which Heian, like the former capitals, was modelled. Later it became known as Kyōto, and it remained the imperial capital for more than a millennium.

It was the emperor's original designation, however, that gave its name to the four centuries or so during which the centre of political activity stayed in or near the city. The Heian period covers an extremely long span of time – about as long as that from the year of Shakespeare's birth until the present day. It is a rather unwieldy period, and historians have enjoyed chopping it up into sub-periods and sub-sub-periods.[1]

1. Kuroita's division of the period is perhaps the most useful:

A. *782–967 Early Heian*
  (i) 782–833 move to Heian Kyō; subjugation of the aborigines; establishment

Most of these divisions are arbitrary, but there is one date that stands out as a clear and useful line of demarcation in the cultural history of the period. That is the year 894, precisely one hundred years after the founding of the capital, when the government decided to stop sending official embassies to China.[2] For almost three centuries envoys had been travelling at fairly regular intervals to the Sui and T'ang courts and had brought back with them a knowledge of government, economic organization, social structure, and culture that had made possible Japan's amazing leap forward during the seventh and eighth centuries. In 894 the famous scholar-statesman, Sugawara no Michizane, was appointed Great Envoy to the T'ang. One month later the mission was cancelled and it was resolved that no further envoys would go to the continent. There were many reasons for this far-reaching decision. Michizane himself was engaged in a struggle for power with the Fujiwara family and feared that, if he undertook the long journey to China, he might return to find his position in the capital undermined. Great man of letters and sinologue though he was, politics had to take precedence over scholarship.

There was, however, a more important motive. The government knew that the T'ang dynasty was reaching the end of its long span (the final

---

of new indigenous institutions such as the Emperor's Private Office and the Imperial Police; founding of the Tendai and Shingon sects of Buddhism.

(ii) 833–87 decline of the emperor's power and emergence of Fujiwara Regents and Chancellors.

(iii) 887–967 struggles between the emperors and the Fujiwara leaders.

B. *967–1167 Late Heian*

(i) 967–1068 monopoly of political power by the Fujiwaras.

(ii) 1068–1156 Cloister Government.

(iii) 1156–67 emergence of the military class as the main factor in the struggle for power. Kuroita Katsumi, *Kokushi no Kenkyū*, i. 6–11.

The world of the shining prince corresponds to subdivision B(i), which represents the high point in the development of Japanese prose literature.

Oka Kazuo breaks the Heian period into 4 divisions of about a century each: (i) 794–887, (ii) 887–986, (iii) 986–1086, (iv) 1086–1185. *Genji Monogatari no Kisoteki Kenkyū*, p. 17, ff.

Sakamoto prefers these 3 periods: (i) 782–930, (ii) 930–1086, (iii) 1086–1185. As will be seen, Japanese scholars are far from agreeing on the opening and terminal dates of the period, let alone on the internal divisions.

2. In art history the year 894 marks the division between the Kōnin and Fujiwara periods.

break-up had started with popular uprisings in the north some twenty years before) and they felt that the missions had, for the time being at least, outlived their usefulness. In fact they were not resumed until over four centuries later.

The lapse of official relations with China marks the beginning of a new phase in the Heian period. The first hundred years is in many ways tied to the preceding Nara period: the prestige of Chinese institutions and culture remained overwhelming and the ruling class was on the whole still adhering to the systems and forms that they had borrowed from abroad. With the beginning of the second hundred-year period the emphasis changed: from then until the end of the Heian period and far later the country developed on increasingly independent lines.

Heian culture reached its full flowering about one hundred years after the official break with China. The apogee corresponds to the rule of Fujiwara no Michinaga, who was the effective head of government during the last decade of the tenth century and the first two decades of the eleventh, and whose resplendent period has been described in a chronicle aptly entitled *Tales of Glory*.[3] Michinaga's daughter and his niece were both consorts of the reigning emperor, and among their maids of honour were two outstanding writers of the period, Sei Shōnagon and Murasaki Shikibu. During their time the remote city of Heian Kyō was the most flourishing cultural centre in the world next to the Chinese capital.

The great days were followed by a long era of decline. Some historians consider that the breakdown of Heian civilization had already started by the beginning of the tenth century. With the shrewdness gained from perspective we can see that the decline progressed like some secret disease long before the people involved realized what was happening. It is true that there is a vague undercurrent of malaise in much of the literature of the time; but in Michinaga's day people would have been most surprised to hear that deadly seeds were already working to bring their magnificent world down in ruins. Towards the end of the eleventh century, when the dangers were becoming more apparent, efforts were

3. *Eiga Monogatari* consists of 40 books. It covers the period from 889 to 1092, but centres on the time of Michinaga. The first 30 books have traditionally been ascribed to Akazome Emon (c. 957–1045), one of the many literary court ladies who flourished in Michinaga's time.

made to shore up the system by a new form of control known as Cloister Government, in which power was held by a retired emperor instead of by a Fujiwara ruler, and the government also tried to stop the spread of the great tax-exempt manors in the provinces. But it was far too late: though there were few to know it, effective power had already passed out of the hands of the old aristocracy into those of an entirely new class with different values and methods of control. Under this new class of military provincials Japan passed from the halcyon days of Heian into a far rougher and harsher period of her history.

Several reasons have been given for the decline and fall of Heian civilization. Japanese scholars of the old school have traditionally emphasized moral factors – the growing self-indulgence and effeteness of the ruling class and their failure to observe Confucian principles of rectitude. On the whole, they have tended to disapprove of the Heian period as being one of licence and immorality, much as the Victorians looked askance at the bawdiness of the Elizabethan age. Nationalist historians have invariably preferred the succeeding Kamakura period with its sterner, more 'masculine' approach. This point of view is not limited to the Japanese. The distinguished Scottish historian, James Murdoch, has summed up his view of the Heian aristocracy in the ringing phrases of the kirk:

An ever-pullulating brood of greedy, needy, frivolous dilettanti – as often as not foully licentious, utterly effeminate, incapable of any worthy achievement, but withal the polished exponents of high breeding and correct 'form'. . . . Now and then a better man did emerge; but one just man is impotent to avert the doom of an intellectual Sodom. . . . A pretty showing, indeed, these pampered minions and bepowdered poetasters might be expected to make.[4]

The most perfervid Confucian moralist could not have put the case more strongly, or worded it as colourfully.

More recently the trend has been to emphasize economic factors – the growth of the manorial system, for example, and the increasing independence of the provinces, or territorial over-expansion. Professor Clough's formula for the decline of civilizations seems especially apt in the case of Heian, where from the beginning we find an imbalance of

4. Murdoch, *A History of Japan*, i. 230.

energies poured into intellectual and artistic pursuits rather than into economic activity.[5] Clearly the breakdown of Heian resulted from a variety of interacting factors; and, as we note the numerous erosive forces that historians have identified, the surprising thing is not that this society collapsed but that, thanks to the law of historical inertia, it lasted as long as it did.

*

In understanding the world of Genji it is particularly important to assess the nature and degree of Chinese influence. The seventh and eighth centuries were one of Japan's great 'borrowing' periods. The official mission to China in 607 included a number of students who remained on the continent for many years and who on their return home helped in the efforts to remodel the primitive island kingdom on the lines of the advanced and sophisticated state that they had admired abroad. The Great Reform of the seventh century, in which some of these students played an important part, was an effort to change the predominantly tribal country into one where, as in China, the emperor would be not merely the most powerful among numerous clan chieftains, but the sole ruler over all the people and all the land.

At the beginning of the eighth century the first permanent capital was established at Nara, and during the so-called Nara period, which lasted until the shift to Nagaoka, every aspect of Chinese culture was avidly adopted. In some ways this can be compared to the early part of the Meiji period, during which Japan tried to transform herself into a Western-type state. The role of the students who returned from China in the seventh and eighth centuries is analogous to that of the young men who were sent to Europe and America in the nineteenth century to learn the modern ways in education, industry, military science, and almost every other field – and who learnt their lesson so well that within fifty years Japan was able to defeat one of the great Western powers in battle.

It would be hard to exaggerate the extent of Chinese influence in Nara. Students and priests accompanied the missions to the continent and came home with fresh technical knowledge and with ever new examples of China's great achievements in art and scholarship. In addition a

5. Shepard Clough, *The Rise and Fall of Civilization*, p. 261 et passim.

stream of Chinese and Korean immigrants and refugees, many of them artists and technicians, helped to build her new urban civilization. Finally, the Buddhist church, with its steadily widening sphere of influence, served to disseminate the sophisticated culture from overseas.

In the provinces, of course, the impact was less overpowering; and for the ignorant, tradition-bound peasant in the fields the riches of China remained as remote as was the civilization of Greece and Rome to the average farmer in Tudor England. But so far as the culture of the capital itself was concerned almost every important aspect had been borrowed more or less directly from abroad. The city was a small copy of Ch'ang-an and the court was modelled on the Chinese emperor's; the system of administration was that of the great T'ang bureaucracy; the language of scholarship and official affairs was Chinese; the national histories were based on the model of the Chinese chronicles; Buddhism, which during this century became a state religion, and which exerted a decisive influence on architecture,[6] sculpture, and painting, had reached Japan by way of China and Korea and had received the stamp of these countries; and, as we can judge from the objects preserved in the great Nara treasure-house,[7] the decorative arts were almost all of alien origin. Rarely in the history of the world has a country, entirely free from external pressure as Japan was during this time, so avidly acquired the fruits of an alien culture.

The process continued unabated after the move to Heian Kyō. Even when official missions had been suspended, priests and scholars still visited China and kept the one-sided cultural relations alive. Throughout the period the Heian court was patterned after that of China. Its elaborate protocol and forms of address were of Chinese origin, and so was its music and dance. (One fortunate aspect is that Japan has remained a repository of many forms of Chinese culture, the stately court dances for example, that disappeared in the country of their origin

6. In 770 Empress Shōtoku ordered one million 3-storied miniature wooden pagodas to be distributed among Buddhist temples throughout the land. Each temple contained a small printed charm; these charms are believed to be the oldest examples of printing in the country.

7 The objects in the Shōsō In show a great variety of influences (including Persian, Greek, and Byzantine), but they had all reached Japan by way of Ch'ang-an, the cosmopolitan centre of the Far East. See Harada Jirō, *The Shōsōin, an Eighth-Century Repository.*

during the Mongol invasions and later disorders.) State activities in Heian as in Nara were modelled on those of T'ang and this continued long after the dynasty itself had disappeared. All official and semi-official documents were written in Chinese or, more usually, in a hybrid form of Sino-Japanese. This too was the principal language that men used for scholarly and literary work, corresponding to the rather debased version of Latin that was current in the West. And, as we repeatedly see in *The Tale of Genji*, a craze for things Chinese (or supposedly Chinese) continued to dominate the aristocracy. Nothing more delighted a court lady than to receive a piece of embroidery brought from China, or to be taught how to play some new tune 'in the Chinese style'; and apt quotations from T'ang poetry remained a sure key to social success. The prefix *kara* ('Chinese') in front of any object was invariably a mark of elegance and value, like the word 'imported' in the more expensive shops of London and New York.

Yet from the ninth century relations with the continent became less intimate and the approach to Chinese culture began to change. This is an early example of the pendulum motion that recurs so often in the island's history: after a period of avid borrowing, during which the country almost indiscriminately imports and imitates things from abroad, the pendulum swings and there follows a period of reaction when Japan tends to turn in on herself and to concentrate on absorbing the foreign forms, adapting them to the indigenous pattern and rejecting those that seem uncongenial. Thus the preponderance of Chinese cultural influence and prestige during the late Ashikaga period and the craze for Western fashions, such as pipes, pantaloons, and crucifixes, that followed the arrival of the Westerners in the sixteenth century are succeeded by a period of insularity and intense Japanization, which for some two centuries involved an almost total rupture with the outside world. Again, in the nineteenth century the frenzied borrowing from the West during the early decades of Meiji gave way to a period of increasing nationalist pride and of stress on indigenous Japanese ways, reaching its dismal climax in the ultra-nationalism and xenophobia of the 1930s.[8]

8. A similar pendulum motion may be recognized in the period following the Second World War:
  'The predilection for novelty – in particular foreign-style novelty – has emerged so often and with such force in the course of Japanese history as to justify our

The reaction that started towards the end of the ninth century was far less intense and deliberate than these. China remained the great mentor, but the influence of her culture was becoming absorbed, indirect, less self-conscious. Japan was in the process of adapting Chinese forms to her own special conditions and needs; and, when some aspect of the imported civilization seemed unsuitable, it would be discarded or quietly allowed to fall into desuetude. The approach, in other words, had become selective: there was no longer the feverish desire to gulp down everything that China had to offer on the principle that what came from the continent must always be superior. The Japanese were now able to pick and choose what they wanted, and their choice was not systematic. One result is that their knowledge was often curiously patchy and out of date. Indeed, their selection sometimes strikes one as arbitrary, even perverse. In the field of literature, for example, the T'ang poet, Po Chü-i, was adulated throughout the period; but the works of the great masters, Li Po and Tu Fu, though more respected in their own country than those of Po Chü-i, were little known, if at all, in Heian times.

Already the world pictured in Japanese literature of the early tenth century suggests considerably less direct Chinese influence than that of the preceding generation, and by the time of Sei Shōnagon and Murasaki Shikibu at the end of the century the process of cultural emancipation has gone further still. Genji and his circle were, to be sure, fervent admirers of China; and no man could count himself cultured unless he had what corresponded to a 'classical education', that is to say, was familiar with Chinese literature and able to produce passable imitations of Chinese poetry and prose. The China to which they looked, however, was that of earlier centuries, rather than of contemporary Sung.[9] More

---

viewing it as a national trait. But no less characteristic are the periods of reaction, following those of wholesale importation, when the more conservative elements in the country have been able to assert themselves and to uphold the value of time-honoured ways in politics, social organization, art, and daily living habits, as against new-fangled foreign fashions. Such a period started during the latter half of the Occupation . . .' Ivan Morris, *Nationalism and the Right Wing in Japan*, p. 123.

9. The same sort of 'cultural lag' occurred in the Muromachi period when the Chinese work that mainly influenced the Japanese was not that of the contemporary Ming dynasty but that of the Sung, which had collapsed one century

important, there was no doubt in their minds that Japan possessed her own characteristic culture and way of life which, though more recent than China's, were not necessarily inferior. Terms like *Yamato-e* (paintings of Japan) and *Yamato-damashii* (the spirit of Japan) now came into use, reflecting the new spirit of national self-consciousness.[10]

Despite the increasing cultural independence of Japan and despite her remarkable advances during the tenth century, a visitor from the continent would not have been greatly impressed by what he saw in Heian Kyō, even if he had chanced to arrive during the palmy days of Michinaga. We know that Chinese travellers commented favourably on certain specific Japanese skills, such as their arts of manufacturing coloured paper and of dyeing material; but this was a case of damning with faint praise. In the really important fields – scholarship, poetry and painting – most educated Chinese found little to arouse their enthusiasm. This, for example, is a contemporary Chinese view of the Yamato-e, which represent the first great flowering of indigenous Japanese painting:

... though one may commend the pictorial method for its ability to express the purpose – for the way it shows the people and customs of a foreign land in an unfamiliar quarter, a country which is rude and out of the way, uncivilized, lacking ceremonies and proprieties – how can one evaluate their skill or awkwardness any more closely, when we think of the cultural splendours of China, which have been attained over so long a period?[11]

---

before. Again, in the Tokugawa period interest was focused on Ming culture rather than that of the contemporary Ch'ing dynasty. It is as though Japan today were to find her principal foreign inspiration in the culture of Europe at about the time of the Congress of Vienna. In a study of works by Japanese poets in Chinese an eminent Tokugawa scholar comments:

'Japan is a great distance from China – separated by myriad *ri* and a great ocean. It is only after a fashion [in poetry] has waned in China that it comes to its height in Japan. Circumstances make this inevitable. In general we are about two hundred years behind.' Emura Hokkai (1713–88), *Nihon Shishi*, iv, 60.

10. The first use of the term *Yamato-e* can be found in 999. *The Tale of Genji* contains the first reference I have seen to *Yamato-damashii*.

11. *Hsüan Ho Hua P'u*, chapter 12, quoted by A. C. Soper in 'The Rise of Yamato-e', *Art Bulletin*, xxiv, 374.

The *Sung Shih* (dynastic history of the Sung) has the following comment on

The reference to 'ceremonies and proprieties' is significant. For it was above all the failure of Heian Japan to conform to the Confucian pattern that earned it the epithet of 'uncivilized'. Many aspects of the world of Genji would be related to this: the cavalier treatment of the emperor, for example, and the prominence of women in society.

A European writer who visited Japan in 1959 has described the irritation he felt at seeing 'Western civilization in a distorting mirror'.[12] The Chinese visitor to Heian Kyō in Murasaki's time might well have experienced a similar reaction, though perhaps he would have been amused rather than annoyed. He would have recognized numerous forms that had clearly been borrowed from his own country at some time or other, but that had by now become absurdly distorted. The literary language affected by the gentlemanly poetasters would have struck him as a laughable caricature of the noble Chinese style, while the palace architecture and the court ceremonial would have seemed like a rather untidy imitation in drab miniature of the glories of his own capital. What might have interested the visitor most would have been that the model the Japanese were so gallantly copying was not contemporary Sung but China some two centuries in the past. This might seem valuable from an antiquarian point of view, and the visitor might well commend the Japanese for faithfully preserving certain aspects of T'ang culture. Yet it seems likely that on his return home he would describe Murasaki's Japan as a poor and hopelessly out-of-date copy of China's great civilization.

If so, he would of course have been missing an essential part of the picture, namely, that for over a century Japan had been developing on increasingly independent lines and in the process was evolving her own original culture, which in some aspects even surpassed that of its parent civilization to the west. In the field of political, social and economic organization the prevalence of strong aristocratic and clan traditions had helped to alienate Japan increasingly from the systems she had taken

---

Japanese poetry: 'Shih-ch'ang [an overseas trader who had returned home in 1002 after a stay in Japan] took this occasion to present [to the Emperor] poems composed by Japanese. They were highly polished in rhetoric but shallow and of no merit.' Ryūsaku Isunoda and Carrington Goodrich, *Japan in the Chinese Dynastic Histories*, p. 59.

12. Arthur Koestler, *The Lotus and the Robot*, pp. 153–60.

over wholesale from China at the time of the Great Reform. New indigenous political institutions had developed to replace the Chinese-type bureaucracy in all but name. The Chinese system of land distribution and taxation, which had also been adopted in the seventh century, had long since lapsed, and the economy was now based on great manorial holdings, for which there was no foreign model. Both political and economic power had become concentrated in the hands of a single family, a state of affairs that was to be characteristic of Japan for many centuries to come.

On the cultural side, new forms of Buddhism had for all intents and purposes displaced the Chinese-type sects of the Nara period; also in Murasaki's time a popular, evangelical Buddhism was coming to the fore; and clerics had elaborated a peculiarly Japanese sort of syncretism, aimed at combining the way of Buddha with Shintō. In painting, the *emaki* picture scrolls, which reached their climax at the end of the Heian period, were developing as an indigenous and important form of art. And in the field of literature, *kanabungaku*, the new type of phonetic writing from which Chinese word constructions were largely excluded, was being used to create some of the greatest works ever produced in the Far East. Among the various genres written in the new script, prose fiction, which was traditionally scorned by Chinese Confucianists, reached a climax of development in tenth-century Heian Kyō, a climax never to be surpassed in either China or Japan.

Significantly this literature in the phonetic script was sometimes known as 'women's writing'. For, although both sexes used *kanabun* to record the native language, most men were still so overawed by the prestige of Chinese writing that they preferred to circumscribe their literary efforts by a foreign idiom, even though the results were almost bound to be derivative and jejune. This put women, who were theoretically debarred from Chinese studies, at a considerable advantage and is the main reason that their sex produced most of the important writers of the time. The preponderance of women in Heian literature represents not only a divergence from the Chinese pattern but an aspect of uniqueness.[13]

*

13. Chapter VIII deals in more detail with the role of women in Heian literature.

The Heian period has two contrasting aspects that must be kept in mind if we are to understand the world of the shining prince. On one side is the love of colour and grandeur, of pomp and circumstance, summed up in the word *eiga*. This involves a fascination with elaborate court ceremonial, with great religious processions, and with those brilliant state functions in which the magnificently accoutred officials move as though performing some stylized dance. Compared to the Chinese court it was all on a small and simple scale, and the descriptions in works like *The Tale of Genji* and *Tales of Glory* no doubt contain a good measure of idealization. Yet Michinaga and the people of his circle loved splendour and display and did their best to infuse the yearly round of ceremonies with the beauty and elegance that were so important in almost every part of their lives.

Never far removed from this delight in the aesthetic joys of the world is the sombre, negative aspect of the period, which is an underlying theme in almost all contemporary literature. Often it is just when some splendid celebration has drawn to an end and images of the dancers and musicians and of the crimson tapestry of blossoms under which they have performed are still fresh in his mind that Genji is most overcome with the gloomy side of reality and that the vanity of human pleasures strikes him with the greatest poignancy. The negative tenor of Buddhist doctrine – its picture of the world as a place of universal suffering – was an important element. This was reinforced, especially in the second half of the period, by the disquieting doctrine that the world was about to enter the hopeless era that the Buddha had predicted when he spoke of 'the latter days of the Law'.[14]

Changing political and social conditions played their part in encouraging this mood of pessimism and melancholia. Among the upper classes of Heian Kyō there appears to have been a vague sense of foreboding, of impending dislocation. Genji himself, and particularly Murasaki's second hero, the rather etiolated young man called Kaoru, are in many ways *fin de siècle* characters. Theirs is not the vigour and ebullience of a new age, but the world-weariness of a great epoch that is entering its period of decline. Though it is not expressed in so many words, we can often recognize in the literature of the time a feeling that the familiar order of things will soon come to an end, a feeling in some ways similar

14. See p. 128.

29

to that of the modern author who wrote of 'closing time in the gardens of the West'.[15]

Fundamentally this was related to the steady weakening of the imperial court and the shift of real power to military clans in the provinces. These trends did not become obvious until a considerable time after Murasaki's death, but in her lifetime there were already ample symptoms of the eventual breakdown. Sporadic revolts and disturbances in the provinces, rampant piracy on the Inland Sea, daylight robbery in the streets of the capital, massive raids by marauding priests from the nearby mountain monasteries – all combined to exert a depressing influence on the more sensitive inhabitants of the world of the shining prince.

Finally there was the great network of superstitious fears – the belief in avenging ghosts, in possession by living spirits, in the fury of the many minor gods who might chastise one for walking in the wrong direction or for washing one's hair on the wrong day or for infringing any of the other innumerable taboos.[16] All this, together with the succession of epidemics, famines, fires, storms, and earthquakes, of which Heian had its full share, was bound to build up a sense of anxiety and to deepen the mood of pessimism that became such a marked feature of the period, tending to neutralize its many gaieties and enjoyments.

15. 'It is closing time in the gardens of the West. From now on an artist will be judged only by the resonance of his solitude or the quality of his despair.' The continuation of Connolly's phrase would have appealed to writers of the late Heian and Kamakura periods with their poignant sense of the 'latter days of the Law'.

16. See Chapter v.

II

The Setting

WHEN Murasaki was born in the seventies of the tenth century, official relations with China and Korea had been in a state of abeyance for almost a hundred years. Merchants and priests continued to risk the dangerous sea voyage to the continent, but other types of travel were forbidden. No ambassadors were sent abroad; nor, as a rule, were any received. When the new Korean kingdom of Koryŏ dispatched missions to Japan, the merchants were allowed to engage in business, but the envoys were regularly sent back without being received at court. With the Khitans and the Golden Tartars in the northern border-lands Japan refused to have any dealings at all; for she regarded them as barbarians from whom there was nothing useful to be learnt.[1]

The centuries of feverish borrowing, during which Japan had almost indiscriminately taken what she could from abroad, were, as we have seen, being followed by a period of national self-confidence and autonomy. So far as direct foreign relations were concerned, the world of the shining prince was isolated to a degree unprecedented in the country's recorded history – a degree that the great island kingdom of the West has never experienced.

The insularity of tenth-century Japan is reflected in the scarcity of foreigners. Whereas the Chinese capital was highly responsive to foreign influences and thronged with visitors from every part of Asia – Indian monks, Zoroastrian priests, merchants from Persia and from the southern seas, envoys from the Arab community in Transoxiana – Heian Kyō had few travellers from abroad, and the rest of Japan virtually none. Near the market there had been a special building where Chinese and other foreigners were lodged, but after the break in official relations it was hardly ever used.

The merchants and occasional scholars who continued to arrive from China in Murasaki's time provided almost the only direct window to the

1. R. K. Reischauer, *Early Japanese History*, A. 67.

31

outside world. One might expect that Heian gentlemen, who spent so much of their time trying to write Chinese, would have welcomed the opportunity to meet people who actually conversed in the language; but from contemporary literature one gathers that they had no such ambition. Evidently they preferred to regard Chinese as a dead language – much like those modern teachers of English and French in Japan for whom inability to speak the language comes near to being a mark of academic distinction.

The Tale of Genji gives a realistic and fairly complete picture of cultural life in the capital. Yet the only foreigners to appear in the course of this immense novel are the Korean visitors in the opening chapter; and it is clear that Murasaki had little interest in these exotic gentlemen. Similarly Sei Shōnagon's *Pillow Book* is a meticulous record of life in Heian Kyō, and she herself was a woman of the greatest curiosity. But never once does she describe a foreigner in the capital. This lack of cosmopolitan life is a remarkable feature of this world and immediately distinguishes Heian from other great civilizations, like those centred in Ch'ang-an, Imperial Rome, and Alexandria, where cultural cross-breeding was so important.

If Prince Genji and his friends had virtually no direct contact with foreigners at home, still less did they dream of travelling abroad themselves. Even if the voyage to China had been far less dangerous than it was, one doubts whether they would have been inclined to spare the time away from Heian Kyō. Never once do they express any curiosity about the appearance or customs of the outside world. They had a sizable store of foreign books at their disposal and were in a position to know a good deal (though in a rather out-of-date and scattered way) even about Central Asia. Yet they had remarkably little interest in what was happening across the seas. The world, to all intents and purposes, consisted of Japan, Korea, and China – and only of an infinitesimal part of even these countries. Their ignorance of points farther west was abysmal. In *The Tale of the Hollow Tree* the hero, who is on his way from Japan to China, performs the remarkable feat of being shipwrecked on the Persian coast. Despite the great role of Buddhism in Heian life, India (Tenjiku) is rarely mentioned – and then as a semi-mythical place where no one but strange hermits or magicians would dream of venturing.

The Setting

The 'Continent Isolated' frame of mind that had developed by Mura-saki's time reinforced the closed, parochial character of her world, which sometimes verges on the stifling. Yet it had a positive result, too. For it was precisely the isolated and self-contained nature of this world that helped to produce the specialized, intense, uniform culture which is its greatest interest. It allowed Murasaki's Japan to go very far in some ways, yet kept it peculiarly backward in others. We can recognize this uneven nature of development throughout Japanese history, but particularly in those periods (of which the world of the shining prince is the first notable example) when the pendulum swings away from the borrowing phase towards the inward-looking extreme.

★

Murasaki's Japan was virtually identical in territory with the present archipelago, except that the great northern island of Hokkaidō was still the preserve of the Ezo aborigines, the putative ancestors of the 'hairy Ainu'. These aborigines had originally been spread all over the islands; but they were driven steadily northwards, and in Murasaki's age they no longer represented a military problem.

The final defeat of the aborigines by the imperial forces had made it possible to bring under cultivation huge new tracts of land in the eastern and northern regions of the main island. This was all theoretically part of the emperor's domain, but, owing to the primitive state of communi-cations and to the strength of local magnates, little of the potential wealth found its way into the imperial coffers. For the inhabitants of Heian Kyō the north-eastern territories of their own island were exceed-ingly remote – even more so, in some ways, than Korea and China.

Japan was divided into sixty-two provinces and two islands, essen-tially the same division that the Portuguese found when they arrived half a millennium later. For Murasaki and her circle by far the most impor-tant region was the Home Provinces; their interest in the country de-clined rapidly when it came to places that were distant from Heian Kyō. In sections 11–18 of her *Pillow Book* Sei Shōnagon lists some one hun-dred famous mountains, lakes, and other places. About three-quarters of them are in the provinces near the capital. Mount Fuji (in the eastern province of Suruga) does not get even a passing mention.

The remaining provinces were grouped in seven circuits, of which the most famous has always been the Tōkaidō, extending north-east from the home provinces to the region where Tokyo is now situated. Each circuit was supposed to have a great highway leading to the capital. Here, as in so many other ways, practice differed sharply from theory: once they had left the home provinces the 'highways' tended to dwindle into mere tracks, and often they were quite impassable.

*

For the cultured inhabitants of Heian Kyō the distant provinces afforded only one mitigating aspect: the varied and dramatic beauties of the Japanese countryside. The young girl who wrote the *Sarashina Diary*, for example, gives some breathless descriptions of Mount Fuji and of the other natural wonders she had seen on her journey to the capital. Yet even in this respect Murasaki and her contemporaries preferred the more familiar environment of the home provinces, where nature seemed less raw and savage, more in harmony with the delicate nuances of human emotion.

In comparison with the wild, grandiose vistas to be found in other parts of Japan, the home provinces were, on the whole, mild and friend-ly. The capital itself was situated in beautiful country, encircled on three sides by thickly forested hills and mountains, often delicately wreathed with trails of mist; in the autumn evenings one could hear the deer's cry in the distance and the desolate call of the wild geese over-head; the landscape abounded in streams and waterfalls and lakes; and into its green slopes and valleys the countless shrines and monasteries blended as if they too had become a part of nature. Even today, after a century of industrialization (which in Japan seems to assume an especi-ally relentless form), the visitor to Kyoto is struck by the splendour of its setting. We can imagine how beautiful it must have been in Mura-saki's day before it had undergone the depredations of civil war and westernization.[2] In whatever direction Prince Genji and his fellow-

2. One of the first Westerners to describe the capital was Kaempfer (see p. 11, note):

'It is surrounded with pleasant green hills and mountains, on which arise numbers of small rivers and agreeable springs. The city comes nearest the mountains on the East side, where there are abundance of temples, monasteries, chapels, and other religious buildings, standing in the ascent . . .' Kaempfer, op. cit., ii. 485.

inhabitants might look, nature appeared in its most delightful forms, subtly varying its beauty and mood with each season. It is small wonder that to be away from the capital, as an exile or even *en poste,* was regarded as a form of living death.

The countryside and climate of Japan have exerted a decisive influence on her literature; and the role of nature in Heian writing can hardly be exaggerated. Japan is a country of marked seasonal changes, a country in which it is particularly hard to be unaware of nature. It is a country, too, where an awesome variety of natural disasters – typhoons, tidal waves, floods, and almost daily earthquakes – has combined to make people highly conscious of the influence of nature on their lives.

The Western world has traditionally been inspired by the ideal of man's boldly pitting himself against the impersonal forces of nature and of eventually subduing them for his convenience – an ideal realized with such success in our own century that, paradoxically, not only man's comfort but his survival as a species is imminently threatened. Less dramatically, the ideal of conquering the physical world is reflected in the modern metropolis, which strives in so many ways to abolish the seasons and thus the influence of nature on its inhabitants. The advertising slogan, 'Cool in summer, warm in winter', seems to sum up much of the Occidental approach.

In the Far East, however, religious and intellectual traditions have stressed the unity of life, in opposition to any idea of duality between man and his natural environment. The indigenous Japanese religion, in which nature worship appears originally to have played a central part, combined with the influence of Buddhism and Taoism to inculcate the sense that man is an integral part of the natural world, his role being not to fight nature, but rather to put himself in harmony with it and, if necessary, to suffer its inconveniences. To a remarkable extent this view persists in Japan even now after a hundred years of Western influence. In Heian times, and far later, any idea that there is an intrinsic opposition between man and the world about him would have seemed as alien as theories of original sin or economic determinism. The inhabitants of the shining prince's world never try to cut themselves off from their natural environment; rather they strive to blend themselves with the nature that surrounds them, believing that thus they can learn to understand themselves and those about them. Sensitivity to the subtle moods of nature, indeed, was an essential attribute of 'good people'. Without such sensitivity it was impossible to enter into the 'emotional quality of things', which was regarded as the basis of aesthetic, and even of moral, awareness.

From the earliest times Japanese poetry was overwhelmingly concerned with the lyrical evocation of nature in its varied aspects. The core of the poem was almost invariably a natural image, used to symbolize some human emotion or experience. This tradition was carried over into prose literature of the Heian period, especially that written by women. Their diaries, notes, and works of fiction show how absorbed they were with the characteristic beauties and moods of the different seasons. Throughout *The Tale of Genji* we are never in any doubt about the time of the year and of the day in which each scene takes place. Murasaki and most writers of her period were fascinated with the calendar and with its effect on people's feelings.

In the famous opening section of her *Pillow Book* Sei Shōnagon evokes the special charms of the four seasons:

In Spring it is the dawn. As gradually the hills come to light, their outline is faintly dyed with red, and wisps of purplish cloud trail over them.

In Summer, the nights. Not only when the moon shines down, but on dark nights, too, when the fireflies flit to and fro, and even when it rains, how beautiful it is!

In Autumn, the evenings – evenings when one is moved to see the brilliant sun sink close to the edge of the hills and the crows fly back to their nests in threes and fours and twos; or, more charming still, a file of wild geese, tiny in the distant sky. And when finally the sun has set, how moving to hear the sound of the wind and the cry of the insects!

In Winter, the early morning. Beautiful indeed when it has snowed during the night, but delightful, too, when the ground is white with frost; or even when it is simply very cold and the attendants hurry from room to room, stirring up the fires and bringing charcoal, how well it fits the season's mood![3]

3. Kaneko Motoomi, *Makura no Sōshi Hyōshaku* (hereafter abbreviated as 'Kaneko ed.'), p. 4.
Unless stated to the contrary, all translations from Japanese and Chinese are my own.

This interest in the phases of nature is also reflected in the 'battles of the seasons', contests in which the participants composed poems and used historical and literary allusions to extol their favourite seasons. By Murasaki's time such contests had become something of a literary convention. In *The Tale of Genji* the battle is waged between spring and autumn, and the leader of the autumn forces is a lady whose association with that season is so conspicuous as to have given her the name of Akikonomu ('Lover of Autumn').

Autumn is the season *par excellence* in *The Tale of Genji* and in much of Japan's classical literature. For it is the autumnal images – the silently falling leaves, the rain gently moistening the last fading flowers, the doleful cry of the deer from the windswept hills, the gathering mists – that most poignantly evoke the pathos of human existence, which is an underlying theme in so much of this literature. It is no coincidence that the most memorable scenes in Murasaki's novel should nearly all take place in the autumn months.

In *The Tale of Genji*, then, the nature of Heian Kyō and its environs is no mere static background which the author introduces for decorative effect. It is a vital force, exerting a constant influence on the characters; and it is in terms of this nature that Prince Genji and the others perceive and express their emotions.

*

In view of the prevailing attitude to the provinces, it is hardly surprising that *The Tale of Genji* and other contemporary literature should have been concerned almost exclusively with life in the capital and its immediate surroundings. In Murasaki's eyes, as in Prince Genji's, only those who were urbane, in the original sense of the word, could be regarded as civilized.

Heian Kyō, like Nara, was modelled on the Chinese city of Ch'ang-an, the great metropolitan wonder of the Eastern world, which had reached the height of its splendour during the T'ang dynasty. Whereas Nara was the capital of Japan for only seventy-five years, Heian Kyō (later known as Miyako and Kyoto) enjoyed the distinction for almost eleven centuries. It was conceived on a far larger scale than Nara, and it had a completely different atmosphere. The great Buddhist centre of Nara represented antiquity and calm; Heian Kyō, at least during its early centuries, stood for all that was new and lively in the country. *Imamekashi* ('up to date') was the keynote of the new age, and the highest term of praise for Murasaki and her friends. Apart from the capital there was no place in all Japan to which the term could properly be applied.

The city of the world of the shining prince was a rectangle about three and a half miles from north to south, and two and a half miles from east to west.[4] A stone wall about six feet high, with a nine-foot ditch on both sides, surrounded Heian Kyō; eighteen gates provided access to the main streets. The wall fell into disrepair at an early stage. Many of the gates remained, however, and some of them, like the famous Rashō Mon, a vast, elaborate structure at the south of the city, became the haunts of thieves, footpads, beggars, waifs, and others who were not privileged to enjoy the amenities of Heian civilization.

Unlike most later Japanese cities, the capital was planned in a perfectly systematic fashion, being divided at regular intervals by parallel streets and avenues crossing each other at right angles. The main avenues running east and west were called *jō*. They were known by numbers, from the First Avenue (Ichi Jō) at the north of the city to the Ninth Avenue (Ku Jō), which constituted its southern extremity. Somewhat confusingly, the word *jō* was also applied to the areas between the avenues; in this sense it is usually translated as 'ward'. Thus the entire district across the city between the Third and Fourth Avenues was known as the Fourth Ward (Shi Jō). Members of the aristocracy, including emperors, were often named after the wards in which they or their families had resided. In *The Tale of Genji*, for example, the pathologically jealous Lady Rokujō owes her name to the Sixth Ward, with which her family was associated.

The streets, compared with those of the later feudal towns, were extremely wide. The avenues varied from about eighty to one hundred and seventy feet across, and the main streets running from north to south were equally spacious. The most impressive of all was Suzaku Ōji, which ran about two and a half miles from the Imperial Palace

4. In other words, about one third of the area of Ch'ang-an, which was 6 × 5 miles. The wall round the Chinese capital was about 20 ft high, and round the Imperial Palace well over 30 ft. In every respect Ch'ang-an was built on a grander scale.

through the centre of the city to the Rashō Mon. 'Red Bird Avenue' (which is what its name means)[5] was almost three hundred feet wide – a fantastic figure when we recall that in Rome the Twelve Tables had prescribed a maximum width of about fifteen feet for the *viae*, and that even the Appian Way was less than twenty feet across; indeed, so far as size is concerned, the Champs Elysées itself is no match for the main thoroughfare of the Heian capital.

Most of the principal streets were lined with trees. Suzaku Ōji was famous for its willows, and from the literature of the time we can judge what an impressive sight it must have been when the imperial processions moved slowly through the centre of the city, the ornate ox-drawn carriages preceded by hundreds of outriders in court costume. A contemporary song celebrates the beauty of the street:

> Light green they shine,
> Dark green they shine,
> Stretching into the distance as far as the eye can see,
> They glitter like jewels.
> Oh, how they glitter – those low-hanging boughs
> Of the willows on Suzaku Ōji![6]

Only the most patrician families were allowed to have residences facing the great avenues. The majority of the inhabitants lived on the narrow streets and still narrower alleys, which ran parallel or perpendicular to the main thoroughfares. The houses, except for those of the nobility, lay close together, permitting a population in Murasaki's time of close on one hundred thousand – far larger than that of any contemporary European city, but inconsiderable when compared with Ch'angan or Imperial Rome.[7]

Heian Kyō was chequered like a vast chess board, and there was an intricate, but delightfully regular, system of subdivisions, and sub-sub-

5. Like the corresponding avenue in Ch'ang-an, Suzaku Ōji was named after the Chinese symbol for the south. The great Chinese avenue was twice as wide as Suzaku Ōji – about 600 ft across.

6. Saibara quoted by Fujiki Kunihiko, *Heian Jidai no Kizoku no Seikatsu*, p. 117.

7. The population of 'greater Ch'ang-an' was almost 2 million; within the 30-square-mile area enclosed by the city walls the population was probably more than a million (Edwin O. Reischauer and John Fairbank, *East Asia: The Great Tradition*, p. 168). Professor Carcopino's minimum estimate for the population

divisions, the basic administrative unit being an area of about fourteen acres. The inhabitants of each unit were responsible for keeping their streets clean, and there were periodic inspections. All sections of the city were numbered systematically, starting from the Imperial Palace; it was possible to give an accurate definition of where any building was situated – a luxury afforded by few modern Japanese towns, in which as a rule the streets have no names and the houses no regular numbers.[8]

Directly in the north centre of the city was an area of some three hundred acres known as the Nine-Fold Enclosure. This was the Greater Imperial Palace, a little town in itself, which contained both the palace buildings and the government offices, and which, as in China, opened to the auspicious southern direction. Some of the buildings, such as the Palace of Administration,[9] were on a huge scale, their great stone base, red lacquered pillars, white walls, stone floors, and elaborate roofs with green glazed tiles being copied directly from Chinese palace architecture. In remarkable contrast were the buildings in pure Japanese style,

---

of Rome under the Antonines is 1,200,000; he assesses the total area of the *urbs* at some 2,000 hectares (*Daily Life in Ancient Rome*, pp. 10–21).

These very approximate figures would yield population densities of about 50 per acre in Ch'ang-an and 250 per acre in Rome, where people were packed together in huge apartment houses; Heian Kyō was relatively uncrowded with less than 20 people to the acre. This last figure is somewhat misleading, however, since less than half of the total area was inhabited in Murasaki's time. If we assume that 600 *chō* were inhabited and if we subtract from this the area occupied by the Greater Imperial Palace and the Imperial Gardens, we find a population density of about 60 per acre. In 1950 the population density of Kyoto was about 100 per acre.

8. The main division, 1 *bō*, was the area bounded by 2 avenues (*jō*) and 2 main north-south streets (*ōji*). Each *bō* was divided into 4 *ho* (the basic administrative unit). The *ho*, in turn, were divided into 4 *chō* (about 3.5 acres each). Finally, the *chō* was broken down into 32 *henushi*, which were bounded by 4 *kō* running north to south and 8 *mon* running east to west. Thus the address of someone's house might be as follows: Sakyō (eastern half of the city), Go Jō (5th Ward), Sambō (3rd *Bō* from Suzaku Ōji), Ichi Ho (1st *Ho*), Hatchō (8th *Chō*), Seihoku Nikō Go Mon (north-east corner of the block formed by the 2nd *Kō* and the 5th *Mon*). Fujiki, op. cit., p. 117.

9. The Great Hall of the Palace of Administration (Chōdō In) is the model for the present Heian Shrine, one of Kyoto's most impressive (though certainly not most attractive) structures; the 9th-century palace, however, was twice the size of the modern building.

which included the emperor's own residence, the Seiryō Den ('Pure and Fresh Palace'); here the plain wood, wattled roofs, and cypress floor-boards reflected the astringent influence of native Shintō architecture. This mixture of foreign and native styles in the same block of buildings provides a notable example of juxtaposition taking the place of cultural assimilation. The entire palace compound was surrounded by a low wall; and the bare grounds were strewn with gravel, in typical Japanese style.

There were few gardens within the precincts of the Great Imperial Palace, and these were of the simplest design, consisting mainly of care-fully raked white gravel and tubbed trees. Apartments in the palace and their inhabitants were sometimes named after these trees; for instance, a literal translation of the name of the Emperor's favourite concubine (and Genji's secret mistress) would be Lady Wistaria Tub (Fujitsubo). The large open space in front of the Ceremonial Palace was used for official celebrations. It was the site of the two most famous trees in the capital, known as the Cherry of the Left and the Orange of the Right; the latter was believed to have been growing in the same place long be-fore Heian Kyō became the capital.

The main imperial garden was the Shinsen En ('Divine Spring Gar-den') south of the enclosure. It covered about thirty acres and con-tained a large lake, a spring, a hill, and a pavilion. The emperor and his court frequently visited the Shinsen En for banquets and poem parties, and it was also used for ceremonies such as the Prayer for Rain. The beauty and splendour of this garden is celebrated in much contem-porary literature,[10] but today all that remains is a little pond on a quiet side street in Kyoto.

There were several 'detached palaces' outside the Greater Imperial Palace. It was here that imperial consorts were lodged during their con-finements, which, according to Shintō beliefs, would have made the imperial residence ritually unclean. Sometimes the emperors them-

10. E.g., the following poem by Shigeno no Sadanushi (785–852) in *Keikoku Shū*, an early 9th-century anthology of Chinese poems by Japanese writers:
'The . . . path [of Shinsen En] is clean swept and shadows of willows lie across it. . . . A sandy white beach winds round the lake. All is calm and clear. The eye catches a pure spring bubbling up, to run off in a narrow streamlet. If we climb the low hill, we may often catch sight of birds, startle the wood doves. . . . In the dragon pond glimmer the sun, moon and stars . . .' Gunsho Ruijū, 6, *Keikoku Shū*, xiv, 172.

selves were obliged to move to these outside palaces, since their own buildings had the unfortunate habit of burning down at frequent intervals.

Most of the leading aristocratic families had their principal residences near the great palace enclosure in the First, Second, and Third Wards. To own a residence close to the palace was an important status symbol, and land in these upper wards was in great demand. The Imperial University was also near the palace walls. Further south, in the Seventh Ward, was the commercial district, centred upon the Eastern and Western Markets; they had a total of some eighty stalls selling foods, clothing, and simple supplies. In each market was a great cherry tree, and it was here that prisoners sentenced to public birching and flogging received their punishments; in the relatively mild atmosphere of the Heian period, however, such harsh displays appear to have been mercifully rare. The Left and Right Prisons were close to the Great Palace Enclosure, but, to judge from the following entry in a contemporary chronicle, they do not seem to have been a conspicuous part of the scene:

The Emperor made a tour of inspection of the city and distributed rice and money to the poor. Coming to the Prison, His Majesty inquired, 'Whose house may this be?' The Minister of the Right replied, 'It is the Prison.' On hearing this, His Majesty was pleased to free all the inmates by means of a special amnesty. They were delighted and greeted the Emperor with great cries of 'Banzai'.[11]

The pleasing symmetry of Heian Kyō did not last long. Earthquakes and fires regularly devastated large parts of the city, and often the sites of the ruined buildings became waste land, or were used as paddy fields or for cultivating onions, parsley, and other homely crops. The original plans for Heian Kyō had envisaged a city in which buildings would occupy 1,215 *chō* (blocks of about three and a half acres), but in fact it appears that less than one half of this area was developed in Murasaki's day. Readers of *The Tale of Genji* will recall that parts of the capital away from the centre are described as being rough and wild, almost like open country. The desolate residence of the red-nosed lady in Books 6 and 15 ('The Saffron-Flower' and 'The Palace in the Tangled Woods' in Waley's translation) is of course an extreme case, but we know that by

11. *Shoku Nihon Kōki*, Kashō II, 12, Kokushi Taikei ed., iii, 231.

Murasaki's time many quarters in the capital had fallen into disuse and were unsafe for travellers.

This applied especially to the 'City of the Right', the area to the west of the Imperial Palace. Despite all efforts to produce a symmetrical pattern, the capital developed unevenly from the very beginning. The eastern half flourished until eventually it spread across its natural boundary, the Kamo River. Meanwhile the western half, which was on lower ground, was falling into decay. Already in 862 an edict of the Great Council of State complains that large sections to the west of Suzaku Avenue have become uninhabited: in the daytime they are being used to graze cattle, at night they become the haunts of thieves; accordingly the Council orders that soldiers under the command of Imperial Guards be posted at each of the western gates to restore confidence to the inhabitants. The measure does not seem to have made the western section any more popular. About one century later (when Murasaki was a girl) we find the following description: 'There are scarcely any houses left in the western half of the city, and it is almost entirely deserted. People pack up and leave, but no one arrives; houses crumble to the ground, but none are built.'[12] The writer stresses the contrast with the remainder of the city: 'The eastern half, north from the Fourth Ward, is thronged with crowds of people, both rich and poor. The halls and gates of the great mansions tower along the avenues; the eaves of the humble cottages make a solid line.'[13] This lopsided development of Heian Kyō continued in the following centuries. The Imperial Palace, instead of overlooking the capital from the centre, came to occupy its north-west corner. The main part of the present city of Kyoto corresponds to the eastern half of the old capital.

Although Heian Kyō failed to develop as its planners intended, there could be no complaint about its site, which was ideal from every traditional point of view. Hills lay to the north, west, and east; and in the north-east, the unlucky direction, the great mountain range of Hiei, on which Buddhist temples and monasteries clustered in endless profusion, proudly defended the city from evil influences – as well as furnishing the aristocracy with an excuse for excursions and trysts. Along the foot

12. Yoshishige Yasutane, *Chitei no Ki*. Entry dated 982. Quoted by Fujiki, op. cit., p. 124.
13. Ibid.

of the eastern hills flowed the Kamo River, which curved round at the south, again as topographical tradition demanded; the Katsura River to the west of the city provided the second of the two essential 'female' elements.[14] The city was on a gentle slope and water from the rivers was diverted into canals, which ran down the centre of many of the main streets, pleasantly reflecting the green willows and the white plum blossoms. The rivers also provided an ample water supply for the artificial streams in the noblemen's gardens, as well as for more prosaic purposes.

Although far more elaborate than anything that had existed previously in Japan, the City of Purple Hills and Crystal Streams, as the poets called it, was of the utmost simplicity when compared with its Chinese model; and, seen next to that of Imperial Rome, the dominant impression of its aristocratic life would be one of Spartan restraint. References in works like *Tales of Glory* to the pomp and splendour of Genji's world, and the use of words like 'palace', 'court', and 'mansion', must not be allowed to obscure this aspect, which was dictated both by Japanese canons of taste and by economic necessity.

The same simplicity marked the domestic architecture of the period. The type of mansion occupied by Genji and those of his class was known as *shinden*. Although originally influenced by Chinese concepts and by Buddhist temple architecture, Heian style had moved steadily away from foreign models during the ninth and early tenth centuries, and by Murasaki's time the *shinden* had assumed a distinctively Japanese air, having sloping bark-shingled or wattled roofs, round pillars of plain wood, deep eaves, and open wooden piling to raise the buildings about one foot from the ground as a protection against humidity. Very few houses had more than a single floor. Despite the elegant Chinese associations of tiles, they were avoided in private dwellings, since they made the rooms uncomfortably hot in the summer; Sei Shōnagon lists heavy tiled roofs among the 'things that give one an uneasy feeling'.

The general effect of the *shinden* mansion must have been light and graceful. It certainly lacked the impressive ornateness of Chinese architecture. On the other hand, it was far from being designed on the miniature scale so often associated with Japanese styles. The standard size of a patrician residence and garden was a block of one *chō* (about three

14. Mountains represented the Yang (male) principle, rivers the Yin (female).

and a half acres) and the mansions of some of the Heian nabobs appear to have been even more spacious.

Centuries of wars, fires, and earthquakes have deprived us of authentic examples of the *shinden* house; but we have numerous reconstructions. The typical mansion consisted of a number of rectangular buildings, joined by long covered corridors – similar to the cloister colonnades of Buddhist temple complexes, and probably cognate. A white stone wall surrounded the compound, and covered entrances were provided for ox-drawn carriages at the east and the west. On three sides there were gates, whose height and ornateness varied in proportion to the rank of the owner; the entire *shinden* formed a large rectangle open to the south.

Here there would be an elegant landscape garden, usually comprising an artificial lake with a line of carefully arranged rocks,[15] a pine-dotted island, and one or two miniature hills. The earth was strewn with fine white sand to reflect the full beauty of the moonlight.

Two parallel streams ran through the whole compound and into the lake. They would wind their way round, and sometimes under, the buildings; the corridors that crossed the water would be arched like miniature bridges. During the Winding Water banquets the guests sat by the stream and, as a wine cup floated by, each in turn would pick it up, drink, recite an elegant poem or cap a verse, and then let the cup pass on. *The Tale of Genji* describes a resplendent garden party during which elaborately carved and painted 'dragon barges' are floated on the artificial lake.

The open, sunny garden was no mere decoration but the very pivot of Heian domestic architecture. Whereas the Chinese palace faced across formal courtyards to the great entrance gate, and usually relegated its gardens to the rear of the main building, the Heian mansion was focused on its outdoor beauties, where so much of the entertainment and ceremony took place. Conditions in the capital were perfect for the Japanese style of garden: the ground was extremely fertile, there was an abundant supply of well-shaped rocks, stones and pebbles, and the nearby rivers

15. These rocks, which are characteristic of the Heian style of garden, were usually placed in a straight line; known as 'night mooring' stones (*yadomairi*), they represented ships anchored at night in a harbour on their way to quest out treasure.

provided ample water for the streams. Sometimes the gardens were designed to evoke famous scenic wonders. In Murasaki's time, for example, one nobleman in the Sixth Ward had an artificial sand-bar built in his lake and planted it with rows of pine trees bent into the fantastic shapes that one finds on Amanohashidate in the Japan Sea. An even more notable garden was in the River Bank Villa of Minamoto no Tōru, a ninth-century nobleman who served as Minister of the Left. It was laid out to suggest the Bay of Matsushima, another of Japan's Three Scenic Wonders, where hundreds of craggy, pine-covered islands rise from the sea. The Minister went to the length of having a salt kiln constructed by his lake in imitation of the Matsushima kiln, which was believed to be the first place in Japan where salt had been made by boiling sea water. He ordered gallons of water to be brought daily from the coast and, while it was being boiled, he and his friends would sit and watch the smoke float across the sky and imagine themselves in the far-off northern region – a region which, of course, nothing short of a ukase would have induced them to visit in person.

Directly facing the Heian garden was the main building of the compound. This was the master's quarters, and it was flanked by eastern and western pavilions, which were occupied by his relations, friends, high-ranking retainers, secondary consorts, and children. Each pavilion in the *shinden* complex consisted basically of a single large room, which could be divided into sections or cubicles as circumstances required. For banquets and other entertainments all the partitions in the main building were removed, thus providing a spacious hall open to the high sloping roof.

The building to the north was inhabited by the principal wife, who accordingly was known as the 'northern person'. Behind the north wing were the servants' quarters, store-rooms, and kitchen. The lavatories and wash-rooms were off the corridors. Whenever necessary, new buildings and corridors could be added behind the main complex. Prince Genji's mansion in the Sixth Ward, where he brought numerous lady friends to live together, must have been a maze of detached pavilions and connecting galleries, liberally interspersed with gardens and courtyards.

The dominant mood of Heian architecture, however, was one of restraint and tranquillity. A desire for understatement and avoidance of ostentation, which characterized Japanese taste many centuries before the influence of Zen Buddhism, discouraged the use of the bright colours, lacquer, and gorgeous designs associated with Chinese architecture. From reconstructions of the imperial residence, on which the *shinden* mansions were based, we may judge that it was one of the most austere palaces in the world.

In Heian times, as today, the furnishings of the typical Japanese house could scarcely have been sparser. The wooden floor was bare, except for the individual straw mats and cushions on which people sat; the custom of covering the entire floor with *tatami* (rush mats) did not come until later. Chairs (*goishi*) had been introduced from the Chinese court in an earlier period, but never came into general use. In Murasaki's day they were employed mainly on ceremonial occasions in Buddhist temples and in the Palace, where they were reserved for the emperor, the imperial princes, the regent and the prime minister. Elsewhere, indoor life, both waking and sleeping, was spent on the floor.

The emptiness of the room was relieved only by an occasional chest, brazier, screen, *go* table, or other movable object. In the centre of the larger apartments was a *chōdai* ('curtain platform'), which served as a sort of bedchamber-*cum*-withdrawingroom. The *chōdai* was a black platform about two foot high and nine foot square; it was covered with straw mats and cushions and surrounded by curtains. Rhinoceros horns were suspended above one end of the platform to ward off illness and opposite them was a pair of mirrors to keep the evil spirits at bay. Despite these precautions the *chōdai* seems to have been a rather insecure form of bedchamber, and supports were often placed on the floor to prevent the platform from slipping, as well as for decoration. The images of a lion and a 'Korean dog' (*komainu*) were regarded as the most elegant type of support – so elegant, in fact, that by Murasaki's time they were reserved exclusively for the emperor and empress.[16]

The sleeping place itself was usually in the centre of the *chōdai*, though any part of the room could be partitioned by screens or curtains and set aside for the purpose. The 'bed' (*yuka*) lacked the associations of comfort and protection that Westerners associate with the word: the Heian

16. These two animals were actually the same, except that the lion was yellow and had an open mouth, while the dog was white and had a closed mouth; both were originally imported from Korea.

aristocrat lay down fully dressed on a straw mat, covering himself with a silk or cotton counterpane or, in the cold weather, with some heavy article of clothing. The Genji scrolls show young Kashiwagi on his death-bed: he is still wearing his stiff court head-dress and, since it is autumn, he is covered with a thick silk robe; his white, emaciated face rests precariously on the hard block that serves as a pillow.

One piece of furniture that plays an important part in the literature of the time was the *kichō*, a six-foot portable frame supporting opaque hangings, which Waley translates as 'screen of state'. The hangings were attractively decorated, the material and the patterns being changed with the seasons. The bottom part was left unsewn, so that objects could be handed through the opening. The main purpose of the screen of state was to protect the ladies of the house from prying eyes. When receiving a gentleman caller, a woman normally ensconced herself behind these curtains, where, at the best, she could be seen only in dim outline. A principal aim of the Heian gallant was to insinuate himself behind the screen of state; once he had achieved this preliminary objective, the rest usually followed with remarkable ease. Yet, despite its flimsy construction, the 'screen of state' could provide a formidable barrier. Readers of *The Tale of Genji* will recall the passage in which Prince Hotaru, seated outside Tamakazura's screen of state, has been making an impassioned declaration to the girl (whom Genji has thoughtfully allowed him to glimpse by the light of fireflies) – only to be informed by a lady-in-waiting that Tamakazura has long since retired to the inner room and that he has been talking into thin air.

A significant aspect of the *shinden* mansion, and of traditional Japanese architecture in general, is the way in which the inside of the house merged into the world outside. Apartments were separated from the open verandas by a series of shutters; in the warm weather these could be removed, and the bamboo blinds rolled up, so that the room would become almost a part of the garden. The separation between 'out of doors' and 'indoors' has never been so strong in Japan as in the West; and Buddhist influence helped to combat the idea of a solid, permanent dwelling-place that might provide a barrier against the outside world of nature.

The insubstantial, 'southern' character of *shinden* architecture combined with Japan's climatic extremes to make the people of Heian Kyō more than ever conscious of nature and its changing moods. Thus in the illustration of the heroine's death-scene in the Genji scrolls there is no visible demarcation between the room and the windswept garden with its desolate clover bushes; and the poems that she, Genji, and the other characters exchange are all built about images taken from the surrounding world of nature to which their emotions are so closely attuned.

The open construction of the *shinden* house and its intimate connexion with the garden were attractive features. Yet, so far as bodily comfort was concerned, the Heian dwellings, even those of the richest aristocrats, could hardly have been less inviting. They were particularly ill-equipped to meet the city's bitter winter months. The round wooden braziers that provided the main form of heating could have little effect on the temperature of the large open rooms and the long draughty corridors.[17] This had an important effect on fashions. Women had to be protected by numerous layers of clothes; since this was an age of taste, they made a virtue of necessity, and the subtle matching of the colours of the different layers became one of the great arts of everyday life.[18]

On bright warm days, when the shutters could be removed and the blinds rolled up, the Heian house was fairly light, but as a rule the overhanging eaves and the absence of windows kept the rooms in semi-darkness. After sunset feeble oil-lamps and occasional tapers (the cause of many a disastrous fire) provided such lighting as there was. When reading *The Tale of Genji* and other works of the time, we must remember how much of the aristocracy's life was spent in a state of semi-obscurity. The gloom that overcomes so many of the characters may well be related

17. So far as comfort was concerned, Japanese architecture did not notably improve during the succeeding ages. Writing at the beginning of the present century, B. H. Chamberlain makes the following acid comments:
'Nothing to sit on, nothing but a brazier to warm oneself by, and yet abundant danger of fire, no solidity, no privacy, the deafening clatter twice daily of the opening and shutting of the outer wooden slides, draughts insidiously pouring in through innumerable chinks and crannies, darkness whenever heavy rain makes it necessary to shut up one or more sides of the house – to these and various other enormities Japanese houses must plead guilty.' *Things Japanese*, pp. 36–7.
Nothing, of course, is more relative than standards of comfort. Many a modern city-dweller would reject the smoke, murkiness, draughts, smells, and clutter of a house in Victorian London almost as indignantly as Chamberlain condemns traditional Japanese architecture.

18. See p. 206.

to the murkiness of their houses. Women in particular lived in a state of almost perpetual twilight. As if the rooms were not already dark enough, they normally immured themselves behind thick silk hangings or screens. All this no doubt added to the aura of mystery and elusiveness by which members of their sex have always sought to intrigue the inquisitive male. We can also imagine what a boon it must have been for those ladies who were not favoured by youth or good looks. If Prince Hitachi's gawky, red-nosed daughter had ever been exposed to the harsh glare of daylight or of modern lighting, one wonders whether even a man as magnanimous as Prince Genji could have brought himself to include her among his mistresses.

The obscurity of the Heian house is the origin of many a complication. Love affairs begin and end in the semi-darkness, and sometimes the lovers are not even sure who their partner is. Genji seduces the Emperor's betrothed without knowing her identity, and thus provides his enemies with an ideal pretext for having him exiled. Towards the end of the novel Ukifune believes – or pretends to believe – that the young man who is joining her in bed is her accepted lover, Kaoru; by the time she discovers that it is in fact his rival, Prince Niou, it is too late to correct the error.

One might expect that this almost perpetual state of semi-darkness would have afforded a good deal of privacy. In fact, not only did the *shinden* house provide little defence from the outside world of nature; it offered scant protection indoors. No architecture could have been better suited to the eavesdropper or the Peeping Tom. The word *kaimamiru* (literally, 'peeping through the hedge') recurs throughout contemporary literature, and many of the plots revolve about conversations that are overheard, or about young ladies who are spied through a lattice by some enterprising gentleman. No reader of *The Tale of Genji* is likely to forget the ubiquitous ladies-in-waiting who, strategically ensconced behind their screens, hear and see everything that is happening in the house and are forever commenting, in a sort of plaintive threnody, on the doings of their unprotected superiors. Certain apartments in the Imperial Palace were provided with 'singing' floorboards to give warning of eavesdroppers and other interlopers; but for most of Murasaki's contemporaries privacy would have been a meaningless term.

*

The difficulty of transport was another important factor in Heian life. Even near the capital the roads were excruciatingly poor, especially during the rainy season when they turned into rivers of mud; and in many of the provinces they were virtually non-existent. Anyone bold enough to undertake a long journey across country (the *Sarashina Diary* provides a good example) was for ever being stopped at barriers and had to manage without inns, posting-houses, or public amenities of any kind.

Travel by sea was uncomfortable, hard to arrange, and risky because of frequent shipwreck and piracy. The tenth-century poet, Ki no Tsurayuki, spent over three months on the short voyage from Tosa to the capital, and his diary vividly evokes its hardships. In *The Tale of Genji* Tamakazura is obliged to languish some fifteen years in the wilds of Kyūshū before she is able to make the sea journey back to the capital.

The speediest method of travel, of course, was horseback. Horses were not used for pulling conveyances, but were ridden by members of the Imperial Guards, messengers, and gentlemen on urgent private business. For the decorous personages of Genji's world, however, this was hardly an appropriate mode of transport; as a rule members of the aristocracy travelled in the unwieldy ox-drawn carriages that lumbered along the streets at about two miles an hour. There was a great variety of such carriages, and imperial edicts had carefully specified what type was appropriate for each rank and how many attendants might escort them. Like the ornamental gardens, carriages provided a convenient form of conspicuous consumption, and the inhabitants of Heian Kyō vied with each other in fitting them out as smartly as possible. The government tried to curb the luxury, but, like most sumptuary laws throughout Japanese history, these edicts had little effect. In 999 it was decreed that no one below the Fifth Rank might use a carriage; this too appears to have been generally disregarded. During all the Heian period the carriage remained an important status symbol, and people never missed a chance to appear in public with a well-appointed equipage. In Murasaki's time there were sometimes as many as five hundred carriages on the main avenues; often they were stuck in massive traffic jams. During processions and other ceremonial occasions people struggled to get their carriages into the most advantageous position, and the repercussions of the brawls between their teams of attendants (*kuruma-arasoi*) are important in contemporary fiction.[19]

In its ponderous way the ox-drawn carriage was certainly a more attractive symbol than the modern motor-car. The most distinguished type, the so-called Chinese carriage, was reserved for members of the imperial family and top officials like the regent and the chancellor. It was immensely elaborate, with a green gabled roof in T'ang style, and so high that a sort of ladder had to be used to climb aboard. The palm carriage was for people of the Fourth Rank and above; it was named after its roof, which was thatched with finely split palm leaves. Among the simpler styles were the stretched-straw and the board carriages. These mini-cars of the carriage hierarchy were assigned to members of the Fifth and Sixth Ranks respectively. Their status-association declined steadily, until they came to be used by families without rank and even for transporting common criminals.

Carriages were normally drawn alongside the veranda of the house and one climbed in from the rear. The spacious compartment accommodated four passengers, who were seated on straw mats according to rank and sex. On reaching the destination the attendants unyoked the ox, and the occupants stepped out from the front. What with the absence of springs and the unevenness of the roads, travel by ox-drawn carriage must have been as rough as the choppiest Channel crossing. Sei Shōnagon describes a visit to the Great Imperial Palace:

As they draw the carriage over the threshold of the Central Gate, it is violently shaken and the heads of all the ladies are knocked together, so that the combs fall out of their hair. When this happens everyone laughs [an interesting point], but if they are not careful the ladies may well find that their combs have been broken, or at least chipped.[20]

This threshold was a particular hazard because of a great horizontal beam fixed on the ground, but the discomfort that Sei describes appears to have been common to most travel by ox-drawn carriage.

19. In Book 9 of *The Tale of Genji* Lady Rokujō is humiliated by Lady Aoi, in a 'carriage quarrel' (*kuruma-arasoi*), and this is one of the reasons that her jealousy turns so fiercely against this particular rival. The wicked stepmother in *The Tale of the Room Below* (see Glossary) suffers similar humiliation. *Kuruma-arasoi* figure in many of the early illustrations.

20. Kaneko ed., p. 7.

Another form of transport was the *teguruma*, a smaller carriage drawn by about six men, mainly within the precincts of the Greater Imperial Palace. It appears to have provided a somewhat smoother form of locomotion than the ox-drawn carriage, and with special permission it could be used by old people and invalids who had to avoid vigorous shaking. The most exalted conveyances of all were palanquins, which were reserved for the sovereign and his principal consort and could not be used even by a retired emperor. During enthronements and other ceremonies the emperor rode in his *hōren*, a magnificently decorated palanquin, carried by thirty-two men and topped by a great golden phoenix.

The slowness and discomfort of travel made people avoid expeditions from the capital unless they were travelling on orders or had some powerful incentive such as a clandestine meeting in a mountain temple. Even a visit to a nearby monastery was regarded as an arduous journey, requiring days of preparation and rest, and further days of recuperation. When we read of Prince Genji's dismay at being banished to Suma, we might have the impression that he has been sent to the antipodes; in fact his place of exile was so near the capital that it can now be reached by train in less than two hours. Uji, the setting of most of the last part of the novel, is viewed as hopelessly remote and inaccessible; but it is actually only some ten miles from the centre of the city. 'Even our deep bond of affection,' Prince Niou tells the girl at Uji whom he is shortly to bring to the capital as his secondary consort, 'can hardly survive the rigours of visiting you at Uji. How on earth can you have chosen such a place?'[21] And when the young lady is ensconced in the Prince's ox-drawn carriage, having finally brought herself to make the journey to the capital, she is appalled to observe the hardships that her lover had had to endure on his visits: 'As she travelled down the long arduous mountain road, she began to see how reasonable had been the Prince's hesitations, which previously she had regarded as the mark of a cold heart.'[22]

The slow pace of *The Tale of Genji*, and of most contemporary literature, is related to this matter of locomotion. In many respects life was

21. Murasaki Shikibu, *Genji Monogatari*, edited by Ikeda Kikan (hereafter abbreviated as 'Ikeda ed.'), vi, 116.
22. Ibid.

attuned to the speed of the ox-drawn carriage; and, whereas a leisurely approach may encourage a delicate, polished, and subtle type of writing, it may also induce a certain monotony, especially for readers who are used to a more rapid movement.

The difficulties of transport also had an effect on the size of the country. For distances are better judged in terms of accessibility than of miles, and in this sense Murasaki's Japan was immense. The great northern island of Hokkaidō, though technically part of the emperor's domain, was not included in the Seven Circuits and might as well have been a foreign land; even the northern provinces of the main island were regarded as a sort of *ultima thule*, about which the less thought and said the better. The journey from Heian Kyō to the great eastern plain that was to be the site of the later military capitals – a journey that can now be done in less than six hours by express train – took several months and involved innumerable risks and discomforts. To be appointed governor in these parts was tantamount to an arduous (though often very profitable) exile.

As a result of poor communications, the continental culture that flourished in the capital scarcely filtered into the provinces at all. Since such indigenous culture as existed in the villages was hardly designed to appeal to Prince Genji and his circle, we can well understand why the Heian city-dweller should have had little interest or knowledge regarding other parts of his country. Yet they would have done well to concern themselves more closely with what was happening beyond the confines of Heian Kyō. For by losing control over the provinces, the source of economic strength in a rice economy, the central government under the Fujiwara oligarchy was eventually to forfeit all real power in the capital city itself. Thus indirectly the backwardness of internal communications helped to bring about the downfall of Murasaki's world.

*

Heian Kyō has disappeared from the face of the earth far more completely than ancient Rome. What could not be accomplished by fires and earthquakes was completed by centuries of warfare, which in later centuries was marked by large-scale arson, looting, and vandalism. The fierce Ōnin Wars in the fifteenth century destroyed virtually all that was left of the old capital. In 1527 a scion of the Fujiwaras lamented: 'The city of Heian that has flourished since the days of Emperor Kammu [reg. 781–806] is now utterly laid waste. What a wretched sight it presents for the capital of our country!'[23] As if things were not bad enough, ten years later the warrior monks of Mount Hiei charged down from their mountain fastness and put the finishing touch to the job of destruction.

Today hardly a single structure remains in Kyoto from Heian days. The largest building from the period (and also one of the most beautiful) is the Phoenix Hall of the Byōdō Temple; it was built by the Fujiwaras in 1053 and is situated in Uji, a few miles to the south of the city. The other famous buildings are all reconstructions, mostly from the Tokugawa and Meiji periods. The 'Old Imperial Palace' which people now visit (often under the happy illusion that it is of immense antiquity) occupies an entirely different site from the palace of Murasaki's day and was built in 1855. Since we do not possess a single picture showing an entire Heian house, we cannot be certain how accurate the reconstructions are; but the Imperial Palace itself is probably a fairly faithful copy of the buildings on which aristocratic life centred in the time of the shining prince. Apart from this, there is the surviving beauty of the natural surroundings, which for Murasaki and her circle were at least as important as any building.

23. Sanjō Sanetaka (Taiei VII). Quoted by Sugimoto Tsutomu, *Kindai Nihongo no Seiritsu*, p. 21.

III

Politics and Society

A. THE EMPERORS

'[The land of Japan] is the region which my descendants shall be lords of. Do thou, my August Grandchild, proceed thither and govern it. Go! and may prosperity attend thy dynasty, and may it, like Heaven and Earth, endure forever.'[1] Such were the ringing phrases in which the Sun Goddess ordered her scion to descend from the Plain of High Heaven and to found the Imperial House of Japan.

The heavenly grandmother's injunction is enshrined in the country's earliest chronicle (written in the eighth century) and provides the mytho-religious basis on which the same family has reigned over Japan from the beginning of her history to the present day. The main purpose of the founding legend was precisely to confirm this authority, which had certainly not been accepted in the country at large. During most of the early period the imperial family had been merely *primus inter pares,* one of the many powerful septs that held sway in different parts of the islands. The movement towards centralization, which culminated in the Great Reform of the seventh century, aimed at putting an end to clan rivalry and creating a centralized bureaucratic state on the Chinese model. In this state the emperor was to have supreme power over all the land and the people, including the former clan chieftains, who had been his rivals in strength; for, as the Reform Edict stated in good Chinese style, 'There are not two suns in the sky, nor two lords on the earth.'

A revolutionary change of this kind, however, cannot be accomplished by proclamations and edicts, especially when these are borrowed, sometimes word for word, from a foreign country. No fiat can make a centralized monarchy function any more than it can create an effective parliamentary democracy. In ancient Japan aristocratic habits of mind

1. W. G. Aston, *Nihongi,* p. 77.

56

and the prevalence of clan traditions prevented social and economic realities from keeping pace with the dramatic institutional changes that the Great Reform put into effect.

The height of imperial power and prestige corresponded to the reign of Emperor Kammu. It was in his time that the capital was shifted to Heian Kyō, the City of the Moon (Tsuki no Miyako) as it was called in reference to the imperial presence; and into the Greater Imperial Palace moved the huge Chinese-style bureaucratic apparatus and the throngs of courtiers, who from their association with the emperor were poetically known as the Gentlemen Who Dwell Among the Clouds (Kumo no Uebito).

Yet even in Kammu's reign it was clear that the emperor's authority was far from being as complete as political theory demanded. During the reigns of his successors the deviations from the Chinese model became more and more conspicuous. This was not primarily because of any personal shortcomings in Kammu's progeny (though it is possible that more vigorous emperors might have stemmed the tide for a while), but resulted from inherent weaknesses in the conception of the Reform and in the way in which it was carried out. To sum up the difficulty in a single sentence: large parts of the Reform were inappropriate to Japan, because they had been designed for a far more developed country and because they conflicted with deeply rooted clan traditions; and, even if they had been appropriate, the paradoxical circumstance that the Reform was instituted and carried out under the auspices of the very aristocratic class whose privileges it was meant to undermine made it inevitable that its underlying principle – namely, government by a supreme ruler under whose authority merit would take precedence over heredity – must sooner or later come to be disregarded. In the event the divergence from the underlying spirit of the Reform came even sooner than one might have expected and was even more complete. As it was put into practice, the new system allowed the aristocracy not only to preserve but actually to strengthen its position. Far from being destroyed by the Reform, the great families – and one of them in particular – were able to use the new prestige of the emperor and his court to reinforce their own status.

By Murasaki's time the process had developed to a remarkable degree. The Reform, and the numerous codes and redactions that sprang from it, continued to be the law of the land; the vast bureaucracy that it had established remained more or less intact; the emperor was still regarded as the source of all power, secular as well as religious. But in effect much of the system had become a façade. Although the cumbrous, and expensive, governmental machinery was allowed to continue, the real process of administration was centred elsewhere. And, although the emperor was theoretically supreme, he had long since been relieved of every jot of political power.

From about the middle of the tenth century only two functions were left to the sovereign – the sacerdotal and the cultural. As the direct descendant of the Sun Goddess and the high priest of Shintō, he was expected to devote a large part of his time to religious ceremonies and observances. The native word for government (*matsurigoto*) meant '[Shintō] ceremonial affairs' and, although the meaning was later extended to cover secular matters, the authority of most of the emperors who reigned after Kammu was, for all intents and purposes, limited to the original sense. In so far as these sovereigns participated in affairs of state, their role was to give formal and religious sanction to the acts that were being carried out in their name. Just as the Sun Goddess had appointed the emperors as her delegates on earth, so they had delegated – or rather, been obliged to delegate – their powers to theoretical subordinates. During the course of Japanese history we find this process of delegation being carried to extraordinary lengths, so that the person who actually exercises power is usually many stages removed from the theoretical source of authority.

The second function that remained to the imperial court was to serve as a centre of aristocratic culture. Many of Kammu's descendants were distinguished artists in their own right, his son, Emperor Saga, for instance, being renowned as one of the Three Great Calligraphers (Sampitsu) of his age. Almost all the subsequent sovereigns were active in one or more of the arts; and during the dark ages of civil war and destruction the imperial court, impoverished and disrupted though it often was by economic and political vicissitudes, played a vital part in keeping the light of traditional culture alive. In the palmy days of the Heian period the wealth and prestige of the palace helped not only to foster the traditional arts – including those, like music and dance, that had been imported from China – but to encourage the development of new forms, such as the romances and the illustrations which culminated in *The Tale of Genji* and the great picture scrolls. It is no coincidence that almost all the notable women writers of the tenth and eleventh centuries were ladies-in-waiting at one or another of the empresses' courts.[2]

Despite this significant role that the Heian emperors continued to play, their total lack of political power and the policy of early abdication combined to give them (and most of the emperors in subsequent periods too) a somewhat asthenic and colourless quality. It is not to the Imperial Palace that we can look for the Japanese equivalent of a Henry VIII or a Charles XII. Let us take as an example the sovereign who figures in Murasaki's diary and in the *Pillow Book*. Born in 980, Ichijō was the offspring of Emperor Enyū and a Fujiwara consort. He came to the throne[3] at the precocious age of six, having 'accepted' the abdication of Emperor Kazan, and he is listed in the chronicles as the sixty-sixth sovereign to reign over the Divine Land. At the age of ten he was married to his first cousin, Fujiwara no Sadako, who was five years older than he; she was named second of the ranking consorts. When the Emperor was nineteen, Sadako gave birth to a son; but in the same year her uncle, Michinaga, succeeded in getting his own daughter, Akiko, into the palace as an Imperial Lady (*Nyōgo*). Just as Siegfried's encounters with women happened to be restricted almost exclusively to his aunts, Ichijō's consorts were chosen from among his first cousins; Akiko, however, did at least have the advantage of being eight years his junior.

In the year 1000 there was a round of promotions: Akiko was named Second Empress (*Chūgū*) and Sadako Empress (*Kōgō*). Owing to Michinaga's political ascendancy, however, Sadako's real position in the palace had already been seriously undermined by the rival Empress; in the following year she died in childbirth. Shortly thereafter the imperial residence burnt down and the Emperor had to move to a 'detached' palace. Two years later the main palace was rebuilt and the Emperor

2. See note on p. 211.

3. 'Crown' and 'throne' should not be taken too literally; it might, however, be noted that the *benkan* was a form of jewelled head-dress worn exclusively by the emperor and that the *hi no goza*, a raised platform with straw mats and cushions where the emperor conducted state formalities, corresponded in some ways to a throne.

returned, only to be dislodged a couple of years later by a new fire, after which he moved into the residence of his father-in-law, Michinaga. These fires occurred regularly at four-year intervals during Ichijō's reign, and the commotion they caused must have provided one of the more exciting breaks in the monotony of palace routine.

The chronicles tell us remarkably little about the Emperor. They record his participation in the regular ceremonies and observances and a series of formal visits to Shintō shrines (the most distant of which is to Nara, some thirty miles from the capital); but none of this throws any light on Ichijō himself. In 1008 Akiko bore him a son (the future Emperor Goichijō) and the Emperor visited the mother and child at his father-in-law's residence; Murasaki's diary starts with a description of this auspicious event. A second child (the future Emperor Gosuzaku) was born in the following year, shortly after the palace had burnt down once again. In 1011 the Emperor was able to return to the rebuilt palace, but it was not long before he fell seriously ill. A general amnesty was proclaimed and Ichijō abdicated. He was now thirty-one, precisely the average age for abdication during the Heian period. Next he 'discarded his fineries', in other words, became a Buddhist priest. He had only three days in which to enjoy this worthy status. He died about a week after his abdication and the imperial cycle started again with his successor, Emperor Sanjō.

Not the faintest whiff of Emperor Ichijō's character comes to us from the official histories. The *Pillow Book*, however, does give a few personal glimpses. He emerges as a gentle and sensitive young man, keenly interested in poetry, a good judge of music and a keen flautist. He must also have had some scholarly interests; for we are told that he had copies of Chinese historical works prepared for his use. Sei relates a pleasant anecdote about the Emperor. One day he was practising the flute in the company of his teacher, a certain Fujiwara bigwig. After some classical airs he played the tune of a popular song that made fun of a recently promoted official called Suketada, who had become the butt of ridicule in court circles because his mother was of humble provincial stock.

'Would Your Majesty be pleased to play a little more loudly?' said the teacher. 'Suketada cannot possibly hear, and even if he did he wouldn't understand.' 'How so?' replied the Emperor. 'I am sure he would recognize the tune.' For a while he continued to play softly. Then he walked towards the Empress's apartments. 'He certainly cannot hear me from here,' explained His Majesty. 'Now I can really let myself go!' So saying, he blew out the tune heartily.[4]

The incident reflects a certain delicacy of feeling, which one likes to imagine as typical of the young monarch.

A life so rigidly circumscribed and a reign so brief as those of most Heian emperors were hardly designed to encourage the development of a vigorous personality, let alone any determination to challenge the political *status quo*. An incident recorded in an early Kamakura history, however, suggests that Ichijō may have retained a certain independence of mind. In the box of personal effects that he bequeathed to his sucessor he is said to have included a piece of paper on which he had paraphrased the words of a famous T'ang emperor:

> That the orchids might blossom in profusion – such was my hope,
> But the Autumn winds destroyed them all.
> That imperial deeds might shine before the world – such was my wish,
> But scheming ministers wrought havoc in the land.[5]

Evidently Michinaga discovered this subversive document and, realizing all too clearly who was meant by 'scheming ministers', destroyed it.

The incident has an apocryphal ring – who, after all, was to know what was written on the paper once it had been destroyed? – but there is no question that by Michinaga's time the emperors had every reason to harbour secret resentment against the Fujiwaras, who had usurped

4. Kaneko ed., p. 156. Suketada had been a Secretary in the Bureau of Carpentry (here and elsewhere, unless stated to the contrary, I normally use R. K. Reischauer's translations for ranks, posts, etc.). This appointment corresponded to the lowly 7th Rank. As a result of being adopted into an influential branch of the Fujiwara family, however, he had been promoted to the dignity of Chamberlain (5th Rank) despite his mother's birth. This was resented in court circles. Suketada was nicknamed the 'rough crocodile' and became the subject of the song that the Emperor was playing on his flute:

> 'He's a master none of us can stand next to –
> Ay, he's the seed of people in Owari!'

5. T'ang Hsüan Tsung. I have given the usual translation of 'orchid' for *lan*, though from a strict botanical point of view it is not correct.

all their actual power and whose clan chieftain was no longer a mere king-maker but the real king of Japan.

B. THE FUJIWARAS

The rise of the Fujiwaras to supreme power had been a slow and arduous process. Their founder was a leading figure in the Great Reform. He and one of the imperial princes (who later came to the throne as Emperor Tenchi) had been the ringleaders of the conspiracy that led to the bloody overthrow of the Sogas, the previous ruling family. According to tradition, Emperor Tenchi gave him his name (*fuji-hara* – 'wistaria plain') in memory of the arbour of wistarias where they had laid their plans; and it was in this arbour that the first of the Fujiwaras was eventually buried.

His descendants were determined to preserve and consolidate their family's position at court. During the next three centuries they kept up a persistent struggle against rival clans and, during the Nara period, against the prepotent Buddhist clergy. They also waged a power struggle within their own proliferous family to determine which of its four main branches should be predominant; in the ninth century the 'northern' branch triumphed over the others.

It was not until well into the tenth century, however, that the family finally achieved hegemony over all contenders. The year 967, in which Saneyori became chancellor, may be taken to mark the full transfer of power to the Fujiwaras. Two years later they succeeded in removing the last of their outside rivals, a certain Minamoto no Takaakira.

The Fujiwara oligarchy was now firmly established, and for at least a century (the period that corresponds to the world of the shining prince) they carried all before them. The extraordinary career of this family has been compared to that of the Frankish Mayors of the Palace; but the Fujiwaras never aspired to the monarchy itself. A more valid parallel can probably be drawn with the Rana family, which until recently held sway in Nepal. Fujiwara noblemen preserved their influence at court long after real power had passed into other hands. Branches of the family survived into our own century; Prince Konoe, who committed suicide in 1945 rather than stand trial as a war crimes suspect, has been described as 'the last of the Fujiwaras'.

How did the Fujiwara family manage to acquire supreme power in the Heian period, and how did they retain it for such a long time? Physical force was the least important of their methods. The Fujiwaras themselves never commanded any significant military strength – certainly not enough to assure them their long dominance. When they did use violence, it was only as a last resort and, one feels, reluctantly. For, above all, they were consummate politicians, and it was mainly by political methods that they achieved their ends.

One of these methods is known by Japanese historians as 'marriage politics'. This was the system whereby the Fujiwara leaders made sure that imperial consorts would be chosen exclusively from among Fujiwara girls. As a result the head of their family was almost invariably the father-in-law or grandfather (or sometimes both) of the reigning sovereign. This policy had been used by their predecessors, the Sogas, but never in such a widespread or systematic fashion. By the tenth century the Fujiwaras had imposed on the emperor a type of life cycle that was almost bound to keep him under the family's thumb. He came to the throne as a callow youth and was promptly married to a Fujiwara girl; their son would be appointed crown prince, and when his father was obliged to abdicate, usually at the age of about thirty, he would succeed him and the cycle would start again.

In Murasaki's time this system of endogamy had forged infrangible links between the imperial family and the Fujiwaras. Michinaga had the satisfaction of seeing no less than four of his daughters married to emperors, and they in turn produced three more emperors. A study of his family tree reveals that he performed the following remarkable genealogical feat: he was father-in-law of two emperors, grandfather of a third, grandfather *and* great-grand-father of a fourth, grandfather *and* father-in-law of a fifth.[6] The emperors themselves, all-powerful as they might be in theory, were of course not consulted about these matrimonial arrangements; else one imagines that at least some of them would have boggled at the fate, a common one during this period, of having to marry their aunts. Historians have speculated about the possible genetic effects of this inbreeding on the imperial stock; and it is interesting, though certainly not conclusive, that the few politically vigorous emperors of the age were those who did *not* have Fujiwara mothers.

If these 'marriage politics' were to function smoothly, it was important that the ruling branch of the Fujiwara family should have a good

6. See Appendix 4.

supply of nubile, philoprogenitive, and reasonably attractive daughters. This condition applied until the eleventh century, when it happened that a series of Fujiwara girls died young, or proved sterile, or had only daughters. As a result a non-Fujiwara emperor came to the throne; and it was he who took the first successful steps to undermine the family's position.

Apart from their skilful use of marriage politics, the Fujiwaras kept the emperors under their control by obliging most of them to abdicate at a young age before they were likely to show any independence of spirit. During their short reigns the sovereigns were so absorbed in ritual, both religious and secular, that there was little time or energy left for political ambitions. The Fujiwaras even managed to turn the frequent palace fires to account by making the emperor and his suite move into his father-in-law's residence while his own was being rebuilt. Since the great Fujiwara mansions had become more imposing and luxurious than the Imperial Palace itself, these moves may often have been quite welcome. When a Fujiwara empress became pregnant, she would normally be moved into her father's house; the emperor would visit her there after the birth; the young prince would be brought up in the Fujiwara household under the watchful eye of the patriarch; and sometimes even his accession ceremony would take place in the family residence rather than in the palace.

Further, as a result of early abdication and polygamy, there were numerous imperial courts at the same time – those of the reigning emperor, the former emperors, the great empress dowager, and the various empresses. In 986, for instance, three former sovereigns were alive in addition to young Ichijō, and each had his own court. This helped to keep imperial authority and wealth divided and to give the Fujiwaras a free hand.

As if all this were not enough, the family found it useful for emperors to come to the throne while they were still children and thus entirely malleable. This allowed them to institute the office of regent which, being outside the cumbrous Chinese-type administrative system, offered them a particularly direct and effective means of political control. The first child-emperor was Seiwa, who acceded in 858 at the age of eight. A Fujiwara regent was appointed for the term of minority, but managed to retain most of his powers even after the emperor came of age. Seiwa was obliged to abdicate when he was twenty-six; so far as the family was concerned he had filled his main function in life, which was to sire a son to his Fujiwara consort. This son now came to the throne at the same precocious age as his father, and a new Fujiwara regent was appointed to exercise his powers. The young emperor in turn was made to abdicate as soon as he came of age.

Now we find an ingenious variation in the pattern. The next sovereign was an incompetent aged fifty-five with the Gilbertian name of Kōkō, and during his brief reign the Fujiwaras were able to establish the precedent that the imperial powers should be delegated to the head of their family even when the sovereign was of age. This act of delegation was the basis of the institution of Chancellor,[7] another vital departure from the Great Reform system and the one that conclusively established the political hegemony of the Fujiwaras. For most of the following two centuries (and during the entire period with which this book is concerned) the country was governed by the emperor's father-in-law or grandfather who ruled as regent while the sovereign was a minor and as chancellor after he came of age. And the incumbents of these crucial posts were the heads of the Fujiwara clan. It is a historic irony that it should have been this particular family that acted as the principal agent in destroying the political structure of the Great Reform which their own revered ancestor had helped to carry out – a reform that had aimed precisely at preventing the domination of the country by any great clan or clans.

Although the twin institutions of regent and chancellor were originally *de facto* posts without any official standing in the hierarchy, they soon came to eclipse all the other organs of government, including the Great Council of State. By Murasaki's time the Administrative Council of the Fujiwara leaders had long since superseded the central administration established by law, and it was from the chambers of this Council

7. R. K. Reischauer translates Kampaku as 'Civil Dictator', which is somewhat misleading as a description and hardly appropriate as a title. Sansom gives 'Regent', but this could be confused with the post of Sesshō. 'Mayor of the Palace' gives a fair idea of the importance of the position, but the analogy with French history must not be pressed too far. On the whole, 'Chancellor' seems to be the least misleading equivalent, but readers of Sansom should be warned that this is his normal translation of Dajō Daijin (which R. K. Reischauer translates as 'Prime Minister').

(Mandokoro) that the real government of the country was carried out. The old machinery of administration was carefully preserved, and the Great Council of State continued to issue regulations and edicts. But for all intents and purposes this had become a matter of form and ceremony. So far as real control was concerned, the orders (*kudashibumi*) of the Fujiwara Council had taken the place of Imperial Decrees (*senji*). In an entry dated 1039 the *Spring Chronicle* comments: 'The Residence of the Chancellor is now in no wise inferior to the Imperial Court itself.'[8] The chronicle might have added (though it would hardly have been prudent) that so far as actual power was concerned the theoretical servant had long since become the master.

Yet never once did the Fujiwaras succumb to the temptation of trying to supplant the reigning dynasty and to put a male member of their family on the throne. Nor did they ever get into the position of having to use force against a hostile emperor or crown prince. In this they profited from the mistake of their predecessors, the Soga family, who came to grief precisely because they aspired (or gave the impression that they aspired) to imperial honour. Astute politicians as they were, the Fujiwaras realized that they could accomplish far more by exploiting the prestige of the imperial family than by becoming emperors themselves.

Although later nationalist historians have looked askance at the Fujiwaras for arrogating to themselves powers that were not rightfully theirs, it could quite justifiably be argued that it was they who saved the throne and helped the Japanese imperial dynasty to become (as it is by far) the oldest in the world. For, by removing all real power from the emperor, while at the same time according him the full honours of sovereignty, they set a precedent that was to be maintained during the succeeding centuries by Japan's military rulers, including as recent a leader as General Tōjō. If the Heian emperors had been allowed to rule as well as to reign, the imperial family might well have been swept away, or at least supplanted by a new dynasty, when the warrior class took over power from the aristocracy.

*

Despite the feeble military resources at their command, the Fujiwaras succeeded for a remarkably long time in detecting and neutralizing

8. *Shunki*, Chōryaku III, quoted by Fujiki, op. cit., p. 89. This is the diary of Fujiwara no Sukefusa; it covers the years 1038–42 and is a valuable source.

potential threats to their position. The first danger was that a strong and active emperor might assert himself and retrieve the powers that were lawfully his. This was effectively forestalled by 'marriage politics', early abdication, and the other devices. Given the actual conditions of the Heian emperor's life, it would almost have required a man of Louis XIV's stature to challenge the hegemony of the Fujiwaras; and for at least two centuries no such emperor came to the throne, or remained there long enough to take the necessary action.

A further danger was represented by other ambitious families; and early Fujiwara history is largely concerned with their successful efforts to remove such rivals from the scene. Early in the eighth century, for example, a certain Prince Nagaya seemed to be standing in their way. The chronicles record his fate in laconic terms:

March 14, 729: It was secretly reported that Great Minister of the Left Nagaya-Ō was engaging in magic and heretical practices with the object of overthrowing the State. [This night] officials were dispatched to guard the Three Barriers. Fujiwara Umakai and others were sent at the head of the troops of the Six Headquarters of the Guards to surround Nagaya-Ō's house.
March 15, 729: Nagaya-Ō was cross-examined by Toneri-Shinnō, Niitabe-Shinnō and Fujiwara Muchimaro [and found guilty of treason].
March 16, 729: Great Minister of the Left Nagaya-Ō was ordered to strangle himself.

There is a pleasantly hypocritical after-touch in the entry for May 5:

It was commanded that those who harmed people by observing unorthodox teachings and practising mysterious arts are to be punished severely.[9]

By far the most famous of the Fujiwaras' rivals was the great savant and calligrapher, Sugawara no Michizane, who by the end of the ninth century had become the leading political figure in the land. He was strongly supported by the retired emperor Uda (one of those few whose mother was not a Fujiwara) and for a time it looked as if the Fujiwaras had finally met their match. They rose to the occasion, however, and evidently succeeded in convincing the young emperor that Michizane was plotting to depose him. An imperial edict was issued in which

9. Reischauer, op cit., A. 181–2.

Michizane was 'removed to the post of Provisional Governor-General of the Government Headquarters in Kyūshū', the kiss of death in Heian politics.[10] The former emperor's efforts to save him were futile, and in 901 Michizane proceeded to the wilds of the western island, where he died two years later – of a 'broken heart', as tradition has it; during his exile he is said to have found his only consolation in climbing up a near-by hill, where he would turn towards the capital and pay obeisance to the emperor who had disgraced him.

Apart from removing Michizane himself from the scene, the Fuji-waras effectively neutralized any danger that might come from his numerous offspring (he had twenty-three in all) by ordering that his daughters be detained and his sons rusticated. Only the two youngest were allowed to accompany their father in his exile. It is to them that he addressed the following well-known poem in Chinese 'to comfort my little son and daughter':

> Your sisters must all stay at home,
> Your brothers are sent away.
> Just we three together, my children,
> Shall chat as we go along.
> Each day we have our meals before us,
> At night we sleep all together.
> We have lamps and tapers to peer in the dark
> And warm clothes for the cold.
> Last year you saw how the Chancellor's son
> Fell out of favour in the capital.
> Now people say he is a ragged gambler,
> And call him names on the street.
> You have seen the barefooted wandering musician
> The townspeople call the Justice's Miss –
> Her father, too, was a great official;
> They were all in their day exceedingly rich.
> Once their gold was like sand in the sea;
> Now they have hardly enough to eat.
> When you look, my children, at other people,
> You can see how gracious Heaven has been.[11]

10. See p. 72.

11. Translated by Burton Watson in Keene, *Anthology of Japanese Literature*, p. 165.

Michizane's death in exile was far from being the end of his career; in fact his greatest success came after. In the years following his demise there was a series of catastrophes in the capital – droughts, floods, and fires; his chief Fujiwara adversary and the crown prince both died prematurely. All this was attributed to the curse of Michizane's angry ghost, and efforts were made to placate him. The documents relating to his exile were burnt, while the Minister himself – now twenty years under the sod – was restored to his former post and promoted to the Senior Second Rank. Even this was not enough to appease the ghost, and seventy years later Michizane was elevated to the supreme post of Prime Minister. Meanwhile a national Shintō shrine had been built in the capital; here his spirit was worshipped as a deity and annual festivals were held in his honour. As so often happens to the 'failures' in Japanese history, Michizane acquired immense prestige among the populace. His reputation as a womanizer in no way detracted from his popularity; he became the patron god of calligraphy, of poetry, and of those who suffer injustice, and later the hero of a well-known Kabuki play.

The Fujiwaras did nothing to prevent the posthumous success of their great rival. So far as they were concerned he was safely out of the way, and they could now return their attention to forestalling other contenders. In the event they had little difficulty in disposing of subsequent challenges from aristocratic families. A far greater potential threat was that of the rising military clans in the provinces. For some two centuries they managed to keep this danger at bay by adroitly using the strength of the Minamotos, though in the end the policy proved disastrous.[12]

A final danger, and one which the Fujiwaras seriously underestimated, was that, having for all intents and purposes disposed of outside aristocratic families, they would be faced with quarrels between rival factions of their own huge clan. This is precisely what happened, and in the long run it weakened the family more than any other single factor, providing the immediate cause of its downfall. After the ninth century much of Heian political history revolves about the struggle for power within the dominant northern branch.

The contest for political ascendancy normally involved intrigues by each contender to have his daughter appointed to the palace as imperial lady, with the ultimate aim that he himself would become regent, chan-

12. See p. 102.

cellor, and the father-in-law of the next emperor. For, although the king himself had little power on the chess-board of Heian politics, to 'capture the king', that is, to have the emperor sire a son with one's daughter, was essential for victory. This meant that the contestant must have a powerful faction at court, including if possible an empress dowager or someone of equivalent importance. To undermine the rival factions he must be prepared to use almost every method except outright violence. These struggles often became blatant and, considering the general elegance of aristocratic life at the time, surprisingly indecorous.

A typical encounter was that between Kanemichi and his wildly ambitious younger brother, Kaneie, about which of the two should succeed to the post of chancellor, which had become vacant in 972.[13] Kaneie was a tireless politician and had managed to obtain greater preferment at court than Kanemichi. On this occasion, however, he appears to have overplayed his hand, and their sister, who now enjoyed the rank of empress dowager, decided that the coveted appointment should go to Kanemichi by virtue of his seniority. She used her influence with the emperor and in 973 the elder brother was duly named chancellor. This setback only spurred Kaneie on to greater efforts. Thwarted in his immediate objective, he now concentrated on marriage politics. One of his daughters became an imperial lady in the Court of Emperor Enyū, while another was married to Reizei, a retired emperor. This was the basis of Kaneie's subsequent triumph; for the offspring of the first match later came to the throne as Emperor Ichijō, and that of the second match was Ichijō's successor, Emperor Sanjō.

Kanemichi was greatly irked by his younger brother's manoeuvres but before he could take any effective counter-action he fell seriously ill. As Kanemichi lay dying, he was told that Kaneie had set out from his mansion in the Third Ward and that his carriage was approaching; presumably his brother had decided to bury the hatchet and was coming to pay his last respects. The next report, however, was that the carriage had passed Kanemichi's house without stopping and was making for the Imperial Palace. Kaneie, it appears, had been told that his brother was already dead, and now he was hurrying to the court to stake out his claim before any rivals got wind of what had happened. This so incensed

13. See Appendix 1 for dates and Appendix 4 for relationships.

the moribund statesman that he rallied his declining powers, rushed to the palace, and announced that he was going to make the last appointments (*jimoku*) of his life. Thereupon he named his first cousin, Yoritada, to succeed him as Chancellor and added insult to injury by reducing his brother to the post of Minister of Civil Administration. He died a few weeks later, no doubt greatly satisfied with his final *démarche*.

The most notable of the many Fujiwara family feuds was waged during the last decade of the tenth century between Kaneie's son, Michinaga, and the latter's attractive young nephew, Korechika. It had wide repercussions in court circles and for a time almost everyone was taking sides. Korechika was an influential and popular young man; his father had served as both Regent and Chancellor; and he himself had the full support of his sister, Sadako, the emperor's principal consort. Indeed Korechika had every reason to expect that in due course he would succeed to the main post in the land.

His uncle, however, was a formidable adversary. Michinaga, now thirty-one years old, was at the height of his energy; he had all his father's ambition, drive, and shrewdness, and when it came to a clash his twenty-two-year-old nephew was no match for him. With the powerful support of his sister, the Empress Dowager, Michinaga managed to undermine the young man's position at court. The Empress Dowager interceded with the Emperor and in 995 Michinaga received the important title of Imperial Examiner. So long as Korechika was in the capital, however, Michinaga could not feel secure, and he now exerted himself to bring about his nephew's disgrace. When the Empress Dowager fell ill, he fanned a rumour that this was due to a curse (*juso*) that Korechika had put on her. He next accused the young man of having officiated in an esoteric religious service, *Daigen no Hō*, that by rights could be performed only by the emperor.

Then in the following year Korechika foolishly presented his uncle with precisely the opportunity he needed to administer the *coup de grâce*. Korechika was in love with a distant cousin of his and was carrying on an elegant intrigue with the young lady when it came to his ears that he had a rival in the unlikely person of the Priestly Retired Sovereign, Kazan. Evidently Kazan's sacerdotal vows did not sit too heavily on his shoulders; for he was in the habit of paying secret visits to the house of Korechika's mistress. As it turned out, the object of the priestly attentions was the girl's younger sister, but by the time that the young man knew this it was too late. In an access of pique Korechika ordered some attendants to hide in the girl's garden during one of Kazan's nocturnal visits. As the Priestly Retired Sovereign emerged from his tryst, they shot arrows at him and members of his suite. One of the arrows brushed the former Emperor's robes.

Korechika's purpose had been to scare his supposed rival, but the plot boomeranged and it was he who was removed from the scene. For when word of the scandal reached the palace Korechika was severely censured. Officially the blame was put on the attendants, but shortly thereafter, owing largely to the machinations of the rival Fujiwara faction, Korechika was given the dreaded appointment of Provisional Governor-General of the Government Headquarters in Kyūshū. This post had become a sinecure (vaguely suggestive of the Chiltern Hundreds) which involved giving up all one's appointments and retiring to the wilds of the western provinces – the most unpalatable fate that could befall a Heian nobleman. So unpalatable was it, indeed, that shortly afterwards Korechika secretly returned to Heian Kyō. He was promptly discovered and ordered back to his post, where he languished for half a year before receiving his pardon.

With his nephew safely relegated to the western wilds, Michinaga set about mopping up what was left of the opposition in the capital. Realizing that Korechika's main support had come from the court of his sister, Empress Sadako, he took steps to weaken her position by promoting bedchamber intrigues and by alienating courtiers from her side. The unfortunate Empress, who had now lost both her father and her brother, found herself more and more isolated. From the *Pillow Book* we can judge that Sadako was a gentle and modest young woman (she was now in her early twenties); but when it came to politics Michinaga was relentless and he treated his niece like an enemy. In 999 he had his pretty eleven-year-old daughter, Akiko, appointed as Imperial Lady, and thereafter he did everything to promote the girl's position at court and to help her win the Emperor's favour with her adolescent charms.

By this time there was an uneasy atmosphere in Sadako's apartments. The Empress herself appears to have borne her misfortunes with good grace, but her ladies, no doubt aware of the bleak future that awaited them, were greatly embittered by their mistress's eclipse. Sei Shōnagon, who belonged to her suite, was suspected of being partial to the 'enemy', that is, to Michinaga's faction, and for some time she was under a cloud. The following passage is from her *Pillow Book*:

I had no way of telling what the Empress thought about all this, but I heard some of the ladies-in-waiting whispering, 'She has connexions with people who are attached to the Minister of the Left [Michinaga].' I was coming from my room when I noticed them all standing there muttering away. When they saw me they stopped talking and each of them went about her own business. I was not used to being treated like this and I found it most painful.[14]

Sei Shōnagon is ambiguous about whether or not the suspicions were justified, but we know from an earlier entry that she was greatly impressed by Michinaga's aura of brilliance.[15]

In 999 Sadako gave birth to a boy and the Emperor visited her. By the time of her next pregnancy, however, Michinaga's machinations had taken effect: she left the palace without any of the normal ceremony, and on her arrival at the house of the low-ranking official where she was to be lodged during her confinement no one of importance was present to greet her. Her death in the following year removed the last potential nest of opposition to Michinaga's hegemony at court. When the Emperor rather pathetically suggested that his son by Sadako be named to succeed him, with the understanding that Michinaga's grandson would be next in line, the request was politely but firmly refused. No mere emperor was to stand in Michinaga's way.

In examining these struggles within the Fujiwara family, we should remember that (much like those that have beset the Japanese conservative party in modern times) they were mainly contests for power between individuals or factions, not clashes about issues, let alone about ideology. The members of the ruling aristocracy were not divided on such questions as whether or not to build up closer relations with China, or how best to control the provinces or to improve communications. What concerned them was to acquire supreme office for themselves and their immediate kin and, having acquired such office and its many delightful trappings, to hold it against all comers. Korechika, and likewise the hero of *The Tale of Genji*, are driven from the capital, not because

14. Kaneko ed., p. 700.   15. Ibid., p. 632.

they advocate any unpopular policy – indeed, so far as we know, neither of them advocated any policy at all – but simply because they stand in the way of more powerful contenders. And, when Prince Genji finally succeeds in restoring his fortunes, what determines appointments in the hierarchy is not whether the candidate agrees with Genji's views on government, still less whether he has any administrative ability, but simply the extent to which he supported the prince at the time of his exile ten years before. As his father-in-law, who backed the wrong side, explains to his embittered wife, 'It is all done in a most casual manner. But the fact is that whether we float or sink depends entirely on the stand we took when Genji fell into disgrace. He has really worked it out beautifully. And I am afraid he remembers only too well where I stood at that time.'[16] This lack of any concrete policy or constructive public service with which we might identify their names gives a somewhat nebulous and interchangeable quality to many of the Fujiwara leaders, even to some of those who were most prominent during the period. When we differentiate between them, it is usually in terms of how strong their ambition was and how great their skill at political intrigue.

By the time that Murasaki Shikibu entered court service the last rumbles of the Korechika-Michinaga clash had subsided and Michinaga ruled supreme in the land. The thirty years during which he was in control represent the high point of Fujiwara power. In establishing this position Michinaga was greatly helped by having among his fourteen children several outstandingly intelligent and attractive daughters, and he used them to forge the strongest possible link with the imperial family. During most of his career he felt no need to take the highest ranks, though any office in the land would have been his for the asking. He never became chancellor and he served as regent for only two years and as prime minister for an even shorter time. Here he helped to establish a precedent; for the most powerful rulers in later Japanese history not only allowed sovereignty to remain with the emperor, but were themselves often content to occupy relatively modest posts in the hierarchy.

It was the reality of power that interested Michinaga, and during the period of his rule he elevated his family to such pre-eminence that at

16. Ikeda ed., iii, 298.

times, it appears, they even hesitated to let their children marry lesser members of the imperial family. Prince Genji complains that his Fujiwara friend, Tō no Chūjō, will not allow the marriage between his daughter and Yūgiri even though the latter is of imperial stock: 'It seems that no outsider is good enough for them any longer. No one is allowed to enter that glittering world they have made for themselves – not even a member of the Blood Royal.'[17]

Though Michinaga was the leading statesman of the Heian period, we know hardly more about the man than about the emperor he was supposed to serve. There is no extant portrait to help us imagine him, and the personal touches in *Tales of Glory* and other contemporary records are not sufficient to produce any well-rounded picture. This is not because he had a self-effacing nature. Whatever Michinaga's virtues may have been, modesty was certainly not one of them. His cousin, the Minister of the Right, mentions in his diary that Michinaga once showed him the following poem that he had written about himself:

> This world, I think,
> Is indeed my world.
> Like the full moon I shine,
> Uncovered by any cloud.[18]

We know that this was no isolated access of euphoria, for we have many similar examples. At the age of fifty-four, shortly after Michinaga had taken his Buddhist vows, he wrote; 'Even if I were to die tomorrow, I should have no cause for regret. I have accomplished all that I could possibly desire and ask nothing of the future – so long as I can continue as I am.'[19] There is something rather refreshing about the way in which Michinaga so blatantly enjoys his power while sparing us the usual cant about its burdens and responsibility.

He loved luxury, pomp, and display – everything that was summed up in the word *eiga* – and he did not hesitate to satisfy this taste at the public expense. When his principal mansion was destroyed in one of the great fires, he ordered some of the rich provincial governors to supply

---

17. Ikeda ed., iii, 194.
18. Fujiwara no Sanesuke, *Shōyūki* (diary covering the years 957–1023).
19. Quoted by Fujiki, op. cit., p. 48.

the men and materials to build an even grander one. Since Michinaga had overriding power of appointment, the governors were at his mercy and had to comply. And we gather that he did little to curb the exuberance of some of the rough bands of workmen who would break into nearby houses and help themselves to pillars, doors, and other materials needed for his building.[20]

Entry into the religious life certainly did not mean the end of his political career; in fact, by giving up his official posts and having his son appointed regent, Michinaga was if anything able to devote even more of his energy to the exercise of power. Nor did his decision to take the tonsure mark the beginning of more austere habits. Some of his most brilliant extravagances were occasioned by the building and dedication of the Hōjō Temple on the western bank of the Kamo River. *Tales of Glory* describes the refulgent ceremony that took place in 1022, when he was fifty-seven years old: 'How auspicious it was! The adornments of heavenly beings must certainly be this. . . . When the Emperor went before the Buddha to bow, His Eminence the Novice [Michinaga] wept without restraint. . . . The sand in the garden glittered . . . with jewels of many kinds . . .'[21] Even making full allowance for the hyperbole that is common in works of this type, we can judge what a resplendent display of Michinaga's wealth and power this must have been.

Now and again the *Pillow Book* and Murasaki's diary give us an authentic glimpse of how the great man appeared to the court ladies of the time. Sei Shōnagon mentions an occasion on which Empress Sadako and her ladies were kept waiting while Michinaga had a new under-robe sewn, because, as the Empress explains, he did not want anyone to see him in the same costume that he had worn when escorting the Empress Dowager.[22] Such vanity, however, was far from discrediting Michinaga in Sei Shōnagon's eyes. Murasaki, who had more opportunity to observe him at close quarters, appears to have been less susceptible to his glamour. She particularly disliked seeing him in his cups. This seems to have been a frequent condition. In 1010, for instance, we find the following entry:

20. Ibid., p. 50.

21. The description is contained in *Eiga Monogatari*, xvii, 387–97. The present translation is from G. B. Sansom, *A History of Japan*, i, 174–5.

22. Kaneko ed., p. 954.

His Excellency [Michinaga] was received in audience by the Emperor and, when they came out of the Imperial Audience Chamber together, they had some refreshments. As usual His Excellency became drunk. I knew what a nuisance this could be and so I tried to keep out of sight, but he noticed me and shouted, 'You *are* a strange creature! It isn't every day that you have a chance to see your Empress's papa taking his ease with the Emperor. And yet you can't get away fast enough.' He went on scolding me for a while and then added, 'By rights I should be composing a poem for this occasion, but you can do it for me. Come on now, write something, write something!' His Excellency kept on urging me, but I was afraid that what I produced might be very lame indeed. I could see now that he was even drunker than usual. His face glowed in the lamplight . . .[23]

Fortunately for Murasaki, the wine soon had its normal effect: Michinaga forgot about making her write a poem and staggered off to have a look at his grandchildren, the little princes, who were asleep in bed.

What worried the prim lady-in-waiting even more than Michinaga's drunkenness was his lechery. Murasaki records a rather suggestive poem that he once addressed to her.[24] Her discouraging reply did not put him off; for shortly afterwards, as she was sleeping in a room near the corridor, she was awakened by a tapping on the shutter. In the world of Heian this could only mean that some gallant was trying to gain admittance. 'I was terrified,' writes Murasaki, 'and lay awake all night without making a sound.' On the following morning she received a poem from Michinaga:

> How sad for him who stands the whole night long
> Knocking on your cedar door
> Tap-tap-tap like the cry of the *kuina* bird.[25]

Murasaki was quick to answer:

> Sadder for her who had answered the *kuina*'s tap,
> For it was no innocent bird who stood there knocking on the door.

23. *Murasaki Shikibu Nikki*, edited by Mochizuki Sekkyō (hereafter abbreviated as 'Mochizuki ed.'), pp. 110–11.

24. See p. 273.

25. Mochizuki ed., p. 108. The *kuina* is a water-rail, whose cry is said to resemble the sound of knocking on a door.

It is doubtful whether this rebuff would have deterred a man of Michinaga's overweening disposition; but the diary ends shortly after and we do not know whether Murasaki ever succumbed.

On the whole, the personal picture that we derive of Michinaga is not an attractive one. Indeed, judged by moral standards, few of the prepotent Fujiwara leaders emerge in a very favourable light. Yet, for all its failings, this family helped to keep the country at peace for a remarkably long period; and they did so without recourse to the dungeons, the torture chambers, and the executioner's sword which became the commonplace means of asserting power in later centuries. For this, and for their encouragement of an indigenous aristocratic culture, they deserve better of historians than has usually been granted.

C. SOCIETY

Heian society was based on a hierarchy of grades as exact as the system devised by Peter the Great and far more rigid than that of the Roman Empire. The earliest Chinese descriptions of Japan (third century A.D.) stress the class feeling that prevailed in the islands; and the Great Reform, though aimed at remodelling the country on the Chinese pattern, did nothing to modify the rigid nature of its social hierarchy. Under the new system the aristocracy was correlated with the civil service in a way that was essentially un-Chinese, and the island's ancient nobility became the ruling officialdom.

The Reform codes and their amendments provided for ten court ranks, the first three being divided into senior and junior, and most of the others being further subdivided into upper and lower, so that there was a total of some thirty grades, apart from the four orders that were reserved for princes of the blood. The main dividing line came between the Third and Fourth Ranks, members of the top three ranks being known as *Kugyō* (High Court Nobles) and receiving all the most valuable privileges. A second division separated members of the Fifth Rank and above, whose appointments were issued by the emperor, from those of inferior rank, who were appointed by the Great Council of State and who were debarred from many important privileges such as appearing in the Imperial Audience Chamber.

The outstanding feature of the new system was that court rank determined both one's post in the government and one's wealth rather than vice versa as was normal in China and in Imperial Rome. And entry into the rank hierarchy was decided exclusively by one's family connexions. Members of the High Court Nobility were recruited from among junior branches of the imperial family and from the great families who had held clan titles (*kabane*) in the pre-Reform days. The Fourth and Fifth Ranks drew their original membership mainly from lesser clans in the Yamato region and from certain distinguished foreign families that had immigrated to Japan during the previous two centuries; the remaining ranks included the heads of other minor clans, particularly those in the provinces.

A glance at some of the privileges accruing to rank-holders will suggest the importance of this system in Heian Japan. Members of the first five ranks received the revenue from special grants of rice land (the source of virtually all income during this period), ranging from about two hundred acres for the Senior First Rank (Prime Minister) to about twenty acres for the Junior Fifth Rank (Minor Counsellor).[26] They were allowed to send their children to the University; these children (and in the case of the top three ranks the grandchildren too) were automatically admitted into the rank system when they came of age. A person of the Fifth Rank or above could wear ceremonial dress and had access to the Imperial Audience Chamber. He was given special allowances of silk and cloth. Sturdy guards and messengers were assigned to his service, the number (and presumably the sturdiness) being precisely correlated with the master's rank. Among the special privileges enjoyed by the High Court Nobles were Sustenance Households, groups of peasant households, ranging from about four thousand for the Prime Minister to about nine hundred for a member of the Third Rank, from which the nobleman was entitled to receive all the dues and taxes that would normally have been paid to the central government. They also had the right to employ house retainers and officials (*keishi*) at government expense and, when they died, to rest beneath a burial mound

26. Fujiki points out that in China the ratio of rank-land (rice land granted in respect of one's court rank) to sustenance rice fields (rice land that was supposed to be distributed equally to the entire population) varied from 5:1 to 60:1; in Japan the ratio varied from 40:1 to 400:1. This points up the crucial role of rank in determining economic position in Nara and early Heian Japan.

(*haka*). Members of all the ranks had privileged status in law: their sentences were lighter and they were spared humiliating punishments like birching. Above all, they were exempt from commuted tax, forced labour, tribute in kind, and conscription, which for several centuries after the Great Reform had placed an increasingly heavy burden on the rest of the population. Even if this had been their sole privilege, it would have been sufficient to turn holders of rank into a race apart.

The details of patrician life were regulated by rank to an almost unbelievable degree. The codes and imperial edicts exhaustively defined the standard of living appropriate to each rank – the height of one's gatepost, for instance, the type of carriage one might own, the number of one's outriders. Costume was rigidly prescribed in terms of rank, down to the type of fan one could hold: twenty-five folds for the first three ranks, twenty-three for the fourth and fifth, twelve for the sixth and below.

Although the details of these regulations were often flouted, court rank continued to be of prime importance in the capital until the very end of the period. The possession of rank was the main criterion that allowed a man or woman to be described as *yoki hito*, a term which can be roughly translated as 'person of quality', yet which retains a great deal of the moral connotation of its literal meaning, 'good person'. Virtually all the characters in *The Tale of Genji* and other contemporary literature are *yoki hito*, and so are the writers of these works and their readers. Even the dead were not immune to the charms of rank. Spirits and vengeful ghosts were occasionally given rank, or promoted to a higher rung, in order to appease them for injuries they had suffered while alive. So important a part did rank play in everyday life that even Emperor Ichijō's pet cat was accorded the theoretical privilege of wearing the head-dress (*kōburi*) reserved for members of the Fifth Rank and above, and was known by the title of Myōbu, which applied to ladies of medium rank.[27]

For the inhabitants of Genji's world, then, court rank determined office, wealth, power, and the myriad details of everyday life; it is small wonder that for many of them promotion to higher rank should have been an obsession. Readers of *The Tale of Genji* will recall the misery of the fourteen-year-old Yūgiri, whose father (Prince Genji) has kept him

27. *Makura no Sōshi*, Kaneko ed., p. 50.

in the Sixth Rank on the principle that this will give the lad more chance to prove himself. Yūgiri is convinced that the indifference of his beloved Lady Kumoi and all his other difficulties are a direct result of the hateful green robe (*midori no sode*) that he has to wear as a member of the Sixth Rank: 'Would the day never come, he used to ask himself, when he could finally change that green costume of his for something better.'[28]

Promotion depended almost entirely on one's family connexions and, particularly after the ninth century, on one's relations with the dominant faction of the Fujiwaras. With his father's help Yūgiri is in due course elevated to the dizziest rungs of the hierarchy and appointed to the high offices that accompany the top ranks. Yet for lack of the proper connexions many an abler man must have languished until his death in the Sixth Rank or below. It seems probable that in Murasaki's day less than one-tenth of one per cent of the population belonged to the rank system, and for some three centuries no fresh blood had been admitted. For in Japan, unlike China, merit was never a passport for entering the hierarchy. The closed nature of the rank system must have kept thousands of the most intelligent and potentially competent men in the country from participating in government service or in any other important activity. This lack of mobility at the centre of power was bound in the long run to produce the same sort of fossilization that occurred in Rome from the time of the Antonines, helping to bring about the decline of the empire.

Heian society manifests in an extreme form features that are common to small aristocratic groups everywhere. Like the characters in Murasaki's novel, members of the upper class are almost all related to each other. They are totally uninterested in everyone outside their own charmed circle and exceedingly sensitive in judging the precise social level of each person who does belong. A glimpse of a girl's handwriting, a snatch of overheard speech, are all that Genji or Kaoru require to 'place' her precisely in the hierarchy. On his clandestine visit to Uji, Prince Niou stands in the darkness outside the shutters and discreetly announces his arrival by clearing his throat. Ukon has no idea who the visitor may be, but 'from the sound of his cough she realized at once that it was someone of noble birth' (*ate-naru shiwabuki to kikishirite*).[29]

28. Ikeda ed., iii, 187.   29. Ibid., vii, 28.

Murasaki and the members of her circle might well have been amused by the English parlour-game that involves classifying people by reference to their use of words, gestures, and table habits. But the modern shibboleths would undoubtedly have struck them as crass, and the dichotomy of 'U' and 'non-U' would have seemed a crude over-simplification of the nuances involved in social status. For in Murasaki's *milieu* to determine a person's precise standing was no simple diversion but a matter of overriding importance.

It is probably this attitude to class that separates us from the world of the shining prince more than any other single factor. The points of view that derive from Heian Buddhism are perfectly comprehensible even if we may not share them; and we can readily understand the network of superstitions that regulated their lives, for the modern world is full of equivalent obfuscations. But the idea that the essential criterion for judging an individual's merit is the aristocratic standing of the family into which he was born has almost disappeared from the world and must strike many readers of Heian literature as ludicrous if not actually repulsive.

Yet it would be a gross oversimplification to condemn Murasaki and her associates as mere snobs. The basis of snobbery may be defined[30] as the choice of irrelevant criteria from among various possible scales of value, as, for example, in judging the beauty of a painting by its age, or a person's wit by his wealth; in Murasaki's world, on the other hand, there was a single overriding criterion by which people were judged: that of birth. Under exceptional circumstances a social group may acquire a 'monolithic' hierarchy of values and such groups are relatively free of snobbery, because there is no other scale of values to interfere with judgement. It is precisely such a hierarchy that we find in the aristocracy of Heian Kyō. Their attitude to provincials and to members of their own class was the natural consequence of an accepted scale of values in which a member of the Third Rank, for instance, automatically took precedence over a provincial governor of the Fifth, and a person without rank (*tadabito* – 'mere person') was in every respect in-

30. I am indebted to Arthur Koestler for his definition and analysis of snobbery (*The Trail of the Dinosaur and Other Essays*, London, 1955, pp. 69–94). Ancient Greece provides an interesting analogy in its use of the terms *kalokagathoi* and *kakoi*, which correspond closely to *yoki* and *waroki hito*.

ferior to one whose birth qualified him for appointment (*yoki hito* –
'good person'). To call this snobbery is to underestimate its scope.

Pace certain post-war critics who have tried to picture Murasaki
Shikibu as a social rebel and her novel as a protest against the rigid class
system of her time, there is every reason to believe that she implicitly
accepted the hierarchical attitudes that were current among the aristocracy of Heian Kyō. Many of the complications in *The Tale of Genji* can
be understood only in terms of these attitudes. The treatment of Prince
Genji's own mother, who was hounded to death by rivals, is a typical
case; for what infuriated her enemies was that she should have achieved
success at court despite her comparatively low status (*ito yamugoto naki
kiwa ni wa aranedo*).

The difference in Genji's handling of two of his youthful mistresses,
Lady Murasaki[31] and Lady Akashi, is also the result of class consciousness. He is unable to take either of these ladies as his official wife, since
they do not have sufficient rank. Lady Murasaki, however, being the
illegitimate[32] daughter of an imperial prince, has a very different status
from Lady Akashi, whose father is a provincial governor. It must therefore have seemed inevitable to contemporary readers of the novel that
the hero's love and respect for Murasaki should have been greater.
When Akashi gives birth to his child, he removes the infant from her
and has it adopted by Murasaki. To the modern reader the hero's behaviour may seem callous, but from the author's point of view it was
perfectly justified, since Lady Murasaki, being on a superior rung of the
hierarchy, was in a better position to provide a good upbringing. Similarly, Kaoru, despite his devotion to Ukifune, cannot possibly put their
relations on an open, formal footing. The reason, though never openly
stated, is perfectly clear: Ukifune's mother is married to a provincial
official. Since Ukifune's half-sister does not suffer from this handicap,
Prince Niou is free to take her as his official concubine; but, when it
comes to selecting his principal wife, no one is good enough but the
daughter of the Minister of the Left, who belongs to the Senior Second
Rank. The hierarchy of consorts (principal wife, open concubine, secret

31. Murasaki no Ue, heroine of the main part of Murasaki Shikibu's novel
(see p. 323).

32. I use the term 'illegitimate' to refer to children born of consorts other than
the principal wife (see p. 231, n. 37).

concubine), and all the emotional complications that it entails, derive from distinctions of rank; and there is no indication that Murasaki Shikibu ever questioned this hierarchy, let alone that she tried to attack it.

D. ADMINISTRATION

Such being the nature of the rank system, its rigid correlation with government office was bound to have a harmful effect on standards of administration. In borrowing the Chinese structure the Japanese conspicuously failed to adopt one of its most valuable features, namely, an examination system that allowed people to enter government service on the basis of intellectual merit as well as of birth.[33] On the other hand, they did take over, virtually intact, the huge, complex administrative system with all its ministries, boards, offices, and bureaux – a system that could hardly have been less appropriate for a small and relatively backward country like Japan.

One result was that already by the beginning of the Heian period many of the organs of government had ceased to have any real administrative function and had often become mere decorations. Since all rank-holders were normally entitled to a corresponding government post, the offices were grossly overstaffed and, as always happens in a bloated bureaucracy, there was a good deal of overlapping. The development of the Heian administration obeyed Parkinson's Law: once a post was established it hardly ever disappeared, however superfluous it might have become. Consequently many of the incumbents had extremely little real work to do in their offices; the boredom that Genji and his friends so often express when referring to their governmental duties is related to this growing emptiness of the system.

The cumbrous government machinery was concerned more and more with ceremony and form. rather than with the practical aspects of ad-

33. I am aware that the Chinese examination system was not fully developed at the time of the Taika Reform and that the schools in Ch'ang-an, like those in Heian Kyō, were largely reserved for the aristocracy. What is significant here is that the Japanese did not make the slightest effort then or later to introduce a system which, however limited its application may have been in early T'ang times, did contain seeds that were to result in a bureaucracy of talent.

ministration. This in turn resulted in inordinate delays and inefficiency. The procedure for issuing Imperial Decrees provides an example of Heian bureaucracy rampant. When the Great Council of State have decided on a proposal, they submit it to the emperor, whose secretaries rewrite it as a State document, drafted of course in Chinese. After the emperor has read it, he automatically approves and signifies this by writing the day of the month in his own hand (the year and the month having already been filled in by the secretaries). The draft is then sent to the Ministry of Central Affairs. The minister makes a Report of Acknowledgement to the emperor. He then examines the document and (approval again being automatic) inscribes the Chinese character for 'Proclaim' under his official title. The next stop is the office of the Senior Assistant Minister, who, after the usual delays, writes the character for 'Received'. The same procedure is followed by the Junior Assistant Minister, except that he writes the character 'Perform'. Now the draft goes to the Scribes' Office, where it is copied. The document is then sent back to the Great Council of State, where the Major Counsellor makes a Report of Acknowledgement. Next the emperor sees the document; this time he writes the character 'Approved' and returns it to the Great Council. Here the document is thoroughly scrutinized and, if no stylistic mistakes are found, it is sent back to the Scribes' Office for multi-copying. Each copy is signed jointly by the Prime Minister and all other officials who are concerned with the matter in hand, and then sent to the palace for the ceremony of affixing the Great Imperial Seal (*Seiin no Gi*). Now finally the decree can be promulgated. Since, as often as not, it is concerned with some such question as the type of head-dress that an official of the Third Rank may wear at court, we can judge the prodigious waste of time and effort involved in government procedure.

As the formal and social aspects of central administration came to overshadow its practical purpose, precedent became all-important and ceremony ever more elaborate. The development of the *Junsei* illustrates the change. Originally these were meetings that took place four times a month between the emperor and officials of the Third Rank and above. They were held in the Imperial Palace and were mainly devoted to reports on government activity; after the business was finished, the officials were invited to a court banquet. By Murasaki's time these meetings had become elaborate affairs, occurring twice a year and consisting exclusively of the banquet.

As the Heian period advanced, there was a significant change in the time at which government functions took place. The Great Reform had stipulated the Hour of the Tiger (about 4 a.m.) as the time when officials should arrive at their offices and the Hour of the Horse (midday) as the time for leaving. It is uncertain how strictly they ever observed this Spartan rule, but we know that by the tenth century a good deal of government work, especially that which involved the higher officials, was carried out at night, that it consisted almost entirely of ceremony, and that its tedium was often relieved by a liberal consumption of wine.

These were hardly conditions in which the virtuous, Chinese-type scholar-administrator, who had been the ideal of an earlier age, was likely to flourish. Appointments to important posts were often made because of pedigree, without the slightest regard to ability. In Murasaki's time, for instance, a young nobleman of fifteen was given the crucial post of Chief of Imperial Police. There was also an increasing amount of corruption, involving the sale of offices and favours. Since more and more government posts had become sinecures, they could be bought for the sake of prestige, in full confidence that no actual work would be involved. The sale of office was particularly common in the Imperial Guards and the Imperial Police. As they were the bodies responsible for maintaining law and order in the capital, venality in these quarters was bound to have serious consequences: it was, for example, the low military standards of the Guards that made possible the terrifying raids on the capital by the warrior priests from Mount Hiei.

Such trends would inevitably have led to the stultification and breakdown of central government if no remedial action had been taken. The reason that so cumbrous, formalized, and corrupt a system could last as long as it did is that real power of administration had passed into the hands of the Fujiwara leaders, who were conducting the effective government of the country through their own private house organs. The old structure was allowed to lumber along intact; but, when it came to making decisions and giving orders, the Supreme Fujiwara Administrative, Military, and Legal Councils were the real seats of authority. Here the Upper Family Officials, unencumbered by the tons of *paperasserie* that weighed down the imperial ministries, were able to conduct affairs in a far simpler and more direct way. It is hard to assess the actual output of the Fujiwara Councils; but we know that Japan's first great Shogun used this type of family organ as the model for his own highly efficient government. The Fujiwaras have been accused of usurping all real power from the ministries and of having governed the country as if it were their private estate. The charge is no doubt just. The Fujiwaras invariably placed their family interests above the common weal, their attitude probably being similar to that of the American Secretary of Defence who, when charged with a 'conflict of interests', explained that what was good for the country was good for General Motors and vice versa. The fact remains that the Fujiwaras gave Japan – or at least the Home Provinces – a relatively simple and effective form of government, which the Chinese-type bureaucracy had been unable to provide.

E. ECONOMY

The Fujiwaras' ascendancy in the administration and their predominant position in the social hierarchy would have availed them little without their wealth. The real basis of the family's power was economic. The control of rice land or its revenue has been a prime factor in determining political and social conditions throughout Japanese history until modern times. The Heian period, for all its emphasis on urban culture, was no exception. It was when the court nobility lost control of the land that power passed from their hands for ever.

In Murasaki's time trade and commerce played a minimal part in the country's economy. Money circulated very little (the minting of coins had ceased by 960) and later it disappeared completely. Almost all payments were made in kind. Material, clothes, musical instruments, medicines, and art objects were all used (the presents given to messengers in *The Tale of Genji* provide numerous examples); but the medium of exchange on which the entire economy rested was rice, the staple of the Far East.

The Great Reform was greatly concerned with the redistribution of economic power, its aim being, on the one hand, to divert the country's wealth from the clan chieftains to the central government and, on the other, to reduce inequalities. All land was declared to belong to the public domain and an ingenious system of 'sustenance rice fields' was taken over from China. This provided that every citizen should receive a grant of rice land when he attained the age of six and should keep it until his death, when it would automatically revert to the public domain. Males were given about five acres, women two-thirds of that amount – generous allotments when we consider that the average size of a farm in Japan today is less than three acres.

Excellent as the system may have been in theory, it never had a chance of working in a country that was ruled by an aristocracy with strong traditions of private ownership.[34] From the very beginning, important areas of rice land were deliberately excluded; and in these exceptions we can detect the seeds that eventually destroyed the entire egalitarian structure. Among the special grants of land were those given in respect of rank and those that accompanied office; the latter, being tax-exempt, were particularly coveted. In addition shrines and temples were granted large tracts of tax-free land in perpetuity. Another exception was the new rice fields that were privately reclaimed with government permission; at first they were regarded as belonging to the crown land, but in due course they too became private, inheritable, and tax-exempt.

The social grants of rice land accorded to members of the ruling class allowed them to accumulate considerable wealth and in effect preserved the inequalities that the system had been designed to correct. It has been calculated that the annual income which a member of the Second Rank derived from his rank land, office land, and sustenance households was almost thirty thousand bushels of rice, equivalent in purchasing power to some £60,000 in present values. Well before the Fujiwaras took over complete power in the tenth century, they held a good proportion of the high ranks and offices, and the income accumulated from these allotments was enough to make them the richest private family in the land. As if all this were not enough, an emperor in the eighth century had given them a grant in perpetuity of thirteen thousand sustenance households as an extra reward for the services that their family had rendered to the state.

The system of 'sustenance rice fields' – or rather, the exceptions to the system – had served the Fujiwaras well; but by Murasaki's time this was no longer the basis of their wealth. The main economic unit was

34. The *chün t'ien* ('equal field') system never worked properly even in the country of its origin and had already begun to break down by the middle of the T'ang period.

now the private manor; and it was Michinaga who controlled by far the largest number of manors in Japan. Observing the situation in 1025, a Fujiwara cousin commented, 'All the land in the realm has become the territory of the First Family [Michinaga's branch]. They do not seem to have left even a speck of earth for the public domain. These are lamentable times indeed.'[35] It was Michinaga's preponderance, however, rather than the principle of private ownership, that distressed the writer; for he himself had inherited lucrative manors from his father, and his mansion in the capital was noted for its opulence.

The manor played a crucial part in Murasaki's Japan, and without a general idea of its function we can no more know her world than we could understand middle-class life in Victorian England if we ignored the role of trade and commerce. It had its origins in the tax-exempt estates granted to religious institutions. These provided a precedent for private ownership and for the alienation of land from government control. With the rapid reclamation of land during the Nara period there was a great expansion of tax-free estates privately held by families; from the eighth century more and more people came to commend their land to these families in order to remove them from the scope of the tax collector, since the dues payable to the consignee were usually less than the government assessment. These private estates are known as *shō*, and by the tenth century they had become the most important source of income for the ruling class. The translation of 'manor', though probably the best available, could well be misleading. For the *shō* differed from the European manor or *Grundherrschaft* in almost every important respect except that of fiscal immunity: it preceded the development of feudal relationships and was never a fief in the Western sense; its proprietor was not a member of the landed aristocracy enjoying outright ownership of his demesne and the loyalty of his vassals, but usually a court nobleman living in the capital and receiving a proportion of the crop from numerous scattered estates.[36]

35. *Shōyūki*, (see p. 75, n. 18).

36. Joüon Des Longrais describes the development of the *shō* and draws some useful comparisons with European manors. *L'Est et l'ouest: institutions du Japon et de l'occident comparées*, Chapter 1. The eminent Japanese authority, Dr Asakawa, is categorical in denying that the *shō* is a manor (e.g. *The Documents of Iriki*, p. 39).

The period that corresponds to the world of the shining prince was marked by the rapid extension of fiscal immunity as more and more families claimed exemption for their estates. Proprietors of manors would obtain charters (*kanshōfu*) from the central government explicitly recognizing their estates as *shō*, defining their boundaries, and, most important of all, exempting them from tax. By the end of the Heian era some eighty per cent of the rice land in the country was included in the manors, which were now not merely private property but virtually extra-territorial. Efforts by the crown to assert its waning right of eminent domain were rudely, and as a rule successfully, flouted by the proprietors.

A peculiarity of the Japanese manor was that a system of rights took the place of actual ownership of the land. These rights (*shiki*) were originally the benefits attached to the various hereditary official posts on the manor; they included rights to use land and to impose dues in kind or labour; but usually they took the form of fixed percentages or shares of the crop. It was a complex system, in which no one enjoyed complete ownership of the land, and in which an individual could hold different rights in different capacities on the same manor or on widely separated manors. The rights could also be transferred upwards or downwards in the hierarchy, and this process of transfer was central to the functioning of the manorial system.

A downward transfer of rights (*onkyū*) was the *beneficium* that the main proprietor of the manor granted to the men who managed and cultivated the land. It was contingent on the satisfactory performance of their duties and could be revoked for disloyalty, disobedience, and (the most frequent case) delay in paying the yearly tribute. The *beneficium* could be increased for meritorious service, especially of a military nature. Here, of course, we have germs of the feudal relationships that gradually developed on the manors after Murasaki's time.

Commendation (*kishin*) refers to an upward transfer of rights and became particularly common in the tenth century. The owner would nominally surrender his rights to some stronger person or institution in return for tax immunity and other forms of protection. In theory he was surrendering his share of ownership while keeping the privilege to use the land; in reality he retained possession and delivered dues to the consignee in the form of an agreed percentage of the crop. The system was further complicated by the practice of re-consignment, according to which rights would be transferred further and further up the hierarchy until they reached the top – some powerful temple or a nobleman of the Third Rank or above. These ultimate consignees were in a position to override the provincial governor and other local officials, and to protect the manor against any demands (however justified) of the imperial government. Each person or institution in the upward chain of commendation would acquire some right in the land. The main proportion of the crop, however, would normally accrue to the *Ryōshu*, who was closest to being the Lord of the Manor in the Western sense, and to the *Honke*, the Legal Guardian, who occupied the highest rung in the ladder of commendation. These enviable positions naturally tended to accrue to the most powerful political figures in the land, who could best protect the manor, namely the leaders of the Fujiwara family; and it was the income that they derived as *Ryōshu* and *Honke*, and the accumulated wealth that they were able to invest in the development of new manors, that provided the economic basis of their hegemony.

The manorial system was a direct violation of the principles that their great ancestor had laid down in the Reform; yet the Fujiwaras, far from preventing its spread, were insatiable in their desire to bring new manors under their control. On one occasion when a certain landowner offered to commend the rights of his manor to Michinaga it was discovered before the documents were signed that the man's grandfather had died as an unpardoned exile. To receive rights from such a source would not have befitted the dignity of the Fujiwaras, but the offer was too tempting to resist; Michinaga accordingly arranged that the man should be adopted into another family and change his name, whereupon he accepted the manor with alacrity.

Sporadic efforts to check the spread of manors served to weaken only the smaller holders, since they would circumvent the decrees by commending their estates to powerful temples or, more usually, to the Fujiwaras. Once land had been lost to the Crown it was rarely recovered. In the eleventh century a non-Fujiwara emperor made a final effort to check the process and demanded that the Fujiwaras present their manorial title deeds for inspection. He was answered with a cavalier refusal by Michinaga's son, the clan head, who pointed out that he had been looking after His Majesty's interests for more than fifty years without having to bother with documents of this kind.[37]

When reading *The Tale of Genji* and other works of the period, we should remember that the shining prince and his patrician circle owe their affluence mainly to the rights they hold as absentee landlords or guardians of various tax-free manors. This, of course, is not a matter on which a writer like Murasaki would be likely to dwell, and it is rare indeed that we come across any reference to the rice income on which the inhabitants of her world depended. When the Prince is winding up his affairs before going into exile, they are mostly of an amatory nature. He does, however, find time for a few practical arrangements:

To Lady Murasaki he handed over all the title deeds of his Manors (*mi-shō*), pasture land (*mi-maki*) and other estates in different parts of the country. His rows of warehouses (*kuramachi*) and his storerooms (*osamedono*) he put in charge of his nurse Shōnagon, in whose reliability he had full trust, and he assigned a few of his closest Family Officials (*keishi*) to help her in these duties.[38]

It is worth while to note, incidentally, that the two people to whom Genji entrusts his vast estates and the wealth that has accumulated from them are both women. The comparatively favourable position that upper-class women enjoyed in the Heian period was partly due to their privilege of inheriting or being given rights in manors, which provided them with an independence they lacked in later ages. Of course, neither they nor the men had the slightest concern with the life and work on the estates from which they drew their sustenance; and they were most unlikely ever to visit them. Like most modern shareholders in business companies, they limited their interest to increases in the value of their various holdings and to their periodical dividends.

The growth of the manorial system has often been decried for leading to the enfeeblement of the imperial government and to a long period of disruption. There is no doubt that by withdrawing ever larger areas of rice land from the national fisc the court nobility so weakened the central government that it was totally unable to withstand the military challenge from the provinces. The rapacity and the success of the Fujiwaras were their own undoing. The poverty of the exchequer was also a grow-

---

37. . . . nanjō bunsho ka wa sōrōbeki. *Gukan Shō*, iv, 130.
38. Ikeda ed., ii, 132.

ing source of corruption; this in turn lowered the standards of provincial administration and weakened the control that the administration could exert outside the capital. Above all, the consolidation of these semi-autonomous units within the state promoted local separatism and, once the manors were armed, brought about the breakdown of central government in most parts of the country.

Yet there is a reverse side to the coin. If literature and the other arts are to flourish in any country there must be either a large public, or else substantial wealth must have accumulated among individuals or groups who are prepared to disburse it for cultural ends. The first condition could hardly be satisfied in tenth-century Japan. The development of the manorial system, however, did permit a sustained concentration of wealth among the aristocracy in the capital. The cultural flowering of the period was made possible mainly by the accumulation of an economic surplus in the hands of one great aristocratic family, which, thanks to the prevalence of peace and to the absence of immediate external challenges, was able to devote this surplus to the patronage and pursuit of the arts and to the creation of a world in which the 'rule of taste' could prevail.

F. PROVINCIALS AND THE LESSER BREEDS

A rough estimate of the population of Japan in Murasaki's time is five million. Of this number probably about one per cent lived in the capital and less than one-tenth of one per cent belonged to the rank hierarchy. It is this last small group, of course, that constitutes almost the entire population of the world of the shining prince. Yet, if we are to understand the aristocracy, we should have at least a general idea of the other classes and of the attitude that the 'good people' had towards them.

The well-known literary ladies of the time wrote almost entirely about high-ranking men and women in the capital and naturally tended to regard the rest of the population through the eyes of the people they described. It is important to remember, however, that almost all these ladies, including Murasaki Shikibu, Izumi Shikibu, the author of the *Sarashina Diary*, and probably Sei Shōnagon, were daughters of provincial officials and theoretically belonged to the provincial, or (as some modern historians call it) middle, class. It is true that their families may often have had distinguished origins (Izumi, for instance, came from the Ōe family, which descended from Emperor Heijō), but such was the rigidity of social attitudes in this period that once a man had been tarred with the brush of the provinces, for example by serving a term of office as governor in some eastern province, he had the greatest difficulty in re-establishing himself in court society. Many of them accordingly preferred, after their terms had expired, to remain in the countryside, where they might consolidate their economic position, rather than return to the capital and face the contumely of high-ranking courtiers. For, however much wealth and local power they might acquire, high rank and office almost invariably eluded their grasp. The governor of a vast province like Iwashiro in the north-east had the same rank (Junior Fifth Upper Grade) as a Junior Assistant Minister in the Ministry of Central Affairs, and far less prestige at court; the governor of a smaller province like Izumi ranked with a mere Junior Secretary in the Department of Shintō.

These provincial officials who remained in their localities and extended their manorial holdings with the help of armed supporters provided one source of leadership in the rising military class; and their descendants frequently built up their strength until they were able to defy all attempts by the central government to control the areas under their command. It was precisely such a family that staged the only large-scale military rising in Murasaki's time. Taira no Tadatsune belonged to a collateral branch of the imperial family that had for a long time been established in the Chiba Peninsula, some thirty miles from the present city of Tokyo, where they held virtually hereditary governorships. He had consolidated his strength in his own province, having brought all the local officials and farmers under his power, and in 1028 (the year of Michinaga's death) he decided that the time had come to expand into the neighbouring territories. He successfully attacked the local seats of government and was preparing to continue his rampages when the court, belatedly as usual, ordered two commissioners of the Imperial Police to take action against him. The imperial levies were no match for Tadatsune's tough local warriors and they soon had to be recalled. The situation was now becoming critical and the government were obliged to call on a member of the Minamotos. This great warlike family had established its role as the 'claws and teeth of the Fujiwara' and was increasingly being used to keep order in the provinces, and even in the capital, when things got beyond the control of the feeble imperial forces. The new general proceeded to the east and started his preparations for attack. Overawed by the prestige of the Minamotos and by the evident determination of the government, Tadatsune shaved his head and surrendered without a fight. He was conducted to the capital, but on the way he died of an illness – possibly of the type that so often afflicted unpopular prisoners in Japanese history. His head was then chopped off and sent to Heian Kyō to be pilloried on the gates of the gaol. This last procedure was a departure from the usual lenient policy of the times and foreshadowed the brutality of the succeeding age of civil warfare.

*

Though the provinces were the source of economic power, and were rapidly building up military strength as well, we should hardly guess their importance from reading *The Tale of Genji* or other contemporary literature. For Murasaki and her friends in the capital they were harsh, dreary, backward places, about which the less said the better.

To be appointed governor of a remote province, however lucrative such a post might be, was regarded as a form of exile. Like the aristocratic denizen of Versailles who had been banished to his *terres*, the provincial governor and other officials who left the capital were cut off from cultural pursuits and from the other pleasures of polite society. Besides, rustication made it virtually impossible for them to be promoted in rank. Often the nominal governor would send a deputy in his place, while he remained in the capital, enjoying the emoluments of his office without its rigours. One result was a serious decline in standards of provincial administration.

In its attitude to the provinces the Heian aristocracy was similar to the eighteenth-century English writer who exclaimed, 'There is not only no knowledge of the world outside a great city, but no decency, no practicable society – I had almost said no virtue.' Perhaps the main difference is that, unlike Horace Walpole, Murasaki and her 'good people' would not have felt the slightest need to qualify the last statement. No harsher pejorative existed in her vocabulary than *inakabitaru* ('countrified'). If Murasaki refers to a girl as having been brought up in 'undesirable surroundings', it usually means that she is the daughter of a governor, and that she has spent her childhood in the provinces. When Lady Akashi learns from her grandmother that she was reared in the provinces – actually a mere sixty miles from the capital – her reaction is one of unmitigated horror: 'Never had she dreamt that she could have been born in a place so cut off from the world.'[39] And the daughter of the Governor of Kazusa, a province near present-day Tokyo, starts her diary with the following doleful entry: 'I was brought up in a remote part of the world – so remote that it lies even beyond the end of the Tōkaidō. I expect that people [in the capital] will regard me as hopelessly outlandish.'[40]

The few provincials who figure in *The Tale of Genji* are usually pictured as boorish upstarts, hopelessly devoid of good taste and standing in exaggerated awe of their 'betters', whose elegance they ape at their peril. Considering the way in which Murasaki describes her provincials, it is amazing that anyone should seriously have represented her as a champion of the 'middle' (provincial) class and her novel as a protest against the treatment of this class by the aristocracy. Here, for example, is her picture of Ukifune's step-father, the former Governor of Hitachi, after he has returned from the provinces to live in the capital:

He was fairly well born [literally, 'he was not a base man'], for his family included Court nobility and there was nothing ignominious about them [literally, 'they were not dirty people']. Having accumulated an immense fortune, he was determined to show off his wealth by living in the style that it permitted, and his residence was decorated in the most luxurious fashion. Yet, the more elegantly he tried to arrange things, the more blatantly was his vulgar, boorish, countrified (*ayashū araraka ni inakabitaru*) nature exposed. He had a rough tone of voice and occasionally he would even allow dialect to intrude into his speech – a result no doubt of his long years in the remote eastern provinces. He stood in great awe of those in authority and was scrupulous in carrying out his duties. He knew nothing of music and the other pleasant sides of life, but he was an excellent shot with the bow.[41]

It is small wonder that Kaoru feels compelled to keep his relations with Ukifune secret.

The 'good people' looked with particular scorn on military men. This

39. Ikeda ed., iv, 83.   40. *Sarashina Nikki*, p. 479.
41. Ikeda ed., vi, 233–4.

was partly because they were connected with the provinces, and partly a reflection of the Chinese contempt for the military that had developed since T'ang times. To be given a post in the Ministry of War was regarded as a most unfortunate development in one's career. The Guards regiments in the capital had never filled any significant military function and by Murasaki's time they had become entirely ceremonial. Kaoru serves as a Major Captain, the highest rank in the Inner Palace Guards, but he would have been incredulous and horrified if the Ministry had asked him to perform any military duty. This attitude of the aristocracy helps to explain why the Fujiwaras were obliged to call on provincial families like the Minamotos despite all the dangers that this dependence involved.

Military men, who were the uncontested heroes of the subsequent age, rarely appear in Heian literature. One of the few in *The Tale of Genji* is Tamakazura's swashbuckling suitor, the Taifu, whose unwelcome attentions force her to escape from Kyūshū and risk the sea voyage back to the capital. The Taifu is described as a warrior (*tsuwamono*) who has built up considerable influence for himself in the central Kyūshū province of Higo, where he serves in the government headquarters. Powerful though he may be, he is woefully lacking in all the attributes of a 'good person', and Tamakazura would no more dream of marrying him than she would a peasant in the fields. When he calls at her house to press his suit, he displays all the boorishness and gaucherie of a North Country parvenu who has crashed into an upper-class Victorian drawing-room. He flatters, cajoles, blusters; then finally he is tripped up in an exchange of poems, and he feels that the time has come to take his leave:

'Ah yes, to be sure, to be sure,' he said, nodding his head. 'A very neat turn of phrase, I must say! Well, no doubt you think of us who live in these parts as rather countrified (*inakabitaru*), but you'd be mistaken if you set me down as some insignificant native (*kuchioshiki tami*). In any case, what's so wonderful about coming from the capital? I know as much as any of your city folk. I'd advise you not to treat me like a fool!' He would have liked to produce a parting poem, but could think of nothing appropriate and had to leave without another word.[42]

*

42. Ibid., iii, 100.

Moving down to the bottom of the social scale, we come to the peasants, fishermen, foresters, and other labourers. Though they constituted the vast majority of the population and the only economically productive class in the country, we have virtually no authentic information about their lives. Heian literature, which gives such a detailed and vivid picture of how the gentry lived, has hardly a word to say about the masses, and it is only by conjecture and reconstruction that we can draw even a tentative picture.[43]

By the beginning of the tenth century the distinction between free-man and slave (never an important one in Japan during the historical period) had lost most of its meaning, the lower strata of free people having absorbed the slaves to make one more or less uniform plebeian class. The majority of its members were peasants working on the rice fields of the lordly estates and manors. They were heavily taxed, either by the government or by the officials of the manor, and it seems probable that during most of the period they were able to keep little above the minimum needed to stay alive, work, and reproduce.

Their lives, we may judge, were close to the Hobbesian state of nature in which the individual's existence is 'nasty, poore, brutish and short'. Totally illiterate, ridden by fears and superstitions, ignorant of anything beyond his narrow experience, the peasant spent his days in unremitting work without profit, the monotony being relieved only by Shintō festivals, marriages, births, and deaths. The riches of Chinese culture, the profound teachings of Buddhism, and the civilized amenities of the capital might as well have belonged to a different planet for all the effect they had on his rough, cheerless life. During the few hours spent away from the fields he and his kind were as a rule crowded together in dark, noisome hovels, where they ate and slept on bare boards. Their food was of the coarsest nature; the authorities were at pains to prevent the peasant from enjoying the fruits of his labour, and the chronicles report numerous sumptuary edicts of the type: 'Farmers [are] forbidden to eat fish or drink wine.'[44] In bad years when their standard of life threatened to sink below even the subsistence level, peasants would sometimes abscond in the hope of finding more tolerable con-

43. Des Longrais gives a vivid reconstruction of peasant life on a manor (op. cit., pp. 61–91), but we have no way of knowing how authentic his picture may be.
44. Reischauer, op. cit., p. 235.

ditions in other parts of the country. At times abscondence presented a
serious economic problem and the officials took energetic measures to
prevent it, for instance by requiring travellers to carry identification.
All in all, rural life in the Heian period was hardly one of Arcadian bliss.
Yet the lot of the peasant was probably better then than in later centuries, when in addition to grinding poverty he so often had to endure
the destruction of his crops, forced levies, harsh military exactions, and
the other inconveniences of civil war.

The attitude of the 'good people' to the plebeians follows naturally
from their monolithic hierarchical approach. If provincial and military
officials and their families were regarded as being beyond the pale,
peasants and labourers could hardly be said to have any human existence
whatsoever. The terms *esemono* and *esebito* that were commonly applied
to them originally connoted 'doubtful, questionable creatures' and
carried the implication that they were not really people at all.[45]

From Murasaki's few references to the lower orders we can judge that
she looked on them as odd and largely incomprehensible. The occasional
peasants who make a fleeting appearance in her novel are shown as
strange, rough creatures who jabber or cackle (*saezuru*) to each other in
uncouth accents. When Genji and Kaoru listen to the labourers setting
out for work in the early morning, it is the strangeness of these people
that most affects them: 'As he looked out at them staggering past in the
dawn light with their loads, they appeared like phantoms.'[46] Acutely
sensitive as the heroes are to their own sufferings and to those of the
people in their circle, they would never dream of sympathizing with the
plebeians, whose hardships were, to say the least, rather more tangible.
This is precisely because members of the lower orders were regarded as
being incapable of understanding the heart of things (*mono no kokoro*

45. Note also the frequent use of the word *ayashi* ('strange' 'grotesque') in
reference to the plebeians.

This attitude is graphically reflected in some of the picture scrolls. For example,
Tenjin Engi Emaki, which illustrates the life of Sugawara no Michizane, depicts
members of the lower orders as wizened homuncules, often engaged in brawls
or grotesquely staggering under loads that are larger than themselves. When
'good people' appear on the same painting, they are usually twice as tall as the
plebeians, and their dignified features are in striking contrast to the hideously
twisted faces of the workers.

46. See p. 280.

shiranu gesu), that is to say, unable to grasp the real meaning of pathos. Kaoru is appalled at the thought of how lonely Prince Hachi's daughters must be in their house at Uji, but the plight of the bargemen on the river could never conceivably inspire his sympathy, since they are, by definition, insensible.

This attitude to the lower orders is not peculiar to Murasaki.[47] Throughout contemporary literature they tend to be regarded as members of a different species – 'uninteresting, useless, and unintelligible', as one writer has expressed it, yet occasionally amusing to observe. When Sei Shōnagon describes some workmen having lunch, one feels that she is looking at a group of strange beasts at their feed:

The way that carpenters eat is really odd. When the roof of the eastern wing was being built, there were several carpenters squatting in a row and having their meal; I went out to have a look. The moment the food was brought, they fell on the soup bowls and gulped down the contents. Then they pushed the bowls aside and polished off all the vegetables. I was wondering whether they were going to leave their rice; a second later there wasn't a grain left in their bowls. They all behaved in exactly the same way and I suppose this must be the nature of carpenters. I should not call it a very charming one.[48]

One of the few references to the hardships of the poorer classes occurs in the Chinese poems of Fujiwara no Tadamichi, a late Heian writer, who with almost Dickensian pathos describes the sufferings of old charcoal-sellers and other unfortunates as they trudge through the wintry streets of the capital. This, however, does not betoken any spontaneous access of sympathy for the lower orders but is a direct result of reading

47. Nor, of course, is it peculiar to Heian Japan. Cf. Count de Tocqueville's observation:
'When the chroniclers of the Middle Ages, who all belonged to the aristocracy by birth or education, relate the tragical end of a noble, their grief flows apace; whereas they tell you at a breath, and without wincing, of massacres and tortures inflicted on the common sort of people. Not that these writers felt habitual hatred or systematic disdain for the people; war between the several classes of the community was not yet declared. They were impelled by an instinct rather than by a passion; as they had formed no clear notion of a poor man's sufferings, they cared but little for his fate.'
48. Kaneko ed., pp. 1075–6.

Po Chü-i's 'social' poems. The fact that Po Chü-i had written about poor people made it a 'respectable' subject.[49]

*

A quick reading of the *Pillow Book* and other writings of the time might give one the impression that the world of *The Tale of Genji* was peculiarly static. It is true that in the pre-scientific age, and especially in the established conservative societies of the East, changes occurred at a snail's pace in comparison with the present period, when a man born while hansom cabs were still clattering over the cobblestones may die with the screech of jet aeroplanes in his ears. Nevertheless there were changes, even in such a seemingly immobile world as that of Heian Japan; and many of the conditions that existed in the lifetime of Murasaki's father had completely altered by the time her daughter had grown up. In her novel Murasaki often refers to the changes thàt have occurred since her hero was a young man.

From the point of view of Murasaki and her group these changes were usually for the worse. During her time an accumulation of factors served to undermine the aristocratic structure that had existed since the seventh century. Several of these factors, such as the fiscal and military weakness of the central government, the fossilization of the social hierarchy, and the corruption of provincial administration, have been mentioned in the present chapter. The final collapse did not come for some one hundred and fifty years after Murasaki's death, but there were numerous symptoms during her lifetime.

Of these the most conspicuous was the failure of the government to maintain law and order, not only in the provinces, but in the capital city itself. The Imperial Police had been created in the ninth century when the inefficiency of the Guards regiments had already grown blatant. By Murasaki's time the Police too were becoming incapable of preventing daylight robbery in the city and of controlling highwaymen outside (as witness Kaoru's terror of being attacked on his way to Uji). The situa-

---

49. Fujiwara no Tadamichi (1097–1164). I am indebted to Professor Burton Watson for calling these Chinese poems to my attention. The *Manyō Shū* contains a long poem about the sufferings of poverty by Yamanoue Okura (660–733) (see Keene, *Anthology of Japanese Literature*, pp. 46–8); but here again the model is Chinese.

tion deteriorated steadily and in 1040 the chronicles record the distressing news that 'robbers broke into the Imperial Palace and stole some of [Emperor Gosuzaku's] clothing'.[50]

Still more disturbing were the raids by mountain priests. Already in 981 soldier-priests from Mount Hiei, the great Buddhist centre that was designed to protect the city from danger, were marching unopposed through the streets of the capital to underline their demands to the government; and later in the period the inhabitants lived in terror of the warrior-monks who would periodically descend from the hills to indulge in arson, loot, and similar un-Buddhist practices.

Here again the Imperial Guards and Police were usually impotent; and it is significant of the steady shift of real power to the provinces that the government should have been obliged to call on families like the Minamotos to suppress such disorders. The weakening of central authority was correlated with the growth of new, more vigorous elements in the countryside, which was eventually to result in the formation of a feudal society. A separate warrior class was not consolidated until well after the period with which we are concerned, but already in Murasaki's time military families based on the manors were developing as a sort of 'second aristocracy'.[51] That there could ever be anything aristocratic about soldiers and provincials would have struck the 'good people' of Heian as nothing short of ludicrous. They were the despised outsiders, who might be used to quell an occasional uprising or to collect taxes from a refractory estate, but who for all important purposes were beyond the pale of civilized society. Yet it was precisely these unpolished provincials who, when they had finally consolidated their strength, were to bring Murasaki's world down in ruins.

50. Reischauer, op. cit., p. 336.
51. *Deuxième noblesse japonaise.* Ref. Des Longrais, op. cit., p. 195 ff.

IV

Religions

WITH Prince Niou's secret visit to Uji in Book 51, *The Tale of Genji* approaches its final climax.[1] Niou has succeeded in finding out about the attractive young girl whom Kaoru has kept hidden in the lonely house by Uji River. Travelling from the capital in disguise, he reaches the place late at night and manages to gain admittance, not only to the house, but to Ukifune's bed, by pretending that he is Kaoru, her 'official' lover. Niou is delighted by Ukifune's charms, and when the night is over, he cannot bear the idea of returning to the capital. The following passage is quoted at some length since it happens to reflect a number of beliefs that were current among the inhabitants of Murasaki's world:

The Prince summoned Ukon[2] and said to her, 'I fear you will think it very inconsiderate of me, but it really does not look as if I can leave here today. Kindly have my attendants lodged somewhere nearby where they will not be seen. Tokitaka[3] had better return to the city and tell them that I am in retreat at a mountain temple or any other excuse that sounds convincing.'

Ukon was dumbfounded.[4] When she remembered how careless she had been on the previous evening, she almost felt that she would go out of her mind. But gradually she managed to calm down, comforting herself with the thought that at this stage it would do no good to make a fuss or to get excited – besides which it would be a breach of etiquette. She reminded herself that the Prince had fallen in love with Ukifune at their very first meeting.[5] Clearly it was his karma from a previous incarnation that things

1. See pp. 284–5.
2. Ukifune's gentlewoman.
3. A young attendant recently promoted to the Fifth Rank.
4. Until seeing Niou in the morning she had been unaware of the imposture.
5. Some months previously Niou met Ukifune at his wife's house in the capital and was instantly captivated; he had no idea that the girl was his wife's half-sister.

should have turned out as they did last night. How could she be blamed?

'But, Your Highness,' she said, 'it was today that they were coming to fetch her.[6] What do you intend to do about that? Evidently it was ordained that Your Highness should behave as he did to my lady, and I have nothing to say on that score. But you could hardly have chosen a worse time. Would Your Highness not consider returning to the capital today? Then, if it is still your pleasure to see my lady at some future time, come back when you can stay quietly.'

Niou was impressed by Ukon's good sense, but he could not agree to her suggestion. 'Your lady has been in my mind for a long time,' he said, 'and now I am hopelessly in love with her. She has become an obsession, and it does not matter to me what people say or how they criticize me. Do you really think that if I cared in the slightest about my position I should have travelled here last night as I did? When they come to fetch her, you had better tell them that she has to stay at home because of a taboo [*monoimi*] . . .'

Ukon's main concern was to avoid letting anyone know that the visitor was Niou. When the watchmen came to her she told them, 'His Highness wishes to keep his movements secret. I gather that he had a bad experience on his way up here last night.[7] He has ordered his attendants to return secretly to the capital at nightfall and fetch a new set of clothes.'

Some of the ladies overheard her. 'Oh, how frightening!' they exclaimed. 'They do say that Mount Kohata is terribly dangerous. What a dreadful thing that His Highness had to come here without his forerunners and in disguise!'

'Hush!' commanded Ukon. 'Not another word! If the servants should get wind of this, it will be a poor lookout for all of us.'

Now she was becoming frightened herself. What on earth would she do in the appalling event that a messenger arrived from Kaoru? 'Bring us safely through this day, O Kannon of Hatsuse!' she prayed in deep earnest.[8]

The other ladies had all been purifying themselves (*sōji*) in preparation for the trip to Ishiyama Temple and they were now [ritually] clean

6. Ukifune's mother had arranged to take the girl on a pilgrimage to Ishiyama Temple on Lake Biwa.

7. Ukon wants the other members of the household to believe that Kaoru was attacked by highwaymen on his way to Uji and had his clothes robbed or dirtied, this being the reason he cannot show himself.

8. Hasedera, the famous Shingon temple south of Nara, is one of the thirty-three centres devoted to the worship of the Bodhisattva Kannon.

(*kiyomawarite aru*). 'Oh, what a shame!' they said. 'Now I suppose our lady won't be able to go to the temple after all.'[9]

Later in the morning Ukon went into Ukifune's room and remained in close attendance. She opened the lattice doors but had the blinds lowered and attached signs to them with the character for 'Taboo' clearly inscribed. It occurred to her that the mother might come herself to fetch the girl and so she reported that Ukifune had had an inauspicious dream . . .[10]

It was towards noon when the people came to fetch Ukifune for the excursion to the temple. The two ox-drawn carriages were accompanied by the usual rough men on horseback who acted as outriders; with them came a number of uncouth servants, who entered the gates of the house, jabbering away in some outlandish dialect. Ukifune's ladies were embarrassed and told the men to wait in some place where they could not be seen . . .

Ukon now took it upon herself to write a message to the mother: 'I regret to report, Madam, that my lady's monthly defilement started yesterday evening.[11] She was greatly distressed about this and kept on saying what a pity it was. Then during the course of the night she had an inauspicious dream. What with one thing and another I felt that she ought to be on her guard, at least for today, and so I declared a taboo. It is a terrible shame, Madam, and I really wonder whether some evil influence isn't interfering with your plans.'

She had the message delivered to the servants with instructions that they should be given something to eat and then sent on their way. She also sent a note to the old nun: 'Today is a taboo day. Our lady is not going out.'[12]

What most impresses one about this passage – apart, perhaps, from the glib cynicism of Ukon's manoeuvres – is the way in which various religions and superstitions have become so inextricably entwined in the minds of the characters that one can hardly tell where one ends and the other begins. Ukifune's visit to a Buddhist temple, for example, is pre-

9. As a result of her recent intercourse with Niou (or, as they believed, Kaoru) she was ritually impure.

10. An inauspicious dream (e.g. about someone's death) would, according to current superstition, make it unwise for Ukifune to meet anyone; the real reason for the taboo could hardly be divulged to her mother.

11. The menses were a standard source of ritual defilement according to Shintoism and would make it necessary to cancel the visit to Ishiyama Temple.

12. Ikeda ed., vii, 30–5.

vented by a defilement (Shintoism) and by a bad dream (superstition). Again, in order to prepare for the visit, Ukifune's ladies have purified themselves according to Buddhist practice by abstaining from meat and fish (*sōji*) and also have rendered themselves ritually clean (*kiyomawarite aru*) by lustration and other Shintoist ritual; yet all their efforts become nugatory because of a taboo. Niou's excuse for spending the day at Uji is that he is on a retreat (Buddhist), while he keeps Ukifune with him on the pretext of taboo (Shintoist).

This facile blending of beliefs reflects the eclecticism that is characteristic of Japanese thought. For Murasaki and her countrymen there was no idea that the acceptance of one set of beliefs (Buddhism) might preclude adherence to another (Shintoism), or that either was incompatible with a mass of complex superstitions deriving both from native tradition and from Chinese folklore.

The remarkable absence of *odium theologicum* between Shintoism and the advanced continental religion, which after the sixth century largely replaced it among the upper classes, is certainly not due to any intrinsic harmony between these ways of thought. Indeed one could hardly imagine two more different approaches. Buddhism, with its stress on the sorrows of the earthly condition, its rejection of transitory pleasures, its preoccupation with decay and death, and its offer of release by retirement from the world and a modification of the human consciousness, would appear in many ways to be the very antithesis of Shintoism, whose central themes are joyful acceptance of the natural world and gratitude for its bounty, coupled with a horror of illness and death, which are regarded as the source of all pollution. Yet during most of Japan's history, including the entire Heian period, the relationship between them has been one of peaceful coexistence – in the proper sense of the term.

This happy outcome owes something to the nature of both religions. On the one hand it results from the strong tendency towards syncretism in the type of Mahâyâna Buddhism that reached Japan from China and Korea. Such conflicts as arose in Japan between proponents of the two religions were basically political. For, unlike Christianity in Europe and Islam in Africa, the Buddhist church had no desire to suppress native beliefs in Japan, and was prepared to accommodate itself to them in a most tolerant fashion, by declaring, for example, that the native gods were avatars of Buddhist deities. This process of syncretism was deliberately fostered during the early part of the Heian period, and in Murasaki's time any idea of a contradiction, let alone of a clash, between Buddhism and Shintoism would have been quite meaningless.

The extreme simplicity of Shintoism is a further reason for the absence of conflict. If it had been a developed religion with a philosophy, a system of ethics, an elaborate ritual, and a great sacerdotal institution, it might well have resisted the inroads of Buddhism, and conversely the foreign religion might have felt a need to suppress it. But this was precisely what Shintoism lacked. It had no philosophical, speculative, or ethical elements; no elaborate ritual or priestly hierarchy; no saints, martyrs, or even a founder; no scripture or exegesis; no interest in education and art – in fact, no positive, constructive aspect whatsoever. So vague and amorphous was the native religion that not until Buddhism appeared in Japan did it even acquire a name – *Shin-tō* ('the way of the gods'), as opposed to *Butsu-dō* ('the way of the Buddha').

Yet, just as the ancient line of emperors, the high priests of Shintoism, survived largely owing to their absence of political power, so it was the lack of any real positive character in the native religion that helped it to persist in the face of all external challenges. In Murasaki's time, although a popular form of Buddhism was slowly beginning to spread, Shintoist attitudes (they can hardly be called ideas) were still the main religious influence among the lower orders, especially the peasants in the provinces, who had been relatively untouched by imports from the continent; and Shintoist festivals and celebrations, which were mainly related to the agricultural cycle, were one of their few distractions. For the aristocracy Buddhism was a far more important force. Yet they too accepted without question the principal Shintoist notions about defilement and abstinence, viewing death, child-birth, intercourse, wounds, and menstruation as sources of ritual uncleanliness, and subscribing to various forms of necromancy and witchcraft in which Shintoist influence was predominant.

This had a considerable effect on their daily life. For ritual uncleanliness, especially when it derived from illness or death, applied not only to the person directly concerned but to all the other members of the household, who were regarded as having been, as it were, infected. The house that was subject to a taboo of this kind was out of bounds to visitors, and willow-wood tags were hung on the shutters to keep them away (Ukon's precautions will be recalled). If a gentleman was obliged to venture abroad despite a taboo, for instance on the anniversary of his father's death, he would attach a taboo tag to his head-dress – women wore them on their sleeves – to keep people at arm's length and protect them from 'infection'.

★

Before examining the role of Buddhism in the world of the shining prince we should briefly assess the influence of the other great doctrine imported from the continent. Knowledge of Confucianism had reached the islands well over a century before the first Buddhist sutras were presented to the court, and a study of the Confucian classics was central to organized education ever since its beginnings in Japan. Here again, the eclectic approach of the Japanese spared them the doctrinal controversies that have afflicted most other countries. The Confucian attitude to the dead, for instance, differed entirely from that of Shintoism. Yet in Japan the two ways of thought were not regarded as incompatible; or rather, the question of incompatibility never appears to have arisen. The addition of yet a third set of doctrines in the sixth century did nothing to undermine Confucianism. Conversely the new Buddhist religion was not regarded as a threat to Confucian ideas, though its approach could hardly have been more different; and it was spared the organized persecution that it suffered in China. In the eighth century, for example, the same empress issued an edict that each household in Japan should provide itself with a copy of *Hsiao Chung*, the Confucian 'Classic of Filial Piety', and also ordered the construction of one million miniature wooden pagodas to be distributed to all the Buddhist temples.

In Murasaki's time Confucian influence on the life of the aristocracy was directed mainly to family relationships. Family solidarity and pride appear to have been strong in Japan ever since the early days of the clan system. They were reinforced and given intellectual backing by Chinese doctrines that stressed the veneration of ancestors, filial piety, and family continuity. The cult of the traditional family and of formalized relationships within it was not properly established in Japan until the seventeenth century, when Confucianism first became a religion in its own right, in many ways taking precedence over Buddhism. The primacy of the family unit, however, has a far longer history. In the Heian period the framework of social activity was always the family or house (*ke*) under the control of the patriarchal head (*kachō*). Heian politics, as we have seen, were largely family or clan politics, and Michinaga's key position during the long period of his hegemony was that of Head of the Clan (*Uji no Chōja*).

It is hard to say how much this stress on the family unit derived from Confucian influence and how much from early native tradition. The circulation of books like the 'Classic of Filial Piety' must have helped to give concrete, systematic form to ideas that until then were somewhat amorphous and ill-defined. The stress on family continuity, and the widespread habit of adoption that it involved, were certainly related to Confucian doctrine, which regarded the absence of posterity as the greatest of crimes. Ancestor worship and its numerous ramifications were mainly of Chinese origin; there is nothing in the native religion that prescribed the worship of deified men by their descendants. The impiety committed by Emperor Reizei in *The Tale of Genji* when he performs rites in honour of the deceased Emperor, who in fact is not his real father, is a heinous breach of Confucian practice and preys painfully on the young man's mind; yet neither Shintoism nor Buddhism would have regarded it as a moral offence, especially since Reizei had never been clearly informed about his paternity. According to Confucian doctrine, the actions of men, particularly of men who are in a position of authority, can have a serious effect on the natural order. A breach of filial piety by a character like Reizei, even if performed unwittingly, could therefore entail the most appalling consequences, not only for the people directly involved, but for the country at large, because nature, in order to right the balance as it were, might respond with floods, earthquakes, and other disasters. It is to avoid such calamities that Emperor Reizei abdicates at the earliest possible opportunity.

Although the main Confucian ideas were familiar to the people of Murasaki's circle and were accepted as an integral part of their intellectual luggage, we often get the impression that the precepts laid down by Confucius and his followers did not weigh too heavily on them when it came to their actual behaviour. Prince Genji, for instance, may have paid lip-service to the theories of the family cult and filial piety, but from a Confucian point of view his life could hardly have been less exemplary.[13] Yet Murasaki presents him as an almost ideal hero and no doubt most of her contemporary readers accepted him as such. It was not until many centuries later that Genji, Fujitsubo, and other characters in the novel were condemned for their flagrant breaches of Confucian ethics.

Sei Shōnagon relates an incident that even to a non-Confucian Westerner would seem to reflect a rather excessive lack of filial respect:

A certain lieutenant of the Headquarters of the Outer Palace Guards (Right Division) looked down on his father[14] and was ashamed for people to see him. When they were journeying up to the capital from Iyo Province he pushed him into the sea [and he drowned]. People were dismayed by his action and regarded it as shameful. [Yet] on the fifteenth day of the seventh month the man said that he was going to celebrate the Bon Festival of the Dead [in honour of his deceased father] and he began to busy himself with preparations.[15]

The commentaries point out that the lieutenant was a rough military provincial of whom one might expect such lapses, and no doubt this was a most exceptional incident. The remarkable aspect, however, is that the man was left at liberty to participate in the Bon Festival. Patricide was the most serious of the eight offences in Confucian law, and in contemporary China or later in Japan when Confucianism had become a state religion the lieutenant would have been condemned to the most painful and humiliating form of execution. In the event his only punishment, so far as we know, was to have a poem written about him by the Fujiwara monk, Dōmei:

> A man who has pushed his father into the ocean's depths
> Now celebrates the festival of Bon[16]—
> Alas, what a grievous sight!

Sei herself, usually so ready with her comments, has nothing to say about the lieutenant's behaviour.

13. See p. 270–71.
14. For being old and ugly, according to the commentaries.
15. Kaneko ed., pp. 1044–5.
16. According to one rather far-fetched theory, mentioned by Kaneko (op. cit., p. 1046) there is a play of words on the word *bon*: (i) the Festival of the Dead, (ii) the splash that the old man made when he hit the water.

A more important field of Confucian influence was education. Here its role was preponderant. 'Learning' referred almost exclusively to a study of the Confucian classics, which was the main subject at the Court University, the provincial schools, and most of the private institutions. The University was also the centre for the performance of ceremonies in honour of Confucius. By Murasaki's time, however, Confucian studies in Japan had become sterile and jejune. Despite the continued paramountcy of Chinese learning for the minute percentage of the Japanese population that was literate, it was not until many centuries later that it began to have that overwhelming effect on the life and thought of the upper classes which it exerted in China.[17] Far more important for the Heian aristocracy was the vast complex of beliefs, related to theories of *yin* and *yang* and the five agents, which had been introduced to Japan together with Confucianism but which did not belong to the original Confucian philosophy.[18]

*

Despite the harmonious blending of different beliefs and traditions, there is no doubt that in the world of *The Tale of Genji* one religion exerted an overriding influence. By Murasaki's time the great Indian faith, which had reached Japan by way of China and Korea some four centuries earlier, had become thoroughly acclimatized. Though it had never sought to exclude, still less to persecute, rival creeds, the Buddhist institution had come to occupy a role in the religious, intellectual, political, and artistic life of Heian which was hardly less impressive than that of the Catholic Church in medieval Europe. Without some knowledge of the varied functions of Buddhism in tenth-century Japan, our understanding of the people of Murasaki's world is bound to be superficial.[19]

The most powerful sect in her time, and the one with which she was mainly associated, was Tendai, named after T'ien-t'ai (Heavenly Terrace) Mountain in China where it originated. With its vast complex of

17. See pp. 184–9.   18. See p. 136 ff.
19. '. . . the most fundamental difference between the Japanese (or, for that matter, any Far Eastern nation) and us is the fact, obvious indeed yet constantly overlooked, that they were not Christians.' Arthur Waley, *The Pillow-Book of Sei Shōnagon*, p. 15.

temples and monasteries on Mount Hiei outside the capital and its close connexion with the ruling Fujiwara family, Tendai came closest to being the national church of Japan. It propounded the standard Mahâyâna doctrine of universal salvation, namely, that the Buddha nature resides in each of us and that it should be our aim in life to develop this nature until ultimately we find release from the cycle of rebirths in the state of Buddhahood. The basic scripture of the sect is the Lotus Sutra, which had been imported to China from India or Central Asia and interpreted by the Grand Master of T'ien T'ai. This sutra was regarded as the final and most complete revelation of Buddhist teaching.

Tendai, however, did not reject the doctrines of other schools or even of other religions. For an outstanding characteristic of the sect, both in China and in Japan, was its syncretic, all-embracing nature. While its main worship was directed to Sâkyamuni (Gautama Buddha), it also revered the Cosmic Buddha (Vairocana) of the Shingon sect, Amida Buddha, Kannon, the Bodhisattva of Mercy, and countless other Buddhas and Bodhisattvas, as well as the many Shintoist deities with whom they were identified. Indeed almost any deity could be fitted into its capacious pantheon and any Buddhist idea (including Esoteric, Amidist, and Zen) into its catholic body of doctrines. The fierce conflicts that Tendai waged with rival institutions and within its own sect almost invariably arose from questions of property and organization; hardly ever were they based on doctrinal disputes, and it was only when they felt their entire structure to be threatened that they attacked rival creeds.

The second great sect in Murasaki's day was almost equally syncretic. Shingon, no less than Tendai, could accommodate itself to the numerous other forms of Buddhist belief and also to Shintoism and Taoism. In the focus of its teachings, however, it differed greatly from Tendai. Both sects reached Japan at about the same time in the early ninth century, but, unlike T'ien-t'ai with its overwhelming Chinese origins, Chên-yen (Shingon=the True Words) was Indian through and through. Its characteristic magic paintings or Mandaras are derived from India: not only is the name itself taken from an Indian word (Mandala), but the compartments into which the sacred picture is divided are filled with Sanskrit letters and with deities who often are not even Buddhist but Hindu. Similarly the importance of certain formalized gestures in Shingon ritual is clearly related to the Indian *mudrâs*.

The Shingon sect is particularly hard to describe in outline. Its plethora of deities, rituals, formulae, and symbols are bound to confuse all but the initiated. Furthermore, its most important doctrines are secret, and can be learnt only from a master who will communicate his knowledge to certain outstanding pupils. This esoteric aspect of Shingon is related to its penchant for magic formulae and ritual, as well as for sexual arcana deriving from Indian Tantrism, which became an increasingly important part of the cult.

The hermetic nature of Shingon teachings is suggestive of Zen, which also stresses the need for direct communication between master and pupil. In Zen, however, the teacher can only guide or prod the student towards an understanding of the truth; the actual awakening (*satori*) must occur within the individual. In this sense Shingon is less demanding, since it does possess certain definite teachings that the master can communicate orally to the happy few, thus enabling them to attain enlightenment.

In another respect Shingon differs diametrically from early Zen. This is in its taste for gorgeous ceremonies and rituals. The most magnificent religious observances in the Heian calendar usually belonged to Shingon, and the impressive pomp and beauty of these displays help to account for the popularity of this sect among members of the Heian aristocracy, who, as we have seen, were much addicted to colour and pageantry. The Shingon sect was also closely associated with art and learning, and this too helped to maintain its prestige in Murasaki's world. The stress on paintings, sculpture, music and literature is related to the obscure nature of its teachings; for, as Kūkai (the founder of Japanese Shingon) wrote, '. . . the Esoteric scriptures are so abstruse that their meaning cannot be conveyed except through art', and again, '. . . the secrets of the sūtras and commentaries can be depicted in art and the essential truths of the Esoteric teaching are all set forth therein. Neither teachers nor students can dispense with it. Art is what reveals to us the state of perfection.'[20] If we are to credit traditional accounts, Shingon is also in a sense responsible for making works like *The Tale of Genji* possible. For the invention of the phonetic syllabary in which most of this literature was written is attributed to Kūkai, who apparently developed it in imitation of Sanskrit usage.

20. de Bary et al., ed., *Sources of the Japanese Tradition*, pp. 145, 142.

Though Tendai may be regarded as the Heian state religion, and though the proximity of the Hiei headquarters to the capital gave it a considerable advantage, its position was far from being exclusive. Shingon also received strong official backing and included many members of the imperial and Fujiwara families among its hierarchy. At times the government was able to make good use of the magic powers commanded by the sect. Some thirty years before Murasaki's time, for example, Masakado, a member of a provincial military clan, staged a successful revolt in the East. He proclaimed himself emperor, set up a court in imitation of Heian Kyō, and appointed governors to the eastern provinces. Government troops were sent against him, but for good measure the emperor also dispatched a Shingon priest (a member of the imperial family) carrying a famous sword called Amakuni no Tsurugi and an image of a certain fierce Shingon deity named Fudō. This image was said to have been brought from India to China; when Kūkai was studying in China, the image informed him in a dream that it wished to proceed further eastwards to Japan: Kūkai accordingly brought it with him on his return home and enshrined it in a temple near the capital. According to another tradition, however, it was carved by Kūkai himself out of an oar of the ship on which he travelled to China. In any case the image clearly possessed supernatural powers; for shortly after its arrival near the insurgents' capital the rebel leader was defeated and killed. When the time came to return the deity to Heian Kyō, however, it was discovered that its weight had increased so much that it could not be moved. The image then appeared in a dream and declared that it wished to remain in the eastern provinces in order to help civilize them. The grateful emperor acceded to the request and built a magnificent Shingon temple in the village of Narita. Here the god is still enshrined, together with the famous sword, which incidentally has the useful virtues of curing both insanity and the disorders that come from being possessed by foxes.[21]

Among the other forms of Buddhism in Murasaki's day there are two that exerted considerable influence on the established sects, though they

21. The present temple, a vast complex of elaborate buildings set in magnificent grounds, was built in 1705. It is fairly near Tokyo and attracts immense throngs of visitors. The image of Fudō, the magic sword, and other treasures can be seen on application to the temple office.

themselves did not grow important until the Kamakura period. Amidism was already becoming the basis of popular Buddhism, and the great Amidist work, *The Essentials of Salvation* (one of the first books printed in Japan), appeared while Murasaki was still a girl. With its vivid descriptions of the horrors of hell and of the paradisian bliss that awaited any believer who was prepared to put his faith in Amida Buddha, the book was bound to appeal to the fears and hopes of the masses, and its author paved the way for the huge Amidist sects that swept Japan in later centuries. The basis of Amidism was the belief that men of this decadent age were no longer able to attain the state of nirvana by means of righteous conduct. Yet the situation was far from hopeless; for in his infinite mercy Amida, when he was a Bodhisattva, had vowed not to enter nirvana himself until every sentient being in the world was saved. In order to achieve this, ritual, scripture, and good works were all otiose. According to the Original Vow, all that was needed was to call on Amida by using a formula that even the simplest peasant could remember: *Namu Amida Butsu* ('I call on thee, Amida Buddha'). After death the believer would then automatically be reborn in the Western Paradise. Here, surrounded by every comfort and delight, he could live in such a way as to attain nirvana; as a rule, however, the Amidists were so absorbed in the expected joys of paradise that they had comparatively small interest in the ultimate release.

The established Nara and Heian sects catered little for the ignorant and the lowly, and it was to them that Amidism directed its main appeal. The 'good people', however, were not immune to its charms. Its adherents included many distinguished prelates, mainly those of the Tendai sect, which was the principal depository of Amidist beliefs during the Heian period.[22] Both Michinaga and Emperor Ichijō believed in salvation by Amida, as did Murasaki, who was an adherent of Tendai. 'Whatever others may do or say,' she writes in her diary, 'I shall recite my prayers tirelessly to Amida Buddha.'[23] Kaoru and many of the other characters in her novel are frequently described as doing *nebutsu* or *nembutsu*, that is to say, meditating on Amida's name and intoning the *Namu Amida Butsu* formula, although at the same time they carried out other

22. Chih K'ai, the founder of T'ien Tai, died repeating the name of Amida; Dengyō Daishi, who introduced the sect to Japan, was also a believer.
23. See p. 269.

forms of Buddhist practice that were entirely irrelevant to Amidism. Shortly after he has lost Fujitsubo, Prince Genji prays to Amida Buddha that after his death they may share the same lotus flower [24]– an ambition that moralists might regard as somewhat questionable inasmuch as this lady was his own father's wife.

When we come to the role of Zen in the Heian period, we are on more dubious ground. Zen is said to have been introduced from China shortly before the Great Reform, and at the beginning of the ninth century we hear of a Chinese priest preaching its doctrines in the capital and being received by the emperor. It was not, however, organized as a separate sect until several centuries later, and Zen as such appears to have had little success among the Heian aristocracy and none at all among the populace. The word Zen (Dhyâna, Ch'an) does not figure a single time in *The Tale of Genji*, nor is it ever mentioned by that great cataloguer, Sei Shōnagon. Tea, which played so important a part in Zen, was brought from China in the ninth century; but tea-drinking was not appreciated, and it more or less died out until reintroduced some three hundred years later by the Zen monk, Eisai.

Yet we should not conclude from this that Zen ideas had no importance in the Heian period. The founder of the Tendai sect in Japan had studied Zen in China and accepted many of its doctrines: 'calm contemplation' (*shikan*), which was important for devout Tendai practitioners, was undoubtedly cognate with the Dhyâna-Zen form of self-trance. Shingon mysticism also was powerfully influenced by the Dhyâna ideas that had percolated into Japan from China, where they had been greatly affected by Taoism. Murasaki gives us only a few hints about the religious conversations between Kaoru and his preceptor, Prince Hachi, and about the periods of meditation to which they devote themselves; yet we can be fairly sure that their practices, though different from those of later Japanese Zen, derived a good deal from Dhyâna.

It is hard to disentwine the various strands of Far Eastern mysticism, and an attempt to do so can produce an artificial and misleading picture. What is certain is that Dhyâna ideas, though often not specifically recognized as such, were an essential ingredient in the mystical aspects of Heian Buddhism. To this extent they exerted an influence on the re-

24. *Genji Monogatari*, Nihon Bungaku Taikei edition (hereafter abbreviated as N.B.T. ed.), vi, 501.

ligious life of the aristocracy. Their great role in Japanese social and cultural development, however, did not come until a later period.

*

A general view of the church in Murasaki's time reveals two significant characteristics. The first is its secular success, which made the Heian Buddhist institution as affluent and well-established as the Church of England in the eighteenth century. This applies particularly to Tendai ('the state in religious form', as Sir Charles Eliot describes it), but also to Shingon and some of the old Nara sects. Though infrangible links still joined the imperial family with Shintoism and though the great Shintō shrine at Ise remained Japan's Holy of Holies, the Buddhist church had the support of the government and the powerful patronage of the Fujiwaras, important Buddhist ceremonies being regularly attended by the emperor and his court. Buddhist affairs were handled by the Ministry of Civil Administration, and the emperor had the right to appoint priests to posts in the ecclesiastical hierarchy and to grant sacerdotal titles. It is significant of the established character of the church that ranks in the priestly and court hierarchies were precisely correlated, and that the superiors of great temple complexes, like Mount Hiei, were usually imperial princes. In Murasaki's time almost all the high ecclesiastical posts in the monasteries were held by court nobles of the Third Rank and above, and about half of the remaining positions were filled by gentlemen of the first five ranks.

By the end of the tenth century many of the Buddhist institutions were becoming sufficiently powerful to resist unpalatable government appointments and to assert their independence in other ways too. Tendai and Shingon in particular were acquiring a degree of political power such as was never achieved by any Buddhist church in China. Despite the noble spiritual and philosophical ideals that underlay their teachings, this power was all too often used for worldly ends. The great Buddhist temples were important landowners, to whom lesser holders would commend their manors in return for tax-exemption and other forms of protection. In consolidating and extending their estates, these temples were often no less predatory and ruthless than members of the rising class of provincial chieftains. When they could not accomplish their ends by political pressure, they would send out bands of warrior monks, whose priestly habit could not conceal the fact that they were often mere mercenaries of the roughest kind. In blatant disregard of the Buddhist injunctions against violence, these armed bands would attack and destroy rival monasteries and, from the eleventh century, they would regularly demonstrate in the streets of the capital, blockading the houses of ministers, and even palace buildings, until their demands were granted. An eleventh-century emperor, who was himself a devout Buddhist, once remarked that the three things in the world he could not control were the floods of Kamo River, the hazards of gambling, and the monks of Mount Hiei.

The strength and prosperity of the great temples continued to grow in subsequent centuries, when many of them became feudal powers in their own right. Already in Murasaki's time Mount Hiei, which 'guarded' the capital from the north-east, contained several thousand Tendai temples and halls, and many were of great beauty and magnificence. The worldly success of the sect eventually proved to be its own undoing; for in the sixteenth century the buildings were all razed to the ground and their thousands of priestly inhabitants put to the sword.

The great cultural role of Heian Buddhism has already been mentioned in connexion with Shingon, but it is certainly not limited to that sect. Sculpture, painting, architecture, and the decorative arts were all deeply indebted to the patronage of the prosperous Buddhist temples, and almost all extant works from Murasaki's time, apart from literature, are of a religious nature. In contrast with the sober restraint that is usually regarded as characteristic of Japanese taste, the ornamental art of this period, especially that associated with the Kegon and Shingon sects, was often of a most sumptuous and colourful style. The sacred writings of the sutras were inscribed on deep blue paper in gold and silver characters; and to help people visualize the relucent glories of the various Buddhist paradises the plastic arts made ample use of ivory, mother-of-pearl, gold, silver, and other precious metals. Like the pomp and splendour of Heian ecclesiastical ceremonial, all this was a far cry from the simplicity of the original religion as symbolized by the Buddha's own renunciation of luxury. In its worldly aspects, indeed, the Buddhist institution in Murasaki's time was no more related to the ancient Indian religion that preached the vanity of mundane things than were the political power, wealth, and cultural splendours of the Renais-

sance Vatican relevant to the life and teachings of the man who was born
in a Bethlehem stable.

*

For Genji and his circle the Buddhist church had many diverse functions. In the first place, the numerous temples surrounding the capital
offered an opportunity for those excursions and pilgrimages that were
one of the main distractions in their somewhat uneventful lives. For
women in particular, these visits provided an occasional escape from the
claustrophobic confines of their crepuscular houses and an opportunity
to glimpse, if only through the heavy silk hangings of their ox-drawn
carriages, the wide bright world outside. Since many of the temples were
situated in places of great scenic beauty, pilgrimages were often mainly
outings to view the cherry blossoms in the foothills of Mount Hiei, for
instance, or to admire the shimmering moonlight on Lake Biwa. Visits
and retreats to outlying temples also served a very secular purpose in the
gallant world of Heian, since they provided an ideal pretext for trysts or
adventures of one kind or another; and it appears that the priests of the
more fashionable temples were quite prepared to accommodate their
aristocratic clients in this respect. In the passage quoted at the beginning
of this chapter it will be recalled how glibly Niou excuses his absence
from the capital by saying that he is in retreat at a mountain temple.

Contemporary literature suggests that for many of the Heian aristocrats religion had become mere mummery. The temples may have been
crowded with visitors, but the motives that brought them there often
had little connexion with the Buddhist faith. This is a subject that lends
itself to satire and, as we might expect, no one has treated it more pun-
gently than Sei Shōnagon, whose mordant wit was, so far as we can
judge, uninhibited by any deep religious feelings. The following passage
from the *Pillow Book* starts with some cynical observations that imply
how lightly the Buddhist faith sat on Sei's shoulders:

A preacher should be good-looking. For, if we are properly to understand the worthy sentiments of his sermon, we must keep our eyes fixed
on him while he speaks; by looking away we may forget to listen.
Accordingly an ugly preacher may well be the source of sin . . .
Time often hangs heavily on the hands of former Chamberlains and
they get into the habit of visiting temples. One will find them there even

on hot summer days, decked out in their bright linen robes and with their loose trousers of light violet or bluish grey spread about them. Some of them have a taboo tag attached to their black lacquered head-dress. One might imagine that these gentlemen would prefer to stay at home [on such an inauspicious day], but apparently they believe that no harm can come to anyone who is bent on so worthy an errand as theirs. They arrive in haste, converse with the priest, look inside the carriages that are being lined up outside the temple[25] – and in general take an interest in everything that is going on.

Now a couple of gentlemen who have not met for some time run into each other in the temple, and great is their surprise. They sit down together and chat away, nodding their heads, exchanging funny stories and opening their fans wide so that they can hold them in front of their faces and laugh more freely. They toy with their elegantly decorated rosaries and, glancing from side to side, criticize some defect they have noticed in one of the carriages and praise the elegance of another. Then they discuss various services that they have recently attended and compare the skill of different priests in performing the Eight Readings or the Offering of the Sutras. Meanwhile, of course, they pay not the slightest attention to the service that is going on. . . .[26]

★

Despite the many secular motives that attracted 'good people' to the Buddhist establishments, we should certainly not assume that they were insensible to its intellectual and spiritual aspects. For some members of the aristocracy the social and aesthetic sides were no doubt all-important; but for many others it was a religion in the full sense of the word. To be familiar with the titles and general content of the Lotus Sutra and other important sacred texts was indispensable for any educated gentleman, and this knowledge was shared by the more cultured court ladies like Murasaki. In their polite conversation they would occasionally introduce stories and ideas from the scriptures, though pedantry and cant were carefully avoided. Thus when Prince Genji talks to Tamakazura

25. Women normally remained in their carriages during the service, and the Chamberlains are not too pious to have a good look. According to Motoori Uchitō, however, they are actually looking at their own carriages to make sure that they have been placed in a good position. In either case their minds are far from religion.

26. Kaneko ed., pp. 172–4.

about the nature of literature he explains his ideas by reference to concepts he has found in the Lotus Sutra.[27]

Studying and reciting the sutras was one of the best ways to acquire spiritual merit. It is doubtful, however, whether many of the aristocrats, apart from devotees of Kaoru's stamp, had the necessary knowledge or training to understand the abstruse complexities of texts like the Lotus. In Murasaki's time the more usual way in which gentlemen 'read' the scriptures was to recite a few lines from the beginning, the middle, and the end, absorbing the remainder by the simple expedient of turning the pages. Sometimes even this seemed too time-consuming and they would pay priests to intone the sutras in their place.

*

However little spiritual pabulum most people of Murasaki's world may have derived directly from the scriptures or from ecclesiastical teaching, there is no doubt that all of them, except the most insensitive and cretinous, were familiar with the fundamental spirit of Buddhism that was common to all the sects: the sense of the transitoriness of worldly things (*mujōkan*). The Japanese Mahâyâna form of Buddhism places somewhat less stress on the theme of suffering than the earlier Hînayâna teachings. Nevertheless, the emphasis on impermanence leads directly to the ideas that all is vanity and that, so long as we cling to the things of this world (including our own mortal lives), we are bound to suffer, since we are, as it were, playing a losing game. Thus we return to the first of the Four Noble Truths preached by the Buddha in his Sermon at Benares, namely, that all existence involves suffering. Though in the Heian period and later the aspects of suffering that most impressed the Japanese derived from the fleeting nature of life, the underlying postulate is essentially the same as in the other parts of Asia where Buddhism made its mark. For a proper understanding of the world of the shining prince we must know what this really signified.

It could well be argued that the ideas of impermanence and suffering are common to other religions, including Christianity. Indeed, what more poignant expression of *mujōkan* could we find than the Biblical threnody, 'Man that is born of a woman hath but a short time to live and is full of misery. He cometh up and is cast down like a flower'? And

27. See Appendix 5, pp. 315–17.

what statement about the sorrow of the human condition could be more conclusive than the sentence in the Church of England burial service that reads, 'We give Thee hearty thanks for that it hath pleased Thee to deliver this our brother out of the miseries of this sinful world'?

Yet the Western approach to these universal themes differs fundamentally from that of Buddhism. A reference to a few of these differences may help to throw light on what the doctrines meant to the people of Murasaki's world. In the first place there was nothing corresponding to the Western idea that we must endure suffering as a duty or in obedience to some divine will, or that suffering improves and ennobles the character. The only thing that people like Kaoru and Prince Hachi learn from suffering is the emptiness of this world and the need to escape from it by meditation or, preferably, by a total withdrawal into a monastic life.

So far as the theme of impermanence was concerned, Buddhism insisted on the total disintegration of our physical being, and by its advocacy of cremation underlined the conclusive nature of death. Certain popular Buddhist writings even seem to gloat on the idea of physical decay. Christianity, on the other hand, holds out the promise of supernatural reconstitution: 'Though worms destroy this body, yet shall I see God in the flesh – and not as another.' The ideas of dissolution and death are far more important in Buddhist-inspired cultures than in the West, and in much Japanese literature the themes of time's ravages and of death are pervasive.

Perhaps the greatest difference is one of emphasis. Christianity, while reminding us of the impermanence and vanity of worldly things, does not as a rule dwell on the theme and prefers to stress the dichotomy of righteousness and sin. Japanese Buddhism, on the other hand, has tended to be preoccupied with the fleeting nature of the phenomenal world and has impressed this idea, perhaps more than any other, on its followers. Ever since the Heian period one of the first things that a Japanese child has learned is an ingenious ABC in which each of the forty-seven phonetic syllables is used once and once only to form a Buddhist poem. This poem is based on the Nirvana Sutra and informs the young pupil that all is transitory in this fleeting world:

> Brightly coloured though the blossoms be,
> All are doomed to scatter.
> So in this world of ours,

Who will last forever?
Today, having crossed the mountain recesses of Samskrita,[28]
I shall be free of fleeting dreams,
Nor shall I be fuddled [by the pleasures of this world].

We can hardly expect that the full impact of these chilling sentiments
has been conveyed to each young Japanese who parrots the syllables.
Yet it is surely significant that the theme of universal impermanence
should have been incorporated into the country's traditional alphabet.
Combined with all the other Buddhist influences, it impressed the sense
of *mujōkan* on the Japanese, just as the opening lines of the Three-
Character Classic memorized by young Chinese students ('Men by
nature are fundamentally good; by nature they share this quality . . .')
must have helped to give them a somewhat more sanguine approach to
the human condition.

The Buddhist stress on evanescence has had a major influence on the
literature of the Heian period and later. It is characteristic of the Japanese absorption with nature that their *memento mori* should be not a
grinning skull nor the crumbling well of a deserted house but live, poignant images like the scattering of blossoms or the yellowing of autumn
leaves, which served to remind them that all beautiful things must soon
pass away.

Whereas the Western reaction to the common lot has often been an
urgent admonition of *carpe diem* – an effort to defy fate by a hasty
gathering of rosebuds – coupled with a stress on individual continuity
in an after-life, the Japanese have tended to adopt a rather more resigned
approach to the universal death sentence. Shintoism, with its horror of
death, clearly had no part in producing this attitude. In the earliest
Japanese poetry we frequently find the most bitter and outspoken
lamentations about illness and death. By Murasaki's time, however,
Buddhism had exerted its influence for over four hundred years, and the
Japanese attitude to the evanescence and uncertainty of life had assumed
its characteristic form. Three Heian poems – one by a Buddhist priest,
the second by Murasaki, and the third by her fellow writer and court
lady, Izumi Shikibu – will suggest this approach better than any
amount of description:

28. i.e. having surmounted the difficulties of freeing oneself from this incon-
stant world.

This world of ours –
To what shall I compare it?
To the white waves behind a boat
As it rows away at dawn.

This world of ours –
Why should we lament it?
Let us view it as we do the cherries
That blossom on the hills.

Out of the dark
Into a dark path
I must now enter:
Shine on me from afar,
Moon of the mountain-fringe![29]

★

A preoccupation with evanescence and death runs through *The Tale of Genji*. One after another, the characters sicken and die, leaving the survivors with an ever deeper sense of the transience of worldly things. According to some Japanese critics, it was the untimely death of Murasaki's husband[30] that caused her to dwell on the theme of impermanence.

29. Yo no naka wo
    Nani ni tatoemu.
    Asaborake
    Kogiyuku fune no
    Ato no shiranami. (Mansei)

    Yo no naka wo
    Nani nagekamashi.
    Yamazakura
    Hana miru hodo no
    Kokoro nariseba. (Murasaki Shikibu)

    Kuraki yori
    Kuraki michi ni zo
    Irinubeki.
    Haruka ni terase
    Yama no ha no tsuki. (Izumi Shikibu)

The last translation is Arthur Waley's; Izumi Shikibu is said to have written the poem on her death-bed, and the first two lines refer to a passage in the Lotus Sutra: 'Out of darkness we enter into darkness.'

30. See p. 265.

Whether or not we accept this somewhat facile explanation, there is little doubt that Murasaki had a sombre disposition. She was well aware of this herself:

If only I could be more adaptable [she writes in her diary] and respond to the pleasures of this fleeting existence with a little more youthful enthusiasm! Whenever I hear of anything delightful or interesting, it only makes me more anxious [to retire from the world]. . . . Thus I was musing one morning when I caught sight of waterfowl playing [on the lake] as if they did not have a care in the world . . .

> 'Like the waterfowl that play there on the lake,
> I too am floating along the surface
> Of a transient world.'

I could not help comparing them with myself. For they too appeared to be enjoying themselves in the most carefree fashion; yet their lives must be full of sorrow.[31]

It is important to remember, however, that this preoccupation with the uncertainty of life was not at all unusual: Murasaki's writing reflects, though perhaps in a rather pronounced form, the Buddhist sense of transience that was common to the people of her world. Most of her fellow-writers, with the notable exception of Sei Shōnagon, are plangent on the theme, and throughout contemporary *belles lettres* we find passages like:

The mourning period [for my mother's death] had come to an end and as usual time was hanging heavily on my hands. I took out my psaltery and, as I dusted it, plucked occasionally at the strings. Now there was no longer any taboo on playing music, and I reflected sadly on the transience of this world . . .

or again,

As I watch the plants pitifully bending in the wind, I think uneasily of my own life – no more lasting than those dewdrops that will be blown away at any moment. The sight of those trees and plants sorrowfully reminds me of my own existence.[32]

31. Mochizuki ed., pp. 34–5.
32. These passages are taken from *Kagerō Nikki*, pp. 146–7, and *Izumi Shikibu Nikki*, p. 420.

Prince Genji and many of the other principal figures in Murasaki's novel are 'tired of the world's impermanence'.[33] Confronted at an early age with the death of their relations and friends, they are keenly conscious of their own short life-expectancy. It is not only funerals and their doleful aftermaths of mourning that impress them with the idea of transience, but the fading blossoms, the falling leaves, and all the other natural images that were associated with it in both Buddhist and secular literature. Despite his youth, Kaoru is probably more preoccupied with the subject than any of the other main characters; this clearly is related to his deep concern with Buddhism. 'Whatever one may say', he remarks on one of his visits to Uji, 'each of us is bound sooner or later to turn into smoke and float up into the sky.'[34] (Here again the practice of cremation added to the sense of insubstantiality.) 'Our life is far too short and uncertain', he says on another occasion, when he is just twenty-four years old, 'for anything in this world to have much importance.'[35] Kaoru's friends are impressed by his feelings, which they recognize as an intense expression of their own sense of evanescence. Prince Niou recalls that Kaoru's emotions are so keenly attuned to the nature of things that the mere cry of a bird flying overhead can plunge him into the depths of gloom, 'for he is a man who is thoroughly absorbed with the idea of the world's impermanence'.[36]

Mahâyâna Buddhism insisted also on the illusory character of all phenomena, and the people of Murasaki's world frequently refer to the nebulous, unreal quality of their lives. The idea that the physical world is an illusion, and our lives no more substantial than dew or gossamer, is most often evoked by the imagery of dreams. The characters in *The Tale of Genji* are forever dreaming, and they keenly recognize that the quality of their dreams is close to that of waking life. 'A night of endless dreams is this my life' (*akenu yo no yume*),[37] writes Lady Akashi in one of her poems to Genji, and the image is used again and again by other characters in the novel. The title of Murasaki's final book, 'The Floating

---

33. Ware akihatenu/ Tsune naranu yo ni. Ikeda ed., v, 108. These are the last two lines of Genji's poem to the Empress after Murasaki's death.

34. Ibid., vi, 198.

35. Ibid., vi, 39.

36. Yo no naka no tsune naki koto wo shimite omoeru otoko. Ibid., vii, 104-5.

37. N.B.T. ed., vi, 360.

Bridge of Dreams' (*Yume no Ukihashi*) was for many centuries regarded as a clue to the entire work. This was disputed by later commentators, like Motoori, who wished to minimize the Buddhist influence. Yet the idea that our life is a dream-like bridge over which we cross from one state of existence to another appears to have been central to Murasaki's conception, and emerges particularly in the last part of the novel, where the Buddhist influence is greatest.[38] The 'bridge of dreams' image is not, however, original with Murasaki. It is taken from an early poem:

> As I walk across the bridge
> That spans the Ford of Yume,
> I see that this world of ours too
> Is like a floating bridge of dreams.[39]

The image occurs frequently in the *Manyō Shū* and other early literature and must have struck a responsive chord among the people of Murasaki's world.

The reference to the evanescence and unreality of the world should not always be taken at face value. In Murasaki's time periodical protestations of melancholy and gloom were essential for people who regarded themselves as sensitive; and *mujōkan* (the sense of impermanence) was often merely a type of conventionalized world-weariness or *Weltschmerz*. When Heian diaries or fictional characters say that they are 'tired of this frail world's decay', their sentiments may be as formalized and specious as those of the romantic poet who claims that he is expiring of unrequited love. On the other hand, we must not go to the extreme of summarily dismissing the expressions of *mujōkan* as insincere formulae. For all its worldly aspects, Buddhism was a vital religious force, and its

---

38. 'The Bridge of Dreams is of course *yo no naka*, Life itself, and the title means something like Calderòn's *La Vida es Sueño*.' (Waley, *The Bridge of Dreams*, p. 16.)

The 'floating bridge of dreams' is probably related to the common Japanese metaphor, 'the floating world', *ukiyo no yume* (N.B.T. ed., vi, 360); in both images the world is regarded as a floating, i.e. a nebulous, place. Written with a different character, *ukiyo* also has the Buddhist sense of 'sad world'. Since Murasaki normally writes the word in the phonetic script, we cannot be certain about which of the two meanings she intends, but most commentators agree that in *ukiyo no yume* she refers to the 'floating' world.

39. Yume: (i) beauty spot on Yoshino River, (ii) dream.

approach to the physical world was bound to have a profound influence on people's thinking, even though it often appeared in the form of platitudes.

Japanese Buddhism not only regarded the human condition in general as a sad, fleeting affair but insisted that it was particularly unfortunate to have been born in the present age. This gloomy conclusion was based on the Mahâyâna belief about the three eras following the Buddha's entry into nirvana – those of the True Law, the Reflected Law, and the Latter Days of the Law. In the third period the Buddha's teachings would finally lose their power and mankind enter an age of decadence. There was no general agreement about the length of these eras, nor for that matter about the year in which the Buddha attained his final release. Chinese clerics during the Six Dynasties (some five and a half centuries before Heian) had calculated that it was their doubtful distinction to be witnessing the beginning of the latter days of the Law. In Japan (where Buddhism was not introduced until the end of the Six Dynasties) the unhappy time was set considerably later. By moving the Buddha's birth back about half a millennium from its historical date and by ascribing a duration of two thousand years to the eras of the True Law and the Reflected Law, they concluded that the latter days of the Law would start in the eleventh century. At the beginning of the Heian period the founder of Japanese Tendai wrote a treatise on the subject in which he said, 'In the Latter Days of the Law there will be none to keep the Buddha's commandments. If there should be such, they will be as rare as a tiger in a market place.'[40]

As the predicted era of decline approached, there was growing apprehension in many quarters. This never approached the frantic sense of doom that at approximately the same period in Europe inspired many Christians to prepare for the millennium by abandoning their homes and taking to the hills. None the less the visible decline of the old system, the increasing breakdown of law and order (emphasized, ironically enough, by the obstreperousness of the priests), and the gradual shift of power to a new class in the provinces, all seemingly provided evidence that the Buddhist prediction was far from fanciful, and made people regard the future with pessimism.

40. Dengyō Daishi, *Mappō Tōmyō Ki*, quoted by Sir Charles Eliot, *Japanese Buddhism*, p. 424.

Another Buddhist idea that profoundly influenced the people of Murasaki's world is that the individual's destiny is determined by his actions in this and previous incarnations. The words *sukuse*, *en*, *gō*, and *inga*, which recur throughout contemporary literature, refer not to Fate in the Western sense but to the Chain of Cause and Effect to which each of us is ineluctably tied and which represents the moral sum of our deeds in successive states of existence. For many centuries it was believed that the principal aim of *The Tale of Genji* was to illustrate this philosophy of karma. Buddhist scholars particularly emphasized that Genji's suffering when he realizes that his young wife has been unfaithful to him is an automatic retribution for his own misdeeds as a youth.[41] Again, Emperor Reizei's childlessness is shown to be the result of the sin that attended his birth. It is surely an oversimplification of *The Tale of Genji* to imagine that its purpose is to expound any particular theory or moral. As a Buddhist, Murasaki was bound to believe that our lives are predetermined by karma; and this pregnant idea is inevitably reflected in her novel. In the passage quoted at the beginning of this chapter Ukon resigns herself to the affair between Ukifune and Niou since it is the result of a predetermined karma (*sukuse*). Later the Assistant High Priest who discovers Ukifune after her attempted suicide knows that this encounter is not a matter of chance but the effect of something that happened in a previous incarnation. He will do his best to help the girl; if she dies despite all his efforts, it will mean that her karma is exhausted (*gō tsukinikeri*), in other words, she will have used up the entire stock of virtue accumulated in previous incarnations. Later, when he sees Ukifune at his sister's house, he is struck by her appearance, and remarks, 'She must have accumulated a great deal of virtue to have been born with such beauty.'[42]

This form of determinism (a highly plausible one, incidentally, if one accepts the idea of reincarnation) provided a ready explanation for even the most secular and trivial events. In the *Sarashina Diary*, for example, the girl's father explains that the reason he has been appointed to govern a distant province instead of some more congenial place near the capital is that he has a bad karma from a previous existence. And in the *Pillow Book*, when Sei describes the cuckoo-hearing excursion and the failure of the ladies-in-waiting to produce adequate verses for the occasion, she remarks that poetry had a bad karma (*sukuse naki*) on that day.[43]

41. See p. 279.   42. Ikeda ed., vii, 162–3.   43. See p. 191.

The long-term effect that this form of fatalism is likely to have on people's thinking need hardly be laboured. It is true that, according to the karma idea, the individual is free to determine his future by the moral quality of his present actions; the trouble is that these actions have themselves already been determined by what he has done in the past and that the causal chain reaches back through innumerable incarnations over which we no longer have the slightest control. The result is almost bound to be a sense of helplessness and resignation, a reluctance to take things into one's own hands or to improve the conditions of one's existence. This was combined with the Buddhist view regarding the fleeting, dreamlike quality of life to produce the somewhat negative and discouraged approach to the world that is prominent in the later books of *The Tale of Genji* and in much subsequent Japanese literature.

Having presented a thoroughly unattractive picture of the physical world and of the human condition, Buddhism offered a solution. If the origin of universal suffering was desire, and if this was inseparable from normal life, then the only answer was to abandon the fleeting world of sorrow (*shaba*) and thereby to eliminate desire, above all the desire for individual survival. By retiring into a monastic existence, and devoting oneself to prayer, meditation, and mystic practices, one could gradually slough off the habit of desire; the sorrows of this transient world would no longer torment one, death would lose its sting, and eventually one could shake oneself free from the chain of causation. The ideal of a complete and final release in nirvana (*nehan*) is never explicitly stated in *The Tale of Genji*, but this of course is the ultimate aspiration of characters like Prince Hachi and Kaoru. For less devout and single-minded men a complete escape might be difficult, and for women it was impossible; yet even they could find surcease from the sorrows of mortal life by retiring to a monastery or convent, and at the same time they would be improving their chances in the next phase of their existence.

In the Heian period these aspirations had little relevance for the illiterate masses, though for them the sorrows of this mortal coil were only too real; but to the people of Murasaki's class they exerted a great appeal, and both in real life and in fiction the idea that one should sooner or later retire into a religious life was never far from the surface of their minds. Towards the end of *The Tale of Genji* we find a moving description of the Buddhist ideal of renouncing the world. Shortly after her attempted suicide, Ukifune, who is now twenty-two years old, has expressed her desire to become a nun. The Assistant High Priest who found her is prepared to administer the vows, but his sister is opposed to this irrevocable step:

'The girl is too young to take the Vows,' she said. 'Far from procuring her salvation, it may lead to greater sin.[44] I really think you might have discussed the matter with me. It's quite outrageous!'

Her words had not the slightest effect on the priest. 'For you,' he said, turning to Ukifune, 'there remains only one thing – to pursue your devotions. Whether we are young or old, this is a world in which we can depend on nothing. You are quite right to regard it as an empty, fleeting place.'

He handed her some figured cloth, thin silk and other materials. 'Use this to make yourself a new habit. And remember, so long as I am alive I shall see that you have what you need. Where such things are concerned, you have nothing to worry about. As for the daily world outside – that fleeting world into which we have all been born – I know it is a hard place to quit. While we are still dazzled by its show and glitter (*eiga*), there seem to be innumerable obstacles that prevent us from leaving it. It was the same for me as for everyone else. Yet I can assure you that living now in these peaceful forest surroundings, absorbed in prayer and meditation, you will be free from all regret and remorse. Life will seem as light to you as a leaf. . . . At dawn you will see the moon hovering over the pine-wood gate.'[45]

Many of Murasaki's characters are sincere when they speak of abandoning the world of desire and retiring to a monastic life. Yet often their protestations on this subject are as stereotyped and conventional as their laments about the fleeting quality of human life, and one feels that they are only too pleased about the obstacles that prevent them from taking the religious plunge. Genji is forever regretting the numerous mundane duties that prevent him from becoming a monk; yet he would no doubt be appalled to spend a single day in a bleak monastic cell, sequestered from the social and cultural delights of the capital. Even Kaoru is not entirely free of hypocrisy on this score. When he complains to the priest about the many troublesome bonds that tie him to this

44. Because she is still likely to succumb to the temptations of the flesh.
45. Ikeda ed., vii, 206. The last two sentences are quotations from a poem of Po Chü-i. As in Izumi Shikibu's poem on p. 124 above, the moon is symbolically associated with the Buddhist Law.

transient world and thwart his desire for a religious life, he seems to be protesting too much; and one cannot help suspecting that, if these obstacles were removed, he would soon find others.[46]

Although it was conventional to express envy for those who had finally succeeded in abandoning the world, few members of the Heian aristocracy had any illusions about the hard, cheerless life that often awaited them in the monasteries and, still more, the convents. The gloom and squalor of a convent appears to them as a sort of living death and, when a girl takes her vows and her long hair is shorn by the priest, the onlookers weep, realizing that she is 'dead to the friendly and human part of life'.

It is true that in many cases the distinction between the world and the cloister was a hazy one. To 'retire' to a monastery often had several practical advantages and involved few restrictions. Kazan, for instance, was far freer to carry on his amorous intrigues after he had become a monk than when he was a reigning emperor;[47] and the priestly condition certainly did nothing to inhibit Michinaga during the last ten years of his life. Yet in many other cases (Emperor Suzaku and Prince Hachi in *The Tale of Genji* are examples) 'discarding one's fineries' and taking the tonsure did mark a genuine determination to embark on a life devoted to religious austerities and winnowed of worldly concerns.

Buddhist renunciation required a far harder sacrifice than giving up the pleasures of the senses: it insisted on total detachment from those one loved. Friends, wives, children – however close they might be and however dependent – had to be removed not only from one's daily life but from one's very thoughts. The Christian scriptures, too, sternly put

46. N.B.T. ed., vii, 843–4. 'Since my youth I have entertained serious religious ambitions. But the Princess, my mother, has in her helplessness been obliged to rely on my inadequate support. I became circumscribed by the stubborn bonds of worldly obligations. I rose in rank and it became hard for me to arrange my life as I should have wished. As time passed, my inescapable duties only increased, and I found myself completely tied down by public and private responsibilities. Nevertheless I have scrupulously respected the Laws of Buddha in so far as I have been acquainted with them. My inner intentions are no less noble than those of a saint . . .'

Kaoru's entire speech is contained in a single Japanese sentence. There is no mistaking the irony in the priest's pithy reply, 'How very noble of you!' (*Ito tōt oki koto.*)

47. See p. 71–2.

family ties in their place ('Who is my mother, or my brethren?'), insisting that they must be submerged in a wider love. In Buddhism, however, the stress is on the need to extirpate human affections in general, since they are the strongest of all the bonds that tie one to this fleeting world of illusions. While we are still bound by human attachments, the Assistant High Priest informs Ukifune, to take the vows, so far from procuring one's salvation, can only lead to disaster.

When put into practice, the Buddhist ideal of renunciation was likely to involve a rupture of human ties that must often strike the Westerner as callous, even egoistic. To be sure, this ideal was aimed not at procuring any selfish advantage, but rather at total self-annihilation (*muga*); and, besides, enlightenment was regarded as the best means of securing spiritual benefit for others. Yet for those who belong to different traditions there can be something curiously chilling and inhuman about the attitude that it involves; and it was certainly the rejection of family bonds that most alienated Chinese Confucianists from Buddhism. In one of the early books of *The Tale of Genji* the moribund old nun who has been looking after Murasaki fears that her affection for the helpless little girl is a worldly tie that may impede her own spiritual promotion. The unyielding Buddhist attitude to family affections emerges most conspicuously in Prince Hachi's treatment of his daughters. When he retires to his monastery, he completely abandons the two unfortunate girls and refuses ever to meet them. After their father's death the daughters request permission to see him for a last time, but the Prince's spiritual mentor, the Holy Teacher, administers a blunt rebuff:

'What good can that possibly do at this stage? Before the Prince died I told him that he must never see you again, and now that he is no longer here it is all the more important that you resign yourself to the inevitable so that all mutual bonds of affection may disappear.'[48]

Murasaki fully realizes how harsh the ideal of renunciation may seem when human emotions are involved:

The girls asked him about their father's life in his mountain retreat, but the holy man was so absorbed in his own pious quest for enlightenment that he could tell them nothing. His attitude struck the sisters as hard and cruel.

48. Ikeda ed., v, 264. 'Holy Teacher' is a translation of *Ajari*, a title given to distinguished priests of the Tendai and Shingon sects.

Among the many other aspects of Buddhism that influenced thought and behaviour in the Heian period was its attitude towards women. The sutras leave no doubt about their inferior spiritual status. For example, in the Lotus, the bible of the Tendai sect, we read that 'no women are to be found' in the Western Paradise; women who call on Amida will be reborn in his paradise as men.[49] Heian Buddhism did not, however, dwell on this subject, and it is only in later centuries, when the social position of Japanese women had drastically deteriorated, that we find passages like: 'Woman is originally an agent of the six devils and has been born as a woman to prevent man from following the way of Buddha', or 'Woman is the emissary of hell; she destroys the seed of Buddha. Her face resembles that of a saint; her heart is like that of a demon.'[50]

The men and women of Murasaki's world were, however, well aware of the innate spiritual difference between the sexes, and they accepted it as one of the facts of life. Thus, when Genji has been confronted with the frenetic jealousy of Lady Rokujō's ghost, he reflects that all women are fundamentally evil (*onna no mi wa mina onaji tsumi fukaki moto*) and that relations with them are almost bound to end in the type of repugnant scene he has just witnessed.[51] Again, when Ukifune's mother enumerates the many difficulties that confront her daughter, she ends by saying that her greatest misfortune is to have been born a woman; for, 'Whatever their station may be, women are bound to have a hard lot, not only in this life but in the world to come.'[52] There is not the slightest evidence that Murasaki herself questioned this gloomy assessment of her own sex.

The Buddhist interdiction of violence and the taking of life also had an effect on behaviour and customs in the Heian period. We have noticed the relative mildness of punishments and the preference of banishment to execution. Buddhism undoubtedly reinforced the disdain of the aristocracy for warfare and its practitioners, and discouraged people from hunting and eating meat. In the eighth century the government had set aside special ponds where fishing was prohibited and where people were encouraged to free and feed fish, crabs, and other water

---

49. *Saddharmapundarîka Sûtra* XXIV, verse 31, and XXII.

50. *Teisetsu Kyōkun Onna Shikimoku* (1745), quoted in Takamure Itsue, *Nihon Josei Shakai Shi*, p. 165. See Joyce Ackroyd, *Women in Feudal Japan*, pp. 54–5.

51. Ikeda ed., iv, 187.   52. N.B.T. ed., vii, 647.

animals in order to acquire Buddhist merit; throughout the Heian period mercy to animals was regarded as a means to spiritual improvement.

The gentleness of the period should certainly not be exaggerated. The 'good people' were on the whole indifferent to the suffering of the lower classes (though no more so than the gentry in Dickens's England), and various forms of violence were frequent – the priesthood itself not being behindhand in this respect when their material interests were at stake. In the *Pillow Book* we read that the dog Okinamaro has been beaten to death for having chased the emperor's cat; to judge from the shock of the empress and her ladies, this must have been unusually severe treatment, but in the provinces, where the lenitive influence of Buddhism was slight, animals and other helpless creatures were no doubt dealt with harshly.[53] It is in contrast with the succeeding centuries of military rule and internecine warfare, when a general could calmly give orders for his enemy's young children to be buried alive[54] and where horrors of every kind became commonplace, that we are impressed by the mildness and forbearance of the Heian period. In later times Buddhism was unable to prevent its adherents from indulging in the most barbarous behaviour; but in Murasaki's day it still appears to have had a mollifying influence on human cruelty and violence.

53. It may be significant that the two men who administer the fatal punishment to Okinamaro both come from a military family in the provinces.

54. *Heike Monogatari*, a pro-Minamoto work, coolly reports the treatment that the Minamotos meted out to the children of their defeated enemies, Taira no Shigemori and Munemori: the younger ones were drowned or buried alive, the older ones decapitated.

V

Superstitions

WHEN it came to regulating the practical details of their daily life, the people of Heian relied far more on superstition than on religion. In Japan as elsewhere the line of demarcation is a tenuous one, especially since many of the superstitions were originally associated with Shintoism, Confucianism, Taoism, and Buddhism. Nevertheless exorcism, divination, and similar practices belong on the whole to a different category from the ideas described in the previous chapter.[1]

In Murasaki's time there was a vast accretion of popular beliefs that had proliferated for many centuries and become closely intertwined. Here there is space to examine only a few of the principal strands that make up the tangled skein of Heian superstition. Some, notably those related to witchcraft, necromancy, and other occult practice, were influenced by Shintoism, and represent the shamanistic strain in the native religion; yet, though their practitioners often invoked Shintō deities, most of them were no longer specifically connected with any particular faith. Other superstitions, including many that are concerned with ghosts and demons, appear to have derived from ancient native folklore whose origin is still obscure.

Still another vast body of beliefs – and for the people of Murasaki's class perhaps the most important – was of Chinese origin. Together with

1. Superstition may perhaps be defined as a belief that is based neither on normally observed fact nor on any moral or ethical system, nor on a search for ultimate truth. Some superstitions may, if held firmly enough, assume a spurious factual validity (e.g. cure by exorcism, appearance of ghosts). Religion, on the other hand, invariably involves the quest for moral or ethical righteousness, or for purity, salvation, or enlightenment, usually in conjunction with some higher or more powerful force or forces (God, Heaven, nature deities, deified ancestors, etc.). It is, of course, possible to have a superstition with deities (e.g. directional taboos) and a religion without them (e.g. Zen Buddhism), and most religions, including Buddhism, are replete with superstitious practices.

Confucianism Japan had imported the vast system of omen lore based on *yin-yang* dualism and the five elements. Although these beliefs formed no part of the original Confucian system, they had thoroughly infiltrated both Confucianism and Taoism by the time that the classics were introduced to Japan. In Murasaki's day people were on the whole far more interested in the idea of a magic order that controlled human affairs by an alternation of the universal *yin* (female, dark, cold, passive, earth, water, moon) and *yang* (male, light, active, Heaven, fire, sun) elements, and in all the ramifications of this pseudo-scientific cosmology, than they were in the ethics of Confucius or the mystic insights of Lao Tzu.

One of the most important and active offices in the Ministry of Central Affairs was the Bureau of Divination (the Yin-Yang Bureau as it was called), which was in charge of astrological, calendrical, and aleatory calculations, the discernment of good and evil omens, and similar activities that were supposed to help the government shape its policy by acting in accordance with the fundamental process of growth and change in the natural world. The Masters of Yin-Yang, who imparted their findings both to the Great Council of State and to members of the nobility, helped to bring ideas about geomancy (*feng-shui*), astrology, and divination into the centre of Japanese practice. Although most of these ideas came from China, by Murasaki's time they had often developed on independent Japanese lines and were not regarded as foreign.

An interesting case of cultural blending is to be found in the idea of directional taboos (*kataimi*), where the native Shintō emphasis on abstinence (*imi*) reappears in the *yin-yang* concept of lucky and unlucky directions. These taboos, which had great practical importance for the aristocracy, can be divided into three main types.[2] First was the permanently and universally unlucky direction, the north-east. It was to guard the capital from this direction that the great complex of Tendai monasteries had been built on Mount Hiei, although the Buddhist religion itself is unconcerned with taboos. The second type was permanently unlucky during specific periods of one's life; at the age of sixteen, for instance, one might (depending on one's sex, the time of one's birth, and other particulars) have to avoid the north-west. The final and most fre-

2. I am indebted to M. Bernard Frank's detailed study of directional taboos, *Etude sur les interdits de direction à l'époque Heian.*

quent type was universally but temporarily unlucky and was based on the position of certain moving divinities. These divinities descended from the heavens and circulated at determined intervals through the various points of the compass. Each time that the divinity stopped in a given direction, that sector was considered 'closed'. In *The Tale of Genji* for example, the hero, who has been visiting Utsusemi, a young married lady on whom he has the usual designs, finds that he cannot return home since his residence lies in a 'closed' direction; conveniently enough, he is obliged to spend the night at her house, just as if he had been caught in a thick November fog.

Certain activities and movements, varying with different divinities and related to the 'closed' direction, were strictly prohibited. It was common knowledge, for example, that Doku (one of the many deities of the Lares-Penates type) spent his springs in the oven, his summers at the gate, his autumns in the well, and his winters in the courtyard. To make repairs in any of these four places while the deity was in residence could be disastrous, and normally one had to wait until he had shifted to his next post. Certain methods had, however, been devised for circumventing the taboos. If repairs were essential, the owner could move out of his house into a temporary dwelling and escape the danger by a complex system of 'converting' the unlucky direction. It was also possible to circumvent a directional taboo by taking a roundabout course (*katatagae*) and avoiding the precise direction that was forbidden at the time. If we transpose the system to London, a person living in Kensington, for example, and wishing to make his way to Hyde Park Corner might avoid the closed eastern direction by first going north-east to Marble Arch (the intermediate point or *tabisho*), spending the night there, and then proceeding south to his destination.[3]

Directional taboos were not observed by commoners until the fifteenth

3. The system of *katatagae* was considerably more complicated than this outline would suggest. It was common practice for people to leave their house for a *katatagae* because they wished to obtain release from some future taboo or prohibition, even though they had no desire to go anywhere. By performing such a seemingly gratuitous *katatagae*, they were freed in advance from the baleful effect that one of the moving divinities might exert if they remained at home or indulged in some tabooed activity like ground-breaking. Furthermore '*katatagae* were not limited to occasions on which people wished to travel abroad, but also took place on those inauspicious days when they had to be absent from

century, but from Heian literature we can judge what a great role they played in the activities of the nobility.[4] One effect was to put a further brake on the already slow pace of life. A provincial governor setting out for his post, a gentleman reporting to his office in a Ministry, an official intending to break ground for the construction of a new government building – all might be inordinately delayed by the fear of violating taboos. At the same time, as we know from *The Tale of Genji*, they provided magnificent excuses for the philanderer.

Taboos also derived from the sexagenary cycle, which was the basis of divination in the *yin-yang* system. The origin of the traditional Chinese chronology that had been imported into Japan was the idea that the all-pervading principles of *yin* and *yang*, as expressed in terms of the five elements, dominated time. By combining the twelve horary characters (rat, ox, tiger, hare, etc.) with the ten celestial stems (pairs of wood, fire, earth, metal, and water), the experts had formed a cycle of sixty, which was applied both to days and to years; it was believed that a proper understanding of this cycle made it possible to foretell future events.

Calendrical divination was one of the main functions of the Masters of Yin-Yang and was regarded most seriously by the government. It also had a considerable effect on the private lives of the aristocracy. The Masters of Yin-Yang used the sexagenary cycle to fix certain taboo days (*monoimi no hi*) when it was essential to stay indoors and, so far as possible, abstain from all activity. Particularly strict rules applied to the

---

their homes [because of the unlucky position of one of the moving divinities]. At such times they would go and stay in the house of an acquaintance – for a couple of days in the case of a short *katatagae*, for seven or even forty-five days in the case of a long one.' (*Kōchū Nihon Bungaku Taikei*, xxv, 211).

Thieves often took advantage of these beliefs to enter their victim's house when they knew that the master and his family would have to be absent because of a *katatagae*.

'. . . le *katatagae*', writes M. Frank (op. cit., p. 55), 'n'avait pas seulement pour but . . . de tourner l'interdiction de se déplacer. . . . Il avait également pour but d'écarter les interdictions . . . concernant le "viol de la terre", l'accouchement et nombre d'autres travaux ou activités sans rapport nécessaire avec l'idée d'un déplacement.' M. Frank suggests (pp. 98–9) that these '*katatagae* préventifs' may actually have been more important than the '*katatagae* de déplacement' though most modern definitions refer exclusively to the latter type.

4. During the civil wars warriors were often guided by directional taboos and divination when choosing the place and time of battles.

emperor's movements on any such *dies nefasti*. Once in every sixty days (on a Day of the Monkey) people were advised to spend the whole night awake, lest they be attacked and killed in their sleep by certain noxious powers that always circulated at that time. Even the most trivial decisions of daily life, such as when to cut one's hair, were made by reference to the sexagenary cycle. In the middle of the tenth century a prominent Fujiwara statesman left the following advice for his grandson: 'When you get up in the morning, first repeat seven times the name of your guardian star. . . . Then take a looking-glass and examine your face. Next you must study the calendar to see whether it is a lucky or an unlucky day. . . .'[5] The day's activities were then carefully determined according to current physiognomic and calendrical theories.

Even urgent affairs of state were delayed by calendrical superstition. An expedition against a dangerous Taira rebel in 1028 had to wait for over a month before an auspicious day could be found to dispatch the troops.

As if these restrictions were not sufficiently onerous, there was a mass of additional taboos derived from miscellaneous sources. Fingernails, for instance, could be cut only on the Day of the Ox and toenails on the Day of the Tiger. Bathing, at best a rather perfunctory process, could take place only once in five days – and then only if the day was auspicious. When Prince Niou visits his consort, Naka no Kimi, he is annoyed to find that she is having her hair washed (an immensely time-consuming operation in the Heian period when a woman's hair was often as long as she was), and he asks her ladies why they had to choose that particular day. 'We normally do it when Your Excellency is not here,' replies one of the ladies, 'but what with one thing or another it has been impossible during the past few days. There are no more auspicious days until the end of this month, and of course the next two months are taboo. So you see, Your Highness, we really could not miss this opportunity.'[6] The two months in question are the Ninth, which was associated with a Buddhist ceremony, and the Tenth, the 'Godless Month' according to

5. Fujiwara no Morosuke, *Kujōdono Yuikai*, xxi, 4a. The 'guardian star' (*zokushō*) is determined by the date of the person's birth and remains unchanged during his entire life. *Renchū Shō* (Kaitei Shiseki Shūran, xxiii, 75, cited by Frank, op. cit., p. 37).

6. Ikeda ed., vi, 266.

Shintoism; to wash one's hair during this time was to court influenza or some other misfortune.

Later in the same book, when Kaoru, in a rare access of determination, is about to abduct Ukifune and has lifted the girl in his arms, her ladies raise a chorus of protest: 'But it's the Ninth Month, Your Highness. Oh, what a terrible thing to do!' Here again, the taboo results from the Buddhist ceremony: to start a love affair at this time was regarded as highly inauspicious. However, the old nun, Ben no Kimi, shrewdly saves the day by pointing out that the actual ceremony does not start until the fourteenth of the month, and that today is only the thirteenth.

Soothsayers also based their pronouncements on the motions of the planets, portents and omens (such as the auspicious discovery of a large tortoise), and also on dreams. Any unusual phenomenon in the skies was promptly reported to the Bureau of Divination for their expert opinion. The following entry in the chronicles is typical: 'On the fourth day of the Eighth Month something (*ki*) appeared in the sky over the Datchi Gate. It looked like smoke, but it was not smoke; it looked like a rainbow, but it was not a rainbow. . . . People declared that nothing like it had ever been seen before.'[7] The Masters of Yin-Yang announced that this odd manifestation presaged a typhoon, floods, and fire, and the terrified people rushed into the streets for safety; shortly afterwards there was an earthquake (the only disaster that had not been predicted).

The year of the Prime Minister's death in *The Tale of Genji* is marked by a series of disturbing portents:

The motion of the moon, sun and stars was irregular, and there were also many peculiarly shaped clouds. People were frightened and consulted the Masters of Yin-Yang. In their report, however, the experts had to confess that these were strange and unprecedented omens [for which they had no ready explanation].[8]

It was not often that the official diviners were reduced to such a candid admission.

Dreams were also regarded as reliable guides to the future, especially when the dreamer was someone of importance; and contemporary works of literature give detailed descriptions of what the characters, or

7. Ninna 3.8.4. *Sandai Jitsuroku*, 1, 637.   8. Ikeda ed., ii, 315.

(in the case of diaries) the authors, have dreamt. As we have seen, the official reason that Ukifune cannot accompany her mother to the temple is that she has had an inauspicious dream (*yumemi sawagashi*). People listened to the pronouncements of the dream interpreter (*yume-toki*) with all the confidence that they nowadays give to the psychiatrist, and among the 'Happy Things' enumerated by Sei Shōnagon is 'to be told by the interpreter that the worrying dream which so frightened one has no particular significance'.[9]

Among the hundreds of miscellaneous superstitions in Murasaki's time were the beliefs that the proximity of chrysanthemums help to prolong life, that a 'human fire' can be seen leaving the body of someone who is about to die (the author of the *Sarashina Diary* is told that such a fire was emanating from her husband when he set out for his province and concludes, quite rightly as it happens, that he does not have long to live), that sorcerers can make themselves invisible by wearing straw cloaks, and that if one wants to have a delightful dream one should go to sleep wearing one's clothes inside out. Sneezing was regarded as ominous and a formula corresponding to the English 'God bless you!' was recited to wish the sneezer long life. If someone sneezed while another person was talking it implied that the speaker was not telling the truth. On one occasion Sei Shōnagon becomes a victim of this superstition. 'The Empress spoke to me for a while and then asked, "Are you really fond of me?" "But Your Majesty," I replied, "how could I possibly not be fond of you?" Just at that moment someone sneezed loudly in the Table Room. "Alas!" said the Empress. "So you're telling a lie. Well, so be it."' The real liar, Sei reflects, is the sneezer's nose, and the incident rankles for some time.[10]

When a man married into a girl's family, her parents would each carry one of his shoes to bed on retiring and hold it when they went to sleep; this (according to a form of sympathetic magic) would hobble the young man should he ever decide to leave his wife. If one wished to put a curse on an enemy, one buried a paper image (*katashiro*) of him and recited certain secret spells and prayers. Carried out effectively, this could result in illness or even death for the victim, and it was of course one of the few methods of redress available against more powerful members of the hierarchy. In order to free oneself from such a curse it was necessary

9. Kaneko ed., p. 944.   10. Ibid., p. 809.

to call on a Master of Yin-Yang. In a typical mixture of religion and superstition, he would take the victim to a river and rub his body with another paper image that had been purified according to Shintō ritual (*misogi*); having thus transferred the evil (*wazawai*) from the man, he would throw the image into the water and it would be carried away by the current together with the curse.

*

The world of Heian was heavily populated with goblins, demons, spirits, and other supernatural beings. Among the visible types were the *tengu*, hideous red-faced dwellers in the hills and forests who were equipped with noses of inordinate length and wings, and who, rather incongruously, were in the habit of carrying feather fans. Foxes were closely associated with the supernatural. They could bewitch people or cast evil spells on them, and also had the disconcerting habit of assuming human form. When the Assistant High Priest's disciples discover Ukifune lying unconscious under a tree at night, they quickly draw their conclusions:

'It's a fox that's gone and changed itself into a girl,' [said one of the priests]. 'You hateful creature! I'll soon make you show your true colours.' He stepped forward, but one of the other priests stopped him. 'That won't do any good,' he explained. 'It's obviously some evil spirit [in human form].' So saying, he began moving his fingers in magic gestures that are designed to discomfit apparitions of this kind and, firmly fixing his gaze on the recumbent figure, he recited certain magic spells.[11]

The disciples soon hurry back to the house and report their exciting discovery to the Assistant High Priest. 'I have always heard about foxes assuming human form,' he says, 'but I've never yet seen it happen.' He gets up from bed and goes out to have a look.

One of the most famous ghost stories in Japan, the Demon of Rashōmon, dates from the late tenth century and, although the extant, elaborated versions belong to a subsequent period, it suggests the type of demonism that stirred people's imaginations in Murasaki's time. In the year 974 several people in the capital have disappeared mysteriously. This is attributed to the maleficent powers of a ghost who has been

11. Ikeda ed., vii, 153.

haunting the region of the Rashō Gate at the southern extremity of the city. Efforts to subdue the creature have so far been unsuccessful and there is growing panic among the inhabitants. A certain doughty young gentleman named Watanabe no Tsuna wagers that he can do the job. He spends several nights by the Rashō Gate, but there is no sign of the demon. One night as he is riding home he meets a beautiful young girl wandering alone in the rain. She speaks to him and eventually invites him to her house. At first Tsuna is suspicious, but the girl gives him various realistic details about her life (her father, she says, is a fan-maker in the Fifth Ward) and finally Tsuna, overcome by her charm and beauty, lets her mount behind him. After they have been riding for some time, Tsuna turns round and is horrified to find the girl in the very act of transforming herself into a loathsome demon. At the same time he feels that he is about to be carried into the air. In an effort to free himself, he draws his famous sword, Higekiri, and cuts off one of the demon's arms, whereupon the creature shoots into the sky like a rocket. When Tsuna recovers, he finds himself lying on the ground with the arm beside him. He returns to his house and, without a word to anyone, locks the gruesome souvenir in a coffer. There are no more disappearances and things have returned to normal in the capital when one day an old woman visits Tsuna. She informs him that she used to be his nurse and tells him familiar stories about his childhood. Soon Tsuna unburdens himself to the kindly old lady, relating his recent terrifying experience and eventually agreeing to show her the severed arm. The moment the chest is open the old woman (somewhat predictably, one feels) changes herself into the demon of the Rashō Gate, snatches the arm, and disappears into the sky – this time for good.

Far more numerous than the visible creatures of this type were the myriad spirits and demons that could not be seen yet had the power to cause every sort of misfortune. People were at great pains to keep these troublesome visitors from their houses by means of charms, spells, and pseudo-religious incantations. Special precautions were observed in the sacred precincts of the palace. At regular intervals the Imperial Guards would twang their bowstrings to scare away any evil spirit who might be lurking in the air. The Masters of Yin-Yang, who among other things were responsible for keeping time by means of clepsydrae, would go every half hour to the courtyard outside the Emperor's Residential

Palace and inscribe the time on a board; they would then strum their bowstrings to warn the spirits that they could do no mischief during the coming period, after which a guard would announce the time in a loud voice to the accompaniment of a variable number of strokes on a gong.

The unappeased spirits of dead people haunted the world of the living and were a prime cause of illness, death, and other disasters. We have seen the misfortunes attributed to the vengeful spirits of exiles like Prince Sawara and Sugawara no Michizane and the posthumous promotions (to the ranks of Emperor and Prime Minister respectively) that were given to appease them. Even people who were still alive might assume a secondary existence as it were and proceed in the form of an invisible spirit to attack their enemies. In such cases the person himself was not consciously aware of what his spirit was doing. No reader of *The Tale of Genji* can forget the terrifying scenes in which Lady Rokujō's 'living ghost' (*ikiryō*) belabours one after another of Genji's mistresses even while the lady herself is still alive; after Rokujō is dead, her implacable spirit, still shackled to this world by her jealous hatred, continues to attack her unfortunate rivals. One reason that jealousy was regarded with such distaste was that it forced the vindictive spirit of the jealous person to work supernatural revenge, both before and after death.[12]

*

A discussion of spirits and ghosts leads us directly to Heian ideas about medicine. In any pre-scientific society beliefs about illness and the physical phenomenon of death are based largely on superstition. Medical theory and practice in Murasaki's day had two main approaches, which, though entirely unrelated, were never regarded as incompatible.

The first set of beliefs derived from China and depended on the old *yin-yang* dualistic system as interpreted by Taoism.[13] The study of

12. See p. 260, n.88.

13. The earliest extant 'medical' work in Japan, so far as I know, is the *Pao P'u Tzu* (*Hōbokushi*), which dates from about A.D. 300. It contains a wealth of Taoist medical lore and was used by Kūkai in his writing. The principal compilation of the Heian period, however, is by Tamba Yasuyori, a Doctor of Acupuncture (*Harihakase*), who from 982 to 984 produced a work called *Ishinhō*. This provides valuable information about Chinese medical science of the T'ang

Chinese medicine had started at the beginning of the seventh century, and a medical faculty was established in the University as part of the Great Reform movement. The reformers also set up a Bureau of Medicine to deal with illness and epidemics. This was hardly a first step towards a Welfare State: the Masters and Doctors of Medicine who were attached to the bureau were responsible for curing only people of the Fifth Rank and above, and significantly their department was placed under the Ministry of the Imperial Household.

A brief survey of their methods of diagnosis and cure would not suggest that commoners suffered any great deprivation as a result of being disqualified for treatment.[14] The basis of physical health was considered to be a harmony between *yin* and *yang*, the two component parts of the universe and the origin of all change. The process of aging was attributed mainly to waning of the *yin* element, and the diseases of age could be cured only by restoring the proper balance, which became increasingly difficult with the years. In explaining the human body, the *yin-yang* theorists referred to a chart of correspondences in which each major organ was related to one of the five elements, to a season of the year, to a colour, and to a taste. The Kidneys, for example, corresponded to the element of Water; this seems appropriate enough, but the other correspondences are a trifle arbitrary: Winter is the Kidney season, Black their colour and Salty their taste. Similarly the Heart corresponds to Fire, Summer, Red, and Bitter.[15]

Dangerous *yin-yang* imbalances were believed to result from a lack of concordance between the elements, the seasons, and human actions. Thus, if a patient suffered from fever in the autumn, the doctor would consult the chart of correspondences to find out which particular organ was involved and whether the cause was an excess of *yin* or *yang*. He would also no doubt refer to one of the many pithy pronouncements embodied in the Chinese treatises, such as, 'Wind causes chills and

---

dynasty and earlier, much of which has disappeared in the country of its origin. Part 28 of *Ishinhō* consists entirely of quotations about erotic techniques taken from old Chinese sex handbooks, medical treatises, etc. For details, and a Latin translation, see R. H. van Gulik, *Sexual Life in Ancient China*, p. 122 ff.

14. The following discussion is based on material contained in W. N. Whitney, *Notes on the History of Medical Progress in Japan* and Y. Fujikawa, *Kurze Geschichte der Medizin in Japan*.

15. Fujikawa, op. cit., p. 15.

fever;... oppressive airs cause insanity; abundant winds cause ulcers.'[16] The next stage in the diagnosis was a palpation of the 'six pulses', an enormously complicated procedure that depended on the various elements of the *yin-yang* system (sex, season, organ) and on Taoist medical lore.

Having determined the nature of the disease, the doctor would refer to the sexagenary table and choose the proper day and time to begin treatment. This consisted mainly of acupuncture and moxabustion. Acupuncture was the insertion of needles into strategic parts of the body where the twelve 'channels' emerged to the surface. These channels are arranged symmetrically on the left and right sides of the body, six belonging to *yin* and six to *yang* and each related to one of the main organs. The blocking of a specific channel could lead to an excess of *yang* and a deficiency of *yin*, and the purpose of inserting needles was to remedy this morbid condition.

Moxabustion was also based on a complex scheme of *yin-yang* correspondences, but in this case the main purpose was to correct an excess of *yin*. The powdered leaf cone (*moe-kusa*=moxa) would be applied to the part of the body that corresponded to the affected organ and would be burnt down until it reached the skin – a process as painful as it was useless. The points of application were determined fancifully, yet with the greatest precision: among the rules of moxa that were elaborated in the course of the centuries we find the following solemn prescription: 'In a difficult delivery burn three cones on the extremity of the little toe of the right foot.'[17]

Herbal medicines were either derived directly from Taoist lore or prescribed by reference to the *yin-yang* table of correspondences. In this case the operative element was taste; 'Salty' for example, corresponds to a hardening of the pulse, and 'Sweet' to an ache in the bones.

The second main approach to illness in Murasaki's day was based on the belief in evil spirits and possessions. Here we often find an interesting, if specious, modernity. For people spoke of 'catching' an evil influence (*mono no ke*) in much the same way as we refer to catching a germ.[18] At times the parallel is quite striking. The following passage

16. Ibid., p. 18.   17. Kaempfer, op. cit., p. 326.

18. Arthur Waley goes so far as to translate the word *mono no ke* as 'infection' (e.g. *Blue Trousers*, p. 260).

provides a homely example. Yūgiri has just awoken from a disturbing dream to find that his little boy is ill and that Lady Kumoi, his wife, is doing her best to comfort him:

The child was crying loudly and would not keep down his milk. His wet nurse had got up and was scurrying about the room in a state of great agitation. Lady Kumoi quickly took charge of the little boy. She tucked her hair behind her ears and, pulling the oil lamp towards her, picked him up in her arms. Her dress was open in front, showing her full, beautifully shaped breasts. . . . She was no longer able to give milk, but she held the child to one of her nipples and soon he had stopped crying.

'Is something the matter with the child?' said Yūgiri, coming up to her. He took a handful of rice and scattered it about the room.[19] What with all this commotion, the unpleasant memory of his recent dream was soon dispelled.

'He seems to be very uncomfortable,' said Kumoi. 'Ever since you've been so fascinated with that fine friend of yours,[20] you've been coming home from your excursions at all hours of the night, throwing open the [lattice-] windows and letting in those evil spirits (*rei no mono no ke no irikitaru*).'

Noticing the solemn frown on her sweet youthful face, Yūgiri could not help smiling. 'How stupid of me to have invited them in!' he said. 'Of course, if I hadn't opened the windows, they could never possibly have found their way indoors, could they? You've certainly acquired a lot of wisdom since you've had all these children!'[21]

One thing that makes the Heian approach to illness seem modern was the recognition that spiritual or mental factors could have a crucial effect on physical health. People were more liable to succumb to evil influences when their spiritual resistance was low; worry and pessimism tended to provoke the very ills one feared, since they provided an opening, as it were, for the *mono no ke* to assert themselves. When Lady Murasaki's final illness takes a turn for the worse and she tells Genji that she has no chance of recovery, he remonstrates with her indignantly:

19. Yūgiri scatters the rice to drive away evil spirits, much as we might spray a room with disinfectant.

20. Yūgiri is having an affair with Kashiwagi's widow, and his wife loses no opportunity to let him know that she is aware of the fact.

21. Ikeda ed., iv, 277–8.

No, no, you must not let yourself think like that. It is most inauspicious. Illness is not always such a serious thing as people imagine. It all depends on what we think. If our thoughts are wide and generous, things will probably go well for us. But if we think in a narrow, timid way we are bound to have ill luck. Often people who have gone far in the world have little time to enjoy their success because, instead of taking a calm, generous approach to life, they are forever worrying about one thing or another [and are soon struck down by illness]. The people who live long are usually those who face things in a tranquil, composed frame of mind.[22]

Familiar as all this may seem to the modern reader, the actual methods of cure were based squarely on primitive shamanistic superstition. As soon as the exorcist (*genza*) had detected a possible possession, he would recite spells and incantations (*kaji*) and attempt to transfer the evil spirit to a shamanistic medium (*yori-mashi*), who was usually a young woman. If this transfer was successful, the spirit would normally 'declare' itself, and finally the exorcist would drive it out of the medium. Contemporary literature contains many vivid accounts of this practice. Here are two such passages, one from the *Pillow Book* and the other from *The Tale of Genji*:

The house had a spacious courtyard and was shaded by tall pine trees. To the south and the east the lattice-windows were all open. It gave a cool feeling when one looked inside. In the main room was a four-foot screen of state and in front of it a round hassock on which a priest was now kneeling. Over his grey habit he wore a fine silk stole – altogether the effect was magnificent. Cooling himself with a clove-scented fan, he recited the Magic Formula of the Thousand Hands.

I gathered that someone in the house was seriously ill, for now a heavily built girl with a splendid head of hair edged her way into the room. Clearly this was the medium to whom the evil spirit was going to be transferred. She was wearing an unlined robe of stiff silk and long, light-coloured trousers.

When the girl had sat down next to the priest in front of a small three-foot screen, he turned round and handed her a thin, highly polished wand. Then with his eyes tightly shut he began to read the mystic incantations (*darani*), his voice coming out in staccato bursts as he uttered the sacred syllables. It was an impressive sight and many of the ladies of the house

22. Ibid., iv, 168.

came out from behind their screens and curtains and sat watching in a group.

After a short time the medium began to tremble and fell into a trance. It was awesome indeed to see how the priest's incantations were steadily taking effect. . . . Everyone who witnessed the scene was overcome with respect. It occurred to me how embarrassed the girl herself would feel [to be exposed like this in front of everyone] if she were in her normal state of mind. She lay there groaning and wailing in the most terrible way, and, though one realized that she was not in any actual pain,[23] one could not help sympathizing with her. Indeed, one of the patient's friends, feeling sorry for the girl, went up to her screen and helped to arrange her disordered clothing.

Meanwhile it was announced that the patient was a little better. Some young attendants were sent to the kitchen to fetch hot water and other requisites. Even while they were carrying their trays they kept on darting uneasy glances at the exorcist. They wore pretty unlined robes and formal skirts whose light mauve colour was as fresh as on the day they were dyed – it made a most charming effect.

By the hour of the Monkey[24] the priest had brought the spirit under control, and having forced it to beg for mercy, he now dismissed it. 'Oh!' exclaimed the medium [as she came to], 'I thought I was inside the screen, and here I am on the outside. What on earth has happened?' In an access of embarrassment she hid her face in her long hair and was about to glide out of the room when the priest stopped her for a moment, and after murmuring a few incantations, said, 'Well, my dear, how do you feel? You should be quite yourself by now.' He smiled at the girl, but this only added to her confusion. 'I should have liked to remain a bit longer,' said the priest, as he prepared to leave the house, 'but I am afraid that it is almost time [for my evening prayers].' The people of the house tried to stop him. 'Please wait a moment,' they said. 'We should like to make an offering.' But the priest was obviously in a great hurry and would not stay. At this point a lady of noble rank, evidently a member of the family, edged her way up to the blinds and said, 'We are most grateful for your visit, Your Reverence. Our patient looked as if she might well succumb [to the evil spirit] but now she is well on the way to recovery. I cannot tell you how delighted we are. If Your Reverence has any free time tomorrow, would you please call again?' 'I fear we are dealing with a very tenacious

23. The groans and wails come from the evil spirit, which has temporarily been transferred to her and is now being painfully subdued by the priest's incantations.
24. About 4 p.m.

spirit,' the priest replied briefly, ' and we must not be off our guard. I am pleased that what I did today has helped the patient.' So saying, he took his leave with an air of such dignity that everyone felt the Buddha himself had appeared on earth.[25]

Possessions and services of exorcism were highly dramatic events, and they inspired some of the most memorable descriptions in *The Tale of Genji*. In the following passage (of which I quote only a small part) Lady Murasaki's illness has reached a crisis. Although Genji does not know it, she has been possessed by the vindictive spirit of Lady Rokujō, which has already killed his wife and other women who have inspired its jealous fury.

The Prince summoned all the most distinguished exorcists to his palace. 'Though she be fated to leave this world at the end of her predetermined span, grant, we beseech Thee, a brief respite at this time. Keep her with us, we pray, if only for the period that Fudō vouchsafed us in his Vow.'[26] Such was the prayer that the exorcists now earnestly recited, and as they stood there by the altar the black candle-smoke seemed to be rising from their very heads. . . .

Then it was as if the Buddha had looked into Genji's heart and pitied him in his terrible grief. For the exorcists finally succeeded in transferring to a young girl [medium] the evil spirit that had refused to manifest itself during all the past months. As the spirit cried out its curses [through the mouth of the medium], Murasaki gradually regained consciousness. Watching the scene, Genji was overcome by mingled emotions of delight and horror.

After the spirit had been thoroughly subdued [by the charms and incantations of the exorcists], it spoke as follows: 'I have something to impart to the Prince alone. Let everyone else leave. . . . You have plagued me mercilessly during all these months with your prayers and spells and I had thought to repay your cruelty in kind. Yet, when I saw the mortal suffering to which you have been prey, I could not but feel pity. For even now when I have been reduced to this wretched condition I still retain the feelings that I had while I was still on earth. I could not close my eyes to your misery and so at last I have manifested myself,[27] though until now

25. Kaneko ed., pp. 1084–7.
26. In his Original Vow the fierce Shingon deity, Fudō, accorded a six-month period of grace to any believer whose life span had reached its end.
27. And thus given Murasaki a chance of recovery.

I never meant to let you know.' As the words issued from the medium's mouth, tears poured out of her eyes and her dishevelled hair fell in cascades over her face. Genji was certain that he had met this spirit before.[28]

It will be noticed that in both these accounts the exorcists were members of the Buddhist clergy. This was normal in the period and represents one of the many anomalies of Heian religious-superstitious practice. Shamanism and the idea of possession by evil spirits formed no part of Buddhist doctrine; and, if logic played any role, we should expect Shintoist priests to officiate on occasions of this kind. Such rational distinctions, however, were alien to the approach of Murasaki and her contemporaries. No more in their thinking than in the structure of their language did the idea of mutually exclusive categories prevail. Seeming incompatibilities of belief could be slurred over by neat syncretic formulae, and the most incongruous practices accepted as if they were an integral part of the faith in question. Not only did the various religious functions overlap, but the religions themselves blended imperceptibly with the vast network of superstitions. Thus it seemed quite natural that the emperors, the high priests of Shintō, should take Buddhist vows, that people should suffer from possessions owing to a bad karma, and that Buddhist priests should believe in nature gods, lucky stars, and goblins. In the West too we can find many cases of incongruity. Renaissance popes practised astrology, and until 1552 the Book of Common Prayer included a service of exorcism preceding the baptism of children.[29] The fact remains that, for better or for worse, the West was rarely prepared to accept the degree of overt syncretism and intellectual permissiveness that was normal in Japan during the Heian period and later.

28. Twenty-six years earlier Lady Rokujō's 'living ghost' had appeared in much the same way at his wife's deathbed. (Ikeda ed., iv, 182–3.)

29. Services for the exorcism of devils from haunted houses may be (and actually still are) carried out by the Church of England with the previous licence of a bishop (72nd Canon of the Church of England, 1603).

VI

The 'Good People' and their Lives

IF the informed Westerner was asked to enumerate the outstanding features of traditional Japan, his list might well consist of the following: in *culture* Nō and Kabuki drama, Haiku poems, Ukiyoe colour prints, samisen music, and various activities like the tea ceremony, flower arrangement, and the preparation of miniature landscapes that are related to Zen influence; in *society* the two-sworded samurai and the geisha; in *ideas* the Zen approach to human experience with its stress on an intuitive understanding of the truth and sudden enlightenment, the samurai ethic sometimes known as *Bushidō*, a great concern with the conflicting demands of duty and human affection, and an extremely permissive attitude to suicide, especially love suicides; in *domestic architecture* fitted straw matting (*tatami*), large communal baths, *tokonoma* alcoves for hanging *kakemono*; in *food* raw fish and soy sauce (*tempura* and *sukiyaki* being judiciously excluded as Western importations). The list would of course be entirely correct. Yet not a single one of these items existed in Murasaki's world, and many of them would have seemed as alien to her as they do to the modern Westerner.

The immense changes that occurred in Japan, especially during the Muromachi and Tokugawa periods, make it hard to reconstruct life in Heian Kyō; and the tidal waves of later Westernization impose a further barrier between us and the world inhabited by Murasaki. We do, however, have a compensating advantage. Vernacular literature, in particular *The Tale of Genji* and the *Pillow Book*, gives us a remarkably detailed picture of daily life in Japanese patrician society during the tenth and eleventh centuries. When it comes to this sort of information, we are probably better served about Japan than about any other country at the time; and in Japan itself it is not until we reach the seventeenth century that we find a body of realistic writing with a similar amount of detail. Of course, it is a one-sided picture, concentrated almost exclusively on the social and cultural aspects of life. From reading works like *The Tale of Genji*, *Gossamer Diary*, and the *Pillow Book* we should hardly guess that the men described were often leading figures in the government of the day and that they spent at least as much of their time in political intrigues as in those of an erotic nature. Still less should we imagine that many of them, especially members of the northern branch of the Fujiwara family, were hard-working officials, seriously devoted to their public duties. The old Minister of the Left in *The Tale of Genji* is one of the few characters in the romantic literature of the time who belongs to the category described by Sir George Sansom when he writes of 'grave and industrious officials, men who were diligent in performing their ceremonial duties, scribbling their memoranda, issuing their orders and despatches, men steeped in official routine'.[1]

One reason is that many of the writers of the vernacular works were women who could have little detailed knowledge of matters like politics from which most of them were excluded.[2] In his study of Sei Shōnagon Arthur Waley refers to the 'extraordinary vagueness of women concerning purely male activities'.[3]

Yet this is only part of the explanation. Writers like Murasaki would, it is true, tend to underplay the 'public' lives of their male characters. Yet from other sources we know that many of the men who attained positions of importance in the Heian administrative hierarchy were in fact singularly uninterested in their official responsibilities and preferred to pass their time in composing elegant poems in Chinese or supervising the punctilios of elaborate ceremonies rather than in carry-

1. George Sansom, *A History of Japan*, i, 144.
2. Some Heian women (especially Dowager Empresses like Higashi Sanjō no In and Jōtōmon In) wielded great political power (see p. 220). But they were exceptions. Most women of the time, including all the writers with whose work we are familiar, were uninvolved in politics, though many of them took a keen interest in palace intrigues, state marriages, and promotions.
3. Arthur Waley, *The Pillow-Book of Sei Shōnagon*, p. 128. But Beaujard considers that Waley is overstating the case: 'On pourrait, tout aussi bien, remarquer par ailleurs que Séi connaissait parfaitement les pétitions officielles et en déduire qu'elle n'était pas tellement ignorante pour tout ce qui regardait l'administration.' (A. Beaujard, *Séi Shōnagon': son temps et son oeuvre*, p. 356.) The fact remains that, for all her curiosity, Sei shows extremely little interest in what took place in the government offices, and none at all in the manors, from which her society derived its sustenance.

ing out the prosaic duties of public office. Still less were most of them prepared to administer their scattered manors in the provinces, which would mean spending precious days away from the capital, and worse still, dealing with dreary, boorish yokels. When Murasaki's gentlemen do venture into the countryside it is not to inspect their estates, or even to enjoy a day of hunting (the common male pastime in most aristocratic societies), but to compose poems on the autumn foliage or to keep a tryst at some mountain temple. Professor Oka emphasizes the debilitating effect on the Heian upper class of being almost totally divorced from the productive life of the country; and the separation of Heian Kyō from the rest of Japan undoubtedly helped to discourage the development of a vigorous, self-reliant approach among the metropolitan aristocrats.[4]

In most of the government departments themselves, overstaffing, cumbrous formalities, and the tendency to turn all business into ceremonial routine had advanced so far by Murasaki's time that even the most energetic official was sooner or later almost bound to succumb to frustration and boredom and to divert his energies to more trivial pursuits. This applied particularly to those who were not related to the dominant faction of the Fujiwaras and were therefore debarred from positions of real power.

Time after time the male characters in *The Tale of Genji* regret the hours that they are obliged to spend in their offices, separated from the activities that really interest them. None is more plangent on the theme than the shining prince himself. By the age of thirty he has reached the lofty post of Great Minister of the Centre. Far from welcoming the promotion, he bitterly begrudges the extra work his new duties involve. Visiting Murasaki's room one day, he discusses the Battle of the Seasons[5] that has recently been engaging the members of his household:

I can well understand the feelings of Lady Akikonomu when she tells us that she likes Autumn best. But, when all is said and done, I think that your own choice of the early morning in Spring is the most reasonable. Oh, if only I could spend more of my time with you here, wandering about the garden and comparing the beauties of the trees and plants in the different seasons! I really was not made for this endless round of official

4. Oka, op. cit., p. 22 ff.   5. See p. 37.

business. Sometimes I wonder if I shouldn't get away from it all and retire to a monastery. . . .[6]

*

The picture of the average Heian aristocrat that appears in literature and painting is likely to strike many Western readers as effeminate. The contemporary ideal of male beauty was a plump white face with a minute mouth, the narrowest of slits for eyes and a little tuft of beard on the point of the chin. This – apart from the beard – was the same as the ideal of feminine beauty, and often in Murasaki's novel we are told that a handsome gentleman like Kaoru is as beautiful as a woman. We know that Fujiwara no Korechika, the great Adonis of the day, had a perfectly round white face; here, as in many other respects, he was probably the model for the hero of *The Tale of Genji*.[7] Having read the scenes in which ladies almost swoon at the thought of Prince Genji's physical charms, most Westerners (and many modern Japanese) are bound to be surprised by his rather epicene appearance in the scrolls, where he is depicted with a pasty complexion, almost imperceptible eyes, and an exiguous tuft of beard. Yet there is every reason to believe that the scrolls are faithful to Murasaki's ideal of male beauty.

We also have a good picture of what a Heian gentleman should *not* look like. The dark, hirsute Prince Higekuro (who is significantly named after his 'black beard') is physically the antithesis of Genji and Kaoru, and when Tamakazura, later to become his wife, looks with aversion at his dark, hairy face, we can judge what Murasaki Shikibu thought about the more masculine-appearing type of man.[8]

The Heian gentleman powdered his face (the faces of badly powdered men remind Sei of dark earth over which the snow has melted in patches)[9] and used a generous amount of scent on his hair and clothes.

6. Ikeda ed., ii, 332. One is reminded of Prince Konoe's frequent statements at the time when he was Prime Minister that he wanted to 'retire from the world of politics and become a priest' (e.g. testimony of General Suzuki Teiichi at the war crimes trial). Konoe was a scion of the Heian aristocracy in more ways than one. See also Ikeda ed., ii, 314, for the passage in which Genji realizes with dismay that the death of his father-in-law, the Prime Minister, is going to force him to devote more of his time to public affairs, which in the past he had managed to delegate to the conscientious old minister.

7. See p. 295.　　　8. Ikeda ed., iii, 237.　　　9. Kaneko ed., p. 8.

The technique of mixing perfumes was highly developed. In an age when very few people bathed carefully[10] and clothing was elaborate and hard to clean, scent served a very useful purpose. It was, of course, no ready-made commodity, but the product of a complex and sophisticated art.[11] Genji himself was much admired for the skill with which he prepared his own incense, whose distinctive aroma always announced his approach and lingered after his departure. In the case of Prince Niou, who on the whole is pictured as one of the more masculine of the male characters, the preparation of scents was something of an obsession. Both he and his friend Kaoru owe their names to this art; and nothing more symbolizes the ideals of this period, and contrasts it with the subsequent age of military heroes, than the fact that two of Murasaki's most respected male characters should be named 'Lord Fragrance' and 'Prince Scent'.

This somewhat feminine impression of the Heian gentleman is confirmed by what we read of his behaviour. During his visits to the nearby village of Uji, Prince Niou, who is certainly not intended to appear more pusillanimous than average, is terrified of being attacked by highway robbers or by men from Kaoru's manor. Few Western readers will fail to be impressed by the unabashed way in which Murasaki's heroes display their softer emotions. Genji and his companions lived in an age when the virtues of male impassivity had not yet come to be valued. Tears, far from being a sign of weakness, showed that a man was sensitive to the beauty and pathos of life. It is true that lachrymose heroes often figure in the history of the military period too; but it is a different sort of situation that reduces these robust men to tears. The warrior will

10. We know very little about Japanese bathing habits during the Heian period, but it appears that very few people took proper baths; the great Japanese love of hot baths did not develop until far later in history. *Shōyū Ki* (Manju 4.11.13) has the following passage: 'The Chancellor [Michinaga] . . . invariably in the evening before the bath begins invocations to the Buddha . . .'; but it is not clear what the 'bath' actually meant. *Eiga Monogatari* (*Tama no Utena*) has an interesting passage about bathing in temples: 'When they looked at a certain place, they saw 22 or 23 priests heating water for the bath tubs and noisily pouring it in. . . . The peasants were uncomprehending of such things, but rejoiced at looking and listening.' The religious horror of bathing that prevailed in the West obviously had no counterpart in Heian Buddhism.

11. See pp. 203–5.

weep at the death of his lord and thus display the sincerity of his grief; but the Heian gentleman is reduced to tears at the prospect of parting from his mistress, at the sight of a magnificent sunrise, or at the thought of someone else's loneliness. In her diary Murasaki describes the great Fujiwara no Michinaga weeping with joy when he sees the emperor arriving at the Gosechi festival; and in her novel the spectators are moved to tears by the beauty of Genji's dance.[12] Love affairs are invariably attended by tears and the man is certainly not behindhand in this respect. After Prince Niou has spent his first night with Ukifune, he weeps at the thought of how hard it will be to arrange future meetings.[13] Here Murasaki is not, as the modern reader might suspect, implying some weakness in the young man's character, but simply reminding us of his exquisite sensibility.

In drawing a picture of the Heian gentleman from a book like *The Tale of Genji* we must of course make full allowance for the fact that it is a work of fiction in which many of the characters, especially the more important ones, are idealized. In her descriptions of Genji, Niou, and Kaoru the author was presenting the ideal man, rather than the flesh and blood creatures whom she met at court, those all too human men who drank to excess, spoke in loud voices, and knocked on her door at night.

For some women the solid, sturdy, impassive male, to whom the grunt or the laconic remark comes easier than the flood of tears, provides a more attractive image; but Murasaki clearly preferred the sensitive and emotional type who might nowadays be described as unmanly. Here, as in her ideas about male physical beauty, she appears to have shared the standards of her time – standards that are reflected not only in women's diaries but in male works of fiction like *The Tale of the Hollow Tree.*

We can be sure that there were many gentlemen in Heian Kyō who worked hard and efficiently in their offices (how else could the Fujiwara Councils have functioned as well as they did?), who were perfunctory in their use of scent and powder, who, like Tachibana no Norimitsu in the *Pillow Book*, did not give a fig for poetry or literary quotations,[14] and

12. See Ikeda ed., vii, 30, and p. 202 below.
13. See p. 198. 14. See p. 193.

who conducted their love affairs expeditiously, with a minimum of tears and elegances. And even among the aristocracy nature no doubt created far more men with Higekuro's attributes than with the smooth features of a Kaoru.

Yet, so long as we are aware of its limitations, Murasaki's picture of the Heian male is valid and historically significant. For it was a man like Prince Genji, with his gentle nature, his sensitivity and his wide range of artistic skills, who represented the ideal of the age and who set the tone for the social and cultural life of the good people.

★

Not much is said about food in the vernacular literature of the time and virtually nothing in the Chinese-style writings. It was regarded as a vulgar subject and, while we hear a good deal about drinking parties, meals are hardly ever described. Sei Shōnagon disliked men who ate heavily; a gentleman, she tells us, should pick daintily at his dishes. One of the most distressing things about the lower orders is the way in which they wolf down their food.[15]

As in China, rice was the staple diet, the polished variety being reserved mainly for the aristocracy. There were several rice dishes, some of which (like *mochi* rice cakes) are still current. Among the food that commonly accompanied the rice was seaweed and radishes. Fruits and nuts were eaten a great deal and also made into cakes; sugar, however, was not used. Ice was stored in special chambers, and in the hot months rich people enjoyed a sort of sherbet made of shaved ice and liana syrup. Fish was boiled, baked, or pickled, but, in the capital at least, it was not as a rule eaten raw until a later period; shell-fish like sea-ear (*awabi*) were especially popular. Meat was normally excluded because of Buddhist influence. Somewhat illogically, pheasant, quail, and other types of game were allowed; but, since there was little hunting, this was not an important part of the menu except in the very richest households. Among the common vegetables were egg-plants, carrots, onions, and garlic (the last having been introduced from Korea). In the reign of Emperor Ichijō a type of butter (*so*) was made of cow's milk, but it did not become popular and soon disappeared from the Japanese diet – so completely, indeed, that when the first Westerners

15. See p. 100.

arrived in the country their outstanding characteristic, apart from having red hair and bulging blue eyes, was that they were 'butter-stinking' (*bata-kusai*).

Heian cuisine was remarkably little influenced by China's. Then as now great stress was placed on presentation, the food always being served with an eye to visual effect. But the dishes themselves lacked the variety and sophistication that, possibly under the influence of Taoism,[16] had already made Chinese cooking among the finest in the world. The joys of the table did not rank high in Heian Kyō, and on the whole the food was poor in both culinary and nutritive value.[17]

Non-alcoholic drink was limited almost entirely to water. Milk had been drunk during the Nara period, but had now lapsed from use and was held in almost the same aversion as in China. Tea was introduced in the ninth century by the founder of the Tendai sect, and was planted on Mount Hiei. The first Japanese sovereign to taste it was Emperor Saga, who was offered a cup by a Buddhist priest in 815. This mark of royal approval did not, however, win success for the new beverage. In Murasaki's time laymen used it almost exclusively for medical purposes, and it did not become popular for more than two hundred years.

In the tenth (as in the twentieth) century the great Japanese drink was rice wine. Already seven hundred years earlier Chinese travellers commented that the Japanese 'are much given to strong drink'.[18] Heian literature provides ample evidence that the gentlemen of the time enjoyed wine and its effects. Drinking parties were extremely popular. Wine was poured for each guest in turn according to his rank; often people were expected to recite a poem or sing a song before raising the cup to their lips. There were several drinking games, in which the losers were obliged to drink the 'cup of defeat' (*basshu*), and these frequently turned into drunken carousals.

Most of the numerous types of *sake* drunk in Murasaki's time were weaker than the present-day varieties; yet (owing, among other things, to the absence of fats from the traditional Japanese diet) they were all highly intoxicating. In her diary Murasaki complains about Michinaga's

16. Ref. Reischauer and Fairbank, op cit., pp. 138–9.
17. For further details about Heian cuisine see Fujiki, op. cit., pp. 156–8.
18. G. B. Sansom, *A Short Cultural History of Japan*, p. 30.

drunkenness, from which she suffered on more than one occasion.[19] His elder brother, Michitaka, shared his taste for drink as we can tell from the following passage in the *Pillow Book*:

The gallery [of the Palace] was full of courtiers. His Excellency [Fujiwara no Michitaka] summoned servants from the Empress's Household and made them bring fruit and other dishes to be eaten with the wine. 'Now let everyone get drunk!' he said. And in fact everyone did get drunk. The ladies-in-waiting began to exchange remarks with the gentlemen and they all found each other extremely amusing.[20]

A common form of entertainment among the officials was a drinking party at which those who had recently been promoted were made to take as much *sake* as they could hold – and sometimes rather more. So bibulous did these affairs become that the custom was repeatedly prohibited. Like most interdictions of this type, however, it had little effect, and the 'promotion parties' went on unabated. The traditional Japanese tolerance towards drunkenness was already well established in the Heian period. Women were not excluded from the pleasures of the cup. Sef Shōnagon expresses her disapproval of women drinkers, but she herself had the reputation of being a tippler.

*

The 'good people' had their two main meals at about ten o'clock in the morning and four o'clock in the afternoon. In Murasaki's time the custom of taking snacks (a piece of dried octopus, for example, or a rice biscuit) had spread upwards from the working class to the aristocracy; also, the first meal was often served a couple of hours later than had been usual in the past, and the day started with a light breakfast.

There was nothing rigid, however, about Heian mealtimes or bedtimes. Time-keeping by the clepsydra was a complicated process. Apart from certain palace officials, few people were ever aware of the exact hour of the day, and on the whole people were free from the tyranny of the clock. The irregularity of hours gives a somewhat amorphous quality to their day. There appears to have been no idea of a normal time, or even of a normal range of hours, at which to go to bed. It is commonplace to read in *The Tale of Genji* that the sun is rising over the horizon

19. E.g. pp. 76–8.   20 Kaneko ed., p. 553.

while the characters are engaged in conversation; and the sight of the dawning light, far from speeding them to their beds for a few hours of belated sleep, is often the occasion for an impromptu concert in which the beauty of the new day is celebrated on the flute or zither.[21] Kaoru on one of his visits to Uji spends all night in desultory talk with Prince Hachi. Towards dawn, hoping to hear something about his host's talented daughter, he brings the conversation round to the subject of music. The indefatigable old prince then calls for his zither and a concert ensues, which in turn is followed by another long conversation. One can imagine how efficiently Kaoru would have carried out his official responsibilities that day if he had bothered to report for duty at the Headquarters of the Inner Palace Guards where he was stationed.

*

The leisured class had a rich variety of games and contests, which allowed people to display their skill, taste, and erudition, and which, particularly for the women, helped to pass the long inactive hours. *Go* (undoubtedly one of the finest games of any country or time) had been introduced from China in the Nara period, and was extremely popular in aristocratic circles. The Genji scrolls picture Kaoru having a game with the Emperor, in which the prize, an unwelcome one as it turns out, is the hand of the Emperor's daughter in marriage; we also see Tamakazura's two daughters enjoying a game of *go* beyond the rich white blossoms of the cherry tree that they have chosen as their stake. Although *go* was often played for bets, the real gambling game of the time was *sugoroku*, a type of backgammon which was periodically (and ineffectively) forbidden. *Sugoroku* was not considered as elegant as *go*, and it is significant that the keenest player in *The Tale of Genji* should be Tō no Chūjō's uncouth illegitimate daughter from the province of Ōmi. There was also a simple dice game called *chōbami*; among the Things that Give One a Pleasant Feeling, Sei Shōnagon includes 'winning a lucky throw of the dice'. Popular among the ladies was the game of *rango*, which involved balancing as many *go* stones as possible on a single finger; they also enjoyed a form of tiddly-winks known as *tagi*.

Several parlour games called for verbal ingenuity and a knowledge of the classics. *Nazo* consisted of a series of conundrums posed by two

21. See pp. 200–201.

opposing teams. In *infutagi* one of the players would cover a character in a Chinese poem, and the aim was to guess the hidden word from the context, the rhythm, and one's own poetic erudition. There was a similar game in which one part of the character was covered while the contestants tried to guess the remainder.

A large category of games was known as 'comparisons' (*awase*). At first they had been mainly 'comparisons of things' (*mono-awase*), such as flowers, roots, seashells, birds, and insects. The root-comparing contest (*ne-awase*), for example, was an ancient and rather formalized game played during the Iris Festival in the Fifth Month. The guests were divided into two teams, left and right. Iris roots were submitted in pairs by members of each team, together with appropriate poems, and carefully compared for beauty, length, and rarity. Specially appointed judges decided which team had produced the finest roots, and prizes were awarded to the winning side. Like most Heian social occasions, this was accompanied by a good deal of music, wine, and amorous dalliance.

The other 'comparisons of things' followed the same general pattern. Thus in the small-birds contest (*kotori-awase*) members of each team produced little song-birds that they had raised at home; they were compared, two by two, in terms of plumage, colour, and voice, and the side that had entered the greatest number of rare and beautiful birds received a prize. The court ladies in particular devoted a great deal of time to preparing their exhibits, and on the eve of one of the great contests the rival teams were in a frenzy of activity. For, as Sei writes in her chapter on Things that Make One Happy, 'If one wins in a contest (*mono-awase*) – no matter what kind it may be – how can one fail to be overjoyed?'[22]

In Murasaki's time 'comparisons' were increasingly devoted to the products of craft and art, like fans, incense, paintings, and poems. Poetry contests (*uta-awase*), which had started in court circles in the ninth century, became particularly popular during the tenth. These contests were no casual parlour-games but keenly fought battles in which a person's reputation as a poet, and accordingly as a man of culture, could be made or broken. The topics were posted several weeks in advance, and even before the announcement the contestants had usually prepared verses on likely subjects – all of which must have removed some of the

22. Kaneko ed., p. 944.

spontaneity from the proceedings. During the contest itself the entries from each of the two sides were recited in pairs by official readers and recorded for posterity; the judge's decisions, and sometimes the reasons for them, were also recorded. Contests of this type were unlikely to produce any very fresh or original verse. They did, however, help to keep poetry in the main stream of social life and had a considerable influence (not, on the whole, a favourable one) on the development of conventional modes of writing.

A somewhat less formal type of poetry contest was the *ensho-awase*, in which the contestants were divided into two teams, with men on one side and women on the other. Each player would recite a love poem to a member of the opposing team, who was then expected to produce a prompt reply using the same mood and imagery. As a rule, the sentiments were conventional and not intended to be taken seriously. The winners received the usual prizes of silk or other valuables, as well as the prestige afforded by poetic fluency.

*

The most popular outdoor pastime for Heian gentlemen was a form of football known as *kemari*. The players arranged themselves in a circle and kicked a leather ball among each other, the aim being to prevent it from touching the ground. The Scrolls of Yearly Observances show a group of noblemen playing *kemari* under a roof of cherry blossoms. They are dressed in elaborate court robes of blue and red silk, and their black lacquered bonnets perch precariously on the back of their heads; two of the gentlemen carry fans. There is a look of great concentration on their white, round faces, but their movements appear to be slow and graceful. *Kemari* tended to become an art rather than a casual game, and some practitioners attained a high degree of skill. The chronicles record that in 905 when a group of young noblemen played *kemari* in the presence of the emperor they passed the ball two hundred and sixty times without letting it touch the ground, which we can safely take to be an all-time record.

The literature of the period frequently describes archery contests. They were especially popular among members of the Guards, who as a rule used a four-foot bow and aimed at a target about one hundred feet away. Like many Heian games, archery came to be a form of gambling.

Horse-racing and a type of polo known as *dakyū* were also enjoyed by Guards officers. Standards of horsemanship, however, declined drastically during the age of court nobles, and at the end of the period we read of an important Fujiwara official trying unsuccessfully to mount his horse while a group of military men stand by jeering.[23] Hunting, as we have seen, was interdicted by the Buddhist church. The ban on taking life extended to falconry, but in this case it was often disregarded, perhaps because some of the emperors themselves enjoyed the sport.

Among spectator games was *sumō* wrestling, performed for the enjoyment of the aristocracy by mountainous fighters from the provinces. The nobility also enjoyed watching horse races and archery contests. The only cruel sport of the time was cock-fighting (*tori-awase*), a popular form of gambling among both nobility and commoners. In the Scrolls of Yearly Observances we see a cock fight in the garden of a patrician mansion. Two cocks are about to pounce on each other. Behind each of them squats a black-bonneted gentleman in elaborate court costume, who looks hardly bigger – and certainly far less fierce – than the bird he has entered in the competition. As usual in the *awase*, there are two teams, one of the left and one of the right; the members are gathered outside gaily coloured pavilions, eagerly waiting for the fight to start. A couple of ladies are seated on the veranda under a spray of cherry blossoms and some others are peeping from behind the blinds of the house. Attached by red strings to two dwarf trees, the next pair of cocks are impatiently waiting to tear each other to pieces.

Since women rarely ventured into the open, there were few outdoor pastimes for their benefit. We know, however, that they enjoyed watching the stately form of boat-racing known as *funakurabe*, and also that in the winter they took great delight in rolling snowballs (*yukikorogashi*) and piling snow in tubs or silver bowls. The *Pillow Book* has a long passage about the huge snow mountain that Empress Sadako's ladies built in the garden of her palace.

*

The Heian year was rich with ceremonies and festivals of every kind.

23. The incident occurred in 1159 and the unfortunate official was Fujiwara no Nobuyori, who among other posts held that of Captain of the Outer Palace Guards.

Indeed, if we were to enumerate all the regular and occasional observances in Murasaki's time, we should have a list no less impressive than that of the *feriae* in ancient Rome. As in Rome, many of these occasions were of religious or folk origin but had become accepted as part of secular, metropolitan life. The greatest differences from Rome were in the scale of the pageantry (even the most gilded Japanese ceremony never approached the grandeur of the affairs described by Suetonius) and in the fact that the celebrations in Heian Kyō concerned chiefly the aristocracy, whereas the Roman authorities arranged *panem et circenses* above all for the plebeians.

The role of these festivals in the lives of Genji and his circle can hardly be exaggerated. Without them daily life, especially for the women, would have been intolerably monotonous. Indeed, when we read a book like *Gossamer Diary*, we sometimes feel that, but for the Festival of the Weaver Star, the Shintō Moon Festival, and similar events with all the preparations they involved, things would have come to an almost complete standstill for the writer and her companions. These observances also satisfied the contemporary taste for colour, grandeur, and display. Many of them involved stately court dances of the *bugaku* type and came close to being artistic performances in their own right. The Yearly Observances were particularly important in the imperial government. For the emperor himself and for many of the High Court Nobles they were so absorbing that there would have been little time for any real political activity even if the ruling Fujiwaras had permitted it.

Among the many occasional ceremonies were those for the installation of a new imperial concubine, childbirth ceremonies, the observances carried out fifty days after the birth, the coming-of-age ceremonies for boys (*Gempuku*) and girls (*Mogi*), and funeral services. In Book 49 of *The Tale of Genji* the Emperor's second daughter (the one whom Kaoru rather reluctantly won as his wife in the game of *go* with the Emperor) proceeds to Kaoru's mansion in the Third Ward:

It was an outstanding ceremony. The Princess was escorted by all the ladies-in-waiting of the Emperor's household, each of whom had eight pages in attendance. She herself rode in a carriage with projecting eaves, behind which came three silken carriages, six gilded carriages, twenty palm-leaf carriages and two of split bamboo. Prince Kaoru sent an escort to meet the Princess. It consisted of several equipages carrying ladies of his own household, whose magnificently coloured sleeves hung elegantly outside the carriages. In addition the Princess was accompanied by a throng of High Court Nobles, Senior Courtiers and officials from the Palace. All in all, it could hardly have been more impressive.[24]

The regular Yearly Observances originated in many different ways. Some had been taken over directly from the Chinese Court, though by Murasaki's time they had mostly undergone considerable adaptation. Others, as we have seen, had their source in folk festivals or local celebrations, but had been absorbed into the court calendar; conversely, many observances that were originally carried out in the Imperial Palace spread to private households, and even came to be practised by commoners and provincials. Still others were religious festivals – Buddhist, Shintō, and Confucianist.

Since they cumulatively played such an important part in Heian life, it may be well to give some examples from the rich array of observances that were carried out in the tenth and eleventh centuries. Rather than divide them into categories (religious and secular, foreign and indigenous, folk and aristocratic), I shall list them in chronological order, which would have seemed more natural in Murasaki's time.

EXTRACTS FROM THE COURT CALENDAR[25]

The First Month

First Day: The Obeisance of the Four Directions.

At the Fourth Watch [about 4 a.m.] His Majesty the Emperor betakes himself to the Eastern Garden of his Residential Palace and, after in-

---

24. Ikeda ed., vi, 223.

25. The Japanese names are as follows (the numbers following the observances being the earliest known dates of their performance in the Japanese Court); as will be seen, few are of any impressive antiquity:

1st Month: Shihōhai (890), Kochōhai (c. 850), O-kusuri and Hagatame (c. 815), Jōi, Aouma no Sechie (c. 725), Wakana no Sekku (911), Nenohi no En (743), Mochigayu (c. 890), Tōka no Sechie (c. 800), Noriyumi (860).

2nd Month: Kinensai (very ancient), Sekiten (701), Kasuga Matsuri (? c. 900), Rekken.

toning the name of his guardian star, looks to the Great Ise Shrine and makes obeisance to the heavens and the earth in the four directions and to the Imperial Mausolea. He prays to the Gods and to his Ancestors for a prosperous reign and for the subjugation of evil spirits.[26]

First Day: The Lesser Obeisance.

After paying their respects at the mansion of the Fujiwara leader [Chancellor or Regent], the High Court Nobles and other gentlemen who are of a rank to be admitted to the Imperial Audience Chamber proceed to His Majesty's Residential Palace and make obeisance.[27]

First to Third Days: The Medicinal Offerings and the Tooth Hardening.

Various types of spiced wine are prepared by the Palace Medicinal Office and, after being tasted by specially appointed virgins, are offered to His Majesty as an elixir of long life. Radishes, mirror-shaped rice cakes, melons, and similar auspicious foods are presented to the Emperor in order to 'harden his teeth' [i.e. ensure his good health] during the coming year.

3rd Month: Jōmi (? 485), Gotō.
4th Month: Koromogae, Kambutsue (? 606), Kamo no Matsuri (667).
5th Month: Tango (611), Shinkō.
6th Month: Ōharai (very ancient).
7th Month: Tanabata Matsuri (734), Urabone (? 608), Sumō (c. 720).
8th Month: Iwashimizu Hōjōe (? 720), Chūshū Kangetsu (897).
9th Month: Fukandenden no Sō (854), Chōyō no En (? 686).
10th Month: Gencho (c. 890).
11th Month: Niiname no Matsuri (very ancient), Gosechi no Mai (743).
12th Month: On-Butsumyō (774), Tsuina (706).
For brief descriptions of the other main observances see Fujiki, op. cit., p. 167 ff., on which much of my material is based; also Beaujard, op cit., pp. 150–66.

26. As a regular palace ceremony Shihōhai dates from the 9th century, but it clearly belongs to far earlier traditions. In Murasaki's time it was being performed by members of the nobility in their own mansions.

27. Kochōhai had recently been substituted for a more elaborate T'ang-style ceremony known as Chōga.

Fifth Day: The Bestowal of Ranks.

Seated in His Majesty's Residential Palace, the Chancellor and the Great Ministers formally confer new ranks on the officials who have been promoted. The ceremony is followed by passing the wine cup.

Seventh Day: Ceremony of the Blue Horses.

Twenty-one white horses from the Imperial Stables are paraded before His Majesty in the great courtyard of the Ceremonial Palace. The inspection is followed by a banquet.[28]

Seventh Day: Festival of the Young Herbs.

Officials of the Imperial Storehouse proceed to the northern plain and pluck the seven lucky herbs. These are mixed with rice to make a gruel, a bowl of which is presented to His Majesty from the Imperial Table Office. Seven-herb gruel is also prepared in private households to ward off evil spirits and to ensure good health throughout the year.[29]

First Day of the Rat: The Feast of the Day of the Rat.

The Emperor and his subjects go into the countryside. Gazing in the four directions, they clear their spirits of evil thoughts; plucking young herbs and drawing pine branches along the ground, they ensure their longevity.[30]

28. Aouma no Sechie was imported from China in the Nara period. Originally the horses were steel grey (hence the name 'blue'), but, since these were very rare in Japan, and since white was regarded as the purest colour, it became customary to parade white horses, even though the name 'blue' was retained. According to *yin-yang* theory, horses are connected with the male (*yang*) principle, and to view the procession on this day was believed to ensure one's health during the coming year. *Aoi* (blue-green) was the auspicious New Year colour. The ceremony was also performed by individual members of the aristocracy.

29. Wakana no Sekku derived from Han China and had become one of the Seven National Festivals as stipulated in the Japanese code of 718.

30. Nenohi no En was an old Japanese folk custom that became influenced by *yin-yang* ideas and was later included among the court celebrations. Originally the emperor simply observed the day by a banquet (hence the name), but after the 9th century he and his court actually went into the countryside for the day. It became a popular form of picnic outing and was later amalgamated with the

Fifteenth Day: The Full-Moon Gruel.

A special gruel is presented to His Majesty from the Imperial Water Office. The same type of gruel is eaten in private households on this day. It is stirred with sticks of peeled elder-wood, and women who wish to conceive male children are struck on the loins with these sticks.[31]

Sixteenth Day: Ceremony of the Poetry Dances.

Poems and songs in honour of the New Year are recited in the Palace gardens to the accompaniment of dancing by a group of forty ladies-in-waiting.[32]

Eighteenth Day: Bowmen's Wager.

The New Year's celebrations are concluded by an archery contest which is held in His Majesty's presence between officers of the Inner and Middle Palace Guards. This is followed by a banquet during which Court dances are performed and prizes awarded to the winning side. Members of the losing side are forced to drink the cup of defeat.

Festival of the Young Herbs. It will be noted that Nenohi no En and many of the other observances were dated in terms of the sexagenary cycle, rather than being fixed on specific days of the month. Each of the 12 horary characters (rat, ox, etc.) gives its name to 3 different days in any single month, so that we get 1st, 2nd, and 3rd Days of the Rat, of the Ox, etc.

31. The preparation of a special gruel on the day of the first full moon (always the 15th in the lunar calendar) was one of the old folk customs that had been incorporated into the court observances. It is significant that the 15th day of the 1st Month was dedicated to Shintō deities representing the male element. Section 3 of the *Pillow Book* describes the women of a certain household chasing each other from room to room and playfully whacking each other with the elder-sticks. The custom, which persisted in certain country districts until fairly recently, probably has phallic origins.

32. In the 7th century Tōka no Sechie was performed by Chinese residents of Japan in conformity with a T'ang custom, but later it became naturalized and was amalgamated with an old folk festival known as *utagaki*. *Tōka* means 'beating time to a song or poem', but the dances were far more elaborate than this would suggest.

The Second Month

Fourth Day: Festival of the Spring Prayer.

One hundred high officials from the Department of Shintō proceed to Kamo Shrine and in the presence of the Great Vestal carry out rituals and recite prayers for good crops. Similar ceremonies are carried out in other shrines in the capital and also in the provinces.[33]

First Day of the Younger Brother of the Fire: Confucian Anniversary Service.

Ceremonies are carried out in the Imperial University in honour of Confucius and his ten disciples. After one of the Princes has made obeisance to Confucius, Imperial Advisers and other high officials join students in the main University building, where they listen to lectures and formal discussions on the [Confucian] classics. This is followed by a banquet during which Chinese poems are recited by Doctors of Literature.[34]

First Day of the Monkey: Kasuga Festival.

At the Fujiwara clan shrine in Nara [Shintō] ceremonies are carried out in the presence of members of the Fujiwara clan and representatives of the Emperor and his family. An Imperial Messenger makes offering to the Gods on behalf of His Majesty.

Eleventh Day: The Examination.

Officials who are to be promoted from the Sixth Rank wear garlands of flowers and are escorted to the Great Council of State, where they are formally examined by the Ministers and their names inscribed on the Roll of Selections. This is followed by a three-by-three exchange of wine cups.

33. Kinensai derives from the old folk custom of holding ceremonies in the 2nd Month to welcome the Rice God down to the fields and in the 11th Month to bid him farewell on his return to the hills. It had become an important part of official observances by the beginning of the 8th century. Shintō was central to most of the celebrations concerned with the agricultural cycle.

34. Sekiten, which was biannual (2nd and 8th Months), was taken over from a similar T'ang observance.

The Third Month

Third Day: Festival of the Snake.

Wine cups are floated down the streams in the gardens of the Imperial Palace and of private households. As the cup passes each guest, he lifts it, drinks, and recites a poem. In households having girl children, elaborately decorated dolls are displayed on shelves.[35]

Third Day: The Holy Light.

To protect the country and avert calamities, His Majesty dedicates a light to the Deity of the North Star. At night tapers are lit in honour of the Great Bear and a feast is held during which young men and women dance and disport themselves.[36]

The Fourth Month

First Day: Change of Dress.

The curtains and other hangings in the Palace and private residences are changed to a lighter material. Summer clothes are worn for the first time.[37]

Eighth Day: The Washing of the Buddha.

In commemoration of the Buddha's birth, a gilt statue of the Buddha and a representation of the scene of his birth are offered to His Majesty.

35. Jōmi (the name of this observance) refers to the 1st Day of the Snake, which was the original date when it was carried out. The custom of Winding Water banquets (see p. 45) was introduced from China. It was originally a purification ceremony, but by Murasaki's time it had lost most of its religious connotation. We know from *The Tale of Genji* (*Suma*) that it was also customary on this day to throw dolls into the water; this too was a form of purification. The display of dolls on this day developed during the Muromachi period into the Doll Festival.

36. Gotō derived from *yin-yang* beliefs about the protective influences of different stars. The dances became a sort of orgy and were later abolished, after which only the lighting of the tapers remained.

37. A similar change to winter materials took place on the 1st day of the 10th Month.

In the Palace, priests pay their respects to the statue; then, while intoning words of praise, they pour coloured water on the statue's head. The Court Nobles also pour water over the statue, make obeisance, and withdraw in a leftward turn. Similar ceremonies are carried out in the temples and private residences.[38]

Second Day of the Bird: Kamo Festival.

Shrines, Palace buildings, private houses, and carriages are decorated with hollyhock; the participants wear garlands of hollyhock and adorn their clothes with it. In the morning ancient dances take place in the Palace. At noon a great procession of Guards, serving as Imperial Envoys, makes its way through the crowds of people and rows of carriages to the Lower Kamo Shrine. The Envoys offer His Majesty's gifts to the Gods, and [Shintō] ceremonies of purification and thanksgiving are performed. The procession then escorts the Great Vestal along the banks of the Kamo River, where on the previous day she has participated i n a Ceremony of Lustration. Reaching the Upper Kamo Shrine, the celebrants carry out further rituals in her presence, including a number of sacred dances. The Great Vestal's return on the following day is attended by similar observances and also by a great banquet in her Palace.[39]

The Fifth Month

Fifth Day: Iris Festival.

Iris is hung on the Palace buildings and private houses to protect the inhabitants from illness, and the roofs are covered with iris leaves and branches of mugwort. The gentlemen of the Court put iris on their head-dress and the ladies wear it in their hair; it is attached to swords and palanquins, and also made into pillows. His Majesty, wearing a gar-

38. The movements performed by the noblemen are, in fact, a highly stylized form of dance. Various schools grew up, each with its own theory about the correct steps.

39. This was the most impressive ceremony of the year and was often known simply as 'the Festival'. According to tradition, it was the god of the Upper Kamo Shrine who originally prescribed the use of hollyhock, and the occasion is also referred to as the Hollyhock Festival (Aoi no Matsuri).

land of iris, graciously offers his high officials wine in which iris leaves have been steeped. Horse races and archery contests are held in the Palace and elsewhere. The officers of the Guards, who have been responsible for providing supplies of iris and mugwort, bring the Festival to a close by twanging their bowstrings to drive away the evil spirits.[40]

Tenth to Thirtieth Days: The Imperial Alms.

Bounty of rice and salt is distributed by the Imperial Police to poor people in different parts of the capital.[41]

The Sixth Month

Last Day: The Great Purification.

An assembly of Imperial Princes and officials, who have attained ritual purity by fasting and continence, gather by the main gate of the Imperial Palace and perform a [Shintō] service to purge all His Majesty's subjects of their impurity and sin.[42]

The Seventh Month

Seventh Day: Festival of the Weaver Star.

Leaves are spread in the garden of the Emperor's Residential Palace and, when it is dark, His Majesty and his Court seat themselves there to

40. Tango (lit. 'First of the Five [Festivals]') appears to have originated in an ancient Chinese festival that was designed to ward off evil spirits. The 5th of the 5th Month was one of the *dies nefasti* (analogous in some ways to the Ides of March), for it was on this day that the great poet-aristocrat Ch'ü Yüan drowned himself. In Japan it was believed that the scent of iris and mugwort provided protection against the evil spirits which were rampant in the 5th Month, particularly on the 5th Day. Archery contests and horse racing were also believed to have prophylactic virtues.

41. Shinkō was probably of Buddhist origin and is comparable to maundy in England.

42. Ōharai services were also carried out on the last day of the 12th Month and in cases of special need, such as epidemics. They included rituals (*norito*) of great antiquity. In addition a life-size figure (*mi-agamono*) of the emperor was washed in a river, so that all imperial impurities might be removed.

watch the meeting of the Weaver and the Herdsman [the stars Vega and Altair]. Poems are dedicated to the two stars, music is played all night, and the Magpie Dance is performed. Similar observances take place in private households, and women pray to the Weaver for help in weaving, sewing, music, and poetry.[43]

Fifteenth Day: Festival of the Dead.

Offerings of food are sent from the Imperial Palace to the temples for the benefit of the spirits of the dead, who return to earth on this day. In the Palace and private households stems of hemp are burnt to light the spirits on their way, and [Buddhist] masses for the dead are recited throughout the day and night.

Twenty-Eighth or Twenty-Ninth Day: Wrestling.

Wrestlers from the provinces are divided into two teams and perform seventeen bouts of *sumō* in the presence of Imperial Princes and gentlemen of the Court, who are offered wine and refreshments during the performance. Afterwards members of the winning team sing special songs and perform Court dances.[44]

43. Tanabata Matsuri is derived from the Chinese legend about the love of the Weaver (Chih-nü) (represented by the star Vega) and the Herdsman (Ch'ien-niu) (represented by the star Altair). Because of her love for the Herdsman, the Weaver neglected her work on the clothes for the gods, while the Herdsman neglected his cattle. As a punishment the Emperor of Heaven put the two stars on opposite sides of the Milky Way, decreeing that they should be allowed to meet only once a year, namely, on the 7th of the 7th Month, when a company of heavenly magpies forms a bridge that the Weaver can cross to join her lover. The magpies will not make their bridge, however, unless it is a clear night; if it rains, the lovers must wait for another year. The festival was adapted by the Japanese Court from the Chi Ch'iao T'ien celebrations in China, and became immensely popular throughout most of the country, possibly because of its romantic connotations.

44. The wrestlers were selected by special envoys from the Inner Palace Guards who travelled about the provinces looking for sturdy fighters. On the day after the fights some of the more energetic young gentlemen of the Court received training in *sumō*.

The Eighth Month

Fifteenth Day: The Liberation.

Court Nobles, Imperial Advisers, Controllers, and Officers of the Guards proceed to the Hachiman Shrine of Iwashimizu with birds, tortoises, fish, and other animals that are to be liberated. The numbers of the animals are announced and, after a reading of the Supreme Sovereign Sutra, they are let loose in their respective elements. This is followed by a performance of *bugaku* dance and some bouts of *sumō* wrestling.[45]

Fifteenth Day: The Great Moon-Viewing.

To the sound of lute and zither music, men and women spend the night in boats on the artificial lakes of the Palace and of private residences, viewing the full moon and composing poems in its honour.[46]

The Ninth Month

Seventh Day: The Submission of Reports on Unfit Land.

The Great Ministers and their assistants assemble in the Palace and humbly present His Majesty with reports from the Provincial Governors about crop failures and land that has fallen out of cultivation because of natural disasters or other causes.[47]

45. The Iwashimizu Shrine is about 8 miles south of the capital. It might seem strange that what is obviously a Buddhist ceremony should take place in a Shintō shrine (especially in one dedicated to the god of war) rather than in a temple; but such was the nature of Heian eclecticism. The origin is traditionally ascribed to the god of the Hachiman Shrine at Usa, who ordered the annual liberation of animals as a retribution for the large number of Hayato aborigines who had been killed by the imperial forces.

46. Chūshū Kangetsu came originally from China. At first it was celebrated only among the aristocracy, but later it spread among the people and it became customary to make offerings of dumplings and potatoes to the moon. The full moon of the 8th Month is traditionally regarded as the most beautiful of the year (see p. 272).

47. The aim of these reports was to secure a remission of tax. Normally a two-thirds remission was allowed on land that had gone out of cultivation, but in

Ninth Day: Chrysanthemum Festival.

The Emperor and his Court inspect the chrysanthemums in the Palace gardens. Afterwards there is a banquet. Poems are composed and the guests drink wine in which chrysanthemums have been steeped.[48] After a performance of dances, Palace Girls present small white trouts to His Majesty, and later the guests are also served dishes of white trout.

The Tenth Month

First Day of the Boar: The Boar.

The day is observed as a holiday and is marked by eating seven special kinds of cakes to ward off illness and other misfortunes. The Senior Courtiers and Ladies each receive a chip-box of glutinous rice as His Majesty's bounty.

The Eleventh Month

Second Day of the Hare: Festival of the First Fruits.

His Majesty offers newly harvested rice to the [Shintō] Gods of Heaven and Earth and then partakes of new rice himself. Thanksgiving rituals and dances are performed and ancient prayers recited.

Second Day of the Dragon: The Gosechi Dances.

In the morning His Majesty attends a [Shintō] service celebrating the newly harvested rice. This is followed by a banquet in honour of the

---

suspicious cases inspectors were sent to examine the situation. The report to the Emperor, though purely ceremonial, was carried out meticulously during the entire period. As Sansom points out, '. . . the participants in the ceremony were but little interested in the substance of the reports, in such points as the area, the position and nature of the rice lands in question. What mattered was the form in which the reports were drawn up, the exact language used in presenting them, the correct placing of signatures and seals, and even the deportment of the officials.' Sansom, *A History of Japan*, i, 167.

48. Chrysanthemums were supposed to promote longevity (see p. 142). It was believed that, if people rubbed their faces with the pieces of silk floss that covered the chrysanthemums on the eve of the festival, they would be spared the ravages of age.

harvest. In the evening the Emperor and his Court attend the annual Gosechi Dances, which are performed by four young girls, three being the daughters of High Court Nobles and one the daughter of a Provincial Governor. Dances are also performed by young gentlemen who have undergone special lustration.

The Twelfth Month

Nineteenth to Twenty-First Days: The General Confession.

A statue of the Goddess of Mercy is moved into the Imperial Dais of His Majesty's Residential Palace, and painted screens depicting the Horrors of Hell are set up under the eaves as a reminder of the need for penitence. In the Palaces and private residences services are held by different priests during each of the three successive nights to expunge the sins committed during the course of the year.

Last Day: The Devil Chase.

On the last night of the year officials from the Ministry of Central Affairs join the Masters of Yin-Yang in a Service of Expulsion, during which special spells are recited. A Devil Chaser, who is selected from among the Imperial Attendants, dons a golden mask and a red skirt. Accompanied by twenty assistants, he makes his way through the Palace buildings and courtyards, twanging his bowstring, shooting arrows into the air, and striking his shield with a spear in order to expel all devils and evil spirits before the beginning of the New Year's celebrations. Similar precautions are taken in private households.[49]

*

The prevailing tone of family life was extremely formal. This was not only in the Imperial Palace, where one would expect ceremonial and punctilio to prevail, but in private households as described by writers of

49. By typical transmutation the devil chaser (*hōsōshi*) himself came to represent the devil. In the 11th century it was customary for gentlemen of the court to shoot arrows at him and his assistants. The *Gōke Shidai*, which mentions this development, does not tell us whether the unfortunate devil-substitutes were ever actually hit.

the time. Important as the family unit was in Heian society, it appears to have provided few of the convivial pleasures. There was nothing corresponding to the cheerful board at which different generations of the family, sometimes joined by friends and acquaintances, can come together to share the joys of food, drink, and conversation.[50] The members of Prince Genji's household in the Sixth Ward, for example, live in almost total isolation from each other. Except on special occasions when they meet for a festival or to take part in some formal activity like an incense competition, they can normally communicate only by exchanges of notes and poems or by messages that Genji himself relays on his tours through the apartments.

Yūgiri has never once met his young stepmother, Lady Murasaki, though they have been living in different wings of the same house for at least ten years. When he finally does catch a glimpse of her it is only because of the confusion prevailing in the house during the great autumn storm. Struck by his stepmother's unexpected beauty, he promptly falls in love – a complication that would doubtless have been avoided if he had been seeing her regularly over the years.

Later in the novel we find that Kōbai has never had a single opportunity to meet his stepdaughter though they too have lived in the same house since she was a small girl:

Kōbai was consumed with curiosity. 'If only I could see what she looks like!' he thought. 'It is really too sad that she should always be hidden.'

On one occasion, when no one was about, he made his way stealthily to the girl's room, hoping to catch a glimpse of her; but, when he peeped through her screen of state, he could not see even the dimmest outline of her figure.

'I thought that in your mother's absence I ought to come and keep you company,' he told her. 'It really makes me very unhappy that you should be so distant with me.'

Since they were separated by thick hangings, Kōbai could barely make

---

50. Among the advice that Fujiwara no Morosuke (d. 960) left to his descendants we find this rather chilling precept: 'Unless it is on public business, or for some unavoidable private affair, do not frequent the houses of others. Social intercourse unless on a strictly formal footing is to be regarded as dangerous, leading to jealousy, quarrels, and slander. You must keep yourself to yourself and so preserve your dignity.' Quoted by Sansom, op. cit., p. 182.

out her answer, but from the elegance and charm of her voice he imagined how attractive she must be and he was deeply moved.[51]

Similar situations occur throughout the novel. Prince Niou, for instance, has never been allowed to converse with his own sister, the Princess of the First Order, except through curtains or from behind a screen; he desperately wishes that he could have a proper look at the girl – and indeed the forced separation makes him regard her with something more than brotherly interest. Eavesdropping and peeping, which were so prevalent during the Heian period, resulted partly from this rigid convention.

Any unfamiliar society presents us with seeming contradictions. The modern reader is bound to find many incongruities in the world of the shining prince, but perhaps none is more striking than the contrast between this formality, which can prevent a brother from ever seeing his sister or a father his stepdaughter, and the remarkable informality that makes it normal for Prince Niou to go to bed with Naka no Kimi on their very first meeting and for Kashiwagi to do the same with Princess Nyosan before they have spoken a word to each other.

Another aspect of upper-class Heian life that must impress any modern reader is its circumscribed, stifling nature. It is to a large extent an indoor life. This applies especially to women, who rarely venture outside the penumbra of their screens and curtains. But the men too, as we have seen, tend to spend as much of their time as possible inside the palaces and houses of the city. Except in those appalling extremities when they are dispatched to the provinces on official business, they eschew travel by land or sea, and their outdoor activities are largely confined to garden entertainments and visits to nearby temples.

Their range of interests is correspondingly limited. Genji and his friends care nothing for the real world outside Japan. Despite their respect for Chinese culture, actual conditions on the continent do not concern them in the slightest, and the lands beyond China may as well have sunk into the ocean for all they would care. This indifference extends to their own country, which, apart from the small area occupied by the Home Provinces, is equally part of the 'outside' world. Their social insularity is even more uncompromising: they are almost totally uninterested in people of other classes, whom they regard without question as being beyond the pale of humanity. In addition they are largely unconcerned with abstract problems or serious intellectual exchanges, and their adherence to Buddhism rarely involves them in metaphysical speculation about questions like the nature of human existence or the origin of evil. The past they regarded as fusty (*furumekitaru*, 'oldish', antique, is invariably a pejorative), and the future concerns them hardly at all except when it directly affects their own interests. Almost entirely, their energy is devoted to the enjoyment of the present – to the enjoyment, that is, of the day-to-day social and cultural pleasures – and, in the case of men, to securing the rank and office that make these pleasures available.

*

In a small, closed society, concentrated almost exclusively on its own activities, conversation is bound to become parochial and many of the interests trivial. The *Pillow Book* pictures a world in which everyone is concerned with everyone else's business – especially if it is of an amatory nature. When Sei receives a gentleman visitor who is carrying an umbrella, all the ladies know about it, and on the following morning the empress sends her a note with a large drawing of an umbrella. The conversation and letters of the aristocracy are larded with teasing innuendoes, artful references to past incidents, and cunningly devised nicknames, which would be meaningless to anyone outside their circle, but which evoke an immediate response among the 'courtly herd'. As a rule it is an innocent sort of fun; but sometimes the humour is edged with malice, and a woman will be nicknamed because of some embarrassing solecism she has committed or a man obliquely ridiculed in a song because of his mother's humble birth.[52]

Absence of real privacy and immense leisure encouraged gossip, especially among the ladies. A good deal of it was unkind. *The Tale of Genji* opens with an account of how the emperor's favourite concubine is hounded to death by the malicious gossip of her rivals; and her successor, Lady Fujitsubo, suffers equally from rumours and backbiting. Since women of high birth had few occasions to meet each other except

52 See pp. 60–61.

on public and ceremonial occasions, much of the tittle-tattle was purveyed by the old ladies-in-waiting who always hover in the background, taking an obsessive interest in the doings of their betters.[53] Princess Nyosan is driven to distraction by the endless gossiping of her nurses and finally escapes to a nunnery.

53. See p. 50.

VII

The Cult of Beauty

IF the lives of the good people had been limited to what we saw in the previous chapter, we should be left with an impression of a small, narrow, and, on the whole, rather dull society (not unlike that of many a minor European court in the nineteenth century), in which an annual round of colourful ceremonies could hardly obscure the essential triviality and monotony of daily existence. What makes the world of the shining prince an engaging and important study is the central role of style and art in the lives of its inhabitants.

Thanks to efficient borrowing and imaginative adaptation Heian Kyō had by Murasaki's time reached a high cultural standard – fantastically high, in fact, when we recall that only some four centuries earlier the entire country had been in an abysmally primitive state, its people almost totally illiterate except for a handful of officials and priests, its organization still largely tribal and its 'capital' a temporary grouping of rude dwellings, centred on the palace, which itself was merely a frail wooden structure roofed with thatch.

The high culture of Heian was admittedly the preserve of a very small number of people. In this respect tenth-century Japan is hardly exceptional among aristocratic societies. What makes Murasaki's world so unusual is the way in which refined standards of cultural appreciation and performance had become generally accepted values among members of the ruling class. Artistic insensitivity damned a gentleman of the Heian court as fatally as did a reputation for cowardice among the nobility of the West. Genji and his friends are all critics, and one of their great pleasures when they meet is to engage in 'judgements' (*sadame*). Sometimes (as when the group of young men meet in the palace on a rainy night) they will exchange critical observations about different types of women; but far more often the objects of their discussions are paintings, books, styles of musical performance. The women are not behindhand in this, and the *Pillow Book* describes the ladies of Empress Sadako's court engaged in heated 'judgements' about books or picture scrolls.

They were fastidious about their surroundings. Though few buildings have survived from the capital city of Murasaki's day, we do have a great many examples of decorative art that they used in their daily lives. From these we know that the Heian aristocracy set a high standard in their choice of decorations and furnishings. The art of embellishing wood was highly developed. There were magnificent gold lacquered boxes for sutra scrolls, and gentlemen like Kaoru would keep their paintings in boxes of sandalwood delicately inlaid with mother-of-pearl. As a rule the most impressive things in the sparsely furnished rooms were the painted screens; but other objects, like mirrors, writing-brushes, ink-stands, musical instruments, and *go* sets, were often works of art in their own right. We also have some beautifully inlaid quivers, decorated with flowers and heraldic paroquets, which were used by the Guards officers during the formal archery contests. Patrician carriages and boats were designed at least as much for aesthetic appeal as for locomotion. The manufacture and dyeing of textiles had reached a high point of achievement, as we can judge from the minute descriptions of dress and colour combinations.

Little of this art would have been likely to impress the cultured traveller from China (the country where most of it originated), though the Japanese technique of manufacturing 'five-coloured' paper did, as we have seen, evoke a few words of approval. What would above all have interested our imaginary Chinese visitor would have been the level of learning and education. A visit to the Imperial University in the Third Ward would have reassured him that Confucian studies were still paramount. The Chinese classics occupied much the same role in Heian education as did Greek literature in ancient Rome, or, until quite recently, Latin literature in England. Libraries of Chinese works were available in Heian Kyō (a late ninth-century catalogue lists over one thousand five hundred titles), and in Murasaki's time the aspiring scholar was favoured with good resources, in addition to a well-established tradition of Chinese scholarship in Japan.

The tenth century, however, had seen a remarkable drop in the prestige of official education and a corresponding decline in scholarly standards.

These trends would hardly have been obvious to the casual visitor, but our evidence is unmistakable. Already in the early part of the century we find a distinguished Confucian scholar complaining in a Memorial to the Throne about the state of education:

The University has come to be looked upon as a place of disappointment, the birthplace of hunger and poverty. Parents do not any longer want their sons to enroll, the quadrangles are overrun with wild grass, the lecture halls are silent. The professors do not trouble to read the papers of candidates, but make recommendations merely by glancing at a list of candidates.[1]

The Memorial did nothing to improve the situation and, as the Heian period continued, Chinese studies at the University became increasingly jejune, depending largely on rote learning and adherence to academic precedent.

This decline in the status of university studies was one of the most significant ways in which the Japan of Murasaki's time had diverged from the Chinese model. A survey of what education and scholarship had come to mean in the lives of the 'good people' will serve as an introduction to a more detailed study of their cult of beauty, and may also throw some light on future developments in the country.

One reason for the downward trend in the prestige of learning was political: when almost all the desirable posts in the land are reserved for members of a single branch of a particular family and are apportioned regardless of individual ability, much of the incentive for scholarly achievement is bound to disappear. The survival of clannish and aristocratic traditions in Heian Japan had a harmful effect, not only on administration, but indirectly in the field of education. While many a capable

---

1. Paraphrased by Sansom, op. cit., p. 148. The examinations had not always been a formality. We have an interesting collection of ten Chinese poems written by Sugawara no Michizane in 882, one addressed to each of the students graduating from the Imperial University. In a poem to a student from the scholarly Wake family Michizane refers to the fact that he has failed thirteen times before finally passing – 'So pray let me see your melancholy face relax its frown this day.' Another student (a Tachibana) has taken some twenty years to pass:

> 'Not till the age of forty-one
> Have you been free to leave these halls.
> [But do not grieve –]
> For great brains ripen late.' *Nihon Shiki*, xvii, 150.

scholar languished in the provinces, well-born duffers occupied coveted posts in the Ministries.

A second factor was the increasing specialization in certain subjects by particular families. The Abe family, for example, concentrated on *yin-yang* studies, the Sugawaras on Chinese history; and later the study of *The Tale of Genji* itself became a family preserve.[2] In order to maintain their traditions many prominent families set up private academies for the training of their sons, and these *shigaku* came to supersede the public institutions for much of the aristocracy. This was part of a general trend according to which private institutions (the Administrative Councils and the manors, for instance) were increasingly replacing national activities. Because of their strict specialization and the very restricted nature of their student body, education in the *shigaku* was even less spontaneous and creative than that provided by the government.

There were several other reasons for the decline of scholarship in Murasaki's time. The relative lack of stimulus from the Continent since the lapse of official relations with China one hundred years earlier was undoubtedly a factor. Perhaps the fundamental cause was the almost exclusive concentration on a foreign language and on foreign patterns of experience, which were static and, for many a young Heian student, dead. Like the pupil of the *grammaticus* and the *rhetor* in ancient Rome, the aristocratic Japanese youth, who struggled to memorize passages about the ancient history of a foreign country written in a language he had never heard (and never would hear) spoken, and who received virtually no other form of instruction, was 'the slave of an artificial literature and the prisoner of a narrow classicism'.[3] In the long run the results were bound to be stultifying.

Considering the lowered prestige of education in Murasaki's time, it is significant that Prince Genji should have been a keen advocate of its benefits. This no doubt is one of the many cases in which Murasaki puts her own views in the mouth of her hero. For she, as we know, came from a family of scholars and was herself uncommonly interested in Chinese literature as well as in the culture of her own country. She makes it clear that Genji's views on education are not those generally held by members of his circle. In the following passage he explains why he is so insistent on giving his son, Yūgiri, a systematic education, rather than simply

2. See pp. 286–7. 3. Carcopino, op. cit., p. 116.

promoting him in rank and offering him an official sinecure, which would have been normal in well-born families. He is speaking to his mother-in-law, who is extremely disgruntled at the thought that her grandson should still be in the humble Sixth Rank even though he has reached the age of twelve:

'I intend that he should study at the University for a few years. . . . I myself was brought up entirely in the Nine-Fold Enclosure and knew nothing about the world outside. Since I was always with my father the Emperor, I did manage to pick up some scraps of knowledge about the Chinese classics. But this was only what I could learn directly from my father, and I did not acquire a really solid learning. As a result I was deficient in both literature and music.

'Now, if I bring this boy up in the same way, what will happen? It is rare indeed for children to be more intelligent than their parents, and I am afraid that, if I simply pass on to him the knowledge I received from my father, and he in turn does the same with his boys, they will be so far removed from the original texts on which all this knowledge is based that they will have a most uncertain future.

'I know that most boys of good families take the world's respect for granted and count on being appointed to whatever office they want. Nothing could be further from the mind of such a lad than to slave away at his studies. Instead of going to the University, he spends his youth in trivial amusements. In due course he receives the appointment he wishes, and soon he is surrounded by a pack of time-servers who flatter him to his face but actually look down their noses at him. The young gentleman is now convinced that he has arrived in the world and he gives himself great airs.

'But times change. The influential person on whom he has counted for support may die and his entire position will be undermined. Then for the first time he realizes what people really think of him. Lacking a proper education, he has nothing to fall back on. For, unless we have a good scholarly basis, the "Japanese spirit" is not of much use to us in this world.

'I know that for the moment it looks as if I am not helping the boy to move ahead very fast. But I want him to have a proper education which in the end will qualify him to become a pillar of our country. Then there will be no cause for concern, even though I shall no longer be here to help him.'[4]

4. Ikeda ed., iii, 43-4.

Shortly thereafter Genji arranges for his son to receive an 'academic name' (*azana*). This was a form of matriculation ceremony performed by Confucian scholars when accepting a new student. Murasaki's description suggests the current attitude of Heian aristocrats to members of the academic profession and, indirectly, to education in general. The scholars are depicted as didactic, peevish, and rather absurd. Their antiquated language abounds in Chinese-type words like 'irregular' (*hizō*) that were avoided in urbane conversation; in almost every way they violate the all-important canon of 'up-to-dateness' (*imamekashisa*):

The professors did their best to appear unconcerned. They were dressed in ill-fitting robes which they had borrowed for the occasion and which hung loosely about their bodies. But this did not bother them in the slightest. With grave looks on their faces, and speaking in solemn tones, they sat down in a row to begin the ceremony.

Everything about it struck the onlookers as extraordinary, and some of the young noblemen could not help giggling. To assist in the actual ceremony Genji had been careful to choose only the most elderly and dignified courtiers – men who would hardly be likely to burst out laughing, however amusing they found the proceedings.

All went well until the time came to pass the wine. Being unfamiliar with the details of the ritual, the gentlemen started pouring in the normal order of precedence, first the Major Captain of the Right Division, then the Minister of People's Affairs. The professors pointed out that this was a grave solecism and roundly denounced the offenders. 'That these persons should be licensed to assist in our exercises,' they said, 'is in the highest degree irregular. Has it not occurred to them that your humble servants have certain academic qualifications that may merit a modicum of respect? Or perhaps these gentlemen are too occupied at Court to appreciate such matters. In any case their behaviour here is preposterous.'

Try as they might, some of the onlookers could not hold back their laughter. This provoked another outburst from the professors: 'This commotion must cease forthwith!' they cried. 'It is all highly irregular. If such displays continue, we shall be constrained to take our leave.'

The members of the audience who were not accustomed to academic ceremonies were greatly diverted by the scoldings and the other strange goings-on. Those among the High Court Nobles who had received training in Confucian studies wore a knowing smile on their faces. It gratified them that Prince Genji should be giving his support to the way of learning by sending his own son to the University, and they felt even more respect for him than they had in the past.

Meanwhile the professors were busy keeping order. The slightest murmur from any member of the audience produced an immediate rebuke and remarks like 'A grave breach of etiquette!' When darkness fell and the lamps were lit, their shabby figures stood out more clearly than ever; and as they sat there, inveighing loudly against their audience, they looked like a group of grimacing clowns in some farce. In more ways than one it was a most peculiar performance.

'No wonder they keep on scolding us,' whispered Genji, 'when they see a wilful, ill-behaved man like myself in the audience!' And he withdrew behind his curtain of state, from where he continued to watch the proceedings.[5]

It is clear that in Murasaki's time 'learning' still referred overwhelmingly to the study of the Chinese classics. Education was confined to an exiguous part of the population, and admittance to the colleges and academies was almost always determined by birth rather than talent, women, of course, being entirely excluded regardless of their qualifications. Even among this restricted group scholarship did not enjoy the prestige that it had in China: the visitor from the Sung capital would have looked in vain for any powerful body of literati such as flourished in his own country. In some ways the Heian attitude comes close to the Renaissance ideal of *sprezzatura*, which disdained the musty and the academic, insisting that learning must be lightly, negligently, worn; in this respect the Heian aristocrat may perhaps be compared to the European gentleman of another age, who knew his Latin and Greek, was familiar with classical mythology, and could quote his Horace and Virgil, but who eschewed anything that smacked of the pedantic.

*

Though most people of Murasaki's class had little interest in learning, and virtually none in abstract speculation, they were almost all addicted to the non-academic forms of culture. Their civilization was, to a quite remarkable extent, based on aesthetic discrimination and, with the rarest of exceptions, every gentleman and lady was an amateur performer in one or more of the arts.

5. Ibid., iii, 45–7.

Among these arts poetry was essential. The composition, exchange, and quotation of poems was central to the daily life of the Heian aristocracy, and it is doubtful whether any other society in the world has ever attached such importance to the poetic versatility of its members. Its key role in the vernacular literature of the time is unmistakable. *The Tale of Genji*, for example, contains some eight hundred original poems, apart from innumerable quotations. For Murasaki and her fellow writers in prose fiction this verse was no casual embellishment but a fundamental aspect of literary style as well as an essential ingredient of any work attempting to describe daily life among the aristocracy.

Much of the verse that has come down to us was of a formal or public nature, such as that written for the poetry contests. Considering the nature of the occasions and the enormous quantity composed (there were sometimes over one thousand competitors), we can hardly be surprised if much of it is trite. There is also a vast category of more private and ephemeral verse of the type exchanged in letters and even in conversations. In Murasaki's time hundreds of such poems must have been composed every day and, though relatively little of it has been preserved, we know a good deal about it from works like the *Pillow Book* and *The Tale of Genji*.

It was a very social type of poetry. Often it cannot be properly understood unless we know the particular occasion on which it was written; for the central image of the poem will frequently refer to some actual incident in the life of the writer, like the tap of the *kuina* bird in the exchange between Murasaki and Fujiwara no Michinaga.[6]

There were many occasions in daily life – a visit to the country, for example, or the sight of the first snowfall of the year – when failure to compose appropriate poems was a grave social solecism. Also, when one received a poem (on these or any other occasions) it was mandatory to send a prompt reply, preferably using the same imagery. As a rule the ladies and gentlemen of Heian rose to the challenge. But there were times, we note almost with relief, when even these indefatigable versifiers faltered. The following passage from the *Pillow Book* (whose author, of course, was among the glibbest poets of her day) describes the return of Empress Sadako's ladies from a cuckoo-viewing expedition, and provides an example of one of these rare deviations from poetic etiquette.

6. See p. 77.

'Well now,' said Her Majesty, 'where are they – your poems?'

We explained that we had not written any.

'Really?' she said. 'That is most unfortunate. The gentlemen at Court will certainly have heard of your expedition. How are we going to explain that you do not have a single interesting poem to show for it? You should have jotted down something on the spur of the moment while you were listening to the cuckoos. But you wanted to make too much of the occasion and as a result you let your inspiration vanish. I'm surprised at you! But you can still make up for it. Write something now! Surely that is not asking too much.'

Everything that Her Majesty said was true and we were really distressed at our failure. I was discussing possible poems with the other ladies when a message arrived from the Fujiwara Gentleman-in-Waiting.[7] His poem was attached to some of the white blossom and the paper itself was as white as the flower:

> If only I had known
> That you were off to hear the cuckoo's song,
> I should have sent my heart to join you on your way.

Since the messenger was no doubt awaiting our reply, I asked someone to fetch an ink-stone from our apartments, but the Empress ordered me to use hers. 'Write something at once,' she said. A piece of paper had been placed in the lid. 'Why don't you write the reply?' I said to Lady Saishō. 'No, I'd rather you did it,' she answered. Meanwhile it had been getting dark, and now the rain started coming down, accompanied by great claps of thunder, which so terrified us that we could think of nothing except closing the lattices. In our confusion we quite forgot about our reply.

The thunder continued rumbling until nightfall. When it finally stopped, we set about writing our poem in earnest. But just at that moment a group of High Court Nobles and Senior Courtiers arrived to ask how the Empress had fared in the thunderstorm, and we had to go to the west entrance and talk with them.

Then at last we could concentrate on our poem. But now the other ladies withdrew on the grounds that no one was responsible for the reply except the person to whom the original poem was addressed. 'Really,' I said laughing, 'poetry seems to be having a bad karma today. We shall simply have to keep as quiet as we can about our outing.' 'I still see no reason,' said Her Majesty, making herself look cross, 'that some of you

7. i.e. the Empress's cousin, Fujiwara no Kiminobu, whom the ladies had met on their outing. He had taken a spray of white deutzia blossom from their carriage.

who went to hear the cuckoos can't write a proper poem about it. I suppose it's because you have set your minds against it.'

'But Your Majesty,' I said, 'by now the whole thing's become a bit dreary.'

'Is it all that dreary?' she said.[8]

There was no more talk about writing a poem for this particular occasion.

Upper-class Heian life was punctuated with poetry from beginning to end, and no important event was complete without it. Birth was attended by an avalanche of congratulatory verse; poetic exchanges were a central part of the formal courting ceremonies; and, when death approached, the Heian gentleman would round out his verse-filled existence with a parting poem.

But poetry was not limited to these formal and momentous occasions. It crops up in the most unexpected situations. For example, when a certain Imperial Prince who is serving as Minister of Military Affairs wishes to ask the newly appointed Assistant Minister why he is so lax in reporting for duty, he does not dream of sending the curt memorandum that would be normal in a more businesslike form of bureaucracy; instead he indites an elegant poem, replete with word-plays, in which he compares the Assistant Minister and himself to two strands that have been coiled together in a single thread and asks his subordinate why he has stopped 'reeling the silk'. There follows a long exchange of increasingly obscure poems, all ringing the changes on the silk-reeling image, in the course of which the two gentlemen appear to have forgotten entirely about the original, rather prosaic, purpose of their correspondence.[9]

In view of its extraordinary wide use, the ability to compose poetry was a *sine qua non* for any self-respecting gentleman or lady. A skilful

8. Kaneko ed., pp. 510–11. I use the conventional translation of 'cuckoo', but the *hototogisu* is a far more poetic sort of bird.

9. *Kagerō Nikki*, pp. 134–5. The Minister is Prince Shōmyō, a son of Emperor Daigo, and the Assistant Minister (Hyōbū no Tayū) is Fujiwara no Kaneie, who received the post in 962. Owing to the low prestige of military affairs in Heian Kyō it was an unwelcome appointment (the Diary refers to the 'distasteful Ministry' – *kokoro mo yukanu tsukasa*); and from the outset Kaneie neglected his duties.

The prince's poem contains puns on *tsuka- -sa, -nu* = (i) Ministry, (ii) to coil, join together, and on *kuru* = (i) to come, (ii) to reel.

verse was often the best way to win a woman's favours or, equally, to obtain a promotion.

Before a deftly turned *Tanka*, [Murdoch writes with unconcealed distaste] the tradition was that female coyness, if not chastity, was bound to yield as readily as the walls of Jericho fell flat before the blasts of the priestly trumpets and the shouts of the Israelitish people, while even the highest Ministers were apt to set infinitely more store by a reputation as an arbiter of taste in the world of *belles-lettres* and polite accomplishments than by renown as a great and successful administrator of the affairs of the nation.[10]

In a society of literary amateurs the occasional person who was unable to turn his hand to poetry laboured under at least as great a handicap as would a gentleman in the court of Henry VIII who could not mount a horse. Such unfortunates receive short shrift from a woman like Sei Shōnagon. A notable case is that of Tachibana no Norimitsu, an intimate of hers, with whom she broke because of his failure as a poet. Norimitsu, who later became governor of a huge northern province, was noted for his physical bravery; but this could hardly make up for his main defect. On one occasion Sei hands him a poem full of allusions that she knows he cannot possibly recognize:

Norimitsu pushed it back to me with his fan. 'Ah,' he said, 'you have been good enough to write one of your poems for me. But when it comes to poetry . . .' and he hurried out of the room. . . . I have heard Norimitsu say, 'People who are fond of me should spare me their poems or I shall have to regard them as enemies. When you feel that the time has come to break our relations, just send me a verse.'[11]

And this is precisely what Sei does.

A good deal of this 'social' poetry was bound to be banal. The poetic vocabulary was so severely limited and the volume of production so enormous that we could not reasonably look for any very high standards of originality. The quality of the recorded poems that have come down to us is, of course, well above the average for the time; and those that are included in the notes of an Izumi Shikibu and a Sei Shōnagon, or that a writer like Murasaki Shikibu puts into the mouth of her characters, are hardly typical of the general poetic output. Examining what has been preserved, and making the necessary adjustments, we should not be far

10. Murdoch, op. cit., i, 515.   11. Kaneko ed., pp. 396–9.

wrong in assuming that much of the verse written by the elegant poetasters of the time was conventional and insincere, replete with trite conceits, stale images, and threadbare *clichés*. The feverish versifying of the time did, however, have a positive effect on the cultural level of the aristocracy. Though truly original and talented poets were as rare as in most other small societies, the fantastic volume of activity served to bring poetry into the centre of people's lives and to impress on even the most ungifted dilettante the significance of style.

At least as important as composing verse was the ability to make and recognize quotations from Chinese and Japanese poems.[12] The language of the aristocracy was full of hints and allusions, and nowhere is this more evident than in their style of enriching conversation, letters, and literature with references to the verse of writers like Po Chü-i or Ariwara no Narihira. The shining prince and his friends had an impressive fund of poetry at their fingertips, and as a rule they needed to quote only a few words for their allusion to be understood. When Ukifune has disappeared, it requires no more than a single word, which her attendants find in one of her letters, for them to recognize the poem from which it is taken and to conclude that she has drowned herself.[13]

The fear of being too explicit always outweighed that of being obscure: the more subtly one could make an allusion, and the more delicately show that one had recognized someone else's, the greater one's prestige in this small, critical world. Much of Sei Shōnagon's social, and even literary, success derived from her skill in recognizing and making quotations. Time after time her erudition is put to the test, but Sei – or so, at least, the *Pillow Book* gives us to believe – always confounds her challengers by promptly recognizing their allusions. On one occasion, however, she comes close to disgracing herself. It is during the time that she is out of favour at Empress Sadako's court because of her suspected partiality for the 'enemy' faction. She is living at home in a state of great suspense when one day a note arrives from the Empress: 'I could see that it was a personal message from Her Majesty and my heart was pounding as I opened it. There was nothing written on the paper. It had been used to wrap up a single petal of mountain rose, on which I read the words, "He who does not speak his love".'

When Sei sees this, all her anxiety of the past weeks evaporates. For

12. See p. 290.   13. See p. 284, n.17.

the Empress's words come from a poem included in an early tenth-century anthology:

> He who does not speak his love
> Yet feels its waters seething underneath
> Loves more than he who prates his every thought.

The mountain rose points to the same poem, because its yellow colour is designated by a word (*kuchinashi-iro*) that is homonymous with 'does not speak'. In other words, the Empress still loves her. Sei is about to dash off her reply, in which she will of course use the same set of images, when suddenly her mind goes blank. The mistress of the most obscure Chinese allusions finds herself defeated by a simple Japanese love poem. ' "Amazing!" I muttered. "How can one possibly forget an old poem like that? I know it perfectly well and yet it just won't come out." Hearing this, a small page-boy, who happened to be in the room, said, " 'Yet feels its waters seething underneath' – those are the words, Madam." Of course! How on earth could it have slipped my mind?'

Later, Sei tells the Empress about her extraordinary lapse: ' "Quite so," said Her Majesty. "It's often these old poems, which one considers too familiar to take seriously, that give the greatest trouble." '[14]

*

The sister art to poetry, in Heian Japan as in China, was calligraphy; and much of the enjoyment that people derived from both poetry and prose depended on the actual handwriting. Arthur Waley goes so far as to say that 'the real religion of Heian was the cult of calligraphy';[15] and there is no doubt that most writers of the time have far more to say about people's chirographic skill than about their piety. A fine hand was probably the most important single mark of a 'good' person, and it came close to being regarded as a moral virtue.

Occupying a key role among the fine arts, calligraphy was bound to be highly regarded in a society of amateur artists and connoisseurs. But there was an even stronger reason for its importance, and that was the belief that a person's handling of his brush was a better guide to his

14. Kaneko ed., pp. 700–701, 702. The pun on *kuchinashi* (= (i) jasmine yellow, (ii) does not speak) comes from a poem in the *Kokin Shū*.
15. Arthur Waley *The Pillow-Book of Sei Shōnagon*, p. 13.

breeding, sensitivity, and character than what he actually said or wrote. In Heian times to have a poor hand was no less ruinous than to be bad at poetry and, as the following passage from the *Pillow Book* suggests, the two were sometimes connected. On this occasion Sei Shōnagon's victim is a certain Fujiwara no Nobutsune, a pretentious young official in the Ministry of Ceremonial:

'Give me any subject,' declared Nobutsune, 'and I'll have no trouble composing a poem either in Chinese or in Japanese.' 'So that's how things are!' I replied. 'Very well, I'll give you a subject and you will kindly write me a poem in Japanese.' 'Splendid,' said Nobutsune. 'But why only one subject? I can just as well handle a whole lot.'

Hearing his boast, the Empress herself proposed a subject, at which Nobutsune promptly took his leave, saying, 'Dear me, how frightening! I'd better be off.'

'He has an appalling hand,' someone explained after he had left the room. 'Whether it's Chinese characters or Japanese script, the results are equally poor. People are always laughing at him about it. That's why he had to escape . . .'

One day when Nobutsune was serving as Intendant in the Office of Palace Works he sent a sketch to one of the craftsmen explaining how a certain piece of work should be done. 'Kindly execute it in this fashion,' he added in Chinese characters. I happened to notice the piece of paper and it was the most preposterous writing I had ever seen. Next to his message I wrote, 'If you do the work in this style, you will certainly produce something odd.' The document found its way to the Imperial apartments and everyone who saw it was greatly amused. Nobutsune was furious and after this held a grudge against me.[16]

Since the people of Genji's world regarded handwriting as the mirror of a person's soul, they awaited the first letter from a potential lover or mistress with the greatest trepidation. For indifferent calligraphy was bound to disqualify people, whatever other charms they might possess. When Prince Genji reads a note from the girl he has known in Akashi, Lady Murasaki is consumed with curiosity – not so much about its contents as about its handwriting. Finally she gets a glimpse of the outer wrapping on which the address is written: 'She saw that there was a great depth of feeling in the penmanship. Indeed, it had a style that

16. Kaneko ed., p. 536.

might give pause to the most distinguished ladies at Court. Small wonder that Genji felt about the girl as he did!'[17]

Several years later, Lady Murasaki has a new rival in the form of Princess Nyosan, the thirteen-year-old girl who has just become Genji's official wife. Once more she anxiously awaits her first sight of the girl's handwriting, knowing that this may determine her entire future. One morning when Genji is lying with Murasaki in her room he receives a letter from the young princess:

It was on fine crimson paper and folded in striking taste. Genji felt his heart beating as he opened the letter. But when he examined the writing he found it extremely childish. He wished that he could stop Murasaki from seeing it for the time being – not that he really wanted to keep anything from her, but in view of Nyosan's rank it seemed a shame that anyone should know how unformed her hand still was. To hide the letter, however, would certainly make a bad impression on Murasaki, and so he unfolded it in such a way that she could glimpse bits of it out of the corner of her eye as she lay there next to him. . . .

Murasaki's first glance told her that it was indeed a childish production. She wondered how anyone could have reached such an age without developing a more polished style. But she pretended not to have noticed and made no comment. Genji also kept silent. If the letter had come from anyone else, he would certainly have whispered something about the writing, but he felt sorry for the girl and simply said, 'Well now, you see that you have nothing to worry about.'[18]

Often it is the sight of a lady's handwriting that first wins a man's affection, sometimes even before he has met her, and women are no less susceptible to the romantic charms of calligraphy.

Since calligraphy is the basis of drawing in the Far East, the people of Murasaki's world were almost all amateur artists. During his exile in Suma one of Genji's great consolations is to make sketches of the sea and hills that surround him; and readers of the novel will recall the great picture competition on Genji's return to the capital, when his drawings are pitted against those that other members of the court have produced for the occasion.[19]

One popular form of drawing consisted of sketches of women (*onnae*)

17. Ikeda ed., ii, 217.   18. Ibid., iv, 57–8.
19. Book 17 of *Genji Monogatari: Eawase* ('The Picture Competition').

and men (*otokoe*). It appears likely that these sketches were often erotic, but no example has come down to us from the period.[20] Having captivated Ukifune by his calligraphy, Niou tells her,

'There will be times when I shall be unable to come and see you, however much I may want to. When that happens, please take out this picture and look at it.' So saying, he picked up his brush and drew a very beautiful man and woman lying next to each other. 'If only you and I could always be like this!' he said and burst out weeping.[21]

Among the other types of amateur drawing in Murasaki's time were illustrations for books, including diaries, *sōshi* (like the *Pillow Book*), and romances. This art appears to have reached a high level, and in the twelfth century it culminated in the great colour scrolls, notably 'The Tale of Genji Picture Scroll', which ranks as one of the glories of Japanese art. (A common way of appreciating works of literature was for an attendant to read the text aloud while one examined the accompanying illustrations.) Another art form practised by the gifted amateurs of the time was to decorate screens and sliding doors with illustrations of poems, accompanied by the texts themselves in beautiful flowing calligraphy.

While most of the artists described in *The Tale of Genji* were amateurs, several of the exhibits produced during the picture competition[22] were the work of well-known painters and calligraphers (like Kose no

20. Ref. Kaneko, op. cit., p. 165, where he quotes a passage from *Eiga Monogatari* in which drawings of the *otokoe* type make the observers blush. Apart from *otokoe*, the Heian period also produced erotic picture scrolls. None are extant, but the *Koshibagakizōshi*, which dates from late Kamakura times, is believed to be a copy of a tenth-century scroll. Cf. Van Gulik, op. cit., pp. 200–201:
'The oldest erotic picture scroll preserved in Japan is the *Kanjō-no-maki* "Scroll of the Initiation", also known as *Koshibagaki-zōshi*. This is a series of sixteen pictures of the sexual act performed in various positions by a courtier and a lady of the Hei-an period ... accompanied by explanations in Japanese. The oldest copy is ascribed to the 13th-century painter Sumiyoshi Kei-on, but it is said that this copy is based on an original of A.D. 900. The scroll is painted in pure Japanese style, including the abnormally enlarged sexual organs characteristic of all Japanese old and later erotic representations. Moreover, the accompanying text contains no reference to the Chinese handbooks of sex.'
21. Ikeda ed., vii, 35–6.
22. See n. 20 above.

Ōmi and Ono no Michikaze) who despite their aristocratic descent were, for all intents and purposes, professional. It is interesting that the work of an out-and-out amateur like Genji should have been submitted together with theirs and that it should have won the prizes. On the whole, the distinction between amateur and professional was still fairly fluid.

*

In a society that put so high a value on poetry and calligraphy a form of everyday communication that combined them was bound to be important. This, of course, was letter-writing, and in Murasaki's time it had come to be regarded as an art in its own right, whose products, ephemeral though they might be, were judged according to the most critical standards. The everyday life of the aristocracy offered endless occasions for writing notes and letters, and the ability to acquit oneself successfully in these exchanges was the ultimate criterion of acceptability. In our age of typewriters, telephones, air-letters, and dictaphones it is hard to imagine that a person's skill in the art of correspondence could make or break his entire reputation. Yet Heian literature leaves us in no doubt that this was the situation in Murasaki's day. There have, of course, been other societies in which letter-writing was highly prized, but none, so far as I know, has ever given it the central cultural role that it acquired in Heian Kyō.

A great body of artistic convention accompanied the preparation and sending of a letter. First it was necessary to choose paper of the proper thickness, size, design, and colour to suit the emotional mood that one wished to suggest, as well as the season of the year and even the weather of the particular day. The calligraphy, of course, was at least as important as the actual message, and often the writer had to make numerous drafts with different brushes before producing the precise effect he wished. The nucleus of the text was usually a thirty-one syllable poem whose central image was some aspect of nature that delicately symbolized the occasion. Having finished his letter, the writer would carefully fold it in one of the accepted styles. The next step was to select the proper branch or spray of blossom to which the letter must be attached. This depended on the dominant mood of the letter and on the imagery of the poem. It was also correlated with the colour of the paper: blue paper for a willow twig, green for oak, crimson for maple, white for an iris root. Finally, the writer would summon a smart, good-looking messenger and give him instructions about delivering the precious document. Then there was nothing but to wait for the reply and discover how skilfully one's correspondent had responded to the challenge.

In the diaries and fictional works of the time there is a constant flow of letters and messages. Day and night, in fair weather and foul, the long-suffering messengers shuttle to and fro between the lordly mansions, carrying now a note on thin, pure white paper about a lady's emotions at the first snowfall, now a 'next morning' letter, attached to a sprig of pine, in which a gentleman tells his mistress that his love will never wither. Since correspondence is regarded as an art form, there is little privacy about these letters; often they are read by the wrong people and this can result in endless complications. Thus Genji catches sight of Kashiwagi's letter to Princess Nyosan and knows that his young wife has been unfaithful; and, by reading Ukifune's letter to Naka no Kimi, Prince Niou's curiosity is aroused – with disastrous results for everyone concerned.

*

Music also played a great part in the daily life of the Heian aristocrats. Not only did they enjoy listening to music, but almost any educated man or woman knew how to play the flute or one of the many types of zither that had originally been introduced from China but that by Murasaki's time had been thoroughly absorbed into Japanese cultural life. Apart from formal musical events, such as those held during the annual ceremonies, we often read about impromptu amateur concerts, which took place in the private mansions of the capital and sometimes out of doors to the accompaniment of birds' songs and the cry of cicadas. After the picture competition, which has lasted during most of the night, the conversation turns to music:

The late moon now emerged. Under the eaves of the building it was still dark, but the sky was beautifully illuminated. An attendant was sent to fetch zithers from the Bureau of Books and Instruments. When they were brought, Tō no Chūjō chose the six-stringed zither, which he, like Genji, played with outstanding skill. Prince Hotaru took the great thirteen-stringed zither, while Genji himself decided on the seven-stringed *kin*. Lady Shōshō accompanied the gentlemen on the four-stringed lute. One of the senior courtiers, who was noted for his musical talents, was asked to conduct, and a delightful concert started. As the light began to spread, the colour of the flowers and the faces of the players gradually came into view. Now the birds joined in with their own gay song. It was a dawn to gladden anyone's heart.[23]

Both *The Tale of the Hollow Tree* and *The Tale of Genji* emphasize the music endowments of their heroes and the success that this brings them at court. Murasaki herself appears to have known a great deal about the history of music and about different styles of performance. Her characters discuss their views on musical styles (especially on various types of zither-playing) at great length, and the novel is a valuable source for the study of Japanese musicology. The diary too reflects her critical interest in the subject. The final scene is a concert in the palace:

The Major Counsellor conducted from a dais. The Controller First Secretary played the lute, Lord Tsunekata the great zither and the Imperial Counsellor (who was Captain of the Guards) the flute. First they accompanied various songs in the double scale . . .; then, as their instrumental music, they did the last two parts of 'The Village in the Forest'. Some of the gentlemen who were listening joined in with their wind instruments. When they were playing 'The Sea of Ise', one of the singers made a mistake in timing and had to be reprimanded. The Minister of the Right was in great spirits, and praised the player of the six-stringed zither with cries of 'Splendid!' Towards the end someone made a serious blunder, sending a chill even to us spectators; it was really rather pathetic. When the concert was finished, the Emperor had two flutes put in boxes and presented to the players as a gift.[24]

There was also a rich variety of dances. Many of them were of foreign origin (Chinese, Korean, and even Indian); others were provincial or folk dances that had been adapted for performance in polite society; still others were associated with Shintō observances, such as *kagura* performed during the Kamo Festival.[25] Among the most eagerly awaited events in the court calendar were the Gosechi dances, which were carried

23. Ikeda ed., ii, 280.   24. Mochizuki ed., pp. 115–16.
25. Of the half-a-dozen dances listed at random in Section 178 of the *Pillow Book*, the Suruga Mai originated in the eastern provinces of Japan, the Taiheiraku came from China, the Tori no Mai from India, and the Komahoko from Korea.

out by specially chosen young girls of good family.[26] These dances, which are frequently described in the literature of the time (Yūgiri, it will be recalled, has a love affair with one of the performers), were supposed to commemorate the occasion when Emperor Temmu, while playing the zither in his palace, was joined by a group of heavenly maidens who danced before him in their feathered robes.

Dancing was an essential accomplishment for any complete gentleman. There were also professional dance masters (*mai no shi*); but, according to Prince Genji's father, the old Emperor, these experts, skilled as they might be, were unable to imbue their dancing with the same impressive elegance that a young man of good family could achieve.[27] Almost every ceremonial occasion, and many an informal gathering, included a performance of dances. The following passage describes the rehearsal for one of the *bugaku* court dances to be carried out during an imperial procession:

Genji danced the Waves of the Blue Sea. His partner was Tō no Chūjō, who, though he excelled most performers in beauty and skill, paled into insignificance next to the prince, like a scrubby bush beside a flower in full bloom. As Genji danced, the rays of the setting sun fell on his body, and at that moment the music swelled up in a crescendo. It was a brilliant climax. Familiar though the dance was to the onlookers, they felt that never before had there been such loveliness of movement and expression; and the accompanying song seemed as melodious as the music of the Kalavinka birds in Buddha's Paradise. Moved beyond words by the beauty of the performance, the Emperor burst into tears, and the High Court Nobles and princes in his suite also wept. When the song was finished, Genji adjusted the sleeves of his robe and waited for the music to start again. Then he resumed his dance to the lively strains of the next movement. Excited by the rhythm of the steps, he glowed with a warm colour, and the name 'Genji the Shining One' seemed even more fitting than usual.[28]

*

Among the many artistic skills that were valued in Heian Kyō there is one that has no equivalent in the West and that depends on a sense which has rarely been exploited in the history of world culture. In most

26. See pp. 177–8.   27. Ikeda ed., i, 369.   28. Ibid., i, 368.

countries and most times the manufacture of perfumes has been re-garded as a trade – and a very utilitarian one at that. But in the world of the shining prince, as we have seen, the blending of incense was one of the great aristocratic arts, which had its own conventions, schools and outstanding connoisseurs.[29] The scent worn by a gentleman was almost as important as his clothes, and the exact method he used in preparing his incense was often a closely guarded secret. Incense competitions were among the most popular and time-consuming of the 'comparisons' carried out in the patrician households. The following account of a competition between the inhabitants of Genji's mansion in the Sixth Ward gives a good idea of the importance attached to this unusual art-form and of the high level it had attained in Murasaki's time. Prepara-tions have been under way for several weeks, each competitor carefully blending his own special combination of incenses and choosing the appropriate bowls, boxes, and burners for the great occasion:

Prince Genji decided that the damp evening air would provide the best conditions for the trial, and he now dispatched messengers to all the apartments where the blending had been going on. The jars and boxes were brought in, each of the contestants having taken care to submit her incense in the most attractive possible style.

'May I ask you to be our judge this evening?' said Genji to Prince Hotaru. 'For, if it be not you . . .'[30] He had the burners placed before the Prince. 'But I am not he who knows,' said Prince Hotaru modestly. Despite his protests it soon became clear that he was a most discerning judge, who could compare the merits of two scents that ordinary people would find nearly indistinguishable, and who, even when confronted with the most unusual blends, could tell whether the contestant had used one of the ingredients wrongly, thus causing some slight imperfection in the final aroma.

29. See pp. 156–7.
30. Genji is quoting from the *Kokin Shū* poem,

> If it be not you,
> To whom can I show the plum tree's flower?
> For, when it comes to blossoms and to scent,
> Only he knows who truly knows.

Hotaru's reply shows that he has duly recognized the allusion.

Now the time came for Genji to produce his own two mixtures. In imitation of the emperor who buried his incense by the moat that runs past the headquarters of the Inner Palace Guards,[31] Genji had buried his exhibit in the ground next to a stream that emerged from the Western gallery of his palace. Koremitsu's son . . . went to dig up the jars and presented them to Yūgiri, who in turn submitted them to the judge.

'It's terribly smoky in here,' complained Prince Hotaru. 'I am finding it very hard to judge these perfumes properly.'

There was little to choose between the various blends of *kurōbo* that had been prepared for the occasion, but the judge decided that Princess Asagao's was outstanding for its calm, elegant scent.[32] When it came to the *jijū* perfumes, the judge picked one of Genji's which had an unusually full and nostalgic quality. Of the three types sent in by Murasaki the judge singled out her *baika* plum scent for special praise. It was a bright, up-to-date scent with a slightly pungent touch. 'Really,' said Prince Hotaru, 'I can imagine nothing more appropriate for the present season than this plum blossom fragrance.'

The lady of the summer garden [Hanachirusato], modest as ever, had hesitated to push herself forward among the contestants and had submitted only a single scent of the type known as Lotus Leaf. It was an unusual blend, however, with a gentle aroma and a certain rather touching tenderness. The lady of the winter garden [Lady Akashi] had decided that, if she followed the normal custom and sent in perfumes that suited her own particular season, she would almost certainly be defeated by ladies who were associated with more fragrant months. This seemed pointless to her, and so she took particular pains to produce some unusual blends of the *kunoekō* variety. She examined the methods that Emperor Uda had used in his preparations, and also referred to the recipe for the Hundred Steps incense, which Lord Kintada had selected when presenting his offering to the Throne.[33] Lady Akashi's unusually thorough studies in

31. This was Emperor Nimmyō (r. 833–50), who was a great practitioner of the art of scent. Burying incense in the ground was believed to improve the aroma.

32. There are no really satisfactory equivalents for adjectives, like *namamekashi* and *shizuyaka*, that are used to describe the different scents. *Namamekashi*, for instance, includes the suggestion of warmth, depth, damp; 'a deep, moist type of elegance' might possibly convey the idea to those whose sense of smell is highly developed.

33. Emperor Uda (r. 887–97) was a noted aesthete. Minamoto no Kintada (889–948) was a statesman-poet, later included among the Thirty-six Poets of Japan.

the subject allowed her to combine various formulae and to produce blends of surpassing elegance. Prince Hotaru declared that each of her exhibits had something special to recommend it, which provoked Genji to remark, 'Our judge seems to have remarkably wide tastes.'[34]

*

If Murasaki's period did little for the intellectual progress of mankind, and still less for techniques of government and social organization, it will always be remembered for the way in which its people pursued that cult of beauty in art and in nature which has played so important a part in Japan's cultural history and which is perhaps the country's greatest contribution to the world. The 'rule of taste' applied not only to the formal arts but to nearly every aspect of the lives of the upper classes in the capital.[35] It was central to Heian Buddhism, making (as Sir George Sansom has put it) religion into an art and art into a religion. In the conduct of a romantic liaison it prescribed not only how the lovers should write their poems and send their letters but the exact manner in which the man should get up in the morning and take his leave.[36] The 'rampant aestheticism' of the period extended even to the day-to-day activities of the government, in which the officials were expected to perform stylized dances as part of their duties, and in which (as we know from a thirteenth-century chronicle) the Intendant of the Imperial Police was chosen for his good looks as much as for his family connexions.[37]

34. Ikeda ed., iii, 320–22. The basic ingredients in the blends submitted during this competition are as follows; certain secret ingredients were usually added:

	aloes	cinnamon	ground conch-shell	Indian resin	sandalwood	musk	sweet pine	tropical tulip	cloves	white gum
kurobō	×	×	×	×	×	×			×	
jijū	×	×	×			×	×	×		
baika	×	×	×	×	×	×	×			
konoekō		×	×	×						×

35. See Chapter IX of Sansom's *A History of Japan* (Vol. I), entitled 'The Rule of Taste'.

36. See pp. 243–4.

37. *Kojidan*, cited by Fujiki, op. cit., p. 221.

The immense leisure enjoyed by members of the upper classes allowed them to indulge in a minute cultivation of taste. Their sophisticated aesthetic code applied even to the smallest details, such as the exact shade of the blossom to which one attached a letter or the precise nuance of scent that one should use for a particular occasion. Taste in colour was developed to a remarkable extent, and the literature of the time is full of colour impressions, like those evoked by the snow falling on a messenger's scarlet tunic or by a gentleman's plum-coloured trousers seen against a background of dark green pines. The art of combining colours was particularly important in men's and women's dress, and when a writer like Murasaki enters into detail about the clothes that her characters are wearing (detail that can become rather tiresome for the modern reader) she is in fact telling us about their artistic sensibility. The following passage from her diary suggests the importance that was attached to taste in colour and the highly critical sense that had developed by her time:

The Empress was wearing the usual scarlet robe, under which she had kimonos of light plum, light green and yellow rose. His Majesty's outer robe was made of grape-coloured brocade; underneath he had a willow green kimono and, below that, one of pure white – all most unusual and up-to-date in both design and colour. . . . Lady Nakazukasa's robe, which was also of grape-coloured brocade, hung loosely over a plain jacket of green and cherry.

On that day all the ladies in attendance on His Majesty had taken particular care with their dress. One of them, however, had made a small error in matching the colours at the openings of her sleeves. When she approached His Majesty to put something in order, the High Court Nobles and Senior Courtiers who were standing nearby noticed the mistake and stared at her. This was a source of lively regret to Lady Saishō and the others. It was not really such a serious lapse of taste; only the colour of one of her robes was a shade too pale at the opening.'[38]

Not only did the rule of taste extend to every sphere of life and apply to the smallest details, but (with the single exception of good birth) it

38. Mochizuki ed., pp. 113–14.

took primacy over all else. Artistic sensibility was more highly valued than ethical goodness. Despite the influence of Buddhism, Heian society was on the whole governed by style rather than by any moral principles, and good looks tended to take the place of virtue. The word *yoki* ('good') referred primarily to birth, but it also applied to a person's beauty or to his aesthetic sensibility; the one implication it lacked was that of ethical rectitude. For all their talk about 'heart' and 'feeling', this stress on the cult of the beautiful, to the virtual exclusion of any concern with charity, sometimes lends a rather chilling impression to the people of Genji's world.

Sensibility also preceded profundity, aesthetic experience invariably being more prized than abstract speculation. We have already noticed the general absence of interest in reasoning and in serious scholarship: erudite as they may be, the Confucian professors are regarded as absurd and unacceptable figures because they lack good, up-to-date taste. The overwhelming interest of the upper classes in the aesthetic side of life enabled Heian culture to make remarkable advances in certain directions, but kept it curiously backward in others.

Finally, the aesthetic cult of the time provided the framework in which the 'good people' not only expressed but even experienced their emotions. Though emotional sensitivity was a mark of the true gentleman, it was kept within the limits of the accepted aesthetic code and rarely developed into wild passion or unrestrained romanticism. Even when Murasaki's characters are plunged into the most agonizing grief over the death of someone who has been close to them, they express their emotions in elegantly turned poems of thirty-one syllables, whose central images of dew and dreams belong to the conventional aesthetic vocabulary.

The accepted pattern of sensibility that was so highly valued in Murasaki's time is summed up by *aware*, one of the many untranslatable (and relentlessly overworked) words that are used to define Japanese aesthetics. In its widest sense it was an interjection or adjective referring to the emotional quality inherent in objects, people, nature, and art, and by extension it applied to a person's internal response to emotional aspects of the external world. The gamut of its use in Heian literature is extremely wide. The word occurs over one thousand times in *The Tale of Genji* (one thousand and eighteen to be exact), and there has been many a learned disquisition on its different shades of meaning.[39] Though in Murasaki's time *aware* still retained its early catholic range, its most characteristic use in *The Tale of Genji* is to suggest the pathos inherent in the beauty of the outer world, a beauty that is inexorably fated to disappear together with the observer. Buddhist doctrines about the evanescence of all living things naturally influenced this particular content of the word, but the stress in *aware* was always on direct emotional experience rather than on religious understanding. *Aware* never entirely lost its simple interjectional sense of 'Ah!'[40]

Often the word appears in the phrase *mono no aware*, which roughly corresponds to *lacrimae rerum*, the pathos of things. It is when people perceive the connexion between the beauty and the sadness of the world that they most poignantly sense *mono no aware*. The sensitive observer is moved to tears by the beauty of nature, or by its embodiment in art (the Emperor's reaction to Genji's dance will be recalled), not only because it is so impressive in itself, but because when confronted with such beauty he becomes more than ever conscious of the ephemeral nature of all that lives in this world of ours. Scene after scene in *The Tale of Genji* reaches its emotional climax in this conjunction of aesthetic enjoyment with sorrow. Thus, when Genji visits the Cloistered Emperor Reizei at night, the gentlemen sit on the veranda nostalgically conversing about old times and about people who have long since died, while one of the courtiers plays the flute to the accompaniment of the bell-insects in the pine trees; the entire scene is suffused with moonlight and evokes an almost unbearable sense of *mono no aware*.

39. In his *Genji Monogatari Jiten* Kitayama Keita suggests the following seven definitions for *aware* and gives examples of how it is used in *The Tale of Genji* in each of these senses: (i) poor, pitiful, wretched, miserable, unfortunate; (ii) lovable, charming, beloved; (iii) sad, mournful, woeful; (iv) happy, pleased; (v) compassionate, benevolent; (vi) effective, charming, tasteful, pleasing, interesting, intriguing, impressive; (vii) exceptional, praiseworthy. 'The spirit of *aware*', writes Hisamatsu Senichi, 'pervades all Heian literature. It is discovered in the feelings inspired by a bright spring morning and also in the sense of sadness that overcomes us on an autumn evening. Its primary mood, however, is one of gentle melancholy, from which it can develop into real grief.' *Kokugo*, x, 152–3.

40. According to Motoori Norinaga, the initial *a* of *aware* is cognate with the same sound that appears in other ancient exclamations like *haya, hamo, atsuhare.*

Yet, powerful though this feeling might become, it was, as we have seen, always circumscribed by a well-defined aesthetic code. Here was no turbulent, romantic emotion, lending itself to wild expressions of melancholy or grief. Rather it was a restrained and elegant form of sensibility, a quiet feeling of resignation that a well-bred man might experience when faced with the combination of the world's beauty and the ineluctable fate of all living things.

The ability to understand this type of aesthetic emotional experience (*mono no aware wo shiru*) was, of course, limited to the 'good people'. It was the equivalent of moral virtue in other societies, but it was a virtue that no member of the provincial or working classes could hope to acquire.[41] Nor did it invariably accrue to people of good birth. Many a well-born character in contemporary literature is irretrievably damned by the comment that he or she does not 'know' *mono no aware*. Such people are 'bad', regardless of their birth, and regardless even of the conventional propriety of their behaviour. This category includes those who assume an understanding of *mono no aware* that they do not really feel. Such false sensibility emerged as a type of fashionable world-weariness which grew increasingly common in the later centuries as the expressions of *aware* became ever more conventionalized.

*

The cult of beauty helped to produce a society of great elegance and charm which, despite its many lacunae and its fatal weaknesses, will always occupy an important place in the world's cultural history. At a time when life in most of the West was unbelievably crude, it provided concepts of the refined life and of the complete gentleman that were not to reach Europe until the Renaissance. Like Castiglione's Il Cortegiano, men like Genji and Niou, with their profound sensibility, their wide connoisseurship of the arts, and their skill in performance, their exquisite manner combined with easy nonchalance, were the ideals of a class and of an age.[42] In practice, no doubt, the men of Murasaki's time, including many of those who inhabited the Nine-Fold Enclosure, often

41. See pp. 99–100.
42. The greatest differences in the Renaissance ideal were the belief that people could *become* gentlemen, and the stress given to courage and other knightly virtues.

retained crude pleasures and vulgar habits, caring little for the aesthetic and emotional elegances that delighted Murasaki's heroes. Yet from our fairly detailed knowledge of Heian upper-class life we can tell that the type of refinement and sensibility reflected in *The Tale of Genji* and the *Pillow Book* were generally accepted as values even by those who could not live up to the ideal.

VIII

The Women of Heian and their Relations with Men

DURING the period of about one hundred years that spans the world of *The Tale of Genji*, almost every noteworthy author who wrote in Japanese was a woman.[1] Such overwhelming literary predominance of women is a rare, if not unique, phenomenon in cultural history; and it is doubly surprising that it should occur in a part of the world where women have traditionally been condemned to a position of irremediable inferiority.

Many reasons have been given. According to some writers, the exclusion of women from all public affairs, combined with the prevailing system of polygamy, gave them an immense amount of free time that they could devote to literary pursuits, whereas men were too busy with

1. These are the principal names: Nakazukasa (daughter of Ise no Go and Prince Atsuyasu), Yoshiko Joō (granddaughter of Emperor Daigo), Michitsuna's mother (author of *Gossamer Diary*), Sei Shōnagon, Murasaki Shikibu, Izumi Shikibu, Sugawara no Takasue's daughter (author of the *Sarashina Diary*), Koshikibu no Naishi (daughter of Izumi Shikibu), Akazome Emon, Ise no Ōsuke, Uma no Naishi, Sagami, Daini no Sammi (Murasaki's daughter).

Of these distinguished ladies the following all served in Empress Akiko's Court: Murasaki Shikibu, Izumi Shikibu, Koshikibu no Naishi, Ise no Ōsuke, and Uma no Naishi.

There were many prominent women writers before and after the period in question (Ono no Komachi in the late 9th century, for example, and Sanuki Tenji in the early 12th), but it was only during the century of the world of the shining prince that women had a virtual monopoly of famous names in Japanese prose and poetry. This century was by far the most important in Heian literature, and in general the rise and decline of this literature was closely associated with the role of women in it. This sexual differentiation extended to the field of painting, Chinese-style works being known as 'men's paintings' and the freer, Japanese style as 'women's paintings'. Ikeda Kikan, *Heianchō no Seikatsu to Bungaku*, p. 160.

their official duties and with satisfying the demands of their numerous wives and mistresses. The trouble with this explanation is, first, that Heian men wrote a great deal and, secondly, that during the next half millennium or so, when men's lives tended to be far more strenuous than in Heian days and when upper-class women still had great leisure at their disposal, not a single woman writer of any real distinction appeared in Japan.

The main reason for the literary predominance of women in Murasaki's time is the role of Chinese language and letters. During the entire Heian period, as we have seen, Chinese remained the language of scholars, priests, and officials, occupying a role analogous to that of Latin in the West. Despite the steady emancipation from foreign tutelage, Chinese characters retained their overwhelming prestige and were the exclusive medium for any serious form of writing among men. Women, on the other hand, were free to make the fullest possible use of the *kana* phonetic script, which allowed them to record the native Japanese language, the language that was actually spoken, in a direct, simple fashion that was impossible either in pure Chinese or in the hybrid form of Sino-Japanese known as *kambun*.

The remarkable growth of vernacular literature during the Heian period – a growth that reached its apex in Murasaki's time – was largely dependent on the use of the phonetic script. Here women held the field. The native syllabary was something called *onnade* or the 'woman's hand' (*otokomoji*, 'men's letters', referring to Chinese characters); and, as one *genre* of literature after another (diaries, travel accounts, romances) came to be written in the Japanese language, it was natural that women should have an advantage. When a certain distinguished man of letters decided to compose a diary in the phonetic script (instead of in Chinese, which until then had been normal), he made it appear that it was being written by a woman and opened with the oblique comment, 'Diaries are usually written by men, but now a woman is going to try her hand at one.'[2]

The cultural success of women in Murasaki's time naturally depended on many factors besides language. The present chapter, which is concerned mainly with women's social position and their relations with men, will, it is hoped, throw light not only on feminine literature but

2. Ki no Tsurayuki, *Tosa Nikki* (935), p. 27.

also on the general subject of upper-class Heian life, in which women played such an unusual part. Two brief warnings are necessary. First, since our knowledge of Heian women is largely based on writings by distinguished members of their own sex, we must be careful not to over-estimate their position. The *Pillow Book*, in particular, suggests a degree of feminine emancipation and self-confidence which, although it was no doubt enjoyed by Sei Shōnagon and by some of her more gifted and assertive contemporaries, can hardly have been common to most upper-class women. Secondly, we must remember that we are dealing with only a minute proportion of the sex. As in most other pre-modern societies, the vast majority of women in Murasaki's day toiled arduously in the fields, were subject to harsh treatment by their men, bred young and frequently, and died at an early age, without having given any more thought to material independence or cultural enjoyments than to the possibility of visiting the moon.

*

Every reader of *The Tale of Genji* and the *Pillow Book* must, at some time or other, have wondered what a typical upper-class Heian woman looked like. Unfortunately we have no contemporary portraits to help us draw an authentic picture. The *emakimono* scrolls belong to a later period; and the women they depict are conventional court beauties whose features so closely resemble each other as to be virtually inter-changeable. Invariably their faces are white and plump, their eyes long, almost closed, slits, from which we can gather no expression, their nose a tiny conventional hook and their mouth a delicate little circle; of their figures we see nothing at all, since they are swathed in voluminous robes. This is how painters of the twelfth century imagined the women of Murasaki's time; their pictures represent the ideal of Heian feminine beauty which itself was greatly influenced by that of T'ang China;[3] but there is no telling how close they came to the reality.

3. According to Van Gulik, T'ang gentlemen liked women 'with round, chubby faces, well-developed breasts, slender waists but heavy hips'. 'This preference', he adds, 'is found also in old Japan; the picture scrolls of the Heian period show ladies as portly as those on T'ang paintings.' Van Gulik, op. cit., p. 188. Descriptions of attractive women in Heian literature almost invariably include phrases like *tsubutsubu to fuetaru* ('she is well-rounded and plump') and *fukuraka naru hito* ('a plump person'). Conversely, the final touch that completes

Nor do we learn much on this subject from literature. Sei Shōnagon and the other women writers were remarkably reticent when it came to detailing the appearance of the members of their own sex. Murasaki's diary contains some sketches of her fellow ladies-in-waiting; but the physical descriptions are perfunctory and stereotyped. One reason for the avoidance of this subject may have been a general lack of interest in the body as such. The humanist idea that the naked body can be a thing of aesthetic joy and significance is alien to the Japanese tradition; the female figure was never included in the contemporary cult of beauty. In Murasaki's case we find not merely indifference to the nude form but actual aversion. In her diary she describes the scene in which two maids-of-honour are robbed of their clothes in the middle of the night. At the sight of the poor naked ladies, their fellow attendants are thrown into pandemonium and rush about ineffectually like frightened barnyard fowl. When things have quieted down, Murasaki comments, 'Unforgettably horrible is the naked body. It really does not have the slightest charm.'[4]

It is not surprising, then, that Murasaki should devote much more time to describing a woman's poetic style or her manner of folding a letter than to telling us what she looked like. When she wishes to impress her heroine's beauty on the reader, she does not catalogue her physical charms but uses the indirect method of describing how a young man reacts on seeing her for the first time.[5]

---

the description of Suetsumuhana's ugliness is this: 'She was pitifully thin and her bony shoulders stuck out painfully above her dress.' Quoted by Ikeda, op. cit., p. 144.

4. Mochizuki ed., p. 74. Fundamentally, no doubt, the aversion for the nude is the result of religious awe (i.e. fear of the magic, and therefore potentially dangerous, properties of the completely exposed human body) rather than of aesthetic taste. What is unclear is why the lack of interest in nude beauty should have persisted in Japan for so many centuries. 'When the Chinese erotic prints of the end of the Ming dynasty were introduced into Japan', writes Dr van Gulik, 'they caused a slight interest in nude beauty, and the early Ukiyoe masters did fairly well in this respect. Before long, however, they again neglected depiction of the [whole] body and concentrated on the private parts, many Ukiyoe booklets resembling medical treatises rather than collections of erotic prints. It was not until the end of the Second World War that the "cult of the nude" came to Japan, being part of the general reaction to traditional inhibitions.'

5. See pp. 179–80.

There is one notable exception to this avoidance of physical detail, and that is the description of a woman's hair. Interest in this particular feature of feminine appearance was so overwhelming in the Heian period as to seem almost obsessive; and as a rule even the most casual reference to a woman is accompanied by some mention of her tresses. The hair of the Heian beauty was straight, glossy, and immensely long. It was parted in the middle and fell freely over the shoulders in great black cascades; ideally, when a woman stood up it reached the ground. Describing Lady Dainagon in her diary, Murasaki writes that 'her hair is three inches longer than her height and she wears beautiful ornaments in it';[6] and in *The Tale of Genji* we read that Princess Ochiba's hair was six foot long. The mere glimpse of a fine head of hair is sufficient to captivate a Heian gentleman. This is probably the main cause of Ukifune's success with men; towards the end of the novel a certain captain becomes hopelessly infatuated with the girl from simply having glanced at her from behind. One reason that taking the tonsure was regarded as such a tragic step for women (the onlookers at the ceremony almost invariably weep) was that her hair could never again grow to its full length.

White skin was also a sign of beauty and, as in most societies, of aristocratic birth. In paintings of gentlemen and ladies of the court it was conventional that people of higher rank had fairer faces. Since nature could not always be relied on to respect these distinctions, generous amounts of powder were used in order to produce the fitting degree of pallor. Over this chalky base married women usually applied a little rouge to their cheeks; and they also painted their lips to give the proper rosebud effect.

Heian women observed two customs that, attractive as they no doubt were to the gentlemen of the time, would hardly add to their appeal for Western men, or indeed for most modern Japanese. They plucked their eyebrows and then carefully painted in a curious blot-like set, either in the same place or about an inch above. They also went to the greatest trouble to blacken their teeth with a type of dye usually made by soaking iron and powdered gallnut in vinegar or tea.[7] During later centuries this

6. Mochizuki ed., p. 76.
7. The custom of plucking or shaving the eyebrows was practised in China during the Former Han dynasty (*chiao mei*), but the fashion of tooth-blackening

bizarre custom spread throughout the country and came to denote a woman's married status;[8] in Heian times it was restricted to the upper classes, but not to married women. The young heroine of *The Lady Who Loved Insects* adds to her general eccentricity by refusing to pluck her eyebrows or blacken her teeth, preferring to leave these features as nature made them. This disgusts her attendants. They do not object so much to their lady's social unconventionality as to the ugliness of the effect – a good example of the relativity of aesthetic standards: '"Ugh!" said one of the maids. "Those eyebrows of hers! Like hairy caterpillars, aren't they. And her teeth! They look just like peeled caterpillars."'[9] A certain Captain of the Guards, who has been interested in the girl, is put off by her dark, thick eyebrows, which give her face an unpleasing boldness, and particularly by her unblackened teeth, which gleam horribly when she smiles.

The importance attached to women's dress has already been noticed as an aspect of the rule of taste. A woman's skill in choosing clothes, and particularly in matching colours, was regarded as a far better guide to her character and charm than the physical features with which she happened to have been born. Feminine clothing was immensely elaborate and cumbersome, consisting *inter alia* of a heavy outer costume and a set of unlined silk robes (twelve was the standard number), all carefully selected with an eye to the most attractive and original colour combinations. So that their fastidious blending of patterns and colours might be properly admired, women wore the robes in such a way that each sleeve was longer as it came closer to the skin. Among contemporary fashions, aimed mainly at attracting male observers, were *oshidashi*, in which the sleeves protruded from beneath the curtain of state: *idashi-uchigi*, in which the bottom of each inner robe extended slightly below the robe above it: and *idashiguruma*, the custom of letting one's full array of sleeves hang outside the carriage for the delectation of passers-by. Women who were going out normally wore either their left or their

---

(*o-haguro*) appears to have been indigenous and, as Van Gulik points out, may well be one of the customs that hark back to the origins of the southern strain in the Japanese race (tooth-blackening being widely spread in the South Seas).

8. In the Tokugawa period, courtesans, who were known as 'brides of one night', also blackened their teeth.

9. Shinshaku Nihon Bungaku Sōsho ed., ii, 569.

right sleeve longer than the other, depending on which side of the carriage they were to occupy.

From our scattered knowledge about the women of Murasaki's day a composite picture emerges. We see her then – the well-born Heian lady – with her vast integument of clothing and her voluminous black hair, with her tiny stature and exiguous features, with her pallid face and darkened teeth. A bizarre, amorphous figure she must have been as she moved about slowly in her twilight world of curtains, screens, and thick silk hangings.

*

According to Confucian and Buddhist doctrine, her position was not a happy one. It is true that the really harsh attitude belongs to later centuries; yet Heian doctrine allowed no room for doubt about her inferior status. On more than one occasion Genji refers to the Chinese teaching about a woman's 'three dependencies' (as a maiden to her father, a wife to her husband, a widow to her eldest son); emancipated though in many ways the Heian woman was, there could be no question about male supremacy in the family hierarchy. Buddhism confirmed the woman's inferiority in the spiritual realm by insisting on her 'five disadvantages': however worthy her conduct in the present life might be, she had no chance of being reborn into any of the higher categories without having first passed through an incarnation as a man.

Despite her low status in religion, the Heian woman enjoyed a remarkably favourable position in law. The current codes guaranteed her right to inherit and keep property (the custom of unitary male inheritance was not established until much later); and in this respect her condition compares very favourably with that of women in the contemporary West.[10] Daughters of the provincial-governor class appear to have been particularly well provided for, usually receiving a share of the inheritance in the form of real property or rights in manorial estates, and being entitled by law to keep their own houses. The resultant economic independence may be one of the reasons that so many of the gifted women writers – Murasaki Shikibu, for instance, and the author of the *Sarashina Diary* – belonged to this class. The literature of the time provides several instances of prospective suitors who are lured by a

10. Des Longrais, op. cit., p. 330; and see above, p. 92.

girl's expectations. In *The Tale of Genji* the parvenu Governor of Hitachi points out the advantages that a certain aristocratic young Guards officer may derive from marrying his daughter, even though she belongs to the despised provincial class:

'I realize that he is not very rich at the moment,' he brashly explained to the matchmaker, 'but that doesn't bother me in the slightest. So long as I'm alive, I'll look after them nicely.... And when I'm gone, my daughter will be handsomely provided for. She will be getting my wealth and my estates (*takaramono ryōjihaberu tokorodokoro*) and there won't be anyone to contest her rights. Of course I have lots of other children, but I've always been especially fond of this girl of mine.

'So long as the young gentleman is sincere about his intentions, he'll be in a position to make a splendid career for himself. Should he want to become a Minister, he'll have to spend a great deal. But this won't present any difficulty, because his wife will be able to provide him with all the wealth he needs. You tell me that the Emperor looks on him with favour. Well, what with that and what with our help, the young man won't have anything to worry about. The marriage will be a blessing for him – and for my own little daughter too. I am sure you agree.'[11]

Since the upper-class Heian wife as a rule continued living in her parents' house during the early part of her marriage, she usually escaped the tyranny of husband and mother-in-law that became traditional in later centuries. This too added to her independence (though of course the system had the balancing disadvantage of making it easier for the husband to decamp). The woman was also protected from physical violence. The codes specifically prohibited the husband from beating his wife – they added, however, that the punishment for this offence should be two grades lower than that imposed for assaulting other people. The husband was also forbidden to kill his wife unless he happened to find her in *flagrante delicto*.

One reason for the relatively favourable position of women was the system of 'marriage politics', which had spread from the Fujiwara family to the aristocracy in general.[12] The prevalence of marriage politics specifically strengthened the position of the principal wife, but indirectly it increased the prestige of women in general. The 'good people' made themselves still better by arranging advantageous marri-

11. Ikeda ed., vi, 242–3. 12. See pp. 63–4.

ages for their daughters – if possible to an emperor or imperial prince, but otherwise into some distinguished family like the Fujiwaras, the Tachibanas, or the Koses. We have noticed how skilfully men like Kaneie and Michinaga used their daughter's matrimonial connexions to secure their political position. As the system developed, daughters became far more useful to the Fujiwaras than sons, and the family could never produce enough of them to satisfy its complicated genealogical needs. When the wife of a Fujiwara leader gave birth to a son, he knew that neither this boy nor the boy's son could ever become an emperor; an attractive daughter, however, had every chance of marrying an imperial prince or an emperor and of giving birth to a future emperor, who would then be a Fujiwara.

The system applied on every level of aristocratic society, women's position in the hierarchy always being more fluid than that of men. Even a girl of humble provincial parentage might enter into a relationship with a man of the highest rank. Thus the young woman from Akashi has a liaison with Genji and gives birth to a daughter, who (having been adopted by Lady Murasaki) becomes the future empress and mother of an emperor. Genji himself, however, though he is the son of an emperor, is irremediably handicapped by his mother's humble birth and can never hope to succeed his father, whatever qualifications he may have.[13] This was the only time in Japanese history when girls were more to be welcomed than boys, and we can well understand Prince Genji's delight when he hears that he has had his first daughter.

In view of the importance of marriage relations, a father would make every effort to have his boy accepted as son-in-law in a highly placed family, and there was keen rivalry for the hand of any attractive girl of good birth. Thus Genji is married to Lady Aoi, the daughter of the Minister of the Left (a powerful Fujiwara), and this connexion is more important for his political success than being the son of an emperor. When Yūgiri, however, tries to marry the daughter of the Fujiwara leader, Tō no Chūjō, the father objects since the boy is not of sufficiently high rank, and it is only after a long delay that he consents to the match. A common theme in Heian literature is the *tsuma-arasoi* ('wife-battle'),

13. In other words, the male child of a 'mixed marriage' (i.e. between a well-born man and a poorly born woman) was normally at a far greater disadvantage than his sister.

in which numerous men compete for a particular girl. The first of the
Heian romances, *The Tale of the Bamboo Cutter*, is centred on a contest
of this kind, and it also plays an important part in *The Tale of the
Hollow Tree*; in *The Tale of Genji* a bevy of distinguished gentlemen
struggle to get Tamakazura's hand in marriage.

When it came to affairs of state, women were normally excluded.
Yet even here some of them held their own. Certain Dowager Empresses,
notably Emperor Ichijō's mother and later Murasaki's own Empress
(Akiko), had considerable power, particularly in matters of promotion,
marriage, and succession. Readers of Murasaki's novel will recall the
influence that the redoubtable Empress Kokiden wields behind the
scenes, and its unfortunate effect on Genji's career. Other important
women of the aristocracy (like Fujitsubo in *The Tale of Genji*) had their
own Administrative Councils, which looked after their property,
retainers, and personal affairs.

While such cases were exceptional, even among the upper classes, the
fact remains that the women at this time were far from being the unfortunate down-trodden creatures that some modern writers have suggested in their effort to represent *The Tale of Genji* as a work of feminine
protest and Murasaki Shikibu as the champion of an exploited class and
sex. From what we know of the ladies in Heian society, they certainly
did not stand in any exaggerated awe of their men. Polygamy, it is true,
made their position insecure, especially if they did not have the fortune
of being an official wife. In this respect, however, the Heian period is
hardly exceptional; for the system has existed in one form or another
throughout Japanese history. On the whole, Heian women were remarkably well off, and it is only since the Second World War that the position
of Japanese women has become better than that of their ancestors a
thousand years ago. It is interesting, and perhaps significant, that the
ladies of the time were not expected to see their husbands off (*mi-okuri*)
with the humble marks of respect that became normal in later times,
and that men like Prince Niou are described as helping their wives in
and out of carriages, an impressive token of consideration in a society
where the tradition of chivalry was unknown.

One important factor that contributed to women's prestige was that
they were all literate and thoroughly at home in a world where music,
belles lettres, the preparation of incense, and other forms of cultural

activity were prized. In these spheres they could hold their own with any man. The following injunction of a tenth-century Fujiwara states-man to his daughter can be taken as typical: 'First you must study pen-manship. Next you must learn to play the seven-string zither better than anyone else. And also you must memorize all the poems in the twenty books of the *Kokin Shū*.'[14] Calligraphy, music and poetry – these were the main components of a woman's education; and together they provided a good basis for the type of cultural life she was expected to lead.

Apart from this, women had come to take a particular interest in the romances known as *monogatari*, though these were not included among the formal requirements. Most of the *monogatari* were probably written by men, but they appear to have been particularly appreciated by women. Not only did they help to while away the leisure hours, but also they provided instructional glimpses of outside life, which was usually hidden from women; for, as Genji remarks in his famous literary discussion with Tamakazura, the *monogatari* describe this world exactly as it is.[15] Girls of the Heian upper class delved into their *monogatari* with the same excitement and with much the same motives that inspired the daughters of strict Victorian families when they read the novels of the Brontë sisters.

It was a very limited form of education (though hardly more so, to be sure, than that offered to most well-born English girls of the nineteenth century). The language of history, law, philosophy, and every other form of scholarship was closed to all but the most enterprising and gifted ladies of the day. The majority of women, including such a talented writer as the author of *Gossamer Diary*, had an exceedingly restricted range of knowledge and interests. It is significant that even an ardent advocate of academic pursuits like Prince Genji should have considered that, when it came to women, a little education went a long way:

'I do not think we need worry too much about her education,' [he remarks one day when discussing the young Princess Akashi]. 'Women should have a general knowledge of several subjects, but it gives a bad

14. Advice of Fujiwara no Morotada (918–69) to his daughter, Yoshiko. Quoted in Kaneko ed., p. 95.
15. Kono yo no hoka no koto narazu. . . . N.B.T. ed., vi, 622. See Appendix 5.

impression if they show themselves to be attached to a particular branch of learning. I would not have her completely ignorant in any field. The important thing is that she should appear to have a gentle, easy-going approach even to those subjects that she takes most seriously.'[16]

*

Despite the many privileges that women of the Japanese upper classes enjoyed in comparison with their successors in later centuries (and also with their contemporaries in the West), we must never forget what a closed and immobile existence most of them were expected to lead if they were not in active court service. There is no need to dwell on this point, since it has already been discussed as a general aspect of Heian life. The woman of Heian Kyō participated in outdoor activities as little as her sister in the Moslem world; and on the rare occasions when she did leave her house the walls of her ox-carriage protected her, more completely than could any yashmak, from the eyes of strangers. Indoors she lived in a condition of semi-obscurity, in which day was barely distinguishable from night. Normally she was hidden behind her screen of state, whose function for the Heian woman was analogous to that of the Islamic *pardah*. Though she might intimate her artistic taste by letting her sleeves protrude outside the curtains, normally she could never show herself to any man except her husband and her father. The 'lady who loved insects' will not allow even her parents to see her face to face: 'Ghosts and women,' she explains to her parents through a small opening in her screen, 'had best remain invisible.' This is not introduced as an example of the lady's eccentricity; for the author comments that it is a 'sensible remark'.[17]

Her state of purdah was rarely relieved by the joys of conversation. The well-bred lady communicated by means of intermediaries or letters; as a rule her only direct exchanges, except with her husband or parents, were with maids and other female attendants.

---

16. Ikeda ed., iii, 131–2. And note the comment of one of the young men in the 'discussion on a rainy night': 'Women should often pretend to be ignorant (*shirazugao*) of things they really know. When they feel like displaying their knowledge of a subject, they should content themselves with a couple of casual comments.' Quoted by Ikeda, *Heianchō no Seikatsu to Bungaku*, p. 173.

17. Shinshaku Nihon Bungaku Sōsho ed., ii, 569.

During most of the time her life must have been one of well-nigh unbelievable monotony and ennui. This is not evident in most of the feminine writings of the time, since their authors were usually court ladies, who had a busy and relatively unrestricted life.[18] In a work like *Gossamer Diary*, however, whose writer was condemned to the inactive stay-at-home life of most upper-class Heian women, the tedium emerges with almost unbearable intensity. The following typical entry is from the Second Month of 972: 'Seventeenth day of the month. There is a slow drizzle. My direction today is unlucky and so I can expect no visitors. The world seems a dreary, cheerless place.'[19]

Surrounded as they were by servants, the women of this class were free from all domestic duties, including the need to look after children. Their existence was almost entirely sedentary: instead of moving about and doing things in the house, they sat for hours on end 'gazing into space' (*tsukuzuku to nagamesasetamau* is a typical phrase[20]) and vaguely waiting for some poem or visit, which, more often than not, fails to come. The word *tsurezure* ('leisure hours') is basic to the vocabulary of the woman's life. Frequently it crops up in phrases like *tsurezure ni kurushimu* ('to suffer from leisure') and *tsurezure wo nagusamu* ('to relieve one's leisure') which suggest that leisure and its effects have come to be regarded almost as a physical ailment.

What, then, were the main reliefs that Heian life offered to these immured women of the upper class? Several have been mentioned in earlier chapters. There was the wealth of time-consuming games like *go* and root-matching competitions, in which women took particular delight. The yearly round of festivals and ceremonies provided them with perennial entertainment; visits to fashionable temples near the capital were a further distraction. Being educated, they were also able to enjoy cultural and artistic pursuits – calligraphy exercises (*tenarai*), poetry exchanges, music practice, and, above all, listening to those numerous *monogatari*, which, as Prince Genji points out, were so ad-

18. Owing to current beliefs about ritual defilement (see pp. 107–8), court ladies were obliged to go home once a month. We can tell from the diaries and the *Pillow Book* that time hung heavily on their hands during these days of enforced idleness.

19. *Kagerō Nikki*, p. 260.

20. Ikeda ed., vii, 18.

mirably suited for 'beguiling the leisure hours'.[21] Many Heian ladies also took an interest in sewing and dyeing materials – or at least in supervising this work; in Murasaki's time dyeing demanded a particularly high degree of skill and artistic sensitivity.

Yet for the vast majority of young, upper-class women the most engaging interest was their relations with men. However independent they may have been economically, however well protected by the law and by their families, however self-confident about their own cultural accomplishments, women like Izumi Shikibu and Michitsuna's mother in real life, or Lady Rokujō and Yūgiri's wife in fiction, were above all absorbed in their relations with their husband or lover, or lovers; and it was the attitude of these men that mainly governed their existence.

The subject of the relationship between aristocratic men and women in the Heian period is complicated and in many ways obscure. But it deserves to be examined in some detail, since it is an important feature of the social, and even the cultural, life of the times. When the people of Genji's circle speak of 'the world' (*yo no naka*), they normally refer to love affairs; and so far as their plots are concerned the Heian *monogatari* are overwhelmingly concerned with relations between the sexes.

*

Because of her secluded life, it was theoretically possible for a woman of the Heian upper class to spend her life without seeing any man except her father. Such indeed would have been the case of the ungainly red-nosed Lady Suetsumuhana in *The Tale of Genji* had it not been for the hero's fortuitous visit and for his magnanimous nature. Suetsumuhana, however, was in almost every way exceptional.[22] On the whole,

21. '. . . without these *monogatari* how on earth would you distract yourself during these tedious hours when you are at your wits' end about what to do?' N.B.T. ed., vi, 621.

22. In her depiction of Prince Hitachi's unfortunate daughter Murasaki was probably satirizing the romantic tradition of a fascinating young woman living in derelict surroundings where she is waiting to be discovered by an enterprising suitor. By the end of the 10th century this figure had become something of a literary *cliché*. In their conversation on the rainy night in Book 2 Genji and his young friends discuss how delightful it must be to meet such a girl. When she does appear in the novel two years later, Murasaki pictures her as gawky and red-nosed.

spinsters and virgins were unusual in well-born families. For one thing, girls of the aristocracy were greatly in demand for the material reasons that we have seen. Also, it was firmly believed that any girl who remained virgin for long had been possessed by an evil spirit, and this was hardly a reputation that a self-respecting family, or the girl herself, would welcome.[23] In *The Tale of Genji* a group of old crones discuss Ōigimi's refusal to become Kaoru's (or anyone else's) mistress:

'Why won't Her Ladyship do as he wants?' said one fearsome-looking old hag through a gap in her teeth. 'Do you suppose she's been possessed by one of those terrible gods (*osoroshiki kami*) people talk about?'

'Yes,' another of them chimed in, 'it's positively eerie. Some evil spirit must have got hold of her . . .'[24]

A cursory reading of a work like the *Pillow Book* might give the impression that the men and women of this world lived in a state of general promiscuity, freely indulging in any sexual activity that their appetites suggested and their circumstances allowed. This, however, was no more true of Heian than it has been of any other human society in recorded history. Relations between the sexes were regulated by an exact system, based largely on class distinctions.[25] To the outsider it may appear somewhat amorphous and confusing – but so do sexual relations in almost any unfamiliar society.

Courting and marriage customs differed according to the particular degree of relationship (principal wife, concubine, etc.); it is nevertheless possible to formulate a general pattern that had been adopted by the upper classes in Murasaki's time. If we remember that there were considerable variations (marriage to the principal wife, for example, was not preceded by the 'three visits' when, as often happened, the bridegroom was a mere stripling of about twelve), we may take the following to be the usual course of events leading up to one of the more permanent types of connexion. First, the man or his family are informed about a suitable girl by a matchmaker (*nakadachi*), who, if properly encouraged,

23. Cf. the ancient Chinese belief that abstention from the sexual act, apart from depriving a person of the physical *yin-yang* benefits that frequent intercourse provided, involved great risks of succumbing to incubi and other evil forces. Van Gulik, op. cit., pp. 105, 152–3.

24. Ikeda ed., vi, 40.   25. See pp. 83–4.

will make the necessary overtures on both sides.[26] (In certain cases the man will have heard about her from a friend or attendant; still more rarely, he may actually have seen her at court or during some ceremony – Kashiwagi, it will be recalled, catches sight of Princess Nyosan while he is playing a game of court football under the cherry trees outside Genji's palace.) If his interest is aroused, he will write the young lady a thirty-one syllable poem expressing conventionally romantic sentiments. This calls for a prompt reply, which will be composed either by the girl herself or, more usually, by a member of her family or even an attendant. The gentleman will examine this reply with the greatest scrutiny; for its calligraphy and poetic skill are a sure indication of the girl's character and charm.[27] If the lady's letter is gauche, he may well decide to cut his losses at this stage and to let the relationship lapse.

If she passes muster, however, he will make arrangements to visit her secretly at her house on the first convenient night. The secrecy is entirely conventional; for by this time the girl's family and attendants know exactly what is afoot – and, besides, Heian architecture provided little effective concealment. This first visit, incidentally, belongs to a type of sexual institution that can be found in certain parts of Asia and Europe, where parents were expected to close their eyes on occasions of this kind. It involves an accepted form of pre-nuptial freedom, which may well have its origins in the idea that there should be a full-scale trial before relations are put on a more official and permanent footing.[28] Heian literature suggests that many conventions (apart from secrecy) attended the first visit. The gallant will, among other things, keep the girl awake all night (at least, it is conventional to speak as if he has), and he will comment on the cock-crow with suitable expressions of dismay. He departs – or, again as convention would have it, drags himself away – at the first sign of dawn. Immediately on his return home he sets about composing his 'next-morning' letter (*kinuginu no fumi*), the reassuring telephone call of the Heian period. In it he laments the long hours that

26. The matchmaker or go-between was also responsible for finding out whether the omens favoured the proposed marriage and for fixing an auspicious day.

27. See pp. 195–7.

28. Edward Westermarck, *A Short History of Marriage*, p. 9. I am indebted to Westermarck for much of the general information in the following paragraphs.

will keep him away from the girl and adds a love poem, usually based on some image of dew-laden flowers or trees. The arrival of this letter is a sign that all has gone well, and the girl's family regales the 'next-morning messenger' with wine and presents. (After Prince Niou's first night with his principal wife, the messenger who has delivered his letter staggers back, full of wine and loaded with costly brocades – much to the dismay of Niou's secondary wife, Naka no Kimi, who realizes that her situation is now hopeless.) The girl sends a reply, using the same imagery and, as a rule, the same messenger.[29]

On the following night the man pays a second 'secret' visit to the girl and again creeps away at dawn. The messenger is kept busy with a further exchange of letters.

The third night is the most important. On this occasion small rice cakes known as 'third-night cakes' (*mikayomochi*) are prepared by the girl's family or attendants and placed in her room. These are in honour of the Shintoist progenitors, Izanagi and Izanami, and the couple's acceptance of the cakes may be regarded as the central marriage rite; for the connexion between the man and the girl now has religious sanction.

29. Sometimes, however, the first night was also the last. After discussing things with their daughter, the girl's parents might agree that the relationship had better be broken off, in which case the matchmaker would be asked to provide suitable excuses. Alternatively, if the man had not sent his 'next-morning' letter by noon, it meant that he had decided not to pursue the liaison. This was naturally a grave insult to the girl and her family, but (possibly owing to the absence of any chivalric tradition) no social stigma attached to the gentleman in these cases. Nor, it would seem, did the girl's loss of virginity irrevocably disqualify her for future matches. By the nature of things, a principal wife was almost bound to be a virgin; early Japanese society did not, however, attach the overriding importance to virginity that had traditionally existed in China and that later came to prevail in Japan.

Although the theoretical right to 'break off an engagement' (if one may use this term to describe a situation in which the relationship ended after the first night) was recognized in Murasaki's time, it was hardly ever exercised in the case of the principal wife (since here the feelings of the partners were normally not taken into consideration) and only very rarely when secondary wives were involved. On the whole, the 'three visits' had come to be regarded as a pre-nuptial convention; the idea of a trial, which was no doubt the origin of the custom, had receded into the background. The laws of human psychology and physiology would suggest that the first night with a virgin bride would be an unreliable form of trial in any civilized society.

One of the main aspects of marriage, as Westermarck points out, is publicity (including publicity about its consummation), and it is significant that this third night in Japan was known as the 'exposure of the event' (*tokoro-arawashi*). As a further mark of open acceptance, the girl's father or guardian would send the couple a formal letter of committal (*mika no yo no goshōsoku*), expressing his official approval of the marriage. On the following morning the man is no longer obliged to make his way home in the dark through the dew-drenched grass but can remain openly with the girl behind her curtain of state. This presentation of rice cakes without ceremony of any kind may seem a rather trivial act. Yet there can be no doubt about its ritual importance: when Prince Genji has become Murasaki's lover and wants to make his marriage to her public and official, he summons his attendant, Koremitsu, and with a smile instructs him to prepare rice cakes for the following evening.[30]

Another universal aspect of marriage is feasting, which is both a means of publicity and a social covenant.[31] By eating and drinking together in the presence of family and friends, the couple openly signify their union. In Heian times the feast normally took place on the evening after the rice cakes or a few days later. Wine and food were prepared at the girl's house, and the bridegroom would be invited together with a few companions (but not, as a rule, with his own parents). On this occasion he would officially meet his bride's family for the first time. At the beginning of the festivities there was usually a simple service, during which a priest would recite *norito* rituals and wave a branch of the sacred *sakaki* tree as a means of purification.[32] The couple normally performed a three-times-three exchange of wine cups. This ceremony, known as *sansan-kudo*, was also a form of Shintō purification, *sake* having since the earliest times been respected in the native religion for its cleansing virtues. In the Muromachi period *sansan-kudo* became the central act of the marriage rites, but in Murasaki's day it was ancillary to the presentation of rice cakes and was not an essential part of the proceedings.

Now the couple was well and truly wed: the man could openly visit

---

30. Ikeda ed., ii, 57–8.   31. Westermarck, op. cit., p. 145 ff.
32. Westermarck mentions prophylactic or cathartic rites as being common to most forms of marriage. This clearly fits in with the Shintō stress on ritual purity.

the girl's house when he pleased and remain with her until late in the morning. Whether or not he eventually moved her into his own house depended on the type of marriage; and at this stage it may be well to distinguish between the three main types of relationship.

First, there was marriage as the principal wife or, as the name literally signified, 'northern person'.[33] In any polygamous system the general rule is that one wife, usually the first, has a higher social position than the rest, and that this wife must be respected by the husband and his concubines because of her dignity and age. This applied throughout Chinese history, and, though the Japanese system diverged in many ways from that on the Continent, the rule prevailed in Japan too until modern times. The principal wife was normally chosen by the bridegroom's family after much discussion and negotiation. Social, political, and economic considerations were paramount, and the marriage was arranged as early as possible. The wishes of the partners were in most cases irrelevant. This, of course, is not peculiar to Heian Japan, but applies to any society (Renaissance Italy, for example) that practises child betrothal and marriage politics.

Though the minimum ages for marriage had been fixed at fourteen for boys and twelve for girls, boys of the upper class were in most cases betrothed shortly after their coming-of-age ceremony, which was normally at the age of twelve. This is the age at which Genji is betrothed to Lady Aoi; Emperor Reizei is only eleven when he marries Akikonomu, and Emperor Ichijō (in real life) was ten.

The wife was often several years older than her boy-husband: Aoi, for example, is sixteen, Akikonomu nineteen, and Sadako (in real life) fifteen. Since women in Heian, as elsewhere, tended to mature at an earlier age than men, the principal wife must often have seemed more of a guardian to her young husband than a bride. When Genji is married to Lady Aoi, her father (the Minister of the Left) is delighted with the lad, who strikes him as being 'quite disgracefully handsome'.[34] The bride, however, has different thoughts: 'Her new husband seemed terribly

33. See p. 46. According to traditional Chinese cosmology, the northern position was the place of the ruler, who faces south. *North* indicated that the principal wife ruled within the house; *east* was the place of the man, who ruled within and without.

34. *Yuyushū utsukushi*. Ikeda ed., i, 181, 182.

young. She felt there was something unsuitable about being married to such a child and she was quite ashamed.' Genji is equally disgruntled: 'He noticed that everyone was treating Aoi with great respect, as if she were the most charming of women; but he saw nothing so special about her.' Such matches, which were arranged for purely political motives, must often have turned out like Genji's with Aoi – a façade, devoid of any depth of friendship or affection.

In marriages of this kind the strictest rules applied to class, and it was only in very exceptional cases that the bride and groom were not of more or less equal rank. Genji is never able to take Murasaki as his principal wife, because, though her father is an imperial prince, her mother is the daughter of a provincial official. When Lady Aoi dies, his next principal wife is Princess Nyosan, a mere child of thirteen, in whom he has not the slightest interest, but who has the overriding advantage of having an emperor for her father and an emperor's daughter for her mother. As a result of this strict endogamy, the number of suitable candidates available, especially in the higher rungs of the aristocracy, was always very limited. One result was an extreme laxity about degrees of relationship permitted in marriage. The Chinese rules of generation could not be applied, and not only were marriages between first cousins quite acceptable, but also those between aunts and nephews, uncles and nieces.[35]

Though betrothal between a man and his principal wife was normally arranged by the parents without any reference to the wishes of the couple, it happened in certain exceptional cases that a man would choose his official wife himself, even against family opposition. *The Tale of Genji* provides a memorable example of a love match of this kind in the story of Yūgiri and Lady Kumoi; it is only after years of waiting and much romantic anguish (of the type that provides a familiar theme in Western literature) that Yūgiri is able to prevail on Kumoi's father to agree to the match.

As a rule the principal wife continued to live with her parents after marriage; so long as the nuptial relations were satisfactory, her husband would visit her there at night, or even move in entirely. This was the ancient Japanese system, and it persisted among most aristocratic

35. See p. 63. The old Chinese kinship system and horror of 'name incest' were of course totally absent in Heian Japan.

families in Murasaki's time.[36] When the man's father died or retired, and he became the head of the family or of a branch, his principal wife would normally leave her parents' house and move into the northern wing of her husband's residence, where she assumed the full dignity of *materfamilias*, administering her own household retainers and, in certain cases, even having her own staff of officials to look after her property.

Her aims and duties were clearly laid down in the Confucian tradition. She must be an obedient, faithful wife, respectful to her husband and his family, and bear him a son, who would maintain the family continuity and perpetuate the ancestral cult.[37] Since the rate of infant mortality was high, she must have as numerous a progeny as possible: the more children she produced, the more secure her position in the family group. She was in particular responsible for the upbringing of her daughters, who must be properly trained in the polite arts, so that when they reached a nubile age they might marry into good families as principal wives or – highest of all ambitions – become the concubine or wife of an emperor and thus secure the family's advancement.

*

36. It was not uncommon, however, for a young husband and his principal wife to live together in their own house, especially after they have had children of their own. It will be recalled that Lady Kumoi moves in with Yūgiri according to this modern fashion.

37. A man's eldest son by his principal wife was normally the heir, all children by other consorts being theoretically equal. (Those familiar with the Chinese system will note how Heian practice diverged in this respect.) If he had no son by his wife, his heir would be a son by some other consort or an adopted child; in either case the principal wife would adopt the child. Sons of lower consorts had a hard time; often they became priests or drifted to the provinces. For a child whose mother was not the principal wife it was particularly important to receive the father's acknowledgement and backing. In *The Tale of Genji* the fathers of Murasaki and of Ukifune (Princes Hyōbukyō and Hachi) refuse to acknowledge their daughters; Genji, however, does acknowledge Akashi's child, thus making possible her meteoric rise in the social hierarchy. As a rule the principal wife would oppose her husband's recognition of children by secondary consorts, and often she would treat these children harshly, especially if it appeared that any of them threatened the primacy of her own brood. The stepmother is a stock villain in Heian fiction, including *The Tale of Genji*, and there was a special *genre* of sentimental works known as *mamako monogatari* ('stepmother tales').

Another great aim – though it would hardly be mentioned in the Confucian manuals – was to avoid being supplanted by a rival, that is, by a
subsidiary consort. This brings us to the next main form of relationship,
marriage to secondary wives or concubines. As in most polygamous
societies, the vast majority of people in Murasaki's Japan practised
monogamy. In the affluent upper classes, however, it was possible for a
man to have a principal wife and several secondary consorts of a more or
less permanent nature; and this was the normal system among the 'good
people' of Heian.[38] Murasaki Shikibu's husband already had three or
four such consorts when he married her, and Fujiwara no Kaneie
divided his attention among some eight wives (one of whom was the
disconsolate author of *Gossamer Diary*) in addition to his principal
wife.

Modern writers sometimes refer to these secondary consorts as 'mistress'; but the term is misleading, for the relationship was officially
recognized and was preceded by forms of courting and marriage that,

38. From the Wei chronicles we gather that this was already the system in the
3rd century: 'All men of high rank have four or five wives; others two or three.'
Quoted by Sansom in *A Short Cultural History of Japan*, p. 30.

A discussion of sexual behaviour in the Heian period raises the question of
whether male homosexuality (which became so prevalent in later centuries
especially among warriors, priests and actors) was widely practised in Murasaki's
time. I have found little evidence on the subject. As we have seen, the gentlemen
described in contemporary literature often give a somewhat epicene impression;
yet nearly all of them, even those who may seem most effeminate, had numerous
involved relations with women. Sei Shōnagon, who would not be likely to remain
silent on this subject if it had ever come to her attention, does not say a single
word about it. The only possible hint that I have found in *The Tale of Genji*
occurs in the scene where the hero, having been turned down by Utsusemi, lies
next to her young brother, who has been acting as his messenger. The lad has
just told Genji that he cannot take him to where his sister is sleeping. ' "Very
well, my boy," said the Prince, laying him down beside him. "But you at least
must not desert me." Utsusemi's brother was delighted to find himself lying
next to the handsome young prince, and Genji for his part found the lad very
sympathetic (*aware*) after his unyielding sister.' (Ikeda ed., i, 229). Even this is
ambiguous; and at most it is a case of *faute de mieux*.

Homosexual relations among the court ladies were probably quite common,
as in any society where women are obliged to live in continuous and close
proximity (cf. Van Gulik, op. cit., p. 48); but here again I have found no specific
evidence.

mutatis mutandis, were the same as with the principal wife. Although the man might meet a secondary wife in private, and over a fairly long period of time, before making the relationship official, the 'third night' cere-mony was identical in form and significance. Thereafter the man was treated as an accepted lover or husband, to whom the girl was expected to remain faithful, and she was his official concubine – to whom, of course, no one expected him to be faithful.

In secondary marriages of this kind there were several degrees of relationship, depending on how open and permanent the man intended the connexion to be. These varied from the type that we find in *The Tale of Genji* between the hero and Lady Murasaki, or later between Prince Niou and Naka no Kimi, which were as open and settled as any marriage could be, to the somewhat furtive sort of connexion that Kaoru envisaged between himself and Ukifune.

The relationship with a concubine often started as a casual affair. Once the 'exposure of the event' had taken place, however, it acquired an official status, though never, it is true, the irrevocability of the princi-pal marriage. At this stage the man had several possible courses of action. His choice would depend on his intentions towards the girl, as well as on his economic means. If he was living in his own house, he might have her brought there and installed in one of the wings. This meant that he regarded the relationship as open and formal, and in this sense the girl and her family would welcome the move. On the other hand, it had the disadvantage of exposing her directly to the hostility and competition of the man's principal wife and of other secondary consorts, past and future. *The Tale of Genji* describes the lethal ordeals that Lady Kiritsubo has to endure at the hands of her rivals after she has become an Imperial Concubine – ordeals from which the adoring emperor himself is unable to protect her. Such rivalries were especially bitter in the Imperial Palace, where the political stakes were high; but they were common too in private households. The following passage from Murasaki's novel suggests some of the difficulties that may confront an official concubine even when she has the protection of men as powerful as Genji and Tō no Chūjō. Among the many suitors who languish so pathetically after Tamakazura (each of whom, incidentally, already has a principal wife and children) the dark, hirsute Prince Higekuro wins the day. During one of his visits he has got the beautiful young lady with child, and now he proudly looks forward to making her his secondary consort and to bringing her home to live in the same house as his principal wife:[39]

Genji deeply regretted what had happened, but at this stage there was nothing to be done about it.[40] Besides, since everyone seemed to approve of the match, it would be most out of place, and also unfair to Higekuro, if he alone showed displeasure. Accordingly he gave instructions that the marriage ceremonies should be carried out in full style.

Higekuro wanted to bring Tamakazura to his house as quickly as possible, but Genji made it clear that he could not agree to her being moved too soon. For, as he explained by way of an excuse, there was already a certain person living in Higekuro's house[41] who must be awaiting Tamakazura's arrival with very little pleasure indeed, and he would feel extremely sorry for his young ward if she had to confront this difficulty without any further preparation.

'Please try to arrange things for her in as quiet and pleasant a way as possible,' he said to Tō no Chūjō one day. 'Whatever happens, Tamakazura must not be subjected to any spite or slander.'

'I think she will be safer this way,' her father replied under his breath, 'than if she had gone into the Palace. I was really extremely worried about her taking service at Court, because I know what a hard time a woman can have unless the emperor is prepared to give her full protection or unless she has powerful backing from outside. Of course I am very fond of the girl and should have done what I could to make things less unpleasant for her. But you have seen how difficult it has been for me to help even my own recognized daughter at Court. What could I possibly have done for a girl in Tamakazura's position?'[42]

Instead of bringing his concubine to live at home, the husband might install her with her attendants in another house, either openly (as Niou does with Naka no Kimi) or secretly (as Kaoru plans to do with Uki-fune).[43] Alternatively, she might continue to live in her own house, like

39. Higekuro's principal wife is the daughter of an imperial prince by his own principal wife; in other words, she is the legitimate granddaughter of an emperor. Despite her talent and beauty, Tamakazura is socially no match for her.

40. It will be recalled that Genji is secretly in love with Tamakazura, whom he has been looking after in place of her real father, Tō no Chūjō.

41. Higekuro's mad wife.

42. Ikeda ed., iii, 278–9.

43. Here again rank was the overriding consideration. Naka no Kimi's mother was Prince Hachi's principal wife and herself the daughter of a State Minister;

the author of *Gossamer Diary*, and her husband would visit her there at more or less regular intervals. There were arrangements to suit all tastes and situations. Yūgiri, for example, that model of respectability, finds the following system most convenient: 'He moved Princess Ochiba [his new secondary wife] into the house in the north-eastern section, and divided his time equally, spending exactly one half of the month with her and the other half in his palace in the Third Ward with Lady Kumoi [his principal wife].'[44] The Minister of the Left in *The Tale of the Hollow Tree* follows the same neat arrangement.

The official concubine may be chosen in various ways. Sometimes she will be a girl with whom the man has started a casual affair and to whom he has grown so attached that he wants to put things on a more permanent footing. In other cases it may be a woman of the same class as the man, or even of a higher class (like Princess Ochiba in *The Tale of Genji*), with whom he has fallen in love when he is already married. In contrast to the strict rules that governed the choice of principal wife, those that prescribed the type of concubine a man might choose were extremely lax. As in all societies, of course, there was an 'outer circle' beyond which marriage was prohibited or considered improper. It would, for example, be inconceivable that a Heian gentleman should take a peasant girl as his official concubine. Apart from this, however, there were few restrictions about class. After Ukifune's supposed death, Kaoru remembers how reluctant he was to put their relationship on an open footing, and it occurs to him that his scruples were unnecessary; for

... even emperors were known to have accepted concubines whose birth was quite as undistinguished as Ukifune's. Sometimes, indeed, because of karma from a previous existence, they had lavished the greatest affection on these girls; yet no one had suggested that such love was misplaced. When it came to people in his own position, there were countless examples of men who had chosen as their concubines girls of humble birth, or women who had already been married.[45]

There was also no definite restriction, such as applied in Moslem law,

---

Ukifune's mother was a secondary consort (who, into the bargain, had lowered herself by marrying an assistant provincial governor), and Prince Hachi had firmly refused to recognize the girl.

44. Ikeda ed., v, 136.   45. Ikeda ed., vii, 122-3.

about the number of wives that a man might have. In practice, however, apart from the emperor and a few immensely rich potentates like Michinaga, the gentlemen of Heian rarely went in for large collections. The exuberant form of polygamy that inspired King Solomon to gather 'seven hundred wives and princesses and three hundred concubines' was unknown in Japan; and the elaborate system of harems and eunuchs was never introduced from China. Kaneie's *ménage* of about ten consorts would seem to have been the maximum for most aristocratic gentlemen of the time. *The Tale of Genji*, in its description of Prince Genji's household in the Sixth Ward, gives us a good idea of how these various wives lived in the same mansion, each having her own set of attendants and occupying her own wing or pavilion, and rarely seeing each other except for special contests and ceremonies.

On the whole, Heian law and social convention allowed men considerable latitude in the management of their marital affairs. One course of action, however, was categorically forbidden: to let a secondary consort take the place of the principal wife. This practice is common in many polygamous societies, but in Heian Japan (possibly because of the overwhelming stress on differences of rank) it was never condoned. Any man who allowed a concubine to supplant his principal wife would have her family down on him and would incur all the public and moral resentment that our society directs against the husband who forsakes his wife and offspring. In this respect Heian custom was stricter than that of China, where it was possible for a man to divorce his principal wife if she was unable to provide him with a son to perpetuate the family cult.[46] When such a case occurred in Japan, the husband would normally arrange for his principal wife to adopt one of his sons by a concubine. (Similarly a higher-ranking concubine who was sterile might adopt the child of a lower concubine.) This was one of the many situations in which the Heian aristocracy, particularly the Fujiwaras, resorted to adoption in order to reconcile the very liberal system of polygamy with the rigid rank hierarchy.

*

46. The Chinese also recognized incurable disease as a valid reason for repudiating the principal wife; and, if a man really wanted a separation, other reasons could be concocted to provide a justification (ref. Van Gulik, op. cit., p. 33).

The third, and numerically most frequent, type of relations between men and women in Heian Kyō were those of a casual and promiscuous nature. This is the sort of affair that the young men in *The Tale of Genji* discuss during their conversation on the rainy night, and that Tō no Chūjō, and later Genji himself, enjoy with Yūgao. The woman is usually someone of a far lower class (like Yūgao), or a lady-in-waiting at one of the palaces. A gentleman might also have a clandestine affair with another man's wife (Kashiwagi with Princess Nyosan, for example), or another man's concubine (Genji with Lady Fujitsubo); and the general obscurity of Heian houses made it possible to have casual encounters (like Genji's with Lady Oborozukiyo) in which, at least to begin with, neither partner knows who the other is.

Few cultured societies in history can have been as tolerant about sexual relations as was the world of *The Tale of Genji*. Whether or not a gentleman was married, it redounded to his prestige to have as many affairs as possible; and the palaces and great mansions were full of ladies who were only too ready to accommodate him if approached in the proper style.[47] From reading the *Pillow Book* we can tell how extremely commonplace these casual affairs had become in court circles, the man usually visiting the girl at night behind her screen of state and leaving her at the crack of dawn.

Such relations entailed no obligation on either side. Occasionally, as we have seen, they might develop into something more permanent and official; but, unless this happened, there was nothing to prevent either man or woman from breaking things off at any time. In practice neither partner was expected to remain faithful, though their poems often contained protestations suggesting the contrary. Unattached women, like Sei Shōnagon herself, tended to be extremely promiscuous. Many of them had their own houses and, being economically independent, were free to have such relations as they wished and also to terminate them. They could refuse their favour to a man; they could keep him waiting;

47. Professional courtesans (*asobi-onna*) were also available in Murasaki's time, and we know that Michinaga was fond of one such girl, who had the name of Kokannon ('Little Goddess of Mercy'). These ladies did not, however, play any important part until the very end of the Heian period, and there were no elaborate gay quarters or hierarchy of courtesans such as had existed in the 'northern quarter' of Ch'ang-an.

they could send him away at any time, or replace him by another lover. It was also possible for them to have more than one lover at a time; the type of triangular situation that developed is often mentioned in contemporary literature, being most effectively treated by Murasaki in her final Uji chapters.

The reputation of carrying on several affairs did not, it is true, add to the lady's prestige as it did to the man's, and women were usually careful to avoid exposure and the consequent gossip. The court ladies, however, were not particularly criticized for their promiscuity; even a relatively strait-laced observer like Murasaki is more likely to censure a colleague for her taste in matching the colours of her robes than for having numerous lovers. A maid-of-honour or a lady in the Office of the Empress's Household would usually have a 'chief lover' who, theoretically at least, had a prior claim to her attentions. In addition, if she was sufficiently attractive and enterprising, she might have a secondary lover and numerous casual lovers, who would be invited behind her screen of state when the occasion permitted. Many women also carried on a sort of platonic liaison with a man whom they described as their 'elder brother'; such is Sei Shōnagon's connexion with the unfortunate Norimitsu in the *Pillow Book*.

In any society, licence of this kind is bound to produce complications and imbroglios. Heian Kyō had its full share. The clash between Korechika and the retired Emperor Kazan is an example of the sort of difficulty that was bound to ensue in a situation where both men and women were free to satisfy their taste for adventure; similarly, though on a less dramatic level, we have Murasaki's description of a certain young gentleman who, when visiting his mistress one evening, is dismayed to find that she is already entertaining another lover. It is natural too that the conversation at court should be full of innuendoes and suggestive badinage, and that much of the poetry exchanged among the aristocracy should refer to casual love affairs and their consequences. A further result is that paternity was frequently confused. Both Emperor Reizei and Kaoru are haunted by the fear (a correct one, as it happens) that their official fathers are not their real ones and that they have therefore been guilty of impiety by performing the Confucian rites in honour of the wrong person. Considering the lax sexual mores that prevailed in the Heian period, we have good reason to doubt the legitimacy of the imperial line. Since it was all-important for the Fujiwaras that their daughters should produce a good supply of imperial princes, and since the imperial bridegrooms were usually extremely young, it would hardly be surprising if there were occasions when somewhat more mature and experienced men performed the boy-emperors' connubial duties. Emperor Reizei's illegitimate succession to the throne may have had many a counterpart in real life.[48]

*

The love life of the Heian aristocracy is marked by a curious mixture of depravity and decorum. The absence of any ideal of courtly love involving fealty, protection, and romantic languishing, and the acceptance of a high degree of promiscuity, frequently give a flippant, rather heartless air to the relations between the men and women of Murasaki's world. One has the impression that, for all the elegant sentiments expressed in the poems, the love affairs of the time, especially at court, were rarely imbued with any real feeling, and that often they were mere exercises in seduction.

There was one factor, however, that saved them from degenerating into something crass and sordid: the dominant part played by the rule of taste.[49] The love affairs of the time were from beginning to end conducted according to an elegant ritual, with a strong aesthetic sense of how things should be done. No doubt many men of the time were impatient with the rules and niceties of courtly dalliance – the endless poems, the 'next-morning letters', the choice of the correct shade of

48. The following passage describes Genji's concern over Emperor Reizei's illegitimate succession: 'In China, instances of irregularity were very numerous, whether revealed or concealed. In Japan he could find none at all. He knew that even if they had existed, such shameful matters would not be handed down to posterity.' (Ikeda ed., i, 623). In Tanizaki Junichirō's modern-language edition that appeared in 1939 even this seemingly innocuous passage had to be omitted owing to censorship. See also Herschel Webb, *The Japanese Imperial Institution in the Tokugawa Period*, Columbia University Press 1968, p. 14, for a discussion of possible breaks in the line of Imperial legitimacy: 'This extraordinary passage [from *The Tale of Genji*] ... if ever so subtly ... gives the observant reader grounds to suspect that the exact lines of descent of the Japanese imperial house may be unprovable.'

49. See p. 205 ff.

flowers and leaves, the application of the proper scent; yet such was the dominance of style that even the rougher males like Higekuro followed the prescriptions carefully, and their inferiors in the provinces did their best to ape them.

Since the vernacular literature of the time is greatly concerned with the amorous doings of the aristocracy, we can get a remarkably clear picture of what a love affair in tenth-century Heian Kyō was like. Admittedly most of the writers were women, and at the same time poets, who, in describing their love affairs, might be inclined to lend them a greater elegance and sensibility than they really had. The caustic brush of Sei Shōnagon, however, provides an ample corrective for any such idealization.

The following typical description is from the diary of Murasaki's colleague, Izumi Shikibu, who was noted not only for her poetry but for her beauty and her passionate temperament. She had been married at the age of twenty-one, but after a few years was separated from her husband and started a love affair with a certain imperial prince. He died in a great epidemic (the same one that killed Murasaki Shikibu's husband), and shortly thereafter Izumi, now aged twenty-eight, became acquainted with Prince Atsumichi. After a suitable exchange of letters and poems, the Prince decided to visit her one evening and bring things to a head:

'Come with me,' he said, 'just for this night. I know a place where we can be alone. There I shall be able to talk to you freely.'

He lost no time in ordering his carriage to be brought up to the veranda and, before I knew what was happening, he had made me get in with him.

As we rode along, I felt sure that we should be overheard, but it was extremely late at night and in fact no one discovered us. Presently we reached a house. The Prince had the carriage quietly drawn up next to a deserted gallery and stepped out. Since the moon was shining brightly, I found it embarrassing to get out myself, [50] but I obeyed and followed him.

'Well, you see what a quiet place I have brought you to,' he said. 'From now on let us meet here, so that we can talk without interruption. At your house I am always afraid that someone may come along while I am with you, and I can never be really at ease.'

There was something very soulful about the way he said this – and about all his other remarks that night.

50. Women were normally heard but not seen (see p. 222).

When dawn came, he ordered the carriage to be brought back to the gallery and made me get in.

'I should like to see you home,' he said, 'but it is getting light and it would be unfortunate if anyone saw me and realized that I had spent the night out.'

He stood there by the gate as the carriage moved away. All the way home I thought about what a strange night it had been. What, I wondered, would people think if they found out? At the same time I remembered how uncommonly handsome the Prince had looked in the light of dawn, and when I returned home I wrote the following poem:

> 'Painful though it were
> To see you leave at night
> Better by far than when the dawn's grey light
> So cruelly tears you from my side.'

To which I added, 'How sad it was!'

The Prince sent this reply:

> 'To leave you while the leaves are moist with dew
> Is bitterer by far
> Than if I were to say farewell at night
> Without a single chance to show my love.'[51]

'Let us hope,' he added, 'that we never have to talk any more of leaving. I cannot stay in your house tonight, since it lies in an unlucky direction for me. But I shall come for you.'

Oh, how disagreeable that it should all have to be so furtive! But that, no doubt, was how things would always be between us. I was thinking this when the Prince arrived in the same carriage. He had it drawn up by the entrance and bade me make haste. I found it all extremely embarrassing, yet I crept out to the veranda and got in beside him.

The Prince took me to the same house as on the previous evening. There we conversed freely and he told me among other things that Her Highness[52] believed he was spending the night at the Reizei Palace.

When dawn came, he whispered to me, 'How cruel the cock's crow!'[53]

---

51. There is a play of words on *oku* = (i) (the dew) settles (on the leaves), (ii) to get up (from bed). The word-play on 'leave' may suggest some of the effect, but it should be remembered that the Japanese are far more tolerant of puns than we are.

52. i.e. his principal wife, the daughter of Fujiwara no Naritoki.

53. The true gallant always had a poetic quotation at his fingertips. This one is from an early 10th-century anthology:

> 'How cruel the cock's crow when it tells the dawn
> To those fond lovers who can rarely meet.'

Then he gently led me to the carriage and got in next to me. On the way to my house he said, 'Whenever I have a chance like this, please come with me.'

'I wonder if that will always be possible,' I replied.

When he had left me at home, he returned to his palace; shortly afterwards I received a letter from him: 'You will remember that this morning we were awakened by the crowing of a cock. I have now had the hateful creature put to death.'

He had attached a cock's feather to his letter and added the following poem:

> 'Now he is dead –
> That heartless bird
> Who broke the dark night's peace with his shrill cry.
> Yet dawn, alas, will always come
> [to end true lovers' joys].'[54]

To this I replied:

> 'A heartless bird indeed!
> None knows it more than I
> Who every morning hears his piercing call.

Do you suppose that I have any love for that cock?'[55]

For an understanding of the etiquette and aesthetic pleasures that attended a well-conducted love affair Sei Shōnagon's *Pillow Book* is by far the most revealing source. She wrote on the subject with an unmistakable width of experience and a striking lack of sentimentality. At times there is something rather superficial and brittle about her approach; yet on the whole we can probably learn more from her than

54. The claim that he has had the cock put to death is a mere conceit, of a type that was frequently affected by the Heian buck.

55. *Izumi Shikibu Nikki*, pp. 408–10. In my translation I have changed Izumi's construction from the third to the first person.

As will be seen, Izumi's affair with Prince Atsumichi (the main subject of her diary) started in the greatest secrecy, and the Prince was evidently very careful to keep it from his principal wife. In the year after it began, however, he moved her to his palace as a concubine (an example, incidentally, of a 'casual' relationship changing to an 'official' one). His principal wife objected strongly to this step and registered her protest by moving back to her family's house (see pp. 255–7). Eventually things became so unpleasant for Izumi that she left the Prince; shortly thereafter she married a governor and went to the province of Tango. In 1008 she returned to the capital and became a lady-in-waiting at the same court as Murasaki Shikibu.

from writers, like Izumi Shikibu and Michitsuna's mother, who were totally involved with their lovers. The first of the passages that I have chosen compares the joys of love affairs in summer and winter:

Summer is indeed a charming time to meet one's lover. The nights are of course terribly short and dawn creeps up before one has had a wink of sleep. Since all the lattices have been left open, the lovers can lie and look out at the garden in the cool morning air. They still have a few endearments to exchange before the man takes his leave, and they are murmuring something to each other when suddenly there is a loud noise. For a moment they are certain they have been discovered; but it is only the caw of a crow flying past in the garden.

In the winter, when it is extremely cold and one lies buried under the bedclothes listening to one's lover's endearments, it is delightful to hear the tolling of the temple bell, which seems to come from the bottom of a deep pit. The first cry of the birds, whose beaks are still tucked under their wings, is also strange and muffled. Then one bird after another takes up the call. How pleasant it is to lie there listening as the sound becomes clearer and clearer![56]

The lover's departure in the morning is a recurrent scene in Heian literature. Perhaps because it is more evocative and poignant – more expressive, in short, of *aware* – the women writers of the time dwell at far greater length on his leave-taking than on his arrival in the evening. Here again the rule of taste is paramount, as Sei Shōnagon makes clear in the following passage from her chapter on Hateful Things:

A lover who is leaving one at dawn announces that he has to find his fan and his paper.[57]

'I know I put them somewhere last night,' he says. Since it is pitch dark, he gropes about the room bumping into the furniture and muttering, 'Strange! Where on earth can they be?'

Finally he discovers the objects. He sticks the paper into the breast of his robe with a great rustling sound; then he snaps open his fan and starts

56. Kaneko ed., p. 322.
57. Elegant coloured paper that gentlemen carried in the folds of their clothes. Among other purposes it served for writing notes and poems. From the seventeenth century this paper always had erotic connotations (see Ihara Saikaku, *The Life of an Amorous Woman and Other Writings*, Ivan Morris, ed., London and New York, 1963, note 134), but in the Heian period its role was ambiguous.

flapping away with it. Only now is he ready to take his leave. What charmless behaviour! 'Hateful' is really an understatement.

Equally disagreeable is the man who, when leaving in the middle of the night, takes care to fasten the cord of his head-dress. This is completely unnecessary; it is perfectly all right to put it gently on his head without tying the cord. In the same way, there is no need to spend time adjusting his cloak or hunting costume. After all, does he really imagine that someone is going to see him at this time of the night and criticize him for not being impeccably dressed?

A good lover will behave just as elegantly at dawn as at any other time. He drags himself out of bed with a look of dismay on his face. The lady urges him on: 'Come, my friend, it's getting light. You don't want anyone to find you here.' He gives a heart-felt sign, as if to say that the night has not been nearly long enough and that it is agony to leave. When he is up, he does not immediately start putting on his trousers. Instead he approaches the lady and whispers to her what remains to be said from their night's exchanges. Though in fact he is doing nothing at the moment, he vaguely pretends to be fastening his sash.

Presently he raises the lattice and the two lovers go and stand by the side door. He tells her how he dreads the coming day, which will keep them apart. Then almost imperceptibly he glides away. The lady watches him go, and this moment of parting will remain among her most charming memories. Indeed, a woman's attachment to a man depends largely on the elegance of his leave-taking. When he jumps out of bed, scurries about the room, tightly fastens his trouser-sash, rolls up the sleeves of his Court cloak, hunting costume or whatnot, stuffs his belongings into the breast of his robe and then briskly secures the outer sash – she really begins to hate him.[58]

In one of the final sections of the *Pillow Book* Sei returns to her description of the perfect lover and shows that his cultural accomplishments are an essential part of his charm:

Being of an adventurous nature, he has still not married, and now at dawn he returns to his bachelor quarters, having spent the night in some amorous adventure. Though he still looks sleepy, he immediately draws his inkstone to him and, after having carefully rubbed some ink on it, starts to write his next-morning letter. He does not let his brush run down the paper in a careless scrawl, but puts himself heart and soul into the calligraphy. What a charming figure he makes as he sits there by himself

58. Kaneko ed., pp. 149–50.

in an easy posture, with his robe falling slightly open! It is a plain unlined robe of pure white, and over it he wears a cloak of yellow rose or crimson. As he finishes his letter, he notices that the white robe is still damp from the dew, and for a while he gazes at it fondly.

Then he makes arrangements for delivering his letter. Instead of calling one of the ladies in attendance, he takes the trouble to get up and select a page-boy who seems appropriate for the task. Summoning the lad to his side, he whispers his instructions and hands over the letter. The page leaves for the lady's house, and for some time the gentleman watches him recede in the distance. As he sits there, he quietly murmurs some appropriate passage from the Sutras.

Now one of his attendants comes to announce that his washing-water and morning gruel have been prepared in the neighbouring wing. The gentleman goes there, and soon he is leaning against the reading-desk and looking at some Chinese poems, from which he will now and then read out a passage that he has particularly enjoyed – altogether a charming sight.

Presently he performs his ablutions and changes into a white Court cloak, which he wears without any trousers. Thus attired, he starts reciting the sixth scroll of the Lotus Sutra from memory. A pious gentleman indeed – or so one might think, except that at just this moment the messenger returns (he cannot have had far to go) and nods encouragingly to his master, who thereupon instantly interrupts his recitation and, with what might strike one as blasphemous haste, transfers his attention to the lady's reply.[59]

This final passage pictures the rather scabrous type of situation that the sexual mores of the time (as well as *shinden* architecture) permitted; yet it reminds us once again that the cult of beauty prevented things from lapsing into mere crassness. It is dawn and a lady is lying in bed, having recently bidden her lover farewell:

She looks as if she is asleep. Under the light mauve costume . . . that she is using as her bedclothes[60] she wears an unlined orange robe and a dark crimson skirt of stiff silk whose cords hang loosely by her side, suggesting that they have been left untied. Her thick tresses tumble over each other in cascades, and one can imagine how long her hair must be when it falls freely down her back.

Meanwhile another gentleman [61] is making his way home in the misty

59. Kaneko ed., p. 1081.   60. See pp. 47–8.
61. Not the one who has spent the night with her.

dawn from some nocturnal visit. He is wearing loose violet trousers, an orange hunting-costume, so lightly coloured that one can hardly tell whether it has been dyed or not, a white robe of stiff silk and a glossy robe of beaten silk. His clothes, which have been thoroughly moistened by the dew, hang loosely about him. From the dishevelment of his side-locks one can tell how negligently he must have tucked his hair into his black lacquered headdress when he got up. He wants to return and write his next-morning letter before the dew on the morning-glories has had time to vanish; the road seems endless, and to divert himself he hums 'The sprouts in the flax fields'.[62]

As he walks along, he passes a house with an open lattice.[63] He is on his way to report for official duty, but he cannot help stopping to raise the blind slightly and peep into the room. It amuses him to think that some other man has probably been spending the night here and has recently got up and left, just as he himself has done. . . .

Looking round the room, he notices near the lady's pillow an open fan with a magnolia frame and purple paper; and at the foot of her curtain of state he sees some narrow strips of white Michinoku paper[64] and also some other paper of a faded colour, which appears to be either orange-red or maple.

The lady senses that someone is watching her and, looking up from under her bedclothes, she sees the gentleman leaning against the wall by the threshold, with a smile on his face. She can tell at once that he is not the sort of man with whom she needs to feel the slightest reserve. All the same, she does not want to enter into any familiar relations with him, and she is annoyed that he should have seen her asleep.

'Well, well, Madam,' says the man, leaning forward so that the upper

62. 'The sprouts of the cherry-flax
      In the flax-fields
      Are heavy now with dew
      I shall stay with you till daybreak
      Even though your parents know.'

In this ancient poem from the *Manyō Shū* the gallant declares that he will not go home until daylight, though this probably means that her parents will find out about his visit. His ostensible reason is that it is hard to make his way through the heavy morning dew (a standard euphuism); the real motive, of course, is his reluctance to leave the partner of his night's pleasures.

63. The house of the lady with the long hair and the orange robe.

64. Thick white paper used for writing love letters, notes, etc. and usually carried in the breast of the *kimono*. It was manufactured in the district of Michinoku in the north of the main island.

part of his body comes behind her curtains, 'what a long nap you're having after your morning adieu! You really are a slug-abed!'

'You call me that, Sir,' she replies, 'only because you're annoyed at having had to get up so early.'

Their conversation may be banal, yet I find there is something rather charming about the scene.

Now the gentleman leans more forward and, using his own fan, tries to get hold of the fan by the lady's pillow. She fears that he is coming too close and, her heart pounding, she moves farther back in her curtain enclosure. The gentleman picks up the magnolia fan and, as he examines it, says in a slightly bitter tone, 'How cold you are being!'

But now it is growing light; there is a sound of people's voices and it looks as if the sun will soon be up. Only a short while ago this same man was hurrying back, so that he might write his next-morning letter before the mists had time to clear. Alas, how easily his intentions have been forgotten!

While all this is afoot, the lady's original lover has been busy with his own next-morning letter, and now, before anyone expected it, the messenger arrives at the lady's house. The letter is attached to a spray of clover, which is still damp with dew, and the paper gives off a delightful aroma of incense. Because of the new visitor, however, the lady's attendants cannot deliver it to her.

Finally it becomes unseemly for the gentleman to stay any longer. As he goes, he is amused to think that a similar scene may well be taking place in the house he left earlier that morning.[65]

*

For the modern reader who inhabits a more or less monogamous society Heian vernacular literature provides valuable insights into the psychological implications of polygamy. It helps us to understand what the system involved emotionally for the people who practised it as their regular form of life.

In the first place, we must remember that the possession of several wives and the frequentation of several mistresses were normal and, in the full sense of the word, respectable behaviour for any Heian gentleman.[66]

65. Kaneko ed., pp. 206–10.
66. This, of course, is peculiar neither to the Heian period nor to Japan. Both the Chinese and the Japanese have traditionally separated their attitudes to marriage, which concerns the welfare of the family, from attitudes to love and

In an aristocracy where a large family was an invaluable advantage, and where women often died young, a man with several fertile wives was performing a valuable social function. As in almost any polygamous society, the possession of numerous attractive concubines and mistresses, in addition to a well-born principal wife, far from labelling the man as a lecher, was an enviable status symbol – an indication of his wealth, skill, charm, and health.[67] The type of disapproval that in Puritan societies is visited on the unfaithful husband was likely in Genji's world to be directed at the man who had only one or two wives; for he would be regarded as not only abnormal but also anti-social. Shortly after Niou has brought Naka no Kimi to the capital as his official concubine, it is

---

sex, which are regarded as needs of the individual. Love, sex, and marriage were never combined into the same set of values as they are, for example, in the Christian marriage service. Far Eastern society rigidly prescribed a man's duty to his family, but was extremely tolerant about how he satisfied his romantic and physical desires, sexual self-gratification never being condemned so long as the man played his proper role in the family. Erotic pleasures (the 'abomination of the flesh' of the medieval Christian Church) were regarded as a natural need, to which it would be absurd to attach any sense of sin or moral guilt. Much of the difficulty that the Jesuits experienced in trying to convert the military leaders of the feudal period came from their insistence that a promiscuous sexual life and polygamy were morally wrong *per se*.

67. The medical advantages of frequent intercourse with several different women were constantly emphasized in Taoist and *yin-yang* literature. The following advice is from *Yü Fang Pi Chüeh* (*Secret Prescriptions for the Bedchamber*), an 8-roll work that is listed among the medical books in the bibliographic section of the Sui dynastic history, and that was almost certainly known in Heian Japan: 'Those who can exercise the sexual act scores of times in one day *sine umquam semen emittendo* will thereby cure all their ills and live to a great age. If the act is performed with a number of different women, its benefit will increase. It is best to engage in the sexual act with ten or more different women on one night.' (Quoted by Van Gulik, op. cit., p. 145.) Similar prescriptions are found in works of the T'ang dynasty and later. As Dr van Gulik has pointed out, we have practically no direct information on the conduct of the sexual act during the Heian period. We do know, however, that a physician of the Japanese Court (i.e. Tamba Yasuyori; see p. 145, n. 13) was familiar with the Chinese handbooks of sex which circulated during the Sui and T'ang dynasties, and that their theories were included in his *Ishinhō*. It therefore seems reasonable to assume that the main points mentioned in the handbooks, such as prenatal care and giving the woman satisfaction during intercourse, were known to the ladies and gentlemen of the Heian Court.

suggested that he should take Yūgiri's young daughter, Roku no Kimi, as his principal wife. He has no objection to Roku no Kimi, but for the moment he would prefer to concentrate on the girl from Uji. His mother, the Empress, loses no time in voicing her shocked disapproval of any such monogamous arrangement:

'... Men of common birth', she told Niou, 'may find it difficult to divide their attentions once they have got married. But for a man in your position things are rather different. Look at the Great Minister [Yūgiri] himself. You could hardly find a more serious-minded gentleman. Yet do you suppose that he has remained faithful to one wife? Of course not. For years he has been living with both Lady Kumoi and Princess Ochiba, and no one has had any ill feelings about it. You have even less reason to hesitate. For, if your career turns out as I hope,[68] having a large number of wives in your household will be anything but a disadvantage.'[69]

The Empress urged him with unusual vehemence. ...

Faced with arguments of this type (which, Murasaki points out, are 'eminently reasonable') the young prince bows to convention, and soon he is respectably married to two wives, whom he visits alternately. He realizes that in the beginning the new arrangements may be hard for Naka no Kimi, and he himself is not entirely satisfied; yet such, he reflects, is the way of the world:

'For the time being,' he said, 'I really should have preferred to continue my peaceful married life without being saddled with these new demands. What a shame that it had to be like this!'

It occurred to him that people of the common class, for whom it was perfectly normal to have only one wife, might well sympathize with Naka no Kimi in her unhappiness about the new situation. But for someone in his walk of life it was hard to have such scruples. This was how things were bound to turn out in the end. After all, he was not only a prince, but a prince with a special future in store for him. Such being his position, he could marry any number of women without being censured. No sensible person could really feel sorry for Naka no Kimi on the grounds that she now had to share his attentions with one other wife.[70]

There is overwhelming evidence that Murasaki Shikibu and the women of her world implicitly accepted this system and the double

68. Niou was expected to become crown prince.
69. Ikeda ed., vi, 138–9.   70. Ibid., pp. 162–3.

standard that it involved. In all their voluminous writings that have come down to us there is never a breath of social protest about it, never the slightest suggestion that the world would be a better place – for women at least – if men had a single wife and remained faithful to her. If she is a principal wife, her great ambition will be, not that her husband should have no concubines (that would be absurd, and even somewhat shameful), but that he should avoid becoming immoderately fond of any one of them. The dangers were that such a woman might receive some of the consideration and respect that were due only to herself; worse still, that the husband might recognize the concubine's children, and (greatest of all menaces) give one of them precedence over his legitimate brood.

So long as she was spared these ordeals, the Heian wife was normally prepared to share her husband's time with such other women as he wished to add to his establishment. The only wife in *The Tale of Genji* who cannot tolerate the idea of her husband's bringing a concubine home to live is Higekuro's – and she is shown to be neurotic to the point of insanity. Izumi Shikibu's diary describes an actual instance in which a wife refuses to accept the installation of a concubine and resorts to the ultimate sanction of returning to her family.[71] In this case, however, it is not the system itself to which the wife objects but the excessive consideration that has been shown to one particular rival.

If the woman is a concubine, the most that she can realistically hope for is that she will occupy first place in the man's affections. At no time does the heroine of Murasaki's novel aspire to become Genji's principal wife; nor does she expect that he will refrain from adding further concubines to his household or from engaging in casual affairs outside. Her one ambition (and this she amply realizes) is to remain his favourite wife – the wife to whom he will continue to give his devotion and friendship whatever new infatuations or matrimonial arrangements the future may bring. Even the author of *Gossamer Diary*, who seems to be less reconciled to the system than most ladies of her time, finally realizes how foolish she has been in hoping to monopolize Kaneie's affections:

It started raining at about noon, and all afternoon as I sat there sunk in gloomy idleness (*aware ni tsurezure*) I could hear it pattering on the eaves. Since nowadays he rarely visited me even when the weather was fine, it was absurd to hope that he might come on such a day, and I

71. See pp. 255-7.

banished the possibility from my mind. Recalling how our relations used to be when first we were lovers, I wondered why they had turned out like this. Perhaps it was not my fault at all, but the result of his fickle nature. But then I remembered that even in the past – even in those days when he used to brave the rain and storm to visit me – I had never for a moment been at ease, but had always been fretting about some future infidelity. So the trouble lay in myself – in my own excessive expectations (*waga kokoro no ōkenaki*). Alas, at the time it had seemed quite reasonable that I should want him to be faithful, but now I could see how unthinkable such a thing really was.[72]

That people should have accepted an institution that had existed since time immemorial, and that was likely to continue for the indefinite future, is hardly unexpected. What may come as a surprise is the way in which the women, and indirectly the men, suffered emotionally from the consequences of polygamy despite their social and intellectual acceptance of the system itself. *The Tale of Genji* and the diaries make it abundantly clear that institutionalized infidelity produced much the same bitterness on the part of women, and much the same need to conceal and prevaricate on the part of men, as we find in monogamous societies where infidelity is, at least in theory, condemned. And this, of course, is one of the reasons that Heian literature is emotionally meaningful to the modern Western reader.

An outstanding aspect of the psychology of Heian women is anxiety about the future. A sense of insecurity and a tendency to worry about each course of action are something that nearly all the women characters in *The Tale of Genji* have in common; and we find it reflected in most other literature of the time, with the notable exception of the *Pillow Book*. This anxiety takes various forms: fear of rumours and gossip, fear of being abandoned by one's lover, fear for one's children's future, fear of committing oneself to a man as his concubine and then being dismissed, fear that one may incur the hostility of the man's principal wife and be subjected to her persecution – these are only a few of the worries that beset the women of Murasaki's novel. Some, of course, exist in any society; but most of them are the specific results of polygamy. Readers of the novel will recall Lady Akikonomu's almost obsessive desire for 'security'; the way in which the ex-Emperor Suzaku's mistress pines

72. *Kagerō Nikki*, p. 209.

away and dies when he removes his protection: and Lady Akashi's terror that Genji may abscond, letting her fall into obscurity and contempt. For all these women romantic feelings and sexual passion are outweighed by fear of what may happen to them if they are not careful. An outstanding exception is Yūgao, whose trusting, uncalculating nature comes as a delightful surprise to Genji. Eighteen years after her death he still thinks of her as the only woman he has met, or even heard of, in whom passion dominates every other motive.

All this suggests that, despite the relatively favourable social and economic situation of Heian women, the conditions of polygamy made their actual position precarious. We must also remember the total absence in Japan of anything corresponding to a tradition of chivalry with its ideals of long unrequited fidelity, its vows of eternal service, and its underlying concept that gentlemen have a duty to honour and protect women because they are women.[73] In Heian Kyō women were respected and courted because of their potential power as an emperor's favourite and the mother of an imperial prince, or because of the backing of an influential family. But, once they had lost such potential or backing, they were often left to fend for themselves. The position of a principal wife was relatively secure, since (like Prince Atsumichi's wife in the passage quoted below) she normally had her relatives behind her. But a concubine or mistress – and she, of course, was in the vast majority – had little reason to be sanguine about the future, unless she was sufficiently attractive and lucky to have a powerful man as her long-term lover.

Heian women, as we have seen, had the right to inherit and retain property. Yet it appears that they needed the support of their family or of some influential man to keep and administer this property effectively. The literature of the time unfortunately throws little light on this crucial subject, which a writer like Murasaki would of course consider as being

73. This could be taken as yet another illustration of Waley's argument that the most fundamental difference between the Japanese and the Westerners is that they were not Christians (p. 111, n. 19). For, if there had been no Mariolatry, the knightly cult of women, and all its consequences in later centuries, would hardly have developed as they did. I am aware that modern historians question the traditional views about Western medieval chivalry and its attitude to women; but the knightly cult of women did exist as an ideal and is historically significant, even if it did not exert as much influence on medieval relations between the sexes as was once believed.

beneath her dignity; but it is clear that the immobile, closeted existence of the upper-class Heian woman hardly lent itself to the efficient super-vision of her manorial estates or to securing the all-important rights of tax exemption from the proper government offices. For matters like these, and also for controlling any refractory retainers or estate officials, she had to rely on some guardian or protector. The reason that Genji finds the red-nosed lady's affairs in such an appalling state (her 'palace in the tangled woods' has, quite literally, begun to crumble about her) is, to put it in the bluntest terms, that she is not sufficiently attractive to secure the male support that was so important for every Heian lady. When the former Emperor Suzaku decides to abandon the world and retire to a mountain monastery, he is consumed with anxiety about the future of his daughter, who, he feels sure, will be entirely helpless with-out him. If such was the situation of an imperial princess – and a Fujiwara to boot – we can imagine how unsure was the position of women who were less well favoured by birth.

It is small wonder, then, that the hope of every Heian woman was to secure the affections of a man who, however many concubines and mistresses he might have, would be sure to protect her from the vicissi-tudes to which she was subject in a polygamous society. Such a man is Prince Genji. It is not just because of his looks, his sensitivity, and his artistic talents that he emerges in Murasaki's novel as the ideal male, but because, once he has given his support to a woman, he never withdraws it, even though he may have lost all interest in her as a mistress.

*

The anxieties that resulted from polygamy had many effects on the in-habitants of Genji's world, but none was more dramatic than the emotion of jealousy. Unquestioningly though they accepted the per-missive sexual customs of their time, they were afflicted by jealousy in all its forms. This applied to both women and men. Owing to the un-equal nature of the situation, however – a situation in which (as one writer has pleasantly expressed it) 'a man had the mobility of a bee [while] a woman was rooted like a flower in her house'[74] – women had far more occasions to suffer from its torments and far less opportunity to mitigate them.

74. Robert H. Brower and Earl Miner, *Japanese Court Poetry*, p. 431.

The Chinese visitors to Japan in the third century, after pointing out that all men of high rank had four or five wives, added that 'the women are faithful and not jealous'.[75] We have little reliable information about conditions in Japan during these early centuries, and none at all about the psychology of women; yet the visitors' final observation must surely be taken with a grain of salt. While deep-rooted traditions have usually inhibited Japanese women from expressing jealousy except in particular types of personal literature, there is certainly no reason to believe that they felt it less keenly than women in other countries; indeed the very taboo that prevented them from giving vent to the emotion may have made them experience it all the more poignantly.[76]

Among the Heian aristocracy, though women were expected to keep their jealousy to themselves,[77] there is every indication that they suffered its pangs in full measure. Their practical dependence on men, their natural desire for the exclusive possession of a husband or lover (a desire no less real for being totally impracticable), their fear of losing him to another woman – all this made it hard for them to bear the uncertainties of the polygamous system and produced a tension that sometimes resulted in hysteria or even madness.

In *The Tale of Genji* jealousy accompanies almost every relationship between men and women and is pictured as the greatest of human torments. Much like Proust, Murasaki is concerned with the origins of jealousy, its development, and its effect on different types of people (though she, of course, concentrates on the ways in which it affects women). In this respect her novel is not unusual for the Heian period: while Murasaki examines jealousy more fully and more expertly than any other contemporary writer, the theme is a common one in the femi-

75. Quoted by Sansom, *A Short Cultural History of Japan*, p. 30.

76. In the 17th century, women had gone so far as to evolve an institutionalized form of expressing jealousy. This was the *Rinki Kō* (Jealousy Meeting), a private gathering of wives, during which each of them in turn would 'let off steam' by reviling her unfaithful husband and his mistresses. Saikaku describes one such meeting in the household of a certain *daimyō*: after voicing their grievances, the women attack a scapegoat in the form of a life-size doll. Ivan Morris, ed., *The Life of an Amorous Woman and Other Writings* (London and New York, 1963), pp. 164–71.

77. Note, for example, Naka no Kimi's reflection about her husband's infidelities: '. . . she resigned herself to enduring her jealousy in silence like other women'. Ikeda ed., vii, 14.

nine literature of the time. *Gossamer Diary,* for example, is one long wail of jealousy by a woman in whom the emotion has attained hysterical proportions, and who gives vent in her writing to all the complaints, all the bitterness, all the tension that have accumulated during the long hours of waiting and that social convention prevents her from expressing in any more direct manner.

Though the current system of polygamy normally allowed the principal wife greater stability than other women, her position, as we have seen, was far from impregnable, and she too could be made to suffer from jealousy. The following passage describes the reactions of Prince Atsumichi's wife, the daughter of an important Fujiwara politician, to the installation of the writer (Izumi Shikibu) as his concubine. As often happens in the case of the principal wife, jealousy is closely tied to a sense of public humiliation; and, typically, it takes the form of scorn for the 'other woman':

A couple of days later the Prince moved me to the northern wing of his palace. People were surprised at this[78] and lost no time in telling the Princess.

'Really,' she said, 'what a thing to do! Even without this he has not treated me as he should. Imagine – a woman of such common birth!'

It particularly upset the Princess that her husband should have gone about things so secretly; for this convinced her that she was confronted with no passing infatuation. She became more disagreeable than ever, and the Prince was at his wits' end. He could not bear to hear the complaints of the attendants or to see their disapproving expressions. As a result he rarely visited the Princess's apartments and spent his time with me.

'Why did you not tell me exactly what you were doing?' the Princess said to him one day. 'There was nothing wrong in it and no one would have tried to stop you. But as it is I've been made into a laughing-stock. You've behaved without any of the consideration due to my rank. You've humiliated me in front of everyone.'

She burst into tears and wept for a long time.

'Simply because I've taken someone into my service,' said the Prince, 'do you really suppose it means that I don't have any consideration for you? Of course I do. The trouble is that you were treating me in such an unfriendly way that the attendants – Lady Chūjō and others – began to

78. The northern wing was normally reserved for the principal wife and for ladies of the highest rank.

take a disliking to me. So I had to get someone who would dress my hair for me and carry out similar duties. Why don't you let her attend upon you also?'

The Prince's words did not improve his wife's mood, but at least she did not reproach him any further. . .

One day the Prince was told that even the common servants were speaking badly about me. He found it most distasteful that his wife should be behaving in such an uncalled-for way and causing all this unpleasantness; as a result his visits to her became even rarer. It embarrassed me that I should be the cause of their estrangement; but there was really nothing I could do about it, and I decided to remain where I was and obey the Prince's wishes.

It happened that just then the Princess's elder sister, who was serving as an Imperial Concubine to the Crown Prince, was staying at home,[79] and now a note came from her. 'Something must be done about this,' she wrote. 'Is it true what people have been telling me these days? If so, I feel that I too am being humiliated. Please leave your house and come here, even if it is in the middle of the night.'

This letter upset the Princess greatly. She knew how people loved to gossip even when they had little grounds for suspicion. What a splendid opportunity they were being given now! 'Thank you for your kind letter,' she wrote. 'I know that marriage (*yo no naka*) rarely goes exactly as one wishes; of late mine has been nothing but a succession of miseries. I shall come home and stay with you for the time being. Perhaps seeing your son, the little prince, will be a comfort to me. Please send someone to fetch me. I also have reached the point where I cannot bear to hear any more unpleasantness.'

After sending the letter, she made her attendants pack what was needed and put everything in perfect order. 'I am moving to my sister's for a time,' she explained. 'There is no point in my staying here. As things are, the Prince is unable to visit me, and no doubt he too finds this situation painful.'

Her ladies joined in a chorus of approval, and one after another expressed her opinion about the Prince's behaviour: 'It's perfectly shocking – that's what I call it. People are taking a very poor view of the way he's been acting.' 'Quite so,' chimed in another of the ladies. 'When she moved in here, His Highness actually went to fetch her himself.'[80] 'Yes, it's more than one can bear to see. That woman sits there in her rooms and the

79. Probably because of a ritual defilement.
80. Normally this would be done only for the principal wife.

Prince comes to visit her during the daytime – sometimes as often as three or four times.' 'It's high time you taught him a good lesson, Madam,' one of them advised. 'It's terrible the way he's been neglecting you.'

As she listened to their remarks, the Princess felt more bitter than ever. 'So be it,' she decided. 'He shall not see me again for a long time.'

Shortly thereafter her brothers arrived in a carriage. 'We have been sent to fetch Her Highness,' they explained. Now finally the Prince realized that she was in earnest. A lady-in-waiting, who had heard from his wife's old nurse that she was taking along a number of important papers and other effects from her Housekeeping Office, visited the Prince.

'You see, Your Highness, she really is leaving. What will the Crown Prince say! Do go to her now and stop her before it is too late. . . .'

When the Prince entered his wife's room, she received him as if nothing had happened. 'Is it true?' he asked. 'They tell me that you are going to stay with Her Highness, your sister. Why did you not ask me to provide a carriage?'

'Because it was arranged that they would send one for me,' she replied; and that was all she said to him.[81]

Of all the upper-class households described in Heian literature none has a homelier and, in some ways, more familiar air for the modern reader than that of Yūgiri and his wife, Kumoi. It will be recalled that this is a love match, Kumoi's family having been opposed to Yūgiri because of his low rank, and also that when the young people finally do get married they adopt the up-to-date fashion of living in their own house rather than with the wife's family. Yūgiri is a most exceptional gentleman for the time and may well be reacting against the rampant polygamy of his father's *ménage*: during the first ten years of his marriage he does not add a single concubine to his household. Instead he lives quietly at home, enjoying his wife's voluptuous charms[82] and fathering a large brood of children, all of whom are to make brilliant marriages.

Yet even this paragon of male fidelity finally succumbs to social convention and the lure of novelty. The object of his infatuation is Princess Ochiba. She is the wife of his best friend, who has died two years earlier (again there is something familiar about the pattern), and Yūgiri seizes every opportunity to visit her, his pretext being to help the young widow

81. *Izumi Shikibu Nikki*, pp. 442–3, 444–6. See p. 242, n. 55.
82. See p. 148.

with practical matters. Kumoi's wifely instinct tells her what is afoot, and her jealousy is all the more intense because Yūgiri has been so faithful in the past. The following scene takes place on the day after the first night that Yūgiri has spent at Princess Ochiba's house – an entirely innocent night, as one of the attendants informs the Princess's old mother, yet the source of many a complication.

Yūgiri spent the day at home. He had decided that it would be impossible to visit Princess Ochiba's house that night. If he went, it would be bound to look as if something had really happened on his previous visit, and this would make a painful impression on everyone concerned. Though he resigned himself to this idea, he was painfully aware that his love was sitting 'like a great weight' on his heart[83] and that his visit on the previous evening, far from improving things, had made it harder than ever to be separated from her.

Kumoi had a shrewd suspicion about where her husband spent the night and it pained her greatly. Yet she pretended that nothing was wrong and passed the day in her room playing with her children.

It was late in the evening that a messenger arrived with a reply to the letter that Yūgiri had sent to Lady Ochiba's mother. The old lady had written in a hand so weak and spindly that her brush strokes looked like a bird's tracks. To read this unusual script was no mean feat, and Yūgiri had to take the letter close to the big lamp.

He had not thought that his wife was nearby, but in fact she had seen the letter arriving and had immediately guessed its origin. Now she crept up behind her husband and snatched the letter from him.

'What on earth are you doing?' he cried in amazement. 'What an outrageous way to behave! This letter happens to be from her ladyship in the Eastern Wing.[84] She caught a cold this morning and was not feeling at all well. I called on her when I arrived in the Sixth Ward and was intending to pay a second visit before I left the house, but instead I returned home directly after my audience with my father. I felt rather concerned about her, and a short while ago I sent her a note asking how

83. The quotation is from a poem by Hitomaro (d. about 710):

> 'My love sits on my heart like a great weight.
> Yet what reason can I give to go and see her –
> The girl whose name I may not tell?'

84. Yūgiri pretends that the letter is from Hanachirusato, one of his father's old flames, who is living in a wing of the great mansion in the Sixth Ward.

she was. Look at this envelope! Is that your idea of a love letter? And yet you permit yourself such a vulgar action.'

'It really distresses me', he continued with a deep sigh, 'to see how you have held me in scorn during all these years. Only someone who did not have the slightest regard for my feelings could have behaved as you did just now.'

Kumoi noticed that her husband did not seem particularly anxious to retrieve the letter, and, instead of examining it as she would normally have done, she simply kept it in her hand.

'If I were you,' she said briefly, 'I should hardly talk about holding someone in scorn.' Her words were serious, but she spoke in a pleasant, youthful manner, hoping to distract him from his gloomy mood. Yūgiri laughed. 'Well, be that as it may,' he said, 'the real point is that the action of which you suspect me is the most commonplace thing in the world. I must be unique. Have you ever heard of a man who enjoys the position in the world that I do, yet never looks at another woman but sticks to one wife, like the proverbial falcon who is terrified of his mate? No wonder I've become a laughing-stock!

'And do you suppose that it adds to your own reputation to have such a single-minded husband? It is when a man has several interests, but makes it clear that he prefers one woman to all the others, that people really admire her. And such a woman is far more likely to keep her own interest in her husband, her relations with him are far more likely to go on being exciting and affectionate, than if he showed that he was blind to other feminine charms. It's really a shame how I have stuck to you, like the dreary old man in the story who could never leave his wife's side. I have given you no challenge to live up to.'

Now Kumoi realized that his real motive was to put her off her guard and to retrieve the letter by pretending not to care about it. 'What a shame that you should have gone to all this trouble to provide a challenge for me when I am too old to do anything about it!' she said with a charming, fresh smile. 'The thing that really hurts me about this new approach of yours,' she added, 'is that I am so unaccustomed to this sort of thing. "You who have never taught me . . ."'[85] Yet, even when she voiced these sad complaints, there was nothing sad about her tone.

85. From an old poem,

> 'You who have never thought me to know jealousy,
> How suddenly you wake me to its pangs!'

Even at the height of their quarrel Yūgiri is careful to show that he has recognized the allusion.

'But really,' said Yūgiri, 'what have I done to produce a "sudden awakening"? Your suspicions are completely unjust. Someone must have been speaking badly about me.[86] It is extraordinary how certain people still refuse to accept me after all these years. They still despise me for that green robe I had to wear[87] and go about planting all sorts of wicked rumours to alienate you from me. It really is a shame – not only for us, but for that unfortunate widow.'

Yet he could not argue the case too vigorously. For, though Kumoi's suspicions about Princess Ochiba were at the moment unfounded, he hoped very much that they would not remain so for long.[88]

---

86. He is alluding to Kumoi's old nurse, Taifu. | 87. See pp. 80–81.

88. Ikeda ed., v, 41–3. I have chosen the example of Kumoi and Yūgiri because it illustrates a typical or 'normal' form of jealousy. Murasaki no Ue's jealousy when Genji visits Akashi, Tamakazura, Nyosan, and other ladies in his household belongs to the same category. In certain cases, however, jealousy assumes a morbid form. The most dramatic instances in *The Tale of Genji* are provided by Higekuro's wife and Lady Rokujō. Higekuro's wife is shown to be mad (readers of the novel will recall the extraordinary scene in which she empties a charcoal brazier on her husband's head in order to prevent him from visiting his new concubine); in Lady Rokujō's case, jealousy assumes so virulent a form as to be lethal. The degree of maleficent power that was attributed to jealousy is suggested by the fact that the only case of a 'living ghost' (*ikiryō*) in *The Tale of Genji* is the spirit of Lady Rokujō, whom jealousy has driven into a murderous frenzy without her being consciously aware of the fact (p. 145). The Taihō Code stipulated jealousy as one of the seven permissible grounds for divorce.

It is clear that the people of Murasaki's time not only disapproved of jealousy as a social solecism but feared it as a spiritual evil. When the Master of Buddhist Asceticism urges Princess Ochiba's mother to stop the relationship between her daughter and Yūgiri, this is his final argument: 'Women are born with a heavy load of guilt. As a retribution for the evil passions in their nature they are condemned to flounder about in the darkness of the long night. If your daughter incurs the jealousy of this man's wife, she will be shackled with fetters from which she can never free herself in this life or the next. I insist that you put an end to this relationship.' (Ikeda ed., v, 34.)

The modern custom of wearing a *tsunokakushi* ('horn-hider') during the wedding ceremony derives from these old fears about female jealousy. The *tsunokakushi* is a white band that women wear to conceal their 'horn of jealousy' and to immunize their husband against the effects of this morbid emotion. Although male jealousy was fully recognized in Japan, and frequently described in the literature of the Heian period and later, it was never believed to have the same sinister implications as the female variety.

A few months later, in fact, Yūgiri realizes his ambition. Ochiba becomes his official concubine and he moves her to a house in the First Ward, where he arranges to spend every other fortnight with her. Kumoi, having once vented her feelings, resigns herself to 'enduring her jealousy in silence like other women'.

IX

Murasaki Shikibu

Pretty yet shy, shrinking from sight, unsociable, fond of old tales, conceited, so wrapped up in poetry that other people hardly exist, spitefully looking down on the whole world – such is the unpleasant opinion that people have of me. Yet when they come to know me they say that I am strangely gentle, quite unlike what they had been led to believe. I know that people look down on me like some old outcast, but I have become accustomed to all this, and tell myself, 'My nature is as it is.'[1]

This is one of the few parts of her diary in which Murasaki turns her acute power of description towards herself. It is a revealing passage. She was what would nowadays be labelled as an introvert and, typically, she was convinced that people misunderstood her. The diary suggests that Murasaki got little pleasure from the casual social relations, the gossip, and the badinage that occupied most of the other ladies at court. She had the reputation of being virtuous (an unusual one in her circle), and we have reason to believe that she was something of a prude.

In this, as in so many other ways, she presents a perfect contrast to that other great literary lady, Sei Shōnagon, who served in the court of the rival empress.[2] Sei was the opposite of timid and gentle. Her greatest pleasure, except perhaps for writing, was the exchange of repartee, especially when this allowed her to display her scattered erudition or to discomfit some unfortunate courtier who had allowed himself to become the butt of her sarcastic wit.

Both women were hypercritical, but in Murasaki's case this trait took a far less blatant form. Whereas Sei was able to give free vent to her tastes, her feelings, her piques, and her curiosity, Murasaki belonged to that more silent breed of writer who stores everything up for later use.

1. Mochizuki ed., p. 98.
2. The Japanese compare Murasaki to the immaculate plum blossom, Sei to the more colourful, yet less pure, cherry.

It is hardly surprising that Murasaki should have disapproved of the uninhibited lady who had made such a name for herself in the rival court. The following passage from the diary contains some of her more scathing comments:

Sei Shōnagon has the most extraordinary air of self-satisfaction. Yet, if we stop to examine those Chinese writings of hers that she so pretentiously scatters about the place, we find that they are full of imperfections. Some-one who makes such an effort to be different from others is bound to fall in people's esteem, and I can only think that her future will be a hard one. She is a gifted woman, to be sure. Yet, if one gives free rein to one's emotions even under the most inappropriate circumstances, if one has to sample each interesting thing that comes along, people are bound to regard one as frivolous. And how can things turn out well for such a woman?[3]

There is an unusual bitterness about the passage, and one cannot help detecting a note of envy – the envy that a shy, serious, solitary woman might feel towards a livelier and more scintillating member of her sex. Be that as it may, Murasaki's prediction was not far off the mark; for, if we are to credit popular tradition, Sei Shōnagon fell on evil days after the death of her empress and ended in the loneliness of a squalid hovel.

To what extent does Murasaki's life provide a clue to her character? Our fund of facts about Japan's first and greatest novelist is soon exhausted.[4] She was born in the seventies of the tenth century into a minor, though very literary, branch of the Fujiwara family. From her earliest youth she lived in a cultured atmosphere among people well versed in the classics, whose pastime it was to compose elegant, if not very original, verses in Chinese. Her father, Tametoki, was an ambitious and fairly successful official, who started his career as a student of litera-

3. Mochizuki ed., p. 94.
4. Several theories about her name (which literally means 'Violet of the Cere-monial') are outlined on pp. 127–32 of Oka, op. cit. *Shikibu* probably refers to the fact that her father had served in the Ministry of Ceremonial (*Shikibu Shō*). The origin of *Murasaki* is a far more moot point. Possibly it refers to the name of her first heroine (Waka Murasaki), but it appears to be connected also with a well-known poem in the *Kokin Shū* to which Emperor Ichijō refers when presenting her to Akiko's Court as a maid-of-honour. In addition *murasaki* is the colour of the *fuji* (wistaria), the first element in her family name.

ture preparing for what roughly corresponds to a D.Lit degree. He had slowly worked his way up the government hierarchy, largely thanks to the influence of his kinsman, the all-powerful Michinaga, to whom he regularly sent appeals in the form of stereotyped Chinese poetry.[5] Tametoki's grandfather was a poet of some note and he in turn was the great-grandson of Fuyutsugu, an illustrious statesman and *littérateur*, who had greatly contributed to establishing the fortunes of the Fujiwara family in the early part of the preceding century.[6] In short, Murasaki had the advantage of belonging to a family with a long tradition of scholarly and artistic interests.

Tametoki had great ambitions for his eldest son and made sure that he had all the benefits of a classical education. A knowledge of Chinese history and literature was essential for any worthwhile political career, and in Murasaki's diary father and son are described poring over Ssu-ma Ch'ien's *Historical Records*. For women this type of study was far from being an asset. Many of the court ladies had a smattering of classical knowledge, but anything more serious might label a woman as being unconventional and, worse still, a blue-stocking. This prejudice did not deter Murasaki, and we find her profiting from her brother's studies to learn what she could herself. Tametoki does not appear to have prevented his daughter from indulging in these odd pursuits, but it is doubtful whether he encouraged her. On one unfortunate occasion (mentioned in the diary) he observed his two children at their lessons and realized that Murasaki was more adept at memorizing Chinese characters than her brother. This inspired the well-known lament, 'If only you were a boy, how happy I should be!' Nobunori, the brother in question, entered government service with a post in the Ministry of Ceremonial (where his father had also served); later he was attached to his father's staff in the province of Echigo, where he died in about 1013 at an early age. Like most well-bred young men of his time he wrote conventional poetry.

> 5. E.g. 'I study hard during the cold nights
> And my sleeves are wet with tears.
> Yet future rewards are in my mind
> Like the blue sky on the horizon.'
> Quoted by Onoe Hachirō in 'Genji Monogatari Kaidai'.

6. Fuyutsugu was the direct ancestor of Michinaga, and Murasaki was Michinaga's fifth cousin. See Appendix 4.

We know little about Murasaki's youth. It seems likely that a good deal of her time was devoted to reading and study; for she became familiar with the standard Chinese and Buddhist classics and was also widely read in the literature of her own country. This may well have deterred potential suitors. In any case she was not betrothed until about twenty, an advanced age for girls of her time.[7] It was of course a *mariage de convenance*: her husband was a kinsman and appears to have been considerably older.

It did not last long. In 1001 (the first fairly definite date in Murasaki's life) her husband died, probably in an epidemic. Japanese commentators have suggested that this untimely separation after a few years of happy marriage had a sort of traumatic effect on the young woman and did much to influence her general outlook on life, in particular the sense of impermanence (*mujōkan*) that dominates the mood of the first and last parts of her novel. It is a pleasant enough hypothesis, but we have no particular reason to believe that Murasaki was devoted to her husband or prostrated by his death. Her diary, which starts only a few years later, does not mention him. Nor – and this is perhaps more surprising – does it refer to their children. We know that she had at least one daughter (who was later to become a well-known author in her own right): but the child does not figure a single time in the diary, though when Murasaki returned to her home in 1008, for example, she cannot have been more than ten years old. We have little ground for accepting the roseate picture of a soft-hearted wife and mother that some of her advocates have conjured up.

For five years after her husband's death Murasaki lived at home in retirement, and it was almost certainly during this period that she began work on her novel. In 1004 her father's poems finally produced the desired effect and he was appointed governor of the province of Echizen, some eighty miles from the capital. Shortly thereafter he arranged for his daughter to enter court as maid-of-honour to Michinaga's daughter, the nineteen-year-old consort of the young Emperor Ichijō. Murasaki began her diary in 1008 and kept it for about two years. It gives a vivid picture of her life at court, but does not help us to fix any

7. *Dai Nihon Shi* gives her date of birth as 974; *Shika Shichiron*, an authoritative 18th-century commentary, prefers 976–7. Her marriage is usually dated 999, but some scholars prefer a slightly earlier date.

accurate chronology; for the Heian diary was an impressionistic literary form rather than a systematic record of events.

Ichijō died in 1011 at the age of thirty-one and was succeeded by his first cousin. The Empress, accompanied by her suite (in which Murasaki was presumably included), moved to one of the 'detached palaces' and embarked on her sixty-year period of staid retirement. In the same year Murasaki's father was made governor of the large northern province of Echigo. His son joined him there, but died after a couple of years. This seems to have cast a pall over Tametoki's life; for in 1016 he retired and took the tonsure. His great patron resigned his official posts shortly thereafter and spent his remaining years as a priest. The Empress Dowager survived most of her generation by living until 1074 and, as Arthur Waley has said, 'reaching an even riper age than Queen Victoria, whom in certain ways she so much resembled'.[8]

During all this time we know absolutely nothing about the life of Murasaki Shikibu. There is little factual basis for the traditional view that she became a nun in 1015 and died in 1031. On the other hand, there is some evidence that she continued in the service of the Empress Dowager; for *Tales of Glory*, in an entry dated the eighth month of 1025, speaks of 'Echigo no Ben, daughter of Murasaki Shikibu, a lady-in-waiting at court'. Six years later, however, Murasaki's name is conspicuously absent from a list of ladies who are mentioned as having travelled in the Empress Dowager's suite on a flower-viewing expedition. It is probable, then, though by no means certain, that Murasaki either died or retired into the seclusion of a convent at some time between 1025 and 1031 at the age of about fifty.[9]

While we have few facts about Murasaki's life, the diary and *The Tale of Genji* do provide ample evidence about her knowledge and her

8. Arthur Waley, *A Wreath of Cloud*, p. 30. For further particulars about Murasaki's life see ibid., pp. 15–30. For a complete but inaccurate translation of Murasaki's diary see Annie S. Omori and Kochi Doi, *Diaries of Court Ladies of Old Japan*, pp. 69–146.

9. Oka's exhaustive study of the question, however, leads him to the conclusion that she died in 1014 at the age of 42 (Oka, op. cit., pp. 143–70). He leans heavily on a poem in a collection by Fujiwara no Yorimune which refers to the death of a 'Shikibu no Kimi'. The new evidence adduced by Professor Oka would not seem to be conclusive, but this is not the place to enter into the details of his argument.

experience of the world. Even the most cursory reading of the novel will suggest how intimately she was acquainted with the aristocratic life of her time, not only at court, but in town mansions and in remoter houses beyond the limits of the capital. Murasaki had keenly observed how different kinds of men and women spoke and behaved, and she had tried to enter into their feelings and to know why they acted as they did. She was sensitive to the natural surroundings in which these people lived and to the subtle effects that these surroundings had on them. Possibly she deserved her reputation for being virtuous (though Michinaga, for one, doubted it); but this did not prevent her from being keenly interested in love between men and women and in all the conflicting emotions and other complexities that it involved. Indeed many people have regarded her novel as primarily a study of the varied manifestations of sexual and romantic love.

When it comes to the type of knowledge that is derived from books, Murasaki never acquired the glittering repute of her great rival, Sei Shōnagon. This was probably due to the difference in their personalities, rather than to any superior erudition on Sei's part. A comparison of literary, historical, and other references in *The Tale of Genji* with those in the *Pillow Book* suggests that there was not much to choose between the two women so far as education was concerned. But, as we can gather from many remarks in Murasaki's diary (her diffidence in replying to Michinaga's poems, for example),[10] hers was not the readiness of wit that permitted the erudite impromptu coruscations for which Sei became famous. The fact is that Sei Shōnagon's renowned erudition was probably no greater than that of most people in her circle.[11] It was rather her extraordinary *présence d'esprit*, her ability to find on the spur of the moment the apt quotation from poetry or the appropriate reference to history, that gave rise to the legend that she was phenomenally learned.

We know from the diary that Murasaki's interest in Chinese literature was no youthful whim. Her husband was a specialist in the subject and at his death he appears to have left a substantial Chinese library. Murasaki mentions that she would occasionally read some of the volumes to

10. N.B.T. ed., iii, 324.
11. M. Beaujard has examined this question at some length and concludes, 'Séi ne semble pas plus savante que les personnes avec qui elle s'entretient d'ordinaire.' Op. cit., p. 350.

while away the long days when she was on leave from court and living at her father's house.[12] Since Chinese studies were socially taboo for her sex, Murasaki's maids expressed dismay, mingled with dire forebodings, when they observed their mistress at this unorthodox pastime: 'My women gather round me and say, "Madam, if you go on like this, there won't be much happiness in store for you. Why should you read books in Chinese characters? In the old days they wouldn't even let women read the sutras." '[13]

At court Murasaki was at great pains to hide her knowledge of the foreign classics; and fear that the other ladies would find out about her interests (as of course they did) seems to have become a sort of complex. The young Empress was also eager to explore these illicit realms, and Murasaki mentions that for some years she has clandestinely been teaching her mistress parts of Po Chü-i's collected works when no one else was present.[14]

If Murasaki had a fair knowledge of Chinese literature – or rather, of that somewhat scattered selection of Chinese literature that circulated in Heian Kyō – she was well versed in the writing of her own country, and we can assume that she was familiar with the principal Japanese works until her time. The diary tells us that when *The Tale of Genji* was read to Emperor Ichijō he commented, 'The person who wrote this must have been reading *The Chronicles of Japan* and is surely very learned.'[15] The Emperor's remark was no doubt well-intentioned, but it was responsible for Murasaki's acquiring the nickname of 'the lady of the Chronicles' (*Nihongi no tsubone*), which she so greatly resented.

Apart from historical works and official court annals, Murasaki was well acquainted with the wealth of Japanese poetry beginning with the vast *Manyō Shū* anthology (*The Collection of Ten Thousand Leaves*) compiled in the eighth century. She was widely read in the vernacular *kanabun* literature, which had developed so brilliantly during the first two centuries of the Heian period – the diaries, the travel records, and

12. N.B.T. ed., iii, 317–18.   13. Ibid., p. 317.   14. Ibid., p. 321.

15. Ibid., p. 320. The Emperor is referring to the *Nihon Shoki*, the first of the Six National Histories. This is the first recorded case in which an influence is attributed to Murasaki's work. The quotation was used by traditional commentators as evidence that the novel was completed by about 1008, the year of the entry in the diary. In fact the Emperor could have made the remark after hearing only the first chapter.

the miscellaneous jottings, of which only a small portion has survived to the present day. Above all, she must have used her long leisure hours at home to steep herself in those voluminous tales or romances known as *monogatari*, the form in which she was to establish her own name.

Murasaki's diary throws considerable light on her knowledge of Buddhism and on her attitude to religion. Her writing shows that she knew a great deal about the intricate Buddhist ceremonial, its hierarchy, and its monastic orders; and we have evidence that she was familiar, not only with the official writings of Tendai (the sect with which she was mainly associated), but with the names, and to some extent the contents, of the other principal scriptures that were known in Japan. Above all, she shows herself to have been imbued with the underlying spirit of Buddhism common to all the sects – the sense of universal impermanence. This is reflected in the thoughts and words of her principal characters; and in the diary itself we find a direct and moving affirmation of faith:

All the things of this world are sad and tiresome. But from now on I shall fear nothing. Whatever others may do or say, I shall recite my prayers tirelessly to Amida Buddha. And when in my mind the things of this world have come to assume no more importance or stability than the vanishing dew, then I shall exert all my efforts to become a wise and holy person.[16]

*

Many an inkstick has been used up, many a brush worn out, in discussing when, why, and whether Murasaki Shikibu wrote *The Tale of Genji*. The last two questions may strike some readers as otiose; but they have exercised Japanese scholars for many a century and it is worth while to note at least a few of the main points that have been raised.

From the early days of Genji criticism there has been a sort of Baconian theory according to which Murasaki's father wrote the outline of *The Tale of Genji*, with his daughter filling in the details, while Michinaga revised the final result. A variant of this theory allows Murasaki the

16. N.B.T. ed., iii, 321. When this was written, the cult of Amida Buddha (Amitâbha) was not associated with any separate sect, but it was practised chiefly by Tendai adherents. Genshin's *Essentials of Salvation* (*Ōjō Yōshū*), which propounds the new Amidist faith, appeared in 985. The book became immensely popular and Murasaki was undoubtedly familiar with it, though she never refers to it in specific terms.

authorship of the main body of the work, but attributes the last ten books (which are often regarded as the best part of the novel) to a different author.

These theories derive more from anti-feminine prejudice than from any systematic study of the text. It galled orthodox Japanese Confucianists that one of the most famous works in their country's literature should have been written by a member of the despised sex and they clutched at any straw to question her authorship. During the past two centuries scholars have tended to restore Murasaki to what is undoubtedly her rightful place as the author of the entire work.[17] There is the evidence of the diary, as well as numerous instances of external reference, to support her claim. The writing of the final books is certainly more careful and delicate than that of the earlier part, but this is an aspect of the progressive improvement in Murasaki's style rather than of multiple authorship.[18]

When we consider the effort that has gone into proving that Shakespeare was merely an ambitious member of an acting troupe, we should perhaps not be too surprised that the question of authorship should have engaged Genji specialists for so long. What does seem peculiar is the great concern of Japanese scholars with the question of why *The Tale of Genji* was written. Early commentators insisted on religious or moral motives. According to one theory, Murasaki undertook her great work as a penance for having written some poem that offended the Buddha. In the Kamakura period, by an interesting historical mutation, to *read* the labyrinthine text of *The Tale of Genji* came to be regarded as a sort of penance – a view that many a hard-pressed Japanese student would still endorse.

During the Muromachi period scholars stressed the Buddhist themes that pervade the work, notably those of retribution and worldly vanity. In the eighteenth century the great nationalist scholar, Motoori Norinaga, rebutted the idea of a religious motive. He pointed out that the 'good' characters in *The Tale of Genji* were often far from good in any conventional sense. Lady Fujitsubo, for instance, is portrayed in a

17. This trend started in the 18th century with Motoori Norinaga, who also combated the idea of a religious motive in Murasaki's work.

18. Ivan Morris, *The Style of Murasaki Shikibu* (Ph.D. thesis, School of Oriental and African Studies, University of London, 1951), p. 212 et passim.

sympathetic light, though she is guilty of the most flagrant adultery and deceit. Murasaki's aim, according to Motoori, was not to preach morality but to evoke a certain pattern of emotional sensibility:

The novel is neither like the Buddhist Way which teaches man to attain enlightenment without deviating from the rightful way, nor like the Confucial Way which teaches man how to govern the country or to regulate one's home or one's conduct. . . . The purpose of *The Tale of Genji* may be likened to the man who, loving the lotus flower, must collect and store muddy and foul water in order to plant and cultivate the flower. The impure mud of illicit love affairs described in *The Tale of Genji* is there not for the purpose of being admired but for the purpose of nurturing the flower of the awareness of the sorrow of human existence.[19]

Motoori's approach helped to clear the air, and certainly it brings us closer to the truth of the matter. More recent scholars have tended to stress personal or psychological motives. For example, the great modern authority, Ikeda Kikan, writes as follows: 'It was the loneliness and the unhappy attitude towards life resulting from the loss of her husband that provided the main impetus for Murasaki's artistic feelings and that caused her to write this great novel.'[20]

There is probably a measure of truth in all these theories (though the penance idea seems rather far-fetched), but it is Murasaki herself who provides the simplest, and perhaps the best, explanation of why the book was written. The scene is the one in which Prince Genji calls on his attractive new ward, Tamakazura, and finds her engrossed in the popular feminine occupation of copying the text from an illustrated romance. He discusses the art of fiction with the young girl and the conversation takes the following turn:

'Of late [said the Prince] I have occasionally stopped to listen while our young Princess's ladies are reading aloud to her, and I have been much impressed by what good authors we have. Perhaps the reason they write so well is simply that they are used to telling lies, but I expect there is more to it than that.'

'I rather imagine,' said Tamakazura, pushing away her inkstone, 'that

19. Quoted in *Sources of the Japanese Tradition*, p. 534, from *Motoori Norinaga Zenshū*, vii, 472–88. But I have changed the translation of 'the Tale' (for *The Tale of Genji*) in the respectful hope that this unpleasing abbreviation may die a rapid death.

20. Ikeda Kikan, 'Genji Monogatari' in *Nihon Bungaku Daijiten*.

it is only those who are themselves in the habit of being deceitful who have to delve like that into the writer's possible motives. Honest people accept what they read as completely true . . .'

[Genji] smiled. '. . . it is a matter of [the writer's] being so moved by things, both good and bad, which he has heard and seen happening to men and women that he cannot keep it all to himself but wants to commit it to writing and make it known to other people – even to those of later generations . . .'[21]

*

Finally, what were the circumstances under which Murasaki wrote her novel? An early Genji commentary has the following account.[22] The great Vestal of Kamo asked Empress Akiko to recommend some interesting book in the phonetic script. The Empress realized that the well-known *monogatari* had become rather stale; besides, many of them were lubricious and hardly suitable for a priestess. Accordingly she asked one of the literary ladies of her acquaintance to try her hand at something new. This lady (who of course was Murasaki Shikibu) went to a temple on the nearby shores of Lake Biwa and stayed there until dawn praying for inspiration. It was the fifteenth of the eighth month, the moonlit night *par excellence* in traditional Japan. Greatly moved by her surroundings, Murasaki received the afflatus she sought and the outline of the novel took shape in her mind. In order not to forget it, she removed the scrolls of the Great Wisdom Sutra from the altar and wrote down two of her most famous chapters. Later, as a penance, she copied out the sixteen scrolls of the sutra in question and dedicated them to the temple. (Even today visitors may be shown the scrolls, and also the room where Murasaki wrote and the ink-slab she used.) Subsequently she added the other chapters until her novel reached its present length of fifty-four, when a fair copy was made by a great court calligrapher and presented to the delighted Vestal.

It is an agreeable (if rather saccharine) story; for many centuries it was accepted as valid, and it became part of the 'Murasaki legend'. Unfortunately, it is as apocryphal as the ink-slab and the scrolls. Scholars are unanimous on this point; but they are still at loggerheads about when the book was actually written. The general tendency has been to discount the tradition that it was completed before Murasaki entered

21. Appendix 5.   22. I refer to *Kakai Shō* (early 14th century).

court service and to attribute an increasing length of time to the writing.

We know from references in the diary that at least part of the book was being circulated at court in 1008. In describing a party given to celebratet he birth of the Empress's first child, Murasaki mentions this incident: ' "Well, now," said the Captain of the Outer Palace Guards, "I expect that little Murasaki must be about here somewhere." "There's no one here like Genji," thought I to myself, "so what should Murasaki be doing in this place?" ' The following entry belongs to 1009:

His Excellency [Michinaga] saw *The Tale of Genji* lying about in the Empress's apartments. He made his usual stupid jibes, and then handed me a poem written on a piece of paper to which he had attached a branch of plum-blossom: 'What with these ardent tales of love, little can I think that men have passed you by, as they might this plum-tree's sour fruit.' And so I replied, 'If no man has tasted, who can say if the fruit is sour, or if the writer of these tales herself has known such love?'[23]

Some of the events in the novel seem to have been taken from things that actually happened at court in 1013 and 1017, but this cannot be accepted as positive evidence. The only other reliable date occurs in the *Sarashina Diary*. I quote the passage at some length, since it gives a good idea of the impression that Murasaki's book made on one young girl at the time, and also of how hard it was to come by a copy:

I read *Waka Murasaki* and a few of the other [early] books in *The Tale of Genji*, and I longed to see the later parts. . . . But we were still new to the capital and it was not easy to find copies. I was burning with impatience and curiosity, and in my prayers I used to say, 'Let me see the whole!' When my parents went to the Kōryū Temple for a retreat, this was the only thing I asked for. Yet all my hopes were in vain.

I was feeling most dejected about it when one day I called on an aunt of mine who had come up from the country. She received me very affectionately and showed the greatest interest in me. 'What a pretty girl you've grown up to be!' said she. Then, as I was leaving, she asked, 'What would you like as a present? I am sure you don't want anything too practical. I'd like to give you something that you will really enjoy.'

And so it was that she presented me with fifty-odd volumes of *The Tale of Genji* in a special case, together with [numerous other *monogatari*]. Oh, how happy I was when I came home with all these books in a bag! In the past I had only been able to have an occasional flurried look at parts

23. N.B.T. ed., iii, 292–3, 324.

of *The Tale of Genji*. Now I had it all in front of me and I could lie undisturbed behind my screen, taking the books out one by one and enjoying them to my heart's content. I wouldn't have changed places with the Empress herself.[24]

Since *The Tale of Genji* consists of fifty-four books, this would seem to be fairly good evidence that most of the novel, if not all, was completed and in circulation by 1022, the date to which this passage refers. It seems plausible that Murasaki started writing shortly after her husband's death when she was living at home, say in about 1002, and that she continued with occasional interruptions during her long period of service at court until about 1020, when she had completed some fifty books. [25]Twenty years may seem a long time to spend on a single novel but, as a modern Japanese scholar has pointed out, many a work far shorter than *The Tale of Genji* has occupied a greater span of its writer's life.[26]

24. Nihon Koten Bungaku Taikei ed., xx, 492–3. Sugawara no Takasue's daughter, the author of the diary, was 13 at the time.

25. See Appendix 3.

26. Tezuka Noboru mentions *La Divina Commedia* (1292–1321), *Paradise Lost* (1640–67), *Hizakurige* (1802–24), and *Faust* (1774–1831) among others. 'Gengo oyobi Nikki yori Mitaru Murasaki Shikibu.' Professor Tezuka divides the writing of *The Tale of Genji* into three main periods and provides a wealth of arguments (none of which, however, is conclusive) to support his chronology:

(i) 1003–5 following her husband's death Murasaki starts work on the novel and continues until she enters court service, by which time she has completed Book 13 (*Akashi*).

1008–10 the diary.

(ii) 1011–c.1016 she completes that part of the novel in which Genji is the hero, i.e. up to Book 41 (*Maboroshi*).

(iii) 1017– she works on the last part of the novel (the Kaoru-Niou sequence), but dies before she is able to complete it.

'Genji Monogatari Chosaku no Jiki', pp. 28–45.

Tezuka places Murasaki's death shortly after 1030 and believes that she was working on her novel until the end. This is a far later date than most scholars would allow. The 18th-century experts, Kamo Mabuchi and Motoori Norinaga, say that the novel was completed by 1004. Modern scholars all give later dates. Ikeda says that most of the novel was finished by 1010; Onoe Hachirō that Murasaki continued writing until her death in the '20s of the 11th century; Oka Kazuo that the books up to Book 41 were written between 1001 and 1008 and the remainder in 1009–10. Considering how little we really know about the facts of Murasaki's life, it is remarkable how precise and dogmatic some of these experts can be.

X

Aspects of 'The Tale of Genji'

THE first psychological novel in the literature of the world is also one of its longest. In its original form *The Tale of Genji* consisted of fifty-four books or chapters, which were separately bound and which, as the complaint in the *Sarashina Diary* reminds us, often circulated independently. Arthur Waley's translation, which does not expand the original (and from which one of the books is missing), has some 630,000 words; this makes Murasaki's novel about twice as long as *Don Quixote*, *War and Peace*, or *The Brothers Karamazov*, though only two-thirds the length of *A la recherche du temps perdu*.

The action is spread over three-quarters of a century and involves four generations. There are about four hundred and thirty characters, not counting messengers, servants, and anonymous members of the working class. Most of these characters are related to each other,[1] and early commentators devoted years to the sisyphean task of producing genealogical tables in which almost every character in the novel was included. The tradition has been maintained by modern scholars: Ikeda's recent *Encyclopaedia of the Tale of Genji* has over seventy closely printed pages of genealogy. Murasaki belonged to a rigidly stratified society in which family connexions were all-important, and while working on the novel she must have kept her own charts to show how her huge cast of characters were related. For never once is she inconsistent about the relationship of even the most obscure people in her book.

This methodical approach is even more striking in Murasaki's time scheme. There is hardly a passage in the entire novel that we cannot identify in terms of year and month and in which we cannot determine the exact age of each of the important characters.[2] Occasionally Murasaki

1. See Appendix 4.
2. These identifications are often extremely complicated. Murasaki does not mar her novel by periodically referring to dates, ages, etc. On the other hand, as

will depart from straight chronological order in telling her story. The events in one chapter, for example, may occur before those in the previous chapter ('flashback'), or two chapters may overlap. But such deviations are deliberate and there is never any confusion. Commentators have subjected the time scheme of the novel to the minutest scrutiny. They are, one feels, almost hoping to find some inconsistency; until now they have been unsuccessful.

This precision is one aspect of Murasaki's talent for organizing her voluminous material in the most effective way. It immediately puts her work in a different category from *The Tale of the Hollow Tree*, the only extant precursor in the field of lengthy prose fiction. For one of the things that makes *The Tale of the Hollow Tree* so hard to read, and ultimately so unreal, is its disorganized construction and its chaotic time scheme.

The Tale of Genji does not ramble on amorphously as a haphazard sequence of loosely connected episodes. It is true that the books tend to be more independent than the chapters of most modern novels, especially since there is often a gap of several years between them; yet to view the work as a series of vaguely related short stories (as some critics have done) seems to me completely off the mark. Like the individual books of which it is composed, *The Tale of Genji* is an artistic unit whose shape has been carefully and deliberately designed. It is so constructed that the entire work can be resolved into certain general divisions, which represent its beginning (Books 1–12), its middle (Books 13–41), and its end (Books 42–54), and into a number of significant sub-divisions whose various chapters are closely bound together by the coherent development of character and event.[3]

Motoori points out in *Genji Monogatari Tama no Ogushi* (pp. 531–63), it appears that in each book she deliberately introduced certain events that can be situated in point of time, usually by reference to the age of the hero. This aspect of her work has been exhaustively examined by Japanese scholars, and most of the standard commentaries contain detailed chronological charts (e.g. Part III of Motoori, op. cit.).

3. Onoe Hachirō finds that the novel falls into six sub-divisions:
    (i) Books 1–7 Genji's life until he is 19;
    (ii) Books 8–13 his disgrace and downfall;
    (iii) Books 14–33 his recall to the capital; the splendour of Genji's life reaches its apex;

Above all, *The Tale of Genji* is constructed about a set of central ideas or themes, the historical theme of Fujiwara power, for example, and the human theme of impermanence, which combine to give it an artistic unity. This is one of the aspects (the use of realistic psychological detail is another) that allow us to describe Murasaki's work as a 'novel', a term that cannot be applied to any of its exact precursors.

One device that Murasaki uses with particular effect is anticipation or build-up. Frequently she will hint at the existence of some character long before that person enters the action of the novel, or she will adumbrate some sequence of events that is to take place many years in the future. There is a scene in one of the early books, for example, in which Prince Genji and his young friends stand on a hill and discuss the beauties of the countryside in the distance. 'If one were to live in such a place,' exclaims Genji, 'one could really ask for nothing more in this world!'[4] Here Murasaki anticipates, not without irony, the events that are to happen eight years (and seven books) later. For the landscape at which Genji gazes so fondly is to be the place of his forlorn exile from the capital. His friend then tells him the story of the strange old lay priest of Akashi and his attractive little daughter. This arouses the young prince's curiosity, as well as the reader's, and paves the way for Genji's love affair with Lady Akashi and for all the complications that this entails in later years.

Sometimes Murasaki will speak about a character never mentioned before as though the reader already knew all about him. In the hands of a skilful writer this device can produce a curiously realistic effect and, as Arthur Waley has pointed out, it was used by Proust. Murasaki's more usual method of build-up, however, is to make different characters

---

(iv) Books 34–41 the decline of Genji's fortunes, owing to a series of emotional shocks (Nyosan's seduction, Murasaki's death, etc.);

(v) Books 42–49 introduction to Kaoru and Niou;

(vi) Books 50–54 Ukifune's appearance on the scene and the tragic rivalry for her affections.

Within each of these sub-divisions there is a definite sequence of events running from book to book, even though there may be time-gaps between the books; and in each case there is a break in the action between one sub-division and the next. Onoe Hachirō, N.B.T. ed., *Genji Monogatari*, vi, 20–33.

4. N.B.T. ed., vi, 116–17.

speak about someone from their respective points of view long before the person in question actually appears on the scene. For example, Kaoru hears various reports about Ukifune, the tragic heroine of the last five books, many years before he actually meets her. It is not until we have formed a fairly clear picture of the girl that she enters the action.

By far the best-known case of anticipation in *The Tale of Genji* occurs in Book 2 when Genji and his young friends meet on a rainy night to discuss the different types of women they have known and to compare their merits. This passage, with its detailed comments on various sorts of women that are to figure in the novel, has often been regarded as a key to the organization of the entire work, not unlike the first movement of a symphony in which the composer may suggest the themes that he intends to develop later.[5] In fact the 'discussion on a rainy night' does not have nearly such a mechanical function as this might suggest. Of the many types of girl that the young gallants describe, only one can be identified with a specific character in the novel. This is Yūgao, the simple young woman whose love affair with Genji and whose weird death are described in the following two books. One of Genji's friends mentions that he has had an illegitimate child with Yūgao; mother and child have both disappeared and he has been unable to track them down. Here is another case of anticipation; for the child in question turns out to be Tamakazura, who enters the action of the novel seventeen years later.

Another aspect of Murasaki's style that serves to tighten the structure of her narrative is the deliberate repetition of situations, settings, and relationships between characters. *The Tale of Genji* contains certain patterns of action that occur with variations at widely separated points of the narrative, not unlike the motifs in a musical composition. Here again we are reminded of *A la recherche du temps perdu*[6] with its subtle use of internal 'rhythms'.

5. Thus, according to Baron Suematsu, the real purpose of *The Tale of Genji* is 'to portray the different shades of female characters, as set forth in [the Judgement on a Rainy Night] and thereby to show the fickleness and selfishness of man'. Suematsu Kenchō, *The Romance of Genji*, Introduction. And so we have yet another 'motive' for Murasaki's novel.

6. Cf. E. M. Forster: '. . . whereas the story appeals to our curiosity and the plot to our intelligence, the pattern appeals to our aesthetic sense, it causes us to see the book as a whole.' Because of its patterns even a vast, rambling novel like

One of the best ways to understand the carefully balanced architecture of Murasaki's novel is to note how she places different characters, or sometimes the same character, in successive situations that 'correspond' with each other. Thus, when Genji finds out that his young wife, Princess Nyosan, has been seduced by Kashiwagi and that the little boy (Kaoru) whom everyone takes to be his own son and heir is in fact the result of this affair, he realizes that history has repeated itself to an uncanny degree. For some thirty years earlier Genji himself had seduced his father's new consort, Lady Fujitsubo, and she had given birth to a boy (Reizei), who was accepted as the Emperor's son and who as a result came to the throne illegitimately. As Genji holds the little child in his arms, it occurs to him that the old Emperor may secretly have known and suffered about Fujitsubo's unfaithfulness, in much the same way that he himself is now tormented by what Nyosan has done.[7] The same pattern continues to unfold in later years. Just as Reizei was racked with doubts about his paternity, to the extent that he eventually resigned the throne, so when Kaoru grows up he is obsessed with the feeling that there was something strange about his birth, and this serves to intensify the neurotic aspect of his character.

There are many cases like this in which a pattern that has been developed in the early part of the novel, when Genji is the hero, is repeated with variations in the Kaoru books. For example, the relationship between Genji and Yūgao finds its echo, as it were, in the love affair between Kaoru and Ukifune some fifty years later. In each case the hero's interest is aroused by hearing about an attractive girl who belongs to a far lower social class than himself. It is only after careful anticipation that Murasaki puts her on the scene. The hero meets her by chance and is almost immediately captivated (Books 4 and 49). The love affair begins in the lady's humble town dwelling; and in the morn-

---

Proust's has an unmistakable unity: 'The book is chaotic, ill constructed, it has ... no external shape; and yet it hangs together because it is stitched internally, because it contains rhythms.' *Aspects of the Novel*, pp. 138, 151.

7. N.B.T. ed., vii, 153–4. The repetition of this particular pattern was emphasized by traditional Genji scholars as an example of the moral intention of the work (the theme of karma and retribution). Motoori indignantly countered their view and insisted that Murasaki's aim was to describe the sense of *mono no aware*, which emerges most poignantly in unhappy love affairs of this kind. Motoori Noringa, op. cit., p. 516.

ing the hero lies listening to the unfamiliar street noises. He abruptly decides to move his mistress to some more isolated place and despite the protests of her attendants he takes her in his carriage to a gloomy country house. In both cases the relationships are marked by a sense of strangeness and end in tragedy. It is not surprising that such closely parallel situations should contain what Waley describes as 'balancing scenes', like those in Books 4 and 50 when Murasaki describes the sounds of the peasants and the pedlars. The emphasis in the two scenes is on the unfamiliarity of the common surroundings in which the hero suddenly finds himself. Both men are fascinated by the street sounds, which in Genji's case are able years later to evoke the memory of his love. These are the scenes:

(Book 4) ... the dwelling, so different from those to which Genji was accustomed, seemed strange to him. It must have been nearly dawn. From the neighbouring houses he could hear the uncouth voices of workers who were just waking up: 'Oh, how cold it is!" We can't count on much business this year. It's a poor look-out for our hauling trade.' 'Hey, neighbour, wake up!' With such remarks they set out noisily, each to his own pitiful job.

(Book 50) Soon it appeared to be dawn, but instead of the song of birds, Kaoru heard the raucous and unintelligible cries of pedlars calling out their wares from near the main street while they passed by in large groups. As he looked out at them staggering past in the dawn light with their loads, they appeared like phantoms. The experience of having passed the night in this simple dwelling seemed most strange to Kaoru.[8]

Murasaki's deliberate repetitions are never as obvious as this may suggest. Nor are they exact. Psychological realism demanded that different types of people react differently in the same situation; however parallel the patterns may be, it is unthinkable that we should, for example, find a resolute character like Genji handling a love affair with the diffidence and deviousness of a Kaoru.

The use of 'sustained imagery' (the repetition, that is, of a single central image in both the narrative passages and the poems) can also serve to connect different parts of the novel that are widely separated in time, or to tighten the structure of a particular series of books. Throughout the novel, for instance, Murasaki rings the changes on the

8. N.B.T. ed., vi, 88 and vii, 669.

image of dreams and thereby evokes one of her central themes – the nebulous, unreal quality of the world about us, and the idea that our life here is a mere 'bridge of dreams' (the title of her final book), over which we cross from one state of existence to the next.[9]

Another example of sustained imagery is the river at Uji, which figures prominently in the last ten books. This section (commonly known as the 'Ten Books of Uji') occupies a special place in the writing of *The Tale of Genji*. It is marked by tightly knit narrative and by a most effective use of psychological detail and of imagery. In almost every sense, indeed, it represents the climax of Murasaki's style. (This having been said, the reader should perhaps be warned that the following discussion is focused on one particular aspect of the Uji books and that their tone is not nearly so monotonous or insistent as an abstract of this kind might lead one to believe.)

The main setting is a house in the little hamlet of Uji, where the religious recluse, Prince Hachi, lives with his two attractive daughters. The Prince's residence, though less than ten miles from the bustle and brilliance of the capital, presents so isolated and depressing an aspect as to become the very crystallization of that mood of melancholy which increasingly dominates the novel and its characters. The theme of death is constantly in the foreground. Indeed, the action of the Uji books centres on the deaths, or supposed deaths, at Uji of the Prince's wife, the Prince himself, his elder daughter, and his step-daughter, Ukifune. Meanwhile the survivors are depicted as becoming more and more imbued with the gloom of the place. They toy with the idea of leaving the house and moving to the capital, but this is hardly easier for the Prince's daughters than it was eight centuries later for the sisters in Chekhov's tragedy.

The very name Uji ('Forlorn') is symbolical of the sorrow that pervades the house. This is not lost on any of its inhabitants; sometimes, in fact, they almost seem to revel in the thought that their village is true to its name.[10]

The mood of Uji is reflected in the imagery. The dreary weather of the village – the winds and rains, the snow flurries and blizzards, the clouds and the gathering mist – mirrors the emotions of the characters, and is contrasted with the relatively benign and cheerful conditions in

9. See pp. 126–7.   10. E.g. N.B.T. ed., vii, 675, 710, 759.

the capital beyond the hills. Murasaki also evokes the atmosphere of the place by numerous sound-symbols that in *The Tale of Genji* are invariably associated with sorrow. Such are the cry of the deer (that strangely poignant sound that has so greatly moved Japanese poets over the centuries), the slow tolling of the distant temple bell, the call of the wild geese, the rush of the waterfall, the wailing of the wind in the oak trees.

Of all the images that symbolize the atmosphere at Uji none is used more consistently and with greater effect than that of the river outside Prince Hachi's house. As the central image of these final books, it serves to evoke the grief and tragedy that dominate the house at Uji and its inhabitants. On his first visit to the place Kaoru is struck by the noise of the river directly outside the Prince's house: 'The fierce sound of the water and the lapping of the waves against the river bank boomed terrifyingly in his ears.'[11]

In the following book the roar of the water is combined with those other doleful aspects of nature into which the girls merge themselves during their grief at Prince Hachi's death:

Now they had reached the ninth month of the year, and the sisters felt that their lives had turned into an unending night. The sight of the rain-swept hills and fields brought tears to their eyes and made the sleeves of their robes still wetter than before. The rustle of the falling leaves as they swirled against each other in the air, the roar of the water in Uji River, the sound of the waterfall like a gushing torrent of tears – it all seemed to blend into a dirge, filling the girls with dismay. How could things go on like this? Was there to be no end to this existence of theirs?[12]

The elder sister is overcome by a particularly intense bout of melancholy: 'Everything seemed unutterably sad, and she felt herself drifting along with the sound of the water.'[13]

Murasaki was always interested in the effects that the same scene could have on different characters. When Kaoru's rival, the comparatively ebullient and extroverted Prince Niou, pays his first visit to Uji,

11 Ibid., pp. 399–400.   12. Ibid., p. 436.

13. Ibid., p. 463. This is a curious use of imagery; I have given a literal translation of *mizu no oto ni nagaresou kokochi shitamau*.

he is delighted by the place; for, as Murasaki points out, 'he was always susceptible to new forms of beauty'. His main objective is to seduce the younger daughter, but as a true Heian gentleman he is bound to be impressed by the natural setting: 'He watched the wreath of mist drifting over the water and the boats laden with brushwood as they sailed along the river leaving white swirls in their wake. A strange place to live, he thought, but not without a charm of its own.'[14] But later in the day the mood of Uji begins to tell on him and he sees the river in a new light: 'The sound of the water seemed to have lost its pleasant tone, and now as the mist cleared and the ancient Bridge of Uji emerged into full view he began to feel that there was something harsh and friendless about these shores.'[15]

Ukifune's tempestuous destiny lends itself perfectly to expression in terms of the river imagery. The girl's life is repeatedly associated with the river that flows ominously outside the house at Uji, where her new lover, Kaoru, has brought her to live. He is rarely able to visit her, and Ukifune spends most of her time in a state of gloomy solitude that is only occasionally interrupted by the arrival of a messenger from the capital. During the rainy season Kaoru sends a poem in which the central image is Uji River. It is hardly a cheering tonic.

> How fare you by those far-off shores
> (Lost no doubt in doleful thoughts)
> While the never-ending rains
> Swell the fierce waves that surge outside your house?[16]

In a subsequent letter Ukifune maintains the image and she also refers to a well-known poem about a gliding boat (which incidentally is the origin of her name):

> So smoothly glides my boat
> That if it were to merge into the waves
> Who would there be to say he saw a ripple on the water's face?

14. Ibid., p. 491.   15. Ibid., p. 492.
16. Ibid., p. 710. The poem contains a conventional play on words: *nagame* = (i) long rains, (ii) lost in thought; *harenu* = (i) does not clear up (of rain), (ii) gloomy, doleful.

For the first time the idea of drowning, of merging with the water in death, is suggested.[17]

When Ukifune finally decides that her predicament has become impossible (her two lovers, Kaoru and Niou, are both expecting to move her to the capital and the dates of departure are only a few days off), it follows both realistically and symbolically that she should decide to drown herself in Uji River, which has become the symbol of her tormented life. Now the image and reality have become a single texture, and the events move fast, with a degree of inevitability that we would never find in a haphazard narrative of actual happenings. Ukifune has overheard her mother, who is visiting her at Uji, tell one of the old ladies in the house that, if her daughter should become involved in any more difficulties, she will never be able to see her again. Ukifune's cup is full. She knows that a most appalling situation is approaching. Although Kaoru and Niou are supposed to be bosom friends, neither has told the other about his relations with Ukifune. Soon they will find out, and then both men will desert her in disgust. And she can no longer count on her mother for support. Clearly there is only one solution: 'Oh that I might lose this body of mine!'[18]

During all this time the roar of the swollen river can be heard outside, and now the girl listens as her mother and the old lady discuss it:

Ukifune's mother had begun to respond to the fearful roar of the river. 'Really,' she said, 'this was an odd place to build a house. Some stretches of the river are far less rough than here. How terrible to have to live year after year with that sound always in one's ears.' Never before had the river seemed so formidable.[19]

It is at once symbol and reality that Ukifune should now resolve to join the large number of people who have ended their lives in Uji River. A recurrent image has become a reality: the fierce waters, which have always represented the mood of sorrow and tragedy at Uji, become the real agent of the culminating disaster.

17. Listed among the love poems later included in the *Shinchokusen* anthology. Later when Ukifune disappears her attendants find a letter that she has written to her mother, and from the single word *majiranaba* ('if it were to merge') recognize the Floating Boat poem and realize that she must have drowned herself. Such were the advantages of knowing one's poetry.

18. N.B.T. ed., vii, 715.   19. Loc. cit.

In one of her last poems Ukifune again uses the river imagery:

> Though this poor body sink into the waves,
> My sinful name, alas, will not stay down,
> But float up to the water's top for all to know.[20]

The river continues to appear as a symbol of tragedy long after Ukifune's supposed suicide. In Book 52 two inhabitants of Uji stand watching the river swirl by outside the Prince's house and hear in its noise a constant rebuke to Ukifune for having committed suicide.[21] Later in the same book Kaoru, unbearably agitated by the noise of the waters, sets out for the capital in the middle of the night, rather than remain alone in Uji with the picture in his mind of Ukifune lying on the river bed: 'So long as he heard that sound he was unable to put his mind to rest for a single moment.'[22]

Yet he cannot keep away from Uji. In the following book a Captain of the Guards tells about having seen Kaoru at Prince Hachi's house:

As His Excellency stood near the river, he gazed into the water and wept. Then he went into the house and wrote a poem which he attached to one of the pillars. It said:

> 'Not even her faintest shadow shows upon the river's face,
> Only my swelling tears that no dam will keep back.'[23]

The scene is spiced with irony; for Ukifune, far from lying at the bottom of Uji River, is safely ensconced in the next room, where she is eavesdropping on the Captain's conversation.

*

Long as *The Tale of Genji* may be, it is the merest ant-hill in comparison with the mountains of commentaries and scholarly studies that have grown up about it. According to Professor Ikeda, more than ten thousand books have been written about *The Tale of Genji*, not to mention innumerable essays, monographs, dissertations, and the like; in addition there are several Genji dictionaries and concordances, and hundreds of weighty works in which Murasaki's novel has been used as material for the study of subjects like Heian court ceremony and music.

20. Ibid., p. 732.   21. Ibid., p. 740.   22. Ibid., p. 758.
23. Ibid., p. 831.

The basic textual commentary belongs to the early thirteenth century and consisted of fifty-four ponderous tomes, one for each of Murasaki's books; of these only a single volume is extant. Subsequent commentaries were rarely less than a thousand pages long; Ikeda's recent *Tale of Genji Encyclopaedia* has some 1,200 large, closely printed pages, of which about one hundred are devoted to listing earlier commentaries. No other novel in the world can have been subjected to such close scrutiny; no writer of any kind, except perhaps Shakespeare, can have had his work more voluminously discussed than Murasaki Shikibu.

This flood of exegesis started about one generation after Murasaki's death, when people were beginning to recognize certain difficulties in understanding her novel. A good deal of the early work was aimed at pointing out the overall unity of the fifty-four books. Genealogies were drawn up to explain how closely the huge cast of characters were related to each other; the systematic sequence of events was demonstrated by means of elaborate chronologies. The next main task was to list the thousands of quotations and references to literature and history that occur throughout the novel. The role of quoted poems was recognized as particularly important in Murasaki's imagery. While civil war raged throughout Japan, many a medieval scholar spent his years patiently ferreting out poems in obscure anthologies or private collections from which Murasaki may have derived her quotations.

As the world of *The Tale of Genji* receded into the distant past, the language of the novel began to present ever greater difficulties. The first Genji dictionary dates from the fourteenth century, and much of the work during the Muromachi period was devoted to linguistic interpretation. The study of manuscripts and the comparison of different versions also became important, as scholars tried to establish a definitive text of the work. By now Genji scholarship had largely become the preserve of certain aristocratic families, and we are confronted with the strange tradition of secret commentaries and secret texts, which would be handed down in particular schools like precious heirlooms. Various 'Genji problems' were listed, and each school would have its own arcane interpretations, jealously guarded from other schools and imparted only to trusted disciples. A good deal of the effort of the medieval scholars was devoted to the exhilarating task of demolishing the work of rival groups.

One of the great centres of Genji studies was the 'southern court' in the richly blossomed hills of Yoshino, where during a good part of the fourteenth century a rival line of emperors maintained itself in opposition to the 'northern court' at Kyoto. Many of the 'southern' emperors were noted for their erudition in the field of Genji scholarship, which of course greatly added to its prestige. It became customary at Yoshino for groups of noble *cognoscenti* to meet in full court dress, often in the presence of the emperor, and for one of them to read aloud from the text, stopping occasionally to interpret an obscure passage or to expatiate on some literary subtlety.

The Yoshino scholars were mainly interested in *The Tale of Genji* as a work of art, whereas the groups in Kyoto tended to use it as a basis for linguistic and historical studies.[24] These two opposing trends have continued throughout the course of Genji scholarship, but the most valuable work, like that of the great nationalist scholars in the Tokugawa period, has always involved a blending of the 'literary' and the 'academic' approaches. The flow of both types of studies has continued unabated until the present day, and Professor Ikeda's voluminous work (both textual and interpretative) will undoubtedly rank among the most valuable in this field during the past eight centuries.

Confronted with this formidable mass of scholarly material, the reader sometimes feels that, far from helping him to enter into the delicate spirit of *The Tale of Genji*, it imposes a block between him and the original novel. Indeed, as one wades through some of the more turgid commentaries, one wonders whether they are not trying to open a fragile persimmon with a hydraulic drill. Of course it would be the height of churlishness to question the value of the work by these generations of patient scholars; without it the novel would be as impenetrable as an Easter Island inscription. But it is important to remember that Murasaki was an artist, not a chronicler (still less a scholar), and that *The Tale of Genji* must be enjoyed above all as a work of literature, not as a source of information.

To what extent can we really understand what she was writing about? It has sometimes been suggested that the modern Western reader is so divorced from Murasaki in time and space, in patterns of thought and

24. Ikeda Kikan, *Genji Monogatari Kōza*.

expression, in custom and in sensibility, that she might as well have belonged to a different planet, and that what we derive from the work of this court lady of tenth-century Japan can be only the palest approximation of what she intended to convey. According to this argument, even the modern Japanese reader, the child of Westernized industrial society, is hardly less cut off from the world of the shining prince than we in the Occident.

I do not subscribe to this view. Indeed, it seems to me, one of the remarkable things about this novel of a millennium ago is how readily we can enter into the thoughts and feelings of its characters and respond to the total vision of life that its author communicated. The more we know about the times – social organization, religious ideas, marriage customs, literary conventions, and so forth – the greater our understanding will be. Yet, even with the most elementary knowledge of the Heian background, the sensitive reader can grasp the psychology of a character like Kaoru, for example, and appreciate the close connexion between beauty and sorrow that is an underlying theme of the novel.

Many things that seemed important to Murasaki (calligraphic skill, for instance, or the court hierarchy) have little relevance in the present day; yet, when it comes to vivifying a character by psychological detail, or using imagery to evoke the feelings that death can inspire, she seems close to us and 'modern' in a way that no previous writer of prose fiction can approach.

But is our present text of *The Tale of Genji* what Murasaki actually wrote? It is a complex matter and this is not the place to discuss it in any detail. The earliest extant manuscript dates from the middle of the twelfth century, over one hundred years after Murasaki was writing; it could hardly be more inaccurate and incomplete. Our first full text of the fifty-four books belongs to the fourteenth century, and varies in many ways from the manuscripts on which most modern texts are based.[25] The rival schools of medieval Genji scholars had their own texts, which they guarded like military secrets. It was not until relatively

25. The two main textual traditions are the *Kawachi Bon*, on which the earliest complete extant manuscript (the *Hirase Bon*) is based, and the *Aobyōshi Bon* (Blue Cover Copy), which is the source of most modern printed texts. Both date from the early 13th century. Ikeda has provided an exhaustive 8-volume correlation of the various texts: *Genji Monogatari Taisei*.

recent times that the various manuscripts could be correlated and compared for accuracy.

Considering this rather confused history and the difficulties of producing reliable copies of Japanese 'grass writing' script, we might expect the most bewildering discrepancies between the different versions. In fact a study of Ikeda's textual correlations suggests that they are remarkably close and that most of the differences are matters of detail which have little bearing on the overall content or significance of the novel. Of course such correlations do not tell us how faithful the texts are to the sentences that Murasaki committed to paper one thousand years ago. Failing a monumental literary discovery, this is something we shall never know. The consensus among modern Japanese scholars, however, is that the printed texts of *The Tale of Genji* may for all literary purposes be regarded as quite close to the original.[26]

The real barrier between the modern reader and *The Tale of Genji* is not any corruption of the text, nor any confusion of theme. It is a far more direct one: the difficulty of the language in which the novel is written. Since this language is virtually pure Japanese, one might expect that at least for Murasaki's countrymen it should present no insuperable hardships. The trouble is that during the past seven centuries both the literary and spoken languages of Japan have become so thoroughly impregnated with Chinese vocabulary and constructions (not to mention the recent flood of linguistic imports from the West) that Heian Japanese has become quite as remote as the Anglo-Saxon of *Beowulf* is for the average Englishman. Most people in Japan who read *The Tale of Genji* nowadays use the modern-language version by the eminent novelist, Tanizaki Junichirō; and some, including as prominent a literary man as Masamune Hakuchō, find Arthur Waley's translation more comprehensible than the original text.

The main trouble does not arise from the length and complexity of the sentences, nor from the massive agglutinative verb forms, the involved honorific usage, and the host of obscure particles. With a certain amount of patience we can work all this out systematically and remember it. What we can never hope to surmount is the fantastic lack of specificity in Heian writing. The Japanese language in general lacks the precision of which Chinese is capable and which is the glory of some

26. Oka, op. cit., p. 560.

Indo-European languages. But in the *kanabun* literature of the Heian period – including, alas, the work of Murasaki Shikibu – this obscurity can reach nightmare proportions. Proper names are rigorously avoided. Direct speech is common, but the speaker hardly ever indicated. As often as not we have to guess at the subject of the sentence, and sometimes the subject will change half-way through without any warning. The mutually exclusive categories that we take for granted in European languages – past and present tense, affirmation and question, singular and plural, male and female (as identified by personal names and pronouns), doubt and certainty – have little relevance in Heian Japanese; sometimes it is not even clear whether the sentence is positive or negative.

This reluctance to be specific, which has given so much trouble to commentators and readers of Heian literature, results partly from the intimate connexion between this literature and classical Japanese poetry – a poetry that is marked by extremely laconic wording and an overwhelming reliance on imagistic suggestion. It also results from the 'closed' nature of upper-class Heian society. The members of Murasaki's society always preferred the allusion to the statement, the hint to the explanation. This applies most conspicuously to poetry and poetic quotations, but it also affected their everyday speech, their occasional writings (diaries and notes), and the vernacular literature in which their lives were described. For people who live in a small, closed society, like that of the Heian court, the entire range of experience will be so familiar that the briefest hint will suffice to convey one's meaning, and any systematic exposition of one's thoughts is regarded as otiose, even boorish. Language becomes a sort of shorthand, immediately understood by those who are 'in', vague and slightly mysterious to the outsider. The same phenomenon can be found in almost any small, closed group, but in the court society of Heian Japan this economy of expression was carried to extraordinary lengths and profoundly influenced the literature, which was an intimate part of that society.

Another reason that Heian writing impresses the modern reader as being so vague is the poverty of the vocabulary that Murasaki and her colleagues had at their disposal. Like many languages in an early stage of development, tenth-century Japanese was endowed with an extremely rich grammatical apparatus but a relatively limited choice of words. This applies especially to abstract adjectives. The result is that certain words tend to be greatly overworked and to lose all precision of meaning. Modern English, of course, has its share of such words ('interesting', 'nice', 'good'), but the conscientious author uses them with the greatest caution. Heian writers, on the other hand, almost seem to revel in the repetition of the same emotive words, whose range of meaning is so widely and thinly spread as to make accurate communication impossible.[27] In the sentence below, for example, the word *ayashi* is used no less than three times, with the successive meanings of 'remarkable', 'outlandish', and 'disagreeable'. This by no means exhausts the possible translations of the word. Among its many other senses is 'absurd', and it is quite possible that this, rather than 'distasteful', is what Murasaki intended here – a typical example of how lack of verbal specificity can obscure meaning for readers of a later age. I have chosen this particular sentence because it illustrates not only the repetition of words but many other characteristics of Heian literary style, and may suggest to what an extent Murasaki's language can act as a barrier to our understanding. It is not regarded as one of the difficult passages.

The scene is that in which Prince Niou secretly sets out for Uji to pay his first visit to Ukifune, whose charms have been vaguely reported to him by Kaoru. Since it was Kaoru who originally introduced him to the Uji household, he feels a certain compunction about seducing his friend's mistress – but not enough to deter him. A fairly literal translation will be followed by a more literary one; the words in square brackets are not in the original, but have to be added if we are to understand anything at all:

... recalling all sorts of things [and thinking] what an underhand thing this is to the person/people who joining [his/their] heart/hearts (*kokoro*) [with me] to a remarkable (*ayashiki*) extent led me and since even in the capital [he] was not under any circumstances able to go about indiscreetly without people/a person knowing wearing an outlandish (*ayashiki*) disguise and though the feelings [of him] who was on the horse were fearful and guilty

27. Typical words of this kind are *aware*, *kokorobososhi*, *okashi* (Sei Shōnagon's favourite), *warinashi*, *namamekashi*, *kuchioshi*. This tendency has not entirely disappeared from modern literature, and is one of the less fortunate legacies of classical Japanese.

since [his] heart (*kokoro*) was advanced in the inquisitive direction thinking
as [he/they] came deep into the hills when how will it become to go back
without even meeting would indeed be unsatisfying (? lonely) and dis-
graceful (? absurd = *ayashi*) [his] heart (*kokoro*) was stirred up[28]

Out of this loose sequence of vague phrases, in which the subject is
never once mentioned, and which of course has no punctuation whatsoever, the following emerges:

Various thoughts occurred to Niou. He recalled how remarkably helpful
Kaoru had been in introducing him to Uji in the first place. Even in the
capital Niou was never in a position to come and go as he pleased without
people knowing about it, and for this expedition he had put on an outlandish disguise. Now as he rode up to Uji his feelings of guilt towards
Kaoru were mixed with a sense of fear. Yet his was an unusually inquisitive
temperament, and as they came deeper into the hills he grew more and
more excited. When would they arrive, he wondered, and how were things
likely to turn out. Perhaps he would have to go back to the capital without
even having met Ukifune. How frustrating that would be – and what a
disgrace!

Heian style poses special problems for the translator. Should he try
to stay close to the original Japanese and convey at least some of its
imprecision to the Western reader? Or should he make everything as
clear and specific as possible, interpreting (and if necessary reorganizing)
the author's thoughts, as well as translating the words? In *The Tale of
Genji*, as in all translation, it is a matter of striking the proper balance
between the extremes. The two versions of the passage above, however,
may suggest that any pedantic attempt at an 'accurate' translation
is doomed to failure. One of the splendours of Murasaki's work is the
beauty of its language, and, unless the translator is able to suggest this
fact, he will not have done his job properly. Paradoxically this means
that he must get away as far as possible from the original language and
recast it in a style of his own that he considers appropriate to the work
in question. In so doing he is bound to obscure the nature and the
character of the original. But, when the main interest of the book is

28. N.B.T. ed., vii, 684. Throughout the novel Murasaki deliberately varies
the length of her sentences. This rather long one is followed by a simple sentence
of about a dozen words. (See also p. 132, n. 46).

literary, an 'accurate' translation will obscure it in a far more damaging way – by making it unreadable.

Arthur Waley's version of *The Tale of Genji* represents the freest possible type of translation. Indeed the word 're-creation' would be more appropriate; for he has brought Murasaki's novel to life as a great work of English literature in its own right. As Waley himself has said, so much is inevitably lost in translating from classical Oriental literature that the translator must give a great deal in return. This is precisely what he has done in *The Tale of Genji*. Purists may object that in the process he has entirely changed the spirit of the original, in particular by making it all seem more modern and 'sophisticated' than it really is. I do not believe that a careful comparison with the Japanese text substantiates this view. Certainly Waley has played fast and loose with the structure of Murasaki's prose and, wherever necessary, has eked out the laconic wording of the original with explanatory phrases and sentences of his own. Yet often when one imagines that he has gone off entirely on his own tack, for instance by ascribing some improbably modern psychological motive to one of the characters, a comparison with the original will reveal that he has been scrupulously faithful to Murasaki's meaning.

Many aspects of Waley's technique will become clear if we compare his version of the passage on p. 291 with the other translations:

It all seemed strangely familiar. Who was he with that second time? Why, of course, with Kaoru; and he became slightly uncomfortable when he remembered all the trouble his friend had taken to bring him and Kozeri together. 'I am afraid he would think this rather an odd way of repaying his kindness,' Niou said to himself. Even in the Capital his position made it extremely difficult for him to amuse himself as he chose, and he was used to going about at night with the utmost secrecy. But the present occasion demanded even greater precautions. He was heavily disguised in clothes of a most awkward and unsightly kind, and was compelled to sit for hours in the saddle – a thing he particularly disliked. But he had a vast fund of curiosity, and as they drew nearer and nearer to Uji his excitement became so intense that he hardly noticed the tedious windings of the mountain road. How was it going to turn out? Was it so certain after all that it was his girl? However, that did not really matter. He only wanted to know. But was that all? Certainly if she proved to be someone different he would feel extremely flat on the way home.[29]

29. Arthur Waley, *The Bridge of Dreams*, pp. 128–9.

Waley's interpretation of the last part of the sentence is different from that of the commentators on whom I have relied; but such is the nature of the original that variants of this kind are all too possible. Leaving aside these moot points of interpretation, we find that, while Waley could hardly be more flexible in his handling of the original, he does not change its essential meaning.

Does he improve on Murasaki's style? This of course is entirely a matter of taste. Waley has produced a new style, totally unrelated to the original, and it would be possible to prefer this style, just as some people profess to find Wilhelm von Schlegel's German better than the English of William Shakespeare. What is certain is that he has exploited Murasaki's writing to the fullest possible advantage, making explicit the many subtle psychological touches that are merely implied in the original. He has changed the loose, meandering language of the Japanese into a precise and limpid idiom, in which we need never stop to wonder about the identity of the speaker or any of the other crucial points that Murasaki fails to specify. The verbal monotony of the original has been overcome by using the bounteous resources of modern literary English.

In doing all this Waley may have lost some of the poetry and the particular charm of Murasaki's writing. In its place he has given us a text that can be readily understood and appreciated for its own admirable style. And it is thanks to this that Murasaki's novel, so long obscure even to its own countrymen, has become one of the few great works of Oriental literature to be widely known, and even read, in the West. Any attempt to reproduce the style of the original would almost certainly have made *The Tale of Genji* the preserve of the specialist – and he in any case could presumably read it in Japanese.

*

One question that has engaged the many generations of Genji scholars is the extent to which Murasaki derived her material from actual life. Should her novel be read as a *roman à clef* in which the characters represent people with whom she was personally acquainted or about whom she had heard? Successive commentators have had their pet theories about the models on whom Genji and the other principal figures are supposedly based. At least twenty people have been named as the source for Prince Genji alone. They include Ariwara no Narihira (the famous ninth-century poet, Adonis, and lover), Emperor Murakami, Sugawara no Michizane, and even such improbable candidates as Po Chü-i and the Duke of Chou.[30]

The main contender for the honour, however, is Michinaga's nephew, Korechika, the attractive young nobleman whose rapid rise in the world was followed by sudden disgrace and exile owing to the machinations of his Fujiwara enemies.[31]

When we come to the heroine of the novel, Murasaki, the obvious identification is with the writer herself. According to early commentators, they both had sensitive, retiring dispositions, both were plagued by disagreeable stepmothers – and above all they had the same name. The trouble with this theory is that the name 'Murasaki' was almost certainly applied to the writer because of the character in her novel, not vice versa. Besides, the Murasaki Shikibu we see in the diary is a very different person indeed from the sweet, gentle girl who figures as the main heroine of *The Tale of Genji*. What seems far more likely is that, in describing her fictional heroine, Murasaki Shikibu projects an ideal – the ideal of the type of woman she would have liked to be and, above all, of the sort of life she would have liked to lead. Prince Genji's lifelong devotion to the heroine also seems to belong to the realm of romantic idealization rather than to the harsh realities of polygamous society.

In discussing the art of fiction with Tamakazura, Genji makes a remark that throws some light on this question of models: 'I am quite sure', he says, 'that the author does not write about specific people, giving all the circumstances of their actual lives.'[32] The trend among modern scholars has been to move away from the simple type of correlation, according to which each character in the novel represents a single historical figure, and to substitute a more complicated system of sources. The character and life of Prince Genji, for example, are shown to be based on those of numerous eminent exiles of the Heian period: his good looks and attractive personality relate him to Korechika; his artistic skill, to the great Michizane; his family name, to Minamoto no Takaaki. In the later books the principal model for the hero may well have been the resplendent figure of Fujiwara no Michinaga himself.

A similar use of multiple models can be found in the case of Genji's

30 Ikeda Kikan, 'Genji Monogatari' in *Nihon Bungaku Daijiten*.
31. See Appendix 4 and pp. 71–4.   32. N.B.T. ed., vi, 261.

pompous son, Yūgiri. So far as personality is concerned he appears to have been based on Michinaga's eldest son (whom Murasaki incidentally mentions in her diary as good potential material for a character in a novel),[33] but his career is closer to that of the younger son.[34]

Although a few of the minor figures in *The Tale of Genji*, especially certain ladies-in-waiting and priests, may have had single, specific models, it is likely that the principal characters are based on a variety of people whom Murasaki had known or heard about, and that often she may not have been aware of these sources. Conversely, several aspects of a single historical person, Michinaga, for example, may have been applied to different characters in the book. The creation of people in fiction is far from being the mechanical process that some commentators and critics seem to suggest. In Murasaki's novel, as in Proust's, it is surely a mistake to identify single individuals as the sources for any of the important characters. In so far as there were models they were almost always composite.[35]

Scholars have also found a number of events in *The Tale of Genji* that appear to be taken directly from actual happenings at court. Genji's exile is given as an example, but, since this was a fairly common form of punishment in Murasaki's time, it is hard to relate it to any particular historical case. The more specific correlations usually refer to somewhat trivial particulars – the Emperor's eye trouble in Book 14, for example, and the details of the ceremony of presenting swords on the Princess's birthday.[36] There are also some entries in Murasaki's diary describing actual events that later find their way into the novel. These too are rather insignificant. A description of an incense competition in Book 32 is

33. Ibid., ed., iii, 269.

34. Tezuka Noboru, 'Genji Monogatari no Moderu' in *Kokugo to Kokubungaku*, i (no. 1), 12–31 and (no. 2) 19–44.

35. Mr Painter's conclusions about the models for characters in *A la recherche du temps perdu* apply remarkably well to *The Tale of Genji*. George Painter, *Marcel Proust*, Vol. I. He finds numerous models for most of Proust's main characters. Baron de Charlus, for example, is related to Baron Doasan, Aimery de la Rochefoucauld, Robert de Montesquiou, and Prince Boson de Sagan. Conversely a single real person may become the basis for more than one character in the novel, e.g. Madame Émile Strauss (née Halévy) for Duchesse de Guermantes *and* Odette Swann, Madeleine Lemaire for Madame Verdurin *and* Madame de Villeparisis.

36. Ikeda, loc. cit.

closely parallel to one in the diary (summer of 1008), and Tō no Chūjō's amazement at finding his daughter asleep in the middle of the day (snoozing was frowned on in aristocratic circles) appears to echo Murasaki's own shock when she comes on a friend of hers indulging in a noonday nap.

There is a more important question than that of specific models for characters and events: does *The Tale of Genji* as a whole present a reasonably faithful picture of Heian society? If we are using Murasaki's novel as a source of social history, the question becomes crucial.

The first point is that the people in *The Tale of Genji* represent only a minute percentage of the inhabitants of tenth-century Japan. With few exceptions they belong to the aristocracy, who numbered a few thousand out of a population of several million. Their lives were as remote from those of the common people as is a Maharaja's from that of an untouchable. A modern scholar (a Russian as it chances) has emphasized the contrast between the elegant luxury in the urban court circles and the poverty and barbarism that prevailed elsewhere in Heian Japan. He compares the flourishing, beautifully planned city of Heian Kyō with the primitive settlements in the provinces, the glittering mansions with the squalid huts, the lofty learning and the exquisite works of art with the bestial ignorance and the primitive household utensils, the magnificent tree-lined avenues with the rough tracks that served for transport in the countryside.[37] He has no doubt exaggerated the splendour of life in the capital by accepting the contemporary idealizations at face value. Yet on the whole his contrast is valid, and we must never forget that what Murasaki describes in her novel was almost totally inapplicable to the vast majority of the population.

Besides, even the aristocratic world is not fully described. Hardly anything is said about affairs of state and politics, let alone about the economic activities that permitted this class to maintain its power. (In exactly what form did they extract income from their land, for instance, and how much did they pay their retainers?)

In short, Murasaki's interest is almost exclusively focused on the private, emotional, and aesthetic lives of a select group of aristocrats. She would no more have thought of entering into the feelings of a peasant than would a novelist nowadays try to describe what a horse or a cow

37. N. I. Konrad, *Yaponskaya Literatura v Obraztsakh i Ocherkakh*, 1, 38.

was thinking; and to discuss the economic life of her people would have seemed as preposterous as for a modern writer to give details about his characters' thymol turbidity.

Far from regretting this, however, we should be grateful that in her novel she did not venture into realms about which she and her female contemporaries could have little reliable information. Murasaki wrote about the sides of life that she knew from her own direct experience; and, if the result is a one-sided representation of a period, so is that of a great modern author like Proust.

Making allowance for a certain measure of idealization, especially in the depiction of a character like Prince Genji, we can be fairly confident that what *The Tale of Genji* does describe it describes realistically. There is no discrepancy between the image that the novel gives us and what we know of contemporary conditions from chronicles, diaries, and other sources. With immense care and detail Murasaki depicts the world as she saw it. She tells us, for instance, exactly what it was like to be a jealous woman in a polygamous society where jealousy was the most scorned of all emotions, and what a sensitive man might experience when confronted with the demands of his various wives. Her novel does not attempt to give a full picture of a period (few successful novels do); but it does provide an authentic picture of a most beautiful world.

Appendix I

PERIODS OF FAR EASTERN HISTORY AND RULERS IN JAPAN DURING THE HEIAN PERIOD

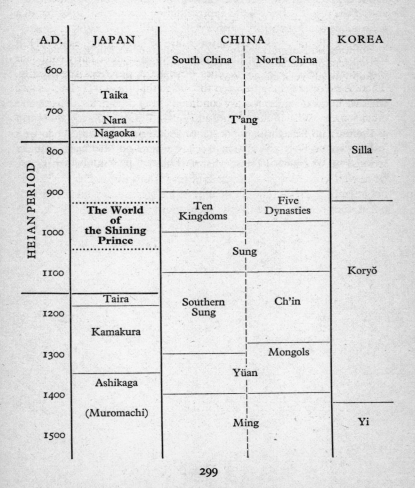

A.D.	JAPAN	CHINA		KOREA
		South China	North China	
600				
	Taika			
700	Nara	T'ang		
	Nagaoka			
800				Silla
900	The World of the Shining Prince	Ten Kingdoms	Five Dynasties	
1000		Sung		
1100				Koryŏ
1200	Taira	Southern Sung	Ch'in	
	Kamakura			
1300			Mongols	
1400	Ashikaga	Yüan		
	(Muromachi)	Ming		Yi
1500				

HEIAN PERIOD

Emperors (Tennō) and years of accession

62nd: Murakami 946
63rd: Reizei 967
64th: Enyū 969
65th: Kazan 984
66th: Ichijō 986

67th: Sanjō 1011
68th: Goichijō 1016
69th: Gosuzaku 1036
70th: Goreizei 1045

Chancellors (Kampaku) and periods of office

Fujiwara no Saneyori 967–9
Fujiwara no Kanemichi 973–7
Fujiwara no Yoritada 977–86

Fujiwara no Michitaka 991–5
Fujiwara no Michikane 995
Fujiwara no Yorimichi 1020–68

Regents (Sesshō) and periods of office

Fujiwara no Saneyori 969–70
Fujiwara no Koretada 970–72
Fujiwara no Kaneie 968–90

Fujiwara no Michitaka 990–91
Fujiwara no Michinaga 1016–17
Fujiwara no Yorimichi 1017–20

Appendix 2

A NOTE ON THE TENTH CENTURY

In Europe the tenth century was a time of great leanness. The waves of invasion during the previous century had left much of the continent in a bleak and exhausted state, and its rulers were hard put to maintain even that sorry level of civilization to which their lands had sunk. It is true that the heritage of the old Roman culture was always present in Europe. There were manuscripts; there were monks and a Church determined to keep the light alive; and occasionally there were laymen who read and remembered the texts. Also in the tenth century the people of the West were finally beginning to contain the terrifying incursions from the southeast and the north, and this, as we now know, was a condition for the stability and wealth that some centuries later were to allow the arts to bloom forth in a great revival.

Yet, if we view tenth-century Europe without the wisdom of hindsight, we must judge that the situation was insecure indeed. England, for example, in the century before the Conquest, was still embroiled in her wasting struggle with the Danes. In Italy, at one time the focal point of European civilization, the century was a troubled one. It is true that Venice succeeded in defeating the Dalmatians, thus enabling her to control the Adriatic and to build up the trade with Byzantium that was to secure her subsequent greatness; it was in 997 that the Doge celebrated the first *sposalizio del mar*. But most of the country was ruled haphazardly by northern foreigners who did little to abate the continuing raids of the Magyars, Huns, and Saracens.

Exhausted though Europe was by the centuries of depredation, the picture is not one of unrelieved gloom. In Germany the Saxon dynasty refounded the Holy Roman Empire, having finally succeeded in 955 in inflicting a decisive defeat on the Magyars. A close alliance between Church and State helped to produce such tenth-century literature as we have, including the first rough draft of *Roman de Renard* and some prose and poetry in the vernacular. The fact remains that 'the scholars of the century can almost be counted on the fingers of one hand; so can the lyrics'.[1]

1. Helen Waddell, *The Wandering Scholars*, p. 71.

To the north of Europe there were hopeful signs. Scandinavia was at the beginning of the first great period of her history. The massive Viking raids along the coasts of western Europe had helped to enrich and refine the rude lives of the Scandinavians, and it was probably during this period that the sagas, which men in the great log houses had for centuries been repeating orally during the long northern evenings, were written down and first entered the realm of conscious literature. The famous works did not come until later, but the tenth century was an important period of germination in Scandinavia.

On the other flank of the continent we find a civilization at a completely different stage of development. Byzantium had withstood the hammerings of the Moslems in the south and of the Slavs and Mongols in the north: despite repeated sieges Constantinople had never fallen. Its empire had been enormously reduced; but now in the course of the tenth century it reconquered Crete, Bulgaria, and other territories, and under a highly organized government it re-established itself as the most powerful force in the eastern Mediterranean. The years of Basil II (the 'Bulgar slayer') were almost exactly those of Murasaki Shikibu. The level of Byzantine civilization remained high and its culture was of course far in advance of anything to the west. Yet by and large it had become a static culture, and the political recovery of the tenth century was not matched by any important fresh achievements in the fields of art or literature.

The same century marks the beginning of the decline of Islam. Politically the huge empire was decaying on its periphery. Yet the varied cultures that Islam had assimilated from India, Persia, Spain, and the other conquered territories had been diffused over much of the vast area it still controlled; and in Baghdad, Damascus, Alexandria, and the other great centres its civilization was flourishing and strong. In the tenth century the Arabs were the most skilled mathematicians that the world had known until then; they were also the best physicians. Islamic literature had absorbed a great deal from Persia and India, and by this time it had reached a high state of refinement, as we can judge from its subtle, finely wrought tone poetry. The most interesting products, however, are the gaudy, glamorous tales whose inspiration is mainly indigenous. The best known, of course, are *The Thousand and One Nights*; these were originally drafted in the middle of the tenth century, exactly at the time that literature in Heian Japan was approaching a peak of refinement.[2]

2. The *Golden Meadows of Masúdi* (A.D. 943) refers to the book of *Hezár Afsáne* ('the thousand tales'). In their present form, of course, the *Arabian Nights* differ greatly from *Hezár Afsáne*: '... the greater part of the stories are of Arabian

Turning to the areas that had succumbed to Islam, we find that by the tenth century Persia had become unimportant as a civilization. Since its conquest three centuries before, the country had been divided into provinces and the various divisions were ruled by caliphs, who were intent on stamping out all sense of the old Persian nationality.

In India the tenth century was an age of considerable literary production; yet there was little in the way of freshness or innovation. 'There is no life in the whole range of literature,' writes an Indian historian. 'It is insipid, artificial and laboured, not spontaneous and natural. The creative age was over by the tenth century, and the process of decadence had already set in.[3] The same writer attributes this decadence, not to the Muslim incursions, but to certain long-standing factors, notably the insular tendency: 'With the loss of contact with the outside world our literature became stagnant and lost freshness of outlook. The general surrounding was uncongenial to the rise of a genius or development of an imaginative spirit.'[4] Yet contemporary Japan, which in most ways was at least as insular as India, produced Murasaki Shikibu.

At the other end of the globe existed the most isolated civilization of all. By the tenth century the Mayan tribes in Yucatan and elsewhere on the American continent were settled, thriving communities. Despite serious gaps in their technological knowledge (they were, for instance, ignorant of the wheel) and despite the total absence of anything corresponding to a Roman tradition, they had evolved a culture that in many ways compared favourably with those of contemporary Europe. They were advanced in architecture, sculpture, and mathematics (they had discovered the value of zero before the Arabs), and their calendar was more accurate than the Julian. The Mayas, however, had not advanced beyond the stage of hieroglyphics, and apparently knew nothing of imaginative literature.

*

In China the beginning of the tenth century saw the final disintegration of the T'ang dynasty, perhaps the most resplendent in all Chinese history. The three centuries of T'ang rule had been a period of unprecedented grandeur during which the Middle Kingdom had developed into the richest and most powerful nation in the world. The vast country was united under a centralized government and administered by a bureaucracy

origin, and the whole is so thoroughly Mohammedan that even the princes of remote ages who are introduced speak and act as Moslems.' (*Encyclopaedia Britannica*, 9th ed., xxiii, 317.)

3. M. A. Mehendale, *The Struggle for Empire*, p. 297.　　　4. Ibid.

depending on a unique examination system in which, theoretically at least, merit took precedence over pedigree. It was a period of economic prosperity, supported by numerous technological advances, the opening of great canals, and the growth of commerce and foreign trade. T'ang China maintained lively contact with the outside world and the capital city of Ch'ang-an became a great cosmopolitan centre. This was an expansive era, marked by military conquest (the entire Korean peninsula came under T'ang suzerainty in the seventh century) and by cultural imperialism, a sort of *mission civilisatrice*, which brought surrounding areas such as Tibet, Korea, and Japan into the Chinese orbit. Above all it was one of the great peaks in the history of world culture. Painting, architecture, and sculpture all flourished (to many Westerners the magnificent three-coloured horses are probably most familiar); there was a great volume of scholarly and historical writings; printing techniques, invented in China in earlier times and not to be known in Europe until the Renaissance, were being used to reproduce Buddhist texts; and in the eighth and ninth centuries Li Po, Tu Fu, Po Chü-i, and other writers of genius brought Chinese poetry to new heights.

The collapse of T'ang was followed by an unstable transitional period which lasted for some fifty years until the Sung dynasty was founded in 960. Despite this break in political continuity and despite the unsettled conditions during a good part of the century, there was no serious disruption of the patterns established under the T'ang dynasty. Culturally the late T'ang and Sung may be regarded as a single period, a golden age that continued until the Mongol invasions.[5]

The Sung dynasty, which lasted from about the time that Murasaki Shikibu was born until some three centuries later, witnessed a steady development in centralized administration and a further flowering of the arts. It was perhaps the greatest period of Chinese painting, and in many other forms, such as porcelain, China continued to lead the world.

The same century saw the collapse of another dynasty. For some two hundred and fifty years the kingdom of Silla had ruled a unified Korea as tributary to China. During this period its rulers had adopted Chinese political institutions and, both socially and culturally, had tried to remodel the peninsula into a little T'ang. The degeneration of Silla paralleled that of the great Chinese dynasty and the end came at about the same

5. J. K. Fairbank describes it as a 'period of renaissance' during which Chinese culture and social organization developed towards a sort of plateau, 'at first high above Western attainments but in later times technologically far below'. Reischauer and Fairbank, op. cit., pp. 183–5.

time. In 936 Wang Kon reunited the country under the Koryŏ dynasty, which survived for almost half a millennium. The tenth century produced Korea's finest religious poet, the Great Master Kyunyŏ, whose biography contains some of the most beautiful verses that faith in the Buddha has ever inspired.

Appendix 3

IS 'THE TALE OF GENJI' COMPLETE?

After centuries of discussion this is still an open question. It is too involved to explore fully in these notes, but readers may be interested to know some of the arguments.

Most of the recent Japanese authorities I have consulted believe that it is unfinished. Fujioka, Onoe, Tezuka, and Ikeda all consider that the writing of *The Tale of Genji* was broken off by Murasaki's death. In fact since the earliest times of Genji criticism the abrupt quality of the ending has prompted the view that, even if Murasaki did not intend to continue the story of Kaoru's life very much further, she cannot have meant it to finish quite so suddenly as it does. It was because the novel appeared to be unfinished that some anonymous writer took it on himself to write a spurious last book called *Yamaji no Tsuyu* ('Dew on the Mountain Road').

A number of considerations incline me to the view that, although with 'The Bridge of Dreams' (Book 54) Murasaki was approaching the end of her story, the book as it stands (and accordingly the entire novel) is incomplete. She was, it seems to me, too great an artist to be satisfied with so casual and weak an ending as that in Book 54. I agree that she would have avoided the traditional sort of ending in which the story is neatly but artificially rounded out. A cheerful outcome to the troublous events, such as we find in the two previous extant works of this type, would clearly be impossible in *The Tale of Genji*, whose surviving hero and heroine are by their characters doomed to a succession of disappointments. Besides, the general theme of Murasaki's novel precludes the type of resolution in which the hero and heroine live happily ever after. As Tezuka says, it was one of Murasaki's greatest merits to have avoided the conventional happy ending, which most of her readers probably expected. For, even if the novel is incomplete (as Tezuka believes), it is sufficiently advanced for us to have a fairly good idea about how Murasaki would *not* have ended it – for instance, by a successful marriage between Kaoru and Ukifune, followed by a flourishing brood of offspring.

Yet, admitting that she did not plan a well-rounded or happy ending, I am unable to believe that she meant her work to finish as it does. I think, for example, that we were meant to know something more about Kaoru's and Niou's reactions to Ukifune's retirement to a nunnery. Also I doubt whether Murasaki would have introduced the fairly prominent character of Ukifune's brother if she had intended her novel to end only a few pages later. Finally, the timing of the last pages seems far too rapid for the end of a book, let alone of the entire novel. Judging from Murasaki's usual style, I should have expected her to end the novel with some sort of *rallentando* description, rather than with a few casual lines summing up Kaoru's thoughts. I am aware of no single convincing reason for regarding the book, as we have it, as complete. I do not, however, believe that it was intended to go on much further; for in Book 54 the action of the Uji sequence is rapidly drawing to its end. I should judge that, at the most, one more book was planned; but possibly only a few pages are missing. Here we might possibly have read of Kaoru's final retirement to a monastery, which would have marked the logical conclusion of his career.

I differ in this view from Dr Waley, who believes that the novel was intended to end exactly as it does in our text. He gives the following three arguments:

(i) the title of the last book sums up the entire novel;

(ii) Book 54 is distinguished from the other 53 books by the fact that its title never occurs in the text;

(iii) it ends with a combination of particles used exclusively to mark the close of a book (Arthur Waley, *The Bridge of Dreams*, p. 17).

If we examine these arguments in reverse order, we note, first, that the particles in question are *to zo*.[1] Now it is quite true that the combination of the conjunctive particle *to* with an emphatic particle (*zo, ya, namu*, etc.) occurring at the end of a sentence normally marks the end of a book. But the use of this combination is *not* restricted to the ending of books; it may simply mark the end of a certain line of action (e.g. N.B.T. ed., vii, 570–1).

Even if it is granted that *to zo* does usually mark the end of a book, there is no reason why some early copyist, finding the manuscript incomplete, should not have taken it upon himself to provide the superficial finishing touch by adding these conventional particles. The unusual construction of the final clause of the sentence would, I believe, support this

1. But Professor Ikeda's text ends with the words, *to zo hon ni haberumeru* ('thus it is written in the [original] text'), which, as he points out (Ikeda ed., vii, 241), is a formula that copyists in the Kamakura period and later frequently used at the end of their manuscripts. This might well have been added to Murasaki's incomplete text.

explanation: in every other use of the combinations *to zo*, *to ya*, and *to namu*, both at the end of books and elsewhere, the *to* is preceded by a verb form (e.g. end of Books 30–2, 37–9, 41, 47, 50–3). But in this case *to zo* is preceded by a simple particle *ni* (. . . *otoshiokitamaerishi narai ni to zo*). *Otishiokitamaerishi narai ni* is an elliptical clause expressing Kaoru's thought ('in the way that I was accustomed to keep her'), *to* is conjunctive, *zo* is emphatic; there is no main verb. This is a most unusual way to end a sentence, especially such a crucial one as this. The most plausible explanation, it seems to me, is that Murasaki broke off with *narai ni*, and that the copyist, finding the book in this incomplete state, added the particles *to zo* to give the novel a specious finality.

Waley's second argument assumes as its premise that Book 54 is complete. If it is not complete, the absence of any explicit reference to the title, far from proving that this is the final book, would in fact suggest that the writing of 'The Bridge of Dreams' was interrupted before Murasaki reached the point of incorporating the title in the text and that, accordingly, both this book and the novel are unfinished. Besides it is hard to understand why Murasaki should have found it necessary to distinguish her final book by so recondite a method as that of failing to repeat the title in the text.

It may be argued that this particular title differs from all the others in that it applies to the entire novel rather than to one specific book. This is the bearing of Waley's first point. Book 41, however, has an equally inclusive title, *Maboroshi* ('Illusion'), which indeed is quite close in feeling to that of Book 54. And, although the title in this earlier book covers a far wider range than those of the other fifty-two books, it *does* occur prominently in one of the poems (N.B.T. ed., vii, 326). It might be argued that there is some significance in the fact that the only two books having 'abstract' titles of this kind should occur at the end of one of the main sections of the novel (*Maboroshi* is the last book to deal with Prince Genji's life). We should remember, however, that the title *Kumogakure* ('Disappearance in the Clouds') follows *Maboroshi*. Accordingly, if there was to be a parallel between the two main sections of the novel, we should conjecture that Murasaki planned a book to follow *Yume no Ukihashi*, in which she would have described the end of Kaoru's career, in the same way that she (presumably) aimed to describe Genji's last years in *Kumogakure*.

Yet, whether or not there were to be one (or even more) additional books, the abrupt ending of *Yume no Ukihashi*, and the absence of any reference to the title, incline me to the view that this book, and accordingly the novel as we have it, is incomplete.

Appendix 4

GENEALOGICAL TABLES

N.B. People whose names appear in capital letters are emperors; ordinal numbers following their names refer to the order of their reigns according to the traditional chronology. Cardinal numbers are for identifying names in the Glossary.)

Chart 1: The Fujiwaras. (*Source:* Kuroita Katsumi, *Kokushi no Kenkyū*, i, 297.)

Chart 2: Principal characters in *The Tale of Genji* listed in the Glossary (Appendix 6). (*Source:* Ikeda Kikan, *Genji Monogatari Jiten*, ii, 418–89.)

(*N.B.* Broken lines indicate certain illicit relationships and children issuing from these relationships.)

The characters can be divided into four generations as follows:

1st Generation	*2nd Generation*
Prince Hyōbukyō (1)	Tō no Chūjō (3)
Empress Kokiden (2)	Yūgao (4)
Lady Kiritsubo (5)	Lady Fujitsubo (6)
	Higekuro (7)
	Lady Rokujō (9)
	Prince Hotaru (10)
	Lady Akikonomu (11)
	Princess Asagao (12)
	Lady Aoi (13)
	Lady Oborozukiyo (14)
	Emperor Suzaku (15)
	Lady Murasaki (16)
	Prince Genji (17)
	Lady Suetsumuhana (19)

2nd Generation

Lady Akashi (20)
Koremitsu (21)
Prince Hachi (29)

3rd Generation	4th Generation
Tamakazura (8)	Kaoru (27)
Emperor Reizei (18)	Roku no Kimi (31)
Princess Nyosan (22)	Prince Niou (32)
Kashiwagi (23)	Naka no Kimi (33)
Yūgiri (24)	Ōigimi (34)
Princess Ochiba (25)	Ukifune (35)
Lady Kumoi (26)	
Princess Akashi (28)	
Governor of Hitachi (30)	

The following is an alphabetical list of these characters, showing their numbers on Chart 2 and their generations:

Akashi, Lady: 20 (2nd)
Akashi, Princess: 28 (3rd)
Akikonomu, Lady: 11 (2nd)
Aoi, Lady: 13 (2nd)
Asagao, Princess: 12 (2nd)
Fujitsubo, Lady: 6 (2nd)
Genji, Prince: 17 (2nd)
Hachi, Prince: 29 (2nd)
Higekuro: 7 (2nd)
Hitachi, Governor of: 30 (3rd)
Hotaru, Prince: 10 (2nd)
Hyōbukyō, Prince: 1 (1st)
Kaoru: 27 (4th)
Kashiwagi: 23 (3rd)
Kiritsubo, Lady: 5 (1st)
Kokiden, Empress: 2 (1st)
Koremitsu: 21 (2nd)
Kumoi, Lady: 26 (3rd)

Murasaki, Lady: 16 (2nd)
Naka no Kimi: 33 (4th)
Niou, Prince: 32 (4th)
Nyosan, Princess: 22 (3rd)
Oborozukiyo, Lady: 14 (2nd)
Ochiba, Princess: 25 (3rd)
Ōigimi: 34 (4th)
Reizei, Emperor: 18 (3rd)
Rokujō, Lady: 9 (2nd)
Roku no Kimi: 31 (4th)
Suetsumuhana: 19 (2nd)
Suzaku, Emperor: 15 (2nd)
Tamakazura: 8 (3rd)
Tō no Chūjō: 3 (2nd)
Ukifune: 35 (4th)
Yūgao: 4 (2nd)
Yūgiri: 24 (3rd)

Appendix 4

The following lists show the relative ages of some of the main characters in terms of the hero's age:

Number of years older than Prince Genji

Aoi, Lady: 4

Suzaku, Emperor: 4

Fujitsubo, Lady: 5

Rokujō, Lady: 8

Number of years younger than Prince Genji

Akashi, Lady: 9

Akikonomu, Lady: 10

Murasaki, Lady: 12

Kashiwagi: 14

Tamakazura: 14

Reizei, Emperor: 18

Kumoi, Lady: 19

Yūgiri: 21

Nyosan, Princess: 26

Akashi, Princess: 28

Ōigimi: 45

Niou, Prince: 46

Ukifune: 52

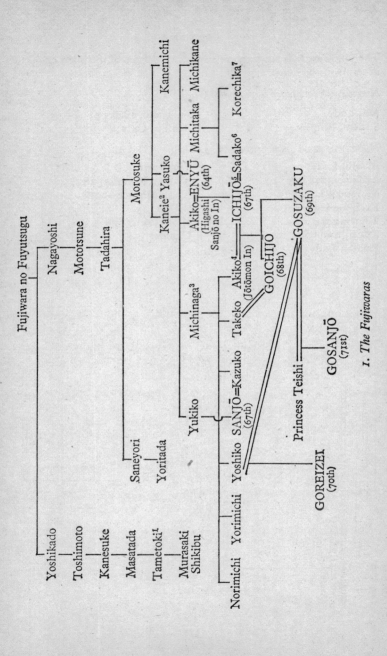

1. *The Fujiwaras*

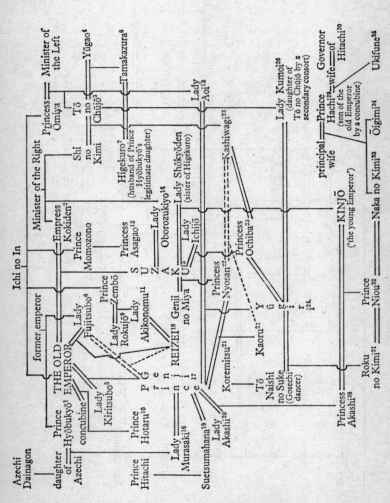

2a. Principal characters in 'The Tale of Genji' listed in the Glossary

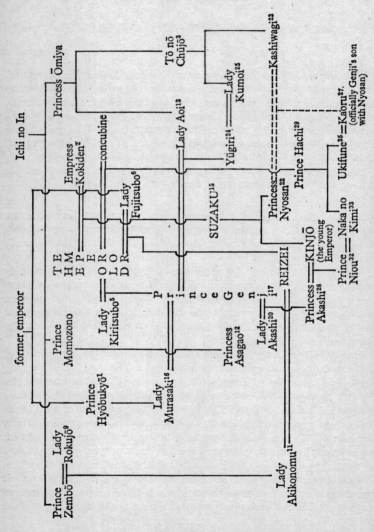

2b. Principal characters and further relationships

Appendix 5

MURASAKI ON THE ART OF FICTION

The following passage from Book 25 of *The Tale of Genji* (Ikeda ed., iii, 181–4) gives Murasaki Shikibu's views on the art of fiction and its importance. It is frequently quoted as one of the earliest and most illuminating examples of informal literary criticism in Japan; since it occupies a significant place in any study of Heian prose fiction, I have made a new translation, which is somewhat more literal (and a great deal less elegant) than that given by Arthur Waley in *A Wreath of Cloud*, pp. 253–7.

Genji's opening remarks reflect the traditional Confucian scorn for fiction; but Murasaki soon makes him set his views to rights.

*

This year the rainy season was more severe than usual. Day after day the rains came down without a let-up, and time hung heavily on the hands of the ladies in Prince Genji's household. As a distraction they had recourse to illustrated romances.

Lady Akashi was proficient in this art and had several such works prepared for her daughter, the little Princess. The greatest enthusiast, however, was Tamakazura, who now spent all day reading and copying romances. Many of her young ladies-in-waiting also took an interest and had accumulated a fascinating collection of stories, some from real life, some fictitious. . . .

One day when Genji came into Tamakazura's rooms he noticed several illustrated romances scattered about the place. 'Really,' he said with a smile, 'you women are incorrigible. Sometimes I wonder whether you haven't been born into this world just so that you can be deceived by people. Look at these books! There probably isn't an ounce of truth in the lot of them – and you know that as well as I do. Yet here you are, utterly fascinated and taken in by all their fabrications, avidly copying down each word – and, I may add, quite unaware that it is a sultry day in the middle of the rainy season and that your hair is in the most frightful mess.'

Genji paused for a while. 'But then,' he continued, 'if it weren't for old romances like this, how on earth would you get through these long tedious days when time moves so slowly? And besides, I realize that many of these works, full of fabrications though they are, do succeed in evoking the emotion of things in a most realistic way. One event follows plausibly on another, and in the end we cannot help being moved by the story, even though we know what foolishness it all really is. Thus, when we read about the ordeals of some delightful princess in a romance, we may find ourselves actually entering into the poor girl's feelings.

'Again, the author may so dazzle us with the brilliance of his writing that we forget about our initial incredulity. Later on, when we think back calmly on the story, we may be annoyed that we should have swallowed its absurdities. But at first hearing we only notice how fascinating it all is.

'Of late I have occasionally stopped to listen while our young Princess's ladies are reading aloud to her, and I have been much impressed by what good authors we have. Perhaps the reason they write so well is simply that they are used to telling lies, but I expect there is more to it than that.'

'I rather imagine,' said Tamakazura, pushing away her inkstone, 'that it is only those who are themselves in the habit of being deceitful who have to delve like that into the writer's possible motives. Honest people accept what they read as completely true.'

'Yes,' said Genji, 'it was rather churlish of me to speak badly about these books as I did just now. For the fact is that works of fiction set down things that have happened in this world ever since the days of the gods. Writings like the *Chronicles of Japan* really give only one side of the picture, whereas these romances must be full of just the right sort of details.'

He smiled and continued, 'The author certainly does not write about specific people, recording all the actual circumstances of their lives. Rather it is a matter of his being so moved by things, both good and bad, which he has heard and seen happening to men and women that he cannot keep it all to himself but wants to commit it to writing and make it known to other people – even to those of later generations. This, I feel sure, is the origin of fiction.

'Sometimes the author will want to write favourably about people, and then he will select all the good qualities he can think of; at other times, when he wants to give a fuller description of human nature, he introduces all sorts of strange and wicked things into his book. But in every case the things he writes about will belong to this actual world of ours.

'Chinese story-tellers differ from our own, both in their learning and in the way they write. Even in Japan, literature has changed greatly since earlier times. And then, of course, there is a large gap between serious and superficial works. To dismiss all these types of fiction as so much falsehood is surely to miss the point. For even in the Law that the Buddha in his great mercy bequeathed to us there are parts known as Accommodated Truths. As a result we find certain seeming inconsistencies, especially in the Vaipulya sutras, which no doubt give rise to doubts in the minds of the unenlightened. Yet in the last analysis these Accommodated Truths tend to the same aim as all the rest of the sutras. The difference between Buddhahood and Earthly Lust as described in the scriptures is precisely the same as that between the good and the bad qualities of fictitious characters.[1] So, when we regard these works of fiction in the proper light, we find that they contain nothing superfluous.'

Thus did Genji show that romances could serve a most useful purpose.

1. The gist of the Buddhist analogy is as follows. There are two elements in fiction to which traditionalists object. First, it contains deception (*soragoto*); secondly, it describes bad things and people (*ashiki mo*). Genji tries to justify the presence of these two elements by comparing fiction to the scriptures. (At the same time, by drawing an analogy between romances and Buddhist writings, he suggests the importance of the former, just as he did earlier by his reference to the *Chronicles of Japan*.) In Genji's analogy the deception in fiction corresponds to the Accommodated Truths (Hōben) in the scriptures: both represent departures from the truth, but both serve good purposes. Secondly, the good and the bad in fiction correspond to Buddhahood (Bodai) and Earthly Lust (Bonnō) as described in the sutras: unless both are included, a complete representation of human life is impossible. Genji concludes from these analogies that in fiction neither deception nor 'bad things' can be considered superfluous: it is all there for a good and useful purpose.

Appendix 6

GLOSSARY

including Characters, Historical Figures, etc.

ADMINISTRATIVE COUNCIL (Mandokoro). Group of family officials employed by the Fujiwaras and other important people to administer their manors and households. The Mandokoro later became an important organ of the Shogunal government.

AKASHI, LADY (Akashi no Ue). **20. The lady from the seaside village of Akashi (daughter of an eccentric lay priest) whom Genji courts during his exile and who later becomes one of his wives.

AKASHI, PRINCESS (Akashi no Chūgū). **28. Genji's daughter with Lady Akashi. She is adopted by Lady Murasaki and eventually attains the rank of Empress (Chūgū) of 'the Young Emperor'.

AKIKO, EMPRESS. See FUJIWARA NO AKIKO.

AKIKONOMU, LADY (Akikonomu Chūgū) (lit. 'lover of autumn'). **11. Daughter of Prince Zembō and Lady Rokujō, she serves as High Priestess of the Ise Shine and later becomes Empress (Chūgū) to Emperor Reizei.

AMIDISM. A form of Buddhism that stressed implicit faith in Amitâbha (Amida='Measureless Light') and the repetition of the Nembutsu formula ('I adore thee, O Lord of Measureless Light'). It was the basis of many of the popular sects that developed in the Kamakura period, but already had considerable influence in Murasaki's time, when it was represented mainly by the Tendai sect.

AOI, LADY (Aoi no Ue) (lit. 'hollyhock'). **13. Daughter of the Minister of the Left, she is married to Genji as his principal wife, and is done to death by Lady Rokujō's 'living ghost'.

ARIWARA NO NARIHIRA. 823–80. Courtier-poet; reputed hero and author of *The Tales of Ise* or parts of it.

ASAGAO, PRINCESS (Asagao no Himegimi) (lit. 'morning glory'). **12. Genji's first cousin, courted by him in vain since his youth. She serves as High Priestess of the Kamo Shrine.

AWARE. A word frequently used in *The Tale of Genji* and other classical literature. Among its wide range of meanings are 'pathetic', 'moving',

---

* see Appendix 4 (Chart 1); ** see Appendix 4 (Charts 2a and 2b)

'beautiful'. The phrase *mono no aware* corresponds to *lacrimae rerum*, the pity of things, which is often taken to be the underlying theme of Murasaki's novel.

BIWA LAKE (Biwa Ko). Large lake near the capital at the eastern foot of Mount Hiei. According to tradition, Murasaki Shikibu started writing her novel in a temple on the shores of this lake.

CHANCELLOR (Kampaku). Leading post in the government during the second half of the Heian period. It was occupied by the chief of the northern branch of the Fujiwara family, who theoretically assisted the emperor but who in fact was the real ruler of the country. Kampaku has also been translated as 'Civil Dictator', 'Regent', and *'maire du palais'*.

CH'ANG-AN. Capital of China during the Early Han, Later Ch'in, Northern Chou, and T'ang dynasties. The Japanese used it as the model for both Nara and Heian Kyō.

'DETACHED PALACE' (*sato dairi*) (lit. 'village palace'). One of many imperial residences outside the main Palace, which were used by imperial consorts and sometimes inhabited by the emperors themselves.

EIGA. Glory, pomp, splendour. A word frequently used to describe the lives of Fujiwara leaders like Michinaga and of glittering fictional heroes like Prince Genji. (Cf. *Tales of Glory*.)

FUJITSUBO, LADY (Fujitsubo no Nyōgo) (lit. 'wistaria tub'). **6. Genji's stepmother and mistress: Lady Murasaki's aunt.

FUJIWARA NO AKIKO. *4. 988–1074. Daughter of Michinaga; married to Emperor Ichijō. She outlived her husband by over 60 years and came to wield considerable influence at Court. Murasaki Shikibu was one of her many literary ladies-in-waiting.

FUJIWARA NO KANEIE. *2. 929–90. A shrewd and ambitious Fujiwara leader, who paved the way for his prepotent son, Michinaga. Among his many concubines was the author of *Gossamer Diary*.

FUJIWARA NO KORECHIKA. *7. 975–1010. Michinaga's popular nephew whose promising career was rudely interrupted by exile; he is frequently mentioned as a possible model for the hero of *The Tale of Genji*.

FUJIWARA NO MICHINAGA. *3. 966–1027. The most powerful leader in the history of the Fujiwara family, he was the undisputed ruler of Japan during most of Murasaki's lifetime. Four of his daughters were married to emperors.

FUJIWARA NO SADAKO. *6. 976–1001. Married to Emperor Ichijō but displaced by Michinaga's daughter, Akiko. Sei Shōnagon served in her court.

FUJIWARA NO TAMETOKI. *1. Father of Murasaki Shikibu; a provincial governor and a versifier. (Scholars do not agree about his dates.)

GENJI, PRINCE (Hikaru Genji). **17. The Shining Prince, son of 'the old Emperor' with his favourite concubine, Kiritsubo. Hero of the first 40 books of *The Tale of Genji*, his name has become a by-word for male beauty and charm.

'GOOD PERSON' (*yoki hito*). A person of good birth; the term also connoted emotional and artistic sensitivity.

GOSSAMER DIARY (*Kagerō Nikki*). The earliest extant diary by a woman; written by the mother of Fujiwara no Michitsuna, it describes her unhappy relations with Fujiwara no Kaneie during the years 954–74.

GREAT REFORM (Taika). Reform movement carried out during the second half of the 7th century, when Japan tried to remodel her political and economic structure on the Chinese pattern.

HACHI, PRINCE (Hachi no Miya). **29. Younger half-brother of Genji; father of Ōigimi, Naka no Kimi, and Ukifune, he figures prominently in the Uji books, where he emerges as a single-minded religious devotee.

HEIAN KYŌ. Capital of Japan from 794 until 1868; known later as Kyoto. It gave its name to the period that covers the 9th-11th and part of the 12th centuries.

HIEI, MOUNT (Hieizan). Mountain range north-east of Heian Kyō; site of the Enryaku Temple, the headquarters of the Tendai sect. Most of the terrifying raids on the capital by warrior monks started from here.

HIGEKURO (lit. 'black beard'). **7. Son of a Fujiwara Minister of State and brother of Emperor Suzaku's consort, Lady Shōkyōden. His principal wife is the daughter of Prince Shikibukyō; later he adds Tamakazura to his household as a secondary consort.

HIGH COURT NOBLE (*Kugyō*). A member of one of the first three ranks or an Imperial Adviser of the Fourth Rank. These Nobles were the ruling class during the Heian period.

HITACHI, GOVERNOR OF (Hitachi no Kami). **30. Ukifune's boorish stepfather; a typical provincial.

HOME PROVINCES (*Kinai*). Heian Kyō and the 5 surrounding provinces of Yamashiro, Yamato, Izumi, Kawachi, and Settsu.

HOTARU, PRINCE (Hotaru no Miya) (lit. 'firefly'). **10. Younger half-brother and close friend of Genji. His principal wife is Empress Kokiden's sister; later he marries Higekuro's daughter.

HYŌBUKYŌ, PRINCE (Hyōbukyō no Miya). **1. Brother of Lady Fujitsubo and father of Lady Murasaki.

ICHIJŌ, EMPEROR (Ichijō Tennō). *5. 66th emperor of Japan (r. 986–1011). A typical Heian puppet-emperor, entirely controlled by the Fujiwaras. He is the emperor described in the *Pillow Book* and in Murasaki's diary.

IMPERIAL LADY (*Nyōgo*). Concubine of the Emperor, ranking below the Empress.

IZUMI SHIKIBU. d. c.1030. Prominent poetess who served in the same court as Murasaki Shikibu and who kept a famous diary.

KAMMU, EMPEROR (Kammu Tennō). 50th emperor of Japan (r. 781–806). An outstanding sovereign, during whose reign the capital was moved first to Nagaoka and then to Heian Kyō. Imperial power and prestige declined rapidly after his death.

KAMO RIVER (Kamogawa). River flowing east and south of Heian Kyō.

KANA. Japanese phonetic syllabary that came into widespread use in the Heian period, encouraging the development of vernacular literature like *The Tale of Genji*. It was particularly associated with women, since Chinese characters were regarded as the preserve and the pride of male writers.

KANEIE. See FUJIWARA NO KANEIE.

KAORU (lit. 'fragrance'). **27. Son of Kashiwagi and Princess Nyosan by an illicit liaison, but officially Prince Genji's son. Principal hero of the last 13 books of *The Tale of Genji*.

KASHIWAGI (lit. 'oak'). **23. Son of Tō no Chūjō; dies at an early age after an illicit liaison with Princess Nyosan.

KAZAN, EMPEROR (Kazan Tennō). 65th emperor of Japan (r. 984–6). Obliged to abdicate and take the tonsure at an early age, but did not abandon his interest in secular affairs.

KIRITSUBO, LADY (Kiritsubo no Kōi) (lit. 'paulownia tub'). **5. Favourite concubine of 'the old Emperor' and mother of Genji. She was persecuted by the other court ladies and died at an early age.

KOKIDEN, EMPRESS (Kokiden no Ōgisaki). **2. Principal wife of Emperor Kiritsubo ('the old Emperor'); she plays the role of 'wicked stepmother' to Genji.

KOKIN SHŪ (*Collection of the Old and the New*). First of the poetic anthologies that were compiled at imperial command. It was produced in 905 by the court noble and writer, Ki no Tsurayuki.

KORECHIKA. See FUJIWARA NO KORECHIKA.

KOREMITSU. **21. Son of Genji's wet-nurse; he becomes the hero's retainer and confidant.

KUMOI, LADY (Kumoi no Kari) (lit. 'cloud'). **26. Daughter of Tō no Chūjō by the former wife of Azechi no Dainagon. She becomes Yūgiri's principal wife despite the long-standing objection of her family.

'*LADY WHO LOVED INSECTS, THE*' (*Mushi Mezuru Himegimi*). One of the 10 stories included in *Tsutsumi Chūnagon Monogatari*, a collection that probably dates from the late 12th century. Its author is unknown. (Translated by Arthur Waley, London, 1929).

LATTER DAYS OF THE LAW (*mappō no yo*). Buddhist idea that after a certain period following the Buddha's death mankind would enter a period of decadence when his teachings would no longer have any effect. In Murasaki's time it was believed that the beginning of this era was imminent.

'LIVING GHOST' (*ikiryō*). Evil spirit of a living person, who haunts people without the conscious knowledge of the 'owner'.

MANOR (*shō* or *shōen*). Estate held by a member of the aristocracy or by a religious institution, whose objective was to secure certain privileges for their land, notably tax-exemption. This became the characteristic economic unit of the Heian period and helped to destroy centralized imperial government in Japan.

MANYO SHŪ (*Collection of Myriad Leaves*). First anthology of Japanese verse; it was compiled during the Nara period and contains some 4,500 poems, mostly written during the period 660–760.

MICHINAGA. See FUJIWARA NO MICHINAGA.

MICHITSUNA'S MOTHER (Michitsuna no Haha). Concubine of Fujiwara no Kaneie, by whom she had a boy, Michitsuna; famous for her *Gossamer Diary*, q.v., but her real name is unknown.

MICHIZANE. See SUGAWARA NO MICHIZANE.

MINAMOTO FAMILY. Outstanding military family descending from the 9th-century Emperor Seiwa. The Fujiwaras relied on them for support, especially in the provinces. In the 12th century the Minamotos became the predominant power in the country and established a proto-feudal administration in Kamakura.

MINISTERS OF THE LEFT AND OF THE RIGHT (Sadaijin, Udaijin). The two senior ministers of state, in charge of all branches of administration according to the Chinese-type system introduced to Japan during the Great Reform. The Minister of the Right was less powerful than the Minister of the Left, but he held the same court rank. The 'left' and 'right' in their titles refer to the seating of the ministers *vis-à-vis* the emperor in the Chinese court.

MONOGATARI. In its broadest sense the term refers to Japanese narrative prose in general, but it is usually limited to prose fiction between the 9th and 16th centuries. The earliest extant *monogatari* belong to the 10th century. The *genre* developed remarkably during the course of the century and culminated in *The Tale of Genji*.

MONO NO AWARE. See AWARE.

MONO NO KE. Evil spirit or influence; in the Heian period believed to be the main cause of illness and other misfortunes.

MOTOORI NORINAGA. 1730–1801. Famous scholar and one of the

leaders of the nationalist-Shintoist revival in the 18th century. He devoted a good part of his career to classical Japanese literature, including *The Tale of Genji*.

MUJŌKAN. The sense of the impermanence of life; a fundamental aspect of the Buddhist approach to the human condition.

MURASAKI, LADY (Murasaki no Ue) (lit. 'violet'). **16. Daughter of Prince Hyōbukyō by a concubine; becomes Genji's official concubine when she is 14 and is the heroine of the first 40 books. Murasaki Shikibu (the writer) was probably named after her.

NAKA NO KIMI. **33. Daughter of Prince Hachi. She leaves Uji to become Prince Niou's official concubine.

NARA. First permanent capital of Japan (710–84.) Lies about 20 miles south of Heian Kyō.

'NEXT-MORNING LETTER' (*kinuginu no fumi*). The elegant letter that a gentleman was expected to send to a lady on his return home after spending the night with her. It was delivered by an equally elegant 'next-morning messenger' (*kinuginu no tsukai*).

NIOU, PRINCE (Niou Miya) (lit. 'scent'). **32. Son of Princess Akashi, and companion of Kaoru. Among his women are Roku no Kimi (principal wife), Naka no Kimi (concubine), and Ukifune (mistress).

NYOSAN, PRINCESS (Nyosan no Miya). **22. Daughter of Emperor Suzaku. She becomes Genji's principal wife, but deceives him with Kashiwagi and gives birth to Kaoru.

OBOROZUKIYO, LADY (Oborozukiyo no Kimi) (lit. 'hazy moonlit night'). **14. Younger sister of Empress Kokiden; she becomes the consort of Emperor Suzaku, but deceives him with Genji.

OCHIBA, PRINCESS (Ochiba no Miya) (lit. 'falling leaves'). **25. Daughter of Emperor Suzaku; she is married to Kashiwagi, but after his death becomes Yūgiri's concubine.

ŌIGIMI. **34. Eldest daughter of Prince Hachi. After being vainly courted by Kaoru, she dies at an early age.

PILLOW BOOK (*Makura no Sōshi*). Lengthy collection of notes, stories, comments, and descriptions of everyday life among the Heian upper classes; written in about 1002 by Sei Shōnagon (q.v.) (Partial translation by Arthur Waley, London, 1928.)

PO CHŪ-I. 772–846. One of the 3 great T'ang poets; in Heian Japan his works were more read than those of any other Chinese writer and his poems are widely quoted in *The Tale of Genji* and other contemporary literature.

PRIME MINISTER (Dajō Daijin). Highest official in the government according to the Great Reform system. He came directly below the

Emperor and above the Ministers of the Left and Right. In fact the post was often not filled and by Murasaki's time it had been superseded by those of Chancellor and Regent.

PRINCIPAL WIFE (*kita no kata*). A wife who normally belonged to a family with the same social standing as the husband's and who took precedence over all his other consorts. According to the Japanese system of polygamy it was normally impossible to displace her in favour of a concubine.

REIZEI, EMPEROR (Reizei In). **18. Son of Genji and Lady Fujitsubo by an illicit liaison, but officially the son of 'the old Emperor'. He succeeds Emperor Suzaku on the throne, but abdicates after a short reign owing to uneasiness about his paternity.

RIGHTS (*shiki*). Part ownership in manor, entitling the holder to a fixed percentage of the annual crop.

ROKUJŌ, LADY (Rokujō Miyasudokoro). **9. Wife of Prince Zembō. She becomes Genji's mistress when he is still in his early youth, and during later years she is implacably jealous of his successive wives.

ROKU NO KIMI. **31. Daughter of Yūgiri by Koremitsu's daughter; becomes Prince Niou's principal wife.

SADAKO, EMPRESS. See FUJIWARA NO SADAKO.

SARASHINA DIARY (*Sarashina Nikki*). Diary by the daughter of Sugawara no Takasue (her real name is unknown); it covers the years 1009–59.

SCREEN OF STATE (kichō). Portable frame with thick decorated hangings behind which women normally sat when receiving callers.

SCROLLS OF YEARLY OBSERVANCES, THE (Nenjū Gyōji Emaki). Scrolls of coloured paintings depicting the annual festivals held at the Imperial Court of Heian. The original series of 60 scrolls was produced in the 12th century; the extant version is 500 years later.

SEI SHŌNAGON. c. 968–c. 1025. One of the two best-known writers of her time (the other being Murasaki Shikibu), she served at the court of Empress Sadako and is the author of the *Pillow Book*, q.v.

SHINDEN (ZUKURI). Style of architecture used by the Heian aristocracy. It consisted of a group of one-storey wooden buildings, each consisting basically of a single room, which could be divided by screens, curtains, etc. The buildings were centred about a main building (the master's quarters) and connected by corridors.

SHINGON. Buddhist sect introduced to Japan in 806 by Kōbō Daishi, one of the greatest religious leaders in the country's history. Shingon, which is often described as 'esoteric Buddhism' (*mikkyō*), gives particular stress to arcane ritual, secret formulae, and mystical experience. Much of it is derived from Indian Tantric Buddhism.

SUETSUMUHANA (lit. 'saffron flower'). **19. Pathetic red-nosed daughter of Prince Hitachi.

SUGAWARA NO MICHIZANE. 845–903. Famous scholar, calligrapher, poet, and statesman who was exiled from the capital owing to Fujiwara rivalry.

SUZAKU, EMPEROR (Suzaku In). **15. Genji's half-brother who succeeds 'the old Emperor' on the throne.

TABOO TAG (*monoimi no fuda*). Willow-wood signs that people hung outside their houses or wore on their clothes to warn others that they were suffering from a taboo and must therefore not be approached.

TALE OF GENJI SCROLLS, THE (Genji Monogatari Emaki). Scrolls of coloured paintings and calligraphy giving scenes from *The Tale of Genji* and the accompanying text. Of the 10 original scrolls that were produced between 1120 and 1140 only 4 remain. They include 19 paintings and 23 pages of text, and are regarded as one of the greatest works of indigenous Japanese art. The styles vary and modern scholars agree on the multiple production of the scrolls. The magnificent calligraphic sections represent the earliest extant text of *The Tale of Genji*; but they are fragmentary and very inaccurate.

TALES OF GLORY (*Eiga Monogatari*). Historical tale (*rekishi monogatari*) that discusses in chronological order the history of the period 889 to 1092. The 'glory' is that of Michinaga, to whose career most of the history is devoted.

TALE OF THE BAMBOO CUTTER, THE (*Taketori Monogatari*). Sometimes known as the 'ancestor of the *monogatari*', it was originally written in the 9th century, but our present texts are based on a later version. It tells the story of a child who is found in a bamboo stem and who grows up to be a beautiful princess courted by numerous distinguished suitors.

TALE OF THE HOLLOW TREE, THE (*Utsubo Monogatari*). The longest extant precursor of *The Tale of Genji*. It is immensely long (20 volumes in all) and, for most modern readers, extremely dull. The date is uncertain, but at least the first part was probably written by 980. The authorship has been variously attributed to Murasaki Shikibu's father and to Minamoto no Shitagau. The heroine, who has been courted by numerous suitors, is eventually married to the Crown Prince. The hero wins great success at court, owing partly to his skill on the zither, and is betrothed to the Emperor's daughter.

TALE OF THE ROOM BELOW, THE (*Ochikubo Monogatari*). The earliest extant *monogatari* on the 'wicked stepmother' theme, it was written in about 980 (authorship unknown) and tells the story of an unfortunate young lady who is maltreated by her stepmother but eventually rescued by an admirer. She marries him and lives happily ever after. The young couple avenge themselves on the stepmother, e.g. by having her publicly humiliated in a 'traffic collision' (*kuruma arasoi*).

TAMAKAZURA (lit. 'jewelled garland'). **8. Tō no Chūjō's daughter by Yūgao; adopted by Genji and married to Higekuro.

T'ANG DYNASTY. Chinese dynasty lasting from 618 to 907. Many of the political, social, and cultural forms in the Nara and early Heian periods were modelled on those of T'ang China.

TENDAI. Syncretic Buddhist sect introduced from China in 805 by Dengyō Daishi, who established its headquarters on Mount Hiei. Tendai was the most powerful sect in Murasaki's time and came closest to being the state religion.

TŌ NO CHŪJŌ. **3. Eldest son of the Minister of the Left and brother of Genji's principal wife, Lady Aoi; Genji's life-long friend and rival.

UJI. District some 10 miles south of the capital. Prince Hachi's gloomy house is situated by Uji River and is the setting of the last 10 books of Murasaki's novel, which are accordingly known as 'The Ten Books of Uji' (*Uji Jūjō*).

UKIFUNE (lit. 'floating boat'). **35. Daughter of Prince Hachi by a secondary consort; heroine of the final book of *The Tale of Genji*.

UTSUSEMI (lit. 'cicada shell'). Young wife of the Assistant Governor of Iyo; courted by Genji, but resists him.

WARD (*jō*). District lying between two east-west avenues in Heian Kyō and named after the avenue to the south.

YAMATO. Name of the province (including Nara) where most of the early Japanese emperors held court; later it came to apply to the entire country.

YIN AND YANG (*onyō*). The female and male principles underlying the ancient Chinese dualistic cosmology, which was generally accepted in Murasaki's time.

YŪGAO (lit. 'moonflower'). **4. Mistress first of Tō no Chūjō, then of Genji; mother of Tamakazura. She dies bewitched when spending the night with Genji.

YUGIRI (lit. 'evening mist'). **24. Genji's son by Lady Aoi. Marries his first cousin, Lady Kumoi, despite her father's objections; later takes Princess Ochiba as his concubine.

Bibliography

WORKS IN JAPANESE

Eiga Monogatari, Kokushi Taikei, 20, Tokyo, 1938.

Engishiki, Kokushi Taikei, 26, Tokyo, 1938.

Emura Hokkai, *Nihon Shishi*, Nihon Jurin Sōsho, Tokyo, 1928.

Fujiki Kunihiko, *Heian Jidai no Kizoku no Seikatsu*, Tokyo, 1960.

Genshin, *Ōjō Yōshū*, Hanayama Shinshō ed., Tokyo, 1937.

Fujiwara no Morosuke, *Kujōdono Yuikai*, Shinkō Gunsho Ruijū, 475, Tokyo, 1929.

Fujiwara no Sanesuke, *Shōyūki*, Dai Nihon Kokiroku, 10.

Hisamatsu Senichi, *Nihon Bungaku Hyōron Shi*, Tokyo, 1938, 3 vols.

Nihon Bungaku Shi, 2, Tokyo, 1956.

Ikeda Kikan, 'Genji Monogatari', *Nihon Bungaku Daijiten*, pp. 974–98.

'Genji Monogatari Keitōron Josetsu', *Nihon Bungaku*, 7, Tokyo, 1933.

Genji Monogatari Kōza, Tōkyō Daigaku Genji Monogatari Kenkyū-kai, Tokyo, 1949.

Genji Monogatari Taisei, Tokyo, 1953–6, 8 vols.

Heianchō no Seikatsu to Bungaku, Tokyo, 1953.

Izumi Shikibu, *Izumi Shikibu Nikki*, Nihon Koten Bungaku Taikei, 20, Tokyo, 1957.

Jien, *Gukan Shō*, Kokushi Taikei, 19, Tokyo, 1930.

Kagerō Nikki, Nihon Koten Bungaku Taikei, 20, Tokyo, 1957.

Kaneko Motoomi, *Makura no Sōshi Hyōshaku*, Tokyo, 1927.[1]

Keikoku Shū, Gunsho Ruijū, 6, Tokyo, 1931.

Ki no Tsurayuki, *Tosa Nikki*, Nihon Koten Bungaku Taikei, 20, Tokyo, 1957.

Kitayama Keita, *Genji Monogatari Jiten*, Tokyo, 1957.

Kuroita Katsumi, *Kokushi no Kenkyū*, Tokyo, 1939, 2 vols.

Motoori Norinaga, *Genji Monogatari Tama no Ogushi*, Motoori Norinaga Zenshū (vii, 46–1785), Tokyo, 1927.

Murasaki Shikibu, *Genji Monogatari*, (1) ed. by Ikeda Kikan, Nihon Koten Zensho, Tokyo, 1958, 7 vols.[1]; (2) Nihon Bungaku Taikei, 6 and 7.[1]

Murasaki Shikibu Nikki, (1) ed. by Mochizuki Sekkyō, Tokyo, 1929;[1] (2) Nihon Bungaku Taikei, 3.[1]

1. See list of abbreviations on p. 329.

Mushi Mezuru Himegimi, in *Tsutsumi Chūnagon Monogatari*, Shinshaku Nihon Bungaku Sōsho, 2, Tokyo, 1931.

Nihon Kōki, Kokushi Taikei, 3, Tokyo, 1934.

Nihon Montoku Tennō Jitsuroku, Kokushi Taikei 3, Tokyo, 1934.

Nihon Shiki, Kokusho Kankō Kai (dainiki kanko), 11, Tokyo, 1911.

Oka Kazuo, *Genji Monogatari no Kisoteki Kenkyū*, Tokyo, 1958.

Ōkagami, Kokushi Taikei, 21, Tokyo, 1939.

Onoe Hachirō, 'Genji Monogatari Kaidai', *Nihon Bungaku Taikei*, vi, 1–44.

Sandai Jitsuroku, Kokushi Taikei, 4, Tokyo, 1934.

Sarashina Nikki, Nihon Koten Bungaku Taikei, 20, Tokyo, 1957.

Sei Shōnagon, *Makura no Sōshi:* see Kaneko Motoomi.

Shoku Nihongi, Kokushi Taikei, 2, Tokyo, 1935.

Shoku Nihon Kōki, Kokushi Taikei, 3, Tokyo, 1934.

Sugimoto Tsutomu, *Kindai Nihongo no Seiritsu*, Tokyo, 1960.

Takeuchi Rizō, *Heian Ibun*, Tokyo, 1947.

Tezuka Noboru, 'Gengo oyobi Nikki yori Mitaru Murasaki Shikibu', *Kokugo to Kokubungaku*, 2, no. 4.

 'Genji Monogatari Chosaku no Jiki', *Kokugo to Kokubungaku*, 1, no. 5.

 'Genji Monogatari no Moderu', *Kokugo to Kokubungaku*, 1, nos. 1 and 2.

WORKS IN OTHER LANGUAGES

Ackroyd, J., 'Women in Feudal Japan', *Transactions of the Asiatic Society of Japan*, 7 (1959).

Asakawa, K., *The Documents of Iriki*, New Haven, 1929.

Aston, W. G., *Nihongi: Chronicles of Japan from the Earliest Times to A.D. 696*, London, 1956.

de Bary, William Theodore, et al., ed., *Sources of the Japanese Tradition*, New York, 1958.

Beaujard, André, *Séi Shōnagon': son temps et son oeuvre*, Paris, 1934.

Brower, Robert H., and Earl Miner, *Japanese Court Poetry*, Stanford, 1961.

Carcopino, J., *Daily Life in Ancient Rome*, London, 1960.

Chamberlain, B. H., *Things Japanese*, London, 1905.

Clough, S., *The Rise and Fall of Civilization*, London, 1951.

Eliot, Sir Charles, *Japanese Buddhism*, London, 1959.

Forster, E. M., *Aspects of the Novel*, London, 1949.

Frank, Bernard, *Kata-imi et kata-tagae: étude sur les interdits de direction à l'époque Heian*, Tokyo, 1958.

Bibliography

Fujikawa, Y., *Kurze Geschichte der Medizin in Japan*, Tokyo, 1911.

van Gulik, R. H., *Sexual Life in Ancient China*, Leyden, 1961.

Harada Jirō, *The Shōsōin, and Eighth-Century Repository*, Tokyo, 1950.

Kaempfer, E., *The History of Japan, Together with a Description of the Kingdom of Siam*, 2 vols., London, 1727.

Keene, Donald, *Anthology of Japanese Literature*, London, 1956.

Konrad, N. I., *Japonskaya Literatura v Obraztsakh i Ocherkakh*, Leningrad, 1927, 2 vols.

Longrais, J. Des, *L'Est et l'ouest: institutions du Japon et de l'occident comparées*, Paris, 1958.

Mehendale, M. A., *The Struggle for Empire*, Bombay, 1957.

Murdoch, James, *A History of Japan* (Vol. 1: to 1542), London, 1949.

Omori, Annie S., and Kochi Doi, *Diaries of Court Ladies of Old Japan*, Boston, 1935.

Painter, George, *Marcel Proust* (Vol. 1), London, 1959.

Reischauer, Edwin O., and John K. Fairbank, *East Asia: The Great Tradition*, Boston, 1958.

Reischauer, R. K., *Early Japanese History*, Princeton, 1937, 2 vols.

Sansom, G. B., *A History of Japan* (Vol. 1: to 1334), London, 1958.

A Short Cultural History of Japan, New York, 1943.

Soper, A. C., 'The Rise of Yamato-e', *Art Bulletin*, 24 (Dec. 1942).

Suematsu Kenchō, *The Romance of Genji*, London, 1882.

Tsunoda Ryūsaku and Carrington Goodrich, *Japan in the Chinese Dynastic Histories*, S. Pasadena, 1951.

Waley, Arthur, *A Wreath of Cloud*, London, 1927.

Blue Trousers, London, 1928.

The Bridge of Dreams, London, 1933.

The Pillow-Book of Sei Shōnagon, London, 1929.

Westermarck, Edward, *A Short History of Marriage*, London, 1926.

Whitney, W. N., 'Notes on the History of Medical Progress in Japan', *Transactions of the Asiatic Society of Japan*, 12 (1885).

ABBREVIATIONS

Ikeda ed.: Murasaki Shikibu, *Genji Monogatari*, ed. by Ikeda Kikan, Nihon Koten Zensho, Tokyo, 1958, 7 vols.

Kaneko ed.: Kaneko Motoomi, *Makura no Sōshi Hyōshaku*, Tokyo, 1927.

Mochizuki ed.: Murasaki Shikibu, *Murasaki Shikibu Nikki*, ed. by Mochizuki Sekkyō, Tokyo, 1929.

N.B.T. ed.: Murasaki Shikibu, *Genji Monogatari*, Nihon Bungaku Taikei, 6 and 7, 1931-2.

Index

Index

(Figures in bold type refer to the Glossary, gen. = genealogical table, Appendix 4.)

abstinence, *see* Shintoism
acupuncture, 147
Administrative Council (Mando-koro), 65, 86, 186, 220, **318**
adoption, 109, 231 n., 236
Ainus, 33
Ajari, 133 n.
Akashi, Lady, **318**; relations with Genji, 83; class, 83, 96, 219; poem, 126; calligraphy, 196; scent, 204–5; anxiety, 252, gene-alogy, gen. 2; age, 311
Akashi, Princess, 221, 231 n., gen. 2, 311, **318**
Akazome Emon, 211 n.
Akiko, Empress, *see* Fujiwara no Akiko
Akikonomu, Lady, 37, 155, 251, gen. 2, 311, **318**
Amakuni no Tsurugi, 114
amayo no shinasadame, see Tale of Genji, The
ancestor worship, 109
animals, 135
Aoi, Lady, 52 n., 219, 229–30, gen. 2, 311, **318**
Aoi no Matsuri, 173 n.
Aouma no Sechi, 167 n., 169 and n.
archery, 164. 170, 174 n., 184
architecture, 40–1, 44–50
Ariwara no Narihira, 194, 294–5, **318**

Asagao, Princess, 204, gen. 2, **318**
asobi-onna, 237 n.
Atsumichi, Prince, 240–2, 255–7
autumn, 36–7, 155
aware, 37, 207–9, 243, 279 n., 291 n., **318–19**
awase, 163–4, 203–5
ayashi, 99 n., 291
azana, 188

baika, 204, 205 and n.
banquets, 45, 85–6
basshu, 160
bathing, 140, 157 and n.
battle of the seasons, *see* seasons
bed, 47–8
bedtime, 161–2
Ben no Kimi, 141
Biwa, Lake, 104 n., 119, 272, **319**
boat-racing, 165
Bon Fesitaval, 110, 168 n., 175
braziers, 49
Bridge of Dreams, The, 127 and n.
Buddhism, general, 105–8, 111–35; cultural role, 23; Sino-Korean imprint, 23; Heian sects, 28, 111–14; Amida Buddha and Amidism, 28; 112, 115–16, 269 and n.; syncretism, 28, 106–7; emotional and intellectual influ-ences, 29, 35–6, 48, 121–7; Zen, 47, 112–13, 116, 136 n., 153;

Buddhism – *contd*
  violent behaviour of priests, 55,
  86, 102, 117–18; karma, 103,
  129–30, 152, 191; Kannon (Bodhisattva),104n., 112,178; Tendai,
  111–12, 115, 116–18, **326**; *Lotus
  Sutra*, 112, 120–1, 124 n., 134,
  245; Gautama Buddha, 112;
  Vairocana, 112; Shingon, 112–14
  116–18, **324**; hierarchy (ecclesiastical), 117; Kegon, 118; pilgrimages and 'pilgrimages', 119;
  Sei Shōnagon, 119–20; *mujōkan*,
  121–7, 265, **323**; Four Noble
  Truths, 121; *Nirvana Sutra*,
  122; attitude to death, 121–6;
  illusory quality of the world,
  126–8, 130; escape (monastic-
  ism), 130–3; nirvana, 130; monasteries and convents, 131–2;
  muga, 133; attitude to women,
  130, 134, 217; attitude to violence and killing, 134–5; attitude
  to animals, 135, 159, 176 n.;
  superstitious elements, 136 n.,
  152; ceremonies, etc., 172–8;
  Supreme Sovereign Sutra, 176;
  Murasaki Shikibu, 269; *Great
  Wisdom Sutra*, 272; Accommodated Truths, 317 and n.; determinism, fatalism, *see* karma
  (above); eclectism, *see* syncretism
  (above); *mappō no yo*, *see* latter
  days of the Law below)
bugaku, 166, 202
bureaucracy, 84–7, 155
Bureau of Divination, *see* Divination, Bureau of
Bushidō, 153
butter, 159–60

Byōdō Temple, 55

calendar, *see* sexagenary cycle
calligraphy, 195–9, 221
carriages, *see* ox carriages
cats, 80
ceremonies and festivals, 165–78,
  223
chairs, 47
Chancellor (Kampaku), 65 and n.,
  66, 69–70, **319**
Ch'ang-An, 18, 23 and n., 32,
  37–40, 38 n., 39 n.–40 n., 304,
  319
chiao mei, 215 n.
Chi Ch'iao T'ien, 175 n.
China (*and see* Ch'ang-An, Confucianism), tenth century, [xii],
  303–4; influence on Japan, [xiii],
  22–9, 137; T'ang dynasty, [xiii],
  303–4, **326**; break in official
  relations with Japan, 19–20;
  attitude to Japan, 25–8; relations
  with Japan during tenth–eleventh
  centuries, 31–3
chivalry, 220, 227 n., 252 and n.
chōbami, 162
chōdai, 47
Chōdō In, 40 n.
Chōga, 168 n.
Chou, Duke of, 295
Chōyō no En, 168 n., 177 and n.
Chronicles of Japan, The (*Nihongi*),
  268, 316, 317 n.
Chrysanthemum Festival, 177
chrysanthemums, 142, 177 and n.
Chūshū Kangetsu, 168 n., 176
  and n.
Ch'ü Yüan, 174 n.
class system, 78–84

Cloister Government, 21
clothing, *see* dress
cock-fighting, 165
colour-matching, 49, 184, 206, 216
coloured paper, 26, 184, 243 n.
'comparisons', *see* awase
Confucianism and Confucian studies, deviations from, 27, 109–11;
influence on Japan, 108–11, 137;
education, 110–11, 184–5; observances, 171; attitude to women,
217, 231–2; *yin-yang*, etc., *see*
yin-yang
contests, *see* awase
corruption, 86–7, 218
cremation, 122

Daigaku, *see* University Imperial
Daigen no Hō, 71
Dai Nihon Shi, 265 n.
Daini no Sammi, 211 n.
Dajō Daijin, *see* Prime Minister
Dajōkan, *see* Great Council of State
dakyū, 165
dances and dancing, 23, 58, 158,
166, 172–3, 173 n., 178, 201–2,
202 n., 205
darani, 149
Datchi Gate, 141
death, attitude to, 121–6
decoration, *see* furnishing
Dengyō Daishi, 115 n., 128 and n.
detached palace, 41, 59, **319**
determinism, *see* Buddhism
directional taboo, *see* taboos
divination, 137
Divination, Bureau of (Onyō Ryō),
141
divorce, *see* women
Doku, 138

dolls and Doll Festival, 172 n.
Dōmei, 110
drawing, 197–9
dream interpreter (*yume-toki*), 142
dreams, 105–6, 105 n., 126–7, 141–2,
281
dress, 49, 184, 206, 216–17
drinking and drunkenness, 76–7,
160–1
dyeing, 26, 184, 224

eavesdropping, 50, 180
education, 111, 184–9, 207
eiga, 20 and n., 29, 44, 75, 113, 131,
166, **319**
Eiga Monogatari, *see* Tales of Glory
Eisai, 116
emaki picture scrolls, indigenous art
form, 28, 59; *Tale of Genji* picture
scrolls, 48, 49, 156, 162, **325**;
Tenjin Engi Emaki, 99 n.; Nenjū
Gyōji Emaki, 164–5, **324**; origins,
198; women, depiction of, 213–
14; lower orders, depiction of,
99 n.
emperors and the imperial institution, general, 56–61; position
according to the Great Reform,
56–7; loss of political power, 58,
66–7, 107; sacerdotal function,
58, 107, 152; cultural function,
58–9, 287; Ichijō as an example
of a Heian emperor, 59–61;
relations with the Fujiwaras,
62–6, 70; illegitimate succession,
238–9
ensho-awase, 164
erotic pictures, 198 and n., 214 n.
Essentials of Salvation, The (*Ojō
Yōshū*), 115, 269 n.

evil spirit (*mono no ke*), 147–52, **322**
examination system, 84 and n.,
    185 n., 304
executions, 17, 95, 134, 135
exorcism and possession, 147–52
eyebrows, plucking of, 215–16
Ezo, 33

falconry, 165
fatalism, *see* Buddhism
feng-shui, *see* geomancy
festivals, *see* ceremonies
feudalism, 89 and n., 90–1, 102
fiction, *see* prose fiction
filial piety, 108–10
fish, 159
folklore, 136–7
food, 159–60
football, *see* kemari
foreigners in Japan, 31–2
foxes, 114, 143
Fudō, 114 and n., 151 and n.
Fuji, Mount, 33
Fujitsubo, Lady, **319**; name, 41;
    immorality, 110, 270–1; rela-
    tions with Genji, 116; victim of
    rumours, 181; material inde-
    pendence, 220; genealogy, gen.
    2; age, 311
Fujiwara family, exploitation of
    Tanetsugu's murder, 17–18; rise
    to power, 61–2; comparisons
    with other great families, 62–3;
    political methods, 62–75; marri-
    age politics, 63–4, 218–19; posi-
    tive contributions, 66–7, 78, 87;
    struggle with Michizane, 67–9;
    struggles within the family,
    69–74; pride, 75; administrative
    organs, 86–7; economic strength,

88–9, 91; dependence on the
    Minamotos, 69, 94–5, 97, 102
Fujiwara no
Akiko (Jōtōmon In), **319**; ap-
    pointment as Imperial Lady,
    59; promoted to be Empress,
    59; political power, 154 n.,
    220; literary ladies-in-waiting,
    20, 211 n.; Empress Dowager,
    266; Murasaki Shikibu, 20,
    266; genealogy, gen. 1
Fuyutsugu, 264 n., gen. 1
Kaneie, 70–1, 192 and n., 232,
    236, gen, 1, **319**
Kanemichi, 70 gen. 1
Kiminobu, 191 n.
Korechika, 71–4, 156, 238, 295,
    gen. 1
Michinaga, **319**; symbolic role,
    20; use of daughters, 59;
    struggle with Korechika, 71–2;
    palmy years, 74–5; character,
    74–8; control of manors, 89–
    92; religion, 76, 115, 132;
    weeps with joy, 158; drunken-
    ness, 160–1; polygamy, 236;
    relations with Murasaki, 76–7,
    264 and n., 273; model for
    Genji, 295–6; genealogy,
    gen. 1
Michitaka, 161, gen. 1
Morosuke, 140 n., 179 n.
Morotada, 221 and n.
Muchimaro, 67
Naritoki, 241 n.
Nobunori, 264
Nobutsune, 196
Norimichi, 296, gen. 1
Sadako, **319**; married to Ichijō,
    59; decline in position, 59,

72–3; opposed by Michinaga, 71, 72–3; relations with Sei Shōnagon, 142, 194–5; genealogy, gen. 1

Saneyori, 62

Sukefusa, 66 n.

Suketada, 60–1, 61 n.

Tadamichi, 100–1, 101 n.

Tametoki, 263–6, gen. 1, **319**

Tanetsugu, 17

Umakai, 67

Yorimichi, 296, gen. 1

Yorimune, 266 n.

Yoritada, 71

Yoshiko, 221 n.

Fujiwara period, 19 n.

Fukandenden no Sō, 168 n., 176 and n., 177 and n.

funa-kurabe, 165

furnishing, 47–8, 184

gambling, 162

games, 162–5, 223

gardens 41, 45–6

Gempuku, 166

Gencho, 168 n., 177

Genji, Prince, **320**; and fireflies, 48; poems, 49; Suetsumuhana, 50, 253; banishment, 53, 74, 277, 297; political power, 74; Lady Akashi, 83, 277; wealth, 92; attitude to lower classes, 99; Confucianism, 109–10; Buddhism, 116, 126, 129, 131–2; Rokujō, 134; ideas about illness, 148–93; attitude to official duties, 155–6; scent, 157, 203–4; idealization, 158–9, 209, 253, 295, 298; arrangement of household, 179; views on education, 186–9, 221–

2; drawing, 197–9; Kashiwagi's letter, 200; dancing, 202; attitude to women, 217, 221–2; birth, 219 and n.; marriage, 219; Lady Murasaki, 83 227n., 230, 233; Lady Aoi, 229–30; Lady Nyosan, 230, 279; relations with a boy, 232 n.; views on literature, 121, 221, 271–2, 295, 315–17; marital arrangements, 236; Fujitsubo, 116, 279; Yūgao, 252, 279–80; models, 294–5; genealogy, gen. 2

Genji scrolls, *see emaki* picture scrolls

Genji, Tale of, see Tale of Genji, The

genza, 149

geomancy, 137

ghosts, etc., 136, 143–5

go (game of), 47 162, 184

'good person' (*yoki hito*), 36, 80, 83, **320**

Gosechi festival, 158, 168 n., 177–8, 202

Gossamer Diary (Kagerō Nikki) and author, **320**; relations with Kaneie, 235, 250–1; gloom and monotony, 125, 166, 223; Kaneie's poem to a Minister, 192 and n.; knowledge and interests, 221; jealousy, 255

gossip, 181–2

Gosuzaku, Emperor, 102, gen. 1

Gotō, 168 n., 172 and n.

Great Council of State (Dajōkan), 65–6, 78, 85, 137, 171

Great Reform (Taika), **320**; aims and principles, 22, 56; deviations from, 28, 57, 65; rank system, 78–9; tax and conscription, 79–

Great Reform – *contd*
80; office hours, 86; land distribution, 87–8; education, 146
guardian star (*zokushō*), 140 and n., 168

Hachi, Prince, 116, 122, 130, 132–3, 162, gen. 2, **320**
Hachiman Shrine, 176 and n.
Hagatame, 167 n., 168
hair, women's, 215
hairwashing, 140–1
haka, 79–80
Hanachirusato, 204, 258 n.
handwriting, *see* calligraphy
Harihakase, 145 n.
Hase Temple, 104 n.
Heian Kyō, **320**; establishment of capital, 18, 57; name, 18; cultural role, 20; foreign visitors, 31–2; natural setting, 18, 34–7, 43–4; plan of city, 37–44; population, 39 and n.; Imperial Palace, 40–1; uneven development, 43–4; survival, 54–5
Heian period, 18–22
Heian Shrine, 40 n.
Heijō, *see* Nara
Heike Monogatari, 135 n.
herbal medicine, 147
Hiei, Mt. (and see Buddhism, violent behaviour of priests) 43, 102, 112, 118, 160, **320**
Higashi Sanjō no In, 154 n.
Higekuro, Prince, and his wife, 156, 233–4, 250, 260 n., gen. 2, **320**
High Court Noble (*Kugyō*), 78–9, **320**
Hitachi, Governor of, 96, 218, gen. 2, **320**

Hitomaro (Kakinomoto), 258 n.
Hōbokushi, *see Pao P'u Tzu*
Hōjō Temple, 76
Hokkaidō, 33, 54
Hollyhock Festival, 173 n.
Home Provinces (Kinai), 33, **320**
homosexuality, 232 n.
Honke, 91
hōren, 53
horse-racing, 165, 174 n.
horses, 51
hōsōshi, 178 n.
Hotaru, Prince, 48, 203–5, gen. 2, **320**
hototogisu, 192 n.
houses, *see* architecture
Hsiao Ching, 108
hunting, 134, 165
Hyōbukyō, Prince, 231 n., gen. 2, **320**

ice, 159
Ichijō, Emperor, 59–61, 70, 115, 268, gen. 1, **320**
idashiguruma, 216
idashiuchigi, 216
Ikeda Kikan, 271, 274 n., 275, 285–6, 287 and n., 306
ikiryō, *see* 'living ghost'
illness, *see* medicine
illustrations, 198
imamekashisa, 38, 188
Imperial Lady *Nyōgo*), 59, **321**
Imperial Police (Kebiishi Chō), 86, 94, 101–2, 174
incense, *see* scent
India, 32, 112–13
infutagi, 163
insularity, 24–6, 31–3, 180–1, 303
Iris Festival, 173–4

iroha, 122
Ise no Ōsuke, 211 n.
Ise Shrine, 117, 168
Ishinhō, 145 n.–146 n., 248 n.
Ishiyama Temple, 104 and n.
Iwashimizu Hōjōe, 168 n., 176 and n.
Izumi Shikibu and her diary, 321; class, 93; last poem, 123–4, 124 n.; transience; 124–6; love affair with Prince Atsumichi, 240–2, 250, 255–7

jealousy, 145, 148 n., 253–61
jijū, 204, 205 n.
jimoku, 71
jō, see ward
Jōi, 167 n., 169
Jōmi, 168 n., 172 and n.
Jōtōmon In, *see* Fujiwara no Akiko
Junsei, 85

kabane, 79
kachō, 109
Kaempfer, Engelbert. 11 n., 34 n.
Kagerō Nikki, see Gossamer Diary
kaji, 149
Kakai Shō, 272 and n.
Kamakura period, 21
Kambutsue, 168 n., 172–3, 173 n.
Kammu, Emperor, 57, 321
Kamo Mabuchi, 274 n.
Kamo (no) Matsuri, 168 n., 173 and n.
Kamo River, 44, 173, 321
Kamo Shrines, 171, 173
Kaneie, *see* Fujiwara no Kaneie
Kannon (Bodhisattva), *see* Buddhism, Kannon
Kaoru, 321; *fin de siècle* character,

29; relations with Ukifune, 50, 83, 103–6, 141, 233, 235, 279–80, 282–5; military duties, 97, 162; attitude to lower classes, 99, 280; fear of highwaymen, 101; Buddhism, 115–16, 122, 126, 130, 132 n.; physical appearance, 156, 158–9; interest in scent, 157; music, 162; doubts about paternity, 238, 279; genealogy, gen. 2
Kampaku, *see* Chancellor
kana and *kanabungaku, see* phonetic writing
Kanjō-no-maki, 198 n.
kanshōfu, 90
karma, *see* Buddhism (karma)
Kashiwagi, 48, 180, 226, gen. 2, 311, 321
Kasuga Matsuri, 167 n., 171
kataimi, see taboos
katatashiro, 142
katatagae, 138 and n.
Katsura River, 44
Kazan, Emperor, 59, 71–2, 132, 321
Kebiishi Chō, *see* Imperial Police
keishi, 79, 92
kemari, 164, 226
kichō, see screen of state
Kinensai, 167 n., 171 and n.
Ki no Tsurayuki, 51, 212 and n.
kinuginu no fumi, see 'next morning' letter
Kiritsubo, Lady, 181, 233, gen. 2, 321
kishin, 90–1
kita no kata, see principal wife
Kōbai, 179–80
Kochōhai, 167–8, 167 n.–168 n.
Kojidan, 206 n.
Kokiden, Empress, 220, gen. 2. 321

Kokin Shū, 195 n., 203 n., 221, 263 n., **321**

Kōkō, Emperor, 65

Komahoko, 202 n.

komainu, 47

Kōnin period, 19 n.

Konoe, Prince, 62, 156 n.

konoekō, 204, 205 n.

Korea and Koreans, 12–13, 31–3, 47 n., 304–5

Korechika, *see* Fujiwara no Korechika

Koremitsu, 204, 228, gen. 2, **321**

Koromogae, 168 n., 172

Kose no Ōmi, 199

Koshibagaki-zōshi, 198 n.

Koshikibu no Naishi, 211 n.

kotori-awase, 163

kubunden system, 88 and n.

kudashibumi, 66

Kugyō, *see* High Court Noble

Kukai, 113, 145 n.

Kumoi, Lady, 81, 148, 230, 257–61, gen. 2, **311, 321**

kurōbo, 204, 205 n.

kuruma-arasoi, 52 and n.

Kyoto, *see* Heian Kyō

Lady Who Loved Insects, The (*Mushi Mezuru Himegimi*), 216, 222, **321**

language, *see Tale of Genji, The* (language)

Lao Tzu, *see* Taoism

latter days of the Law (*mappō no yo*), 29, 30 n., 128, **322**

letters and letter-writing, 199–200, 258–9

literary criticism, *see* Genji, Prince (views on literature)

'living ghost' (*ikiryō*), 145, 260 n., **322**

Lotus Sutra, *see* Buddhism

lower classes, 97–101, 209, 279–80, 297

mai no shi, 202

mamkko monogatari, 231 n.

Mandokoro, *see* Administrative Council

manors (*shōen*), **322**; general, 89–93; efforts at control, 21, 91; effect of growth, 21, 91–3; indigenous aspect, 27–8, 186; ownership, 89–91; commendation, 91; *beneficium*, 90; life in, 98 n.; interest of aristocracy in, 92, 154 n., 155

Mansei, 124 n.

Manyō Shū, 246 n., 258 n., 268, **322**

mappō no yo, *see* latter days of the Law

marriage, *see* women

marriage politics, *see* women

Masakado, *see* Taira no Masakado

Masamune Hakuchō, 289

mealtimes, 161

meat, 159

medicine and medical knowledge, 145–52, 160

Medicine, Bureau of (Kusuri no Tsukasa), 146

mediums, *see* exorcism

Meiji period, 22

menstruation, 105 and n., 107, 223

mi-agamono, 174 n.

Michinaga, *see* Fujiwara no Michinaga

Michinoku paper, 246 and n.

Michitsuna's mother, *see Gossamer Diary*

Michizane, *see* Sugawara no Michizane

mika no yo no goshōsoku, 228

mikayomochi, 227

Military Affairs, Ministry of (Hyōbu Shō), 192 and n.

military men, *see* warrior class

milk, 160

Minamoto family, 69, 95, 97, 102, 135 n., **322**

Minamoto no
  Kintada, 204–5, 205 n.
  Takaaki, 62, 295
  Tōru, 46

Minister of the Left (Sadaijin), 154, 156 n., **322**

misogi, 143

mochi, 159

Mochigayu, 167 n., 170 and n.

Mogi, 166

money, 87

mono-awase, 163

monogatari, *see* prose fiction

monoimi, *see* taboos

monoimi no hi, *see* taboos

mono no aware, *see* aware

mono no ke, *see* evil spirit

moon (imagery), 131 n., 176 n.

Motoori Norinaga, 127, 208 n., 270 n., 270–1, 274 n., 276 n., 279 n., **323**

moxa, moxabustion, 147

mudra. 112

mujōkan, *see* Buddhism

muko, 231

Murakami, Emperor, 295

Murasaki, Lady (Murasaki no Ue), **323**; relations with Genji, 83, 250; economic situation, 92; illness, 148–9, 151–2; death, 49,

126 n.; jealousy, 196–7, 260 n.; name, 83 n., 295; models, 295–6; age, 311; genealogy, gen. 2

Murasaki no Ue, *see* Murasaki, Lady

Murasaki Shikibu (*and see Tale of Genji, The*), general, 262–74; position at court, 20; relations with Michinaga, 76–8, 264 and n., 273; class, 93, 217; religion, 115, 269; poetry, 124 n.; attitude to death and impermanence, 124–5; education and knowledge, 186–7, 263–4, 267–9; music, 201; absence of social protest, 82–4, 96, 134, 250–1; model for heroine of novel, 294–6; character, 262–3; life, 263–6, 274 n.; Sei Shōnagon, 262–3; name, 263 n.; diary, 265–6, 266 n., 274 n., 296; date of death, 274 n.; genealogy, gen. 1; authorship of *Tale of Genji*, *see Tale of Genji, The*; views on literature, *see* Genji, Prince views on literature)

Murasaki Shikibu Nikki, *see* Murasaki Shikibu (diary)

Murdoch, James, 21

Muromachi period, 25 n., 153, 270, 286

Mushi Mezuru Himegimi, *see Lady Who Loved Insects, The*

music, 58, 162, 200–2, 220–1

mysticism, 116

Nagaoka, 17, 18

Nagaya, Prince, 67

nakadachi, 225–6, 226 n.

Naka no Kimi, 83, 140, 234 and n., 248–9, 254 n., gen. 2, **323**

Nakazukasa, 211 n.

napping, 297

Nara and Nara period, 17, 20, 22–3, 43, **323**

Narita, 114 and n.

nature and natural beauty, 34–7, 48–9, 55

nazo, 162–3

ne-awase, 163

nembutsu, 115

Nenohi no En, 167 n., 169 n., 169–70

'next morning' letter (*kinuginu no fumi*), 200, 226–7, 244–5, 247, **323**

Nihongi, see Chronicles of Japan, The

Niiname no Matsuri, 168 n., 177

Nimmyō Emperor, 204 n.

Niou, Prince, **323**; Ukifune, 50, 103–6, 198, 282–5; Naka no Kimi, 53, 140, 180, 227, 233, 234, 248–9; visits to Uji, 81, 103–5, 119, 291–2; marital arrangements, 83–4; Kaoru, 126; interest in scent, 157; idealization, 158, 209; interest in his sister, 180; drawing, 198; given to tears, 157–8, 198; reads Ukifune's letter, 200; Roku no Kimi, 249; age, 311; genealogy, gen. 2

norito, 174 n.

Noriyumi, 167 n., 170

nudity, ideas about, 214 and n.

Nyōgo, see Imperial Lady

Nyosan, Princess, 180, 182, 197, gen. 2, 311, **323**

Oborozukiyo, Lady, 237, gen. 2, **323**

Ochiba, Princess, 148 n., 215, 235, 257–61, gen. 2, **323**

Ochikubo Monogatari, see Tale of the Room Below, The

Ōe family, 94

o-haguro, see tooth-blackening

Ōcharai, 168 n., 174 and n.

Ōigimi, 225, 282, gen. 2, 311, **323**

Ojō Yōshū, see Essentials of Salvation, The

Okinamaro, 135

O-kusuri, 167 n., 169

omens, 141–2

Ōmi no Kimi, 162

On-Butsumyō, 168 n., 178

Ōnin Wars, 54

onkyū, 90

onnade, 212

onnae and *otokoe*, 198 and n.

Ono no Komachi, 211 n.

Ono no Michikaze, 199

Onyōji, see Yin- Yang, Master of

Onyō Ryō, *see* Divination, Bureau of

oshidashi, 216

otokomoji, 212

ox carriages (*gissha*), 51–4, 184

Palace, Imperial (Dairi), 40–1

Palace of Administration (Chōdō In), 40

palanquins, 53

Pao P'u Tzu, 145 n.

paper, *see* coloured paper, Michinoku paper

parties, *see* banquets

peasants, *see* lower classes

perfume, *see* scent

phonetic writing (*kana* literature), 28, 113, 212, 268, 290, **321**

pictures, *see* drawing

picture scrolls, *see emaki* picture scrolls

Pillow Book (*Makura no Sōshi*) (*and see* Sei Shōnagon), **323**; historical value, 14, 153–4, 213; foreigners, 32; lack of interest in provinces, 33–4; the four seasons, 36; tiled roofs, 44; travel by carriage, 52; Emperor Ichijō, 60–1; Fujiwara no Michinaga, 73, 76–7; workmen at their feed, 100; story of the unfilial lieutenant, 110; importance of good looks for a preacher, 119–20; cuckoo-hearing excursion, 129, 190–2; the dog Okinamaro, 135; sneezing, 142; exorcism, 149–50; badly-powdered men, 156; Tachibana no Norimitsu, 158, 238; gentlemanly eating, 159; poetry, 190–1; dice and other games, 162–3; Fujiwara no Michitaka, 161; temple visit, 119–20; Fujiwara no Sadako, 72–3; snow mountain, 165; Full-moon Gruel, 170 n.; gossip, 181–2; 'judgements', 183–4; dances, 202 n.; love affairs, 225, 237–8, 239–40, 241–7; *muko*, 231 n.

Po Chü-i, 25, 101, 131 n., 194, 268, 295, 304, **323**

poetry, natural imagery, 35–6; social importance, 97, 190–4; about poverty, 100–1, 101 n.; contests, 163–4, 190; importance in prose literature, 190; occasional, 190–3; conventional, 193–4; quotations, 189, 194–5, 284 n.; letters, 199–200; importance for women, 221; role in courting customs, 225–6

police, *see* Imperial Police

polo, *see dakyū*

polygamy, *see* women

population, 39–40, 39 n.–40 n., 93

portents, *see* omens

possession, *see* exorcism

Prime Minister (Dajō Daijin), 69, **323–4**

principal wife (*kita no kata*) 46, 229, 255 and n., **324**

prisons, 42

privacy, lack of, 50

professors, 188–9, 207

prose fiction (*monogatari*), **322**; scorn of Confucianists, 28; indigenous art form, 28; role of nature, 36; slow pace, 53; influence of court, 58–9; interest of women, 221, 223–4, 269; Murasaki Shikibu's views, 315–17

prostitutes, 237 n.

Proust, Marcel, 254, 277, 278, 278 n.–9 n., 296 and n., 298

provinces and provincials, general, 93–7; attitude of aristocracy, 33–4, 37, 54, 60, 72, 93–7, 209; growth of power, 94–5

rank system, 78–82

Rashō Mon, 38, 39, 144

Regent (Sesshō), 64–5, 65 n., 69

Reizei, Emperor, 109, 129, 208, 238–9, 239 n., 279, gen. 2, 311, **324**

Rekken, 167 n., 171

rice, 159

rights (*shiki*), 90, **324**

roads, 51

Rokujō, Lady, 38, 52 n., 134, 145, 151–2, 260 n., gen. 2, 311, **324**

Roku no Kimi, 83, 249, gen. 2, **324**

Ryōshu, 91

Sadako, *see* Fujiwara no Sadako
sadame, 183
Saga, Emperor, 58, 160
Sagami, 211 n.
Saishō, Lady, 191
sake, 160–1
Sampitsu, 58
Sanjō, Emperor, 60, 70
sansan-kudo, 228
Sanuki Tenji, 211 n.
Sarashina Diary and author, **324**; references to *Tale of Genji*, 273–4, 275; descriptions of nature, 34; travel, 51; class (of author), 93–4, 217–18; attitude to provinces, 96; karma, 129; supersitition, 142
Sawara, Crown Prince, 17–18, 145
scent, and incense competitions, 157, 203–5, 296–7
scholarship and scholars, *see* education
screen of state (*kichō*), 48, 222, **324**
screens, 47, 184, 198
scrolls, picture, *see* *emaki* picture scrolls
seasons, battle of, 37, 155–6
sea travel, 31, 51
Sei Shōnagon (*and see Pillow Book*), **324**; position at court, 20; Fujiwara no Michinaga, 73, 77; class, 93–4; religion, 119–20; ignorance of politics, etc., 154 and n.; reputation for tippling, 161; poetry, 193; quotations, 194–5; calligraphy, 196; promiscuity, 237–8, 243; comparison with Murasaki Shikibu, 262–3, 267; education and knowledge, 267
Seiin no Gi, 85

Seiryō Den, 41, 144–5
Seiwa, Emperor, 64–5
Sekiten, 167 n., 171 and n.
senji, 66, 85
Sessho, *see* Regent
sex handbooks, techniques, etc., 146 n., 248 n.
sexagenary cycle and table, 139, 147, 170 n.
shamanism, 136, 152
shigaku, 186
Shihōhai, 167–8, 167 n.–8 n.
shikan, 116
Shika Shichiron, 265 n.
shiki, *see* rights
Shinchokusen Shū, 284 n.
shinden, 44–50, **324**
Shingon, *see* Buddhism
Shinkō, 168 n., 174 and n.
Shinsen En, 41
Shintoism, general, 106–8; architecture, 40–1; sources of pollution, 41–2, 105 n., 256 n., role of emperor, 58; festivals, etc., 98, 170 n., 171 and n., 173, 174, 177–8; attitude to death, 107, 108, 123; superstitions, 107, 136; abstinence, 137; taboos, 107–8; purification, 142–3; agriculture, 171 n.; dances, 201–2; marriage rites, 227–8; relations with Buddhism, *see* syncretism (below)
shō(en) *see* manors
Shōmyō, Prince, 192 and n.
Shōsō In, 23 n.
Shōtoku, Empress, 23 n.
Shōyūki, 75 and n., 89, 157 n.
Shunki, 66 and n.
slaves, 98
sneezing, superstition about, 142

snobbery, 82–3
snowballs, 165
so, 159
social protest, *see* Murasaki Shikibu
Soga family, 62, 64, 66
sōji, 104
soothsayers, 141–2
spirits, *see* ghosts
Ssu-ma Ch'ien, 264
Sudō, Emperor, 18
Suetsumuhana, 42, 50, 214 n., 224
    and n., 253, gen. 2, **325**
sugar, 159
Sugawara no Michizane, 19, 67–9,
    145, 185 n., 295, **325**
Sugawara no Takasue, 211 n., 274 n.
sugoroku, 162
Suma, 53
sumō, 165, 168 n., 175 and n.
superstitions, 30, 136–52
Suruga Mai, 202 n.
Suzaku, Emperor, 132, 253, gen. 2,
    311, **325**
Suzaku Ōji, 39
syncretism, 28, 106–7 108, 112,
    152, 176 n.

tabisho, 138
taboo day, *see* taboos
taboos (*monoimi*), Ukifune subject
    to, 104–6; tags, 105, 108, 120,
    325; mourning period, 125;
    directional, 136 n. 137–9, 223,
    241; calendrical (and taboo days),
    139–41
Tachibana no Norimitsu, 158, 193,
    238
tadabito, 82
Taifu (Kumoi's nurse), 260 n.
Taifu (Tamakazura's suitor), 97

Taiheiraku, 202 n.
Taihō Code, 260 n.
Taika, *see* Great Reform
Taira no Masakado, 114
Taira no Tadatsune, 94, 140
*Taketori Monogatari, see Tale of
    the Bamboo Cutter, The*
*Tale of Genji, The (Genji Monoga-
    tari) (and see* Murasaki Shikibu),
    general, 275–98; realism and
    idealization, 158, 297–8; music,
    200–1, 286; poetry, 190; *mono no
    aware*, 208 and n.; jealousy, 254;
    authorship, etc., 265, 268–74;
    love, 267; Baconian theory, 270;
    Uji chapters ('ten books of Uji'),
    238, 270, 281–5, **326**; purpose,
    269–72, 278 n., 279 n., dates,
    273–4; availability, 273–4; length,
    275; precision, 275–7; 'flash-
    back', 276; construction, 275–7;
    themes, 277. 279 n., 288; antici-
    pation, 277–8; *amayo no shina-
    sadame* (rainy night judgement)
    183, 222 n., 224 n., 237, 278;
    repetition of patterns, 278–81;
    sustained imagery, 280–5;
    dreams, 280–1; symbols, 281–2;
    river (Uji) symbolism, 281–5;
    commentaries, 285–7; genealo-
    gies, 286; quotations, 190, 286;
    language, 286–7, 289–92; prob-
    lems, 286; comprehensibility,
    287–92; texts, 288–9; translation,
    292–4; *Kumogakure*, 308; models,
    294–7; attitude to lower classes,
    279–80, 297–8; ending (complete
    or incomplete?), 306–8; *The
    Bridge of Dreams (Yume no Uki-
    hashi)*, 127, 306–8; *Maboroshi*,

Tale of Genji – contd.
308; motive, *see* purpose (above);
sources, *see* models (above)
Tale of Genji picture scrolls, *see*
emaki picture scrolls
Tale of the Bamboo Cutter, The,
(*Taketori Monogatari*), 220, **325**
*Tale of the Hollow Tree, The (Utsubo
Monogatari*), 32, 158, 201, 220,
235, 276, **325**
Tale of The Room Below, The
(*Ochikubo Monogatari*), 52 n.,
325–6
Tales of Glory (Eiga Monogatari),
20 and n., 29, 75, 76, 157 n.,
198 n., 266, **325**
Tamakazura, **326**; courted by Hotaru, 48; life in Kyūshū, 51;
courted by Taifu, 97; relations
with Higekuro, 156, 233; courted
by many men, 220; insecure
position, 234; build-up, 278;
genealogy, gen. 2; age, 311;
interest in *monogatari*, 315–17
Tamba Yasuyori, 145 n.
Tanabata Matsuri, 168 n., 174–5,
175 n.
T'ang dynasty, *see* China
T'ang Hsüan Tsung, 61 n.
Tango, 168 n., 173–4, 174 n.
Tanizaki Junichirō, 289
Taoism, 116, 137, 145–6, 146 n.,
147, 160, 248 n.
tatami, 47, 153
tea, 116, 160
tears, 157–8, 198, 202
teguruma, 53
Temmu, Emperor, 202
tenaria, 223
Tenchi, Emperor, 62

Tendai, *see* Buddhism
tengu, 143
Tenjin Engi Emaki, *see emaki*
picture scrolls
tenth century, 11–13, 301–5
time and time-keeping, 144–5, 161–2
Tōjō, General, 66
Tōkaidō, 34, 96
Tōka no Sechie, 167 n., 170 and n.
Tokikata, 103 and n.
tokoro-arawashi, 228, 233
Tokugawa period, 26 n., 153, 216 n.
Tō no Chūjō, 75, 219, gen. 2, **326**
tooth-blackening (*o-haguro*), 215–17
tori-awase, see cock-fighting
Tori no Mai, 202 n.
Tosa Nikki, 212 and n.
trade and commerce, 87–8
transport, 51–4
travel, 31–2, 52–3, 180
Tsuina, 168 n., 178 and n.
tsuma-arasoi, 219–20
tsunokakushi, 260 n.
tsurezure, 223, 250

Uda, Emperor, 67, 204, 205 n.
Uji, 53, 55, 101, **326**
Uji chapters ('ten books of Uji'),
see Tale of Genji, The
Uji no Chōja, 109
Ukifune, **326**; relations with Kaoru
and Niou, 50, 83, 96, 103–6, 141,
158, 197, 234, 282–5; attempted
suicide, 129, 143, 194, 283–5;
Buddhism, 131, 133; mother's
regrets, 134; inauspicious dream,
142; hair, 215; class, 235 n.;
build-up, 278; river imagery,
283–5; genealogy, gen. 2; age,
311

ukiyo, 127 n.
Ukon, 103–5
Uma no Naishi, 211 n.
University, Imperial (Daigaku), 42,
    79, 111, 146, 171, 184–5, 187
Urabon(e), *see* Bon Festival
uta-awase, 163
Utsubo Monogatari, *see* Tale of the
    Hollow Tree, The
Utsusemi, 138, **326**

vegetables, 159

Wakana no Sekku, 167 n., 169 and
    n.
Waley, Arthur, his statements
    about: religion, 111 n., 195,
    252 n.; translation, 293; women's
    knowledge, 154; calligraphy, 195;
    style (construction) of Murasaki
    Shikibu's novel, 277, 280; end-
    ing of Murasaki Shikibu's novel,
    307–8; translation of *Genji Mono-
    gatari*, etc., 124 n., 147 n., 275,
    289, 293–4
ward (*jō*), 38, **320**
warrior class, 97, 102
Watanabe no Tsuna, 144
weeping, *see* tears
Winding Water banquets, 45–6,
    172
women, general, 211–61; role in
    literature, 28, 59, 211–13; econo-
    mic situation, 92–3, 217–18, 253;
    status in religion, 130, 134, 217;
    role in politics, 154 and n., 220;
    cloistered, idle lives, 50, 180,
    221–4; physical appearance, 213–
    16; dress, 216–17; position in
law, 217–19; marriage politics,
    63–4, 218–19; 'wife battles',
    219–20; general status, 220–1,
    252–3; general attitude to men,
    220; cultural interests, 220–1;
    education, 221, 268; distractions,
    223–4; virginity, 225 and n.,
    227 n.; courting and marriage
    customs, 225–9; wives, concu-
    bines, etc., 229–39; polygamy,
    229–39, 247–52; divorce, 236;
    prostitutes, 237 n.; promiscuity,
    237–8; love affairs, 239–47;
    anxiety and jealousy, 251–61;
    hysteria, 254, 260 n.; marriage,
    see courting and marriage cus-
    toms (above)
workmen, *see* lower classes

Yamaji no Tsuyu, 306
Yamato-damashii, 26 and n., 187,
    326
Yamato-e, 26 and n.
yin-yang, **326**; mountains and
    rivers, 44 n.; Confucianism, 111;
    Ministry of, 137; Masters of,
    137, 139, 141, 143, 144, 178;
    medical theories, 146–7; horses,
    169 n.; Nenshi no En, 169 n.–
    170 n.; stars, 172 n.; Abe family,
    186; ideas about sexual activity,
    225 n., 248 n.
Yin-Yang, Master of (*Onyōji*), *see*
    yin-yang
yoki hito, *see* 'good person'
yo no naka, 224, 256
yorimashi, 149
Yoshiko Joō, 211 n.
Yoshino, 287
Yu Fang Pi Chüeh, 248 n.

Yūgao, 252, 278, 279, gen. 2, **326**
Yūgiri, **326**; marriage to Kumoi, 75, 219, 230, 235, 257–61; unhappiness about his rank, 81, 260; ideas about illness, 148; captivated by Murasaki, 179, 214; education, 186–7; affair with Gosechi dancer, 202; marital arrangements, 235, 249; affair with Ochiba, 148 n., 235; models, 295–6; genealogy, gen. 2; age, 311

yukikorogashi, 165
Yume, 127 and n.
Yume no Ukihashi, see Bridge of Dreams, The
yume-toki see dream interpreter

Zen, *see* Buddhism
zokushō, see guardian star

A selection of books published by Penguin is listed on the following pages.

For a complete list of books available from Penguin in the United States, write to Dept. DG, Penguin Books, 299 Murray Hill Parkway, East Rutherford, New Jersey 07073.

For a complete list of books available from Penguin in Canada, write to Penguin Books Canada Limited, 2801 John Street, Markham, Ontario L3R 1B4.

If you live in the British Isles, write to Dept. EP, Penguin Books Ltd, Harmondsworth, Middlesex.

THE PILLOW BOOK OF SEI SHŌNAGON

Translated and edited by Ivan Morris

Sei Shōnagon was a court lady in tenth-century Japan at the height of the Heian culture. In her Pillow Book she notes all the things in daily life that attract, displease, or interest her. She was an enthusiast for good manners and good taste – whether this applied to dress, servants, or the correct behavior of lovers. This is by far the most detailed source of factual material on the daily life of the time and is also a work of great literary beauty, full of lively humor and subtle impressions of the world she lived in. Shōnagon's life after her service in the court of the empress is totally obscure. There is a tradition that she died in lonely poverty, but this is probably an invention of moralists who were shocked by her promiscuity and thought she deserved retribution.

THE PENGUIN BOOK OF JAPANESE VERSE

Translated with an Introduction by Geoffrey Bownas
and Anthony Thwaite

Says Geoffrey Bownas in his Introduction: 'Poetry is in a real sense a living part of the culture of Japan today. Most Japanese, without much effort, can – and many do – compose poems that, if no more, are at least technically correct. . . . The clichés of everyday speech are often to be traced to famous ancient poems. . . . The emperor's poetry prize attracts tens of thousands of entries each New Year, while most large towns have their *tanka* or *haiku* clubs which publish quarterly magazines.' This collection, with its comprehensive introduction of background to language and prosody, covers Japanese poetry from its earliest primitive beginnings to the mid–twentieth century.

A HISTORY OF MODERN JAPAN

Richard Storry

The rise, fall, and renaissance of Japan within the space of less than a hundred years is one of the most curious and dramatic stories of our time. This history begins by describing the historical background to Japan's emergence as a modern state in the sixties of the last century. It then discusses in detail the stages of Japan's advance as a world power up to the tragedy of the Pacific war. This struggle and its aftermath – the Occupation – are vividly described and analysed. The last chapter, bringing the account right up to the present day, is a fascinating study of the new Japan that has come into being since the San Francisco Peace Treaty of 1951. 'There has long been a need for an up-to-date general survey of Japanese history. This book . . . admirably fills the gap. . . . Mr Storry has provided a succinct, well-written, and accurate account' – *International Affairs*.

THE FALL OF JAPAN

William Craig

At the end of World War II, Japan chose surrender instead of annihilation. Using unpublished diaries, memoirs, and documents, as well as interviews with key figures in the United States and in Japan, William Craig tells the full story of the events behind that choice: Admiral Takijiro Onishi, the fanatical Vice-Chief of Staff, organizes the infamous suicide squadrons, or kamikazes; General Curtis Lemay launches low-altitude fire-bomb attacks on Tokyo; Japanese Intelligence penetrates the American invasion plan of the Home Islands and discovers the strength of every American military unit in the Pacific – except the one designated to drop the two nuclear bombs. Illustrated with over 50 black-and-white photos.

THE NARROW ROAD TO THE DEEP
NORTH AND OTHER TRAVEL SKETCHES

Matsuo Bashō

Translated with an Introduction by Nobuyuki Yuasa

This volume contains five travel sketches written in later life by
Matsuo Bashō (1644–1694), the greatest of the Japanese *haiku* poets.
Bashō's genius had already given new freedom and energy to the strict
haiku form of seventeen syllables, elevating it to a level of miniature
perfection. Zen Buddhism was a leading influence in the school of
poetry he founded. His journeys through Japan are recorded in linked
prose and verse, and the title piece of these sketches is a bid by the poet
to discover a vision of eternity in nature and the ephemeral world
about him.